My-HiME

Volume 2

Written by Kimura Noboru
Illustrated by Sato Ken-etsu

HAMBURG // LONDON // LOS ANGELES // TOKYO

My-HiME Vol. 2
Written by Kimura Noboru
Illustrated by Sato Ken-etsu

Translation - Jeremiah Bourque
English Adaptation - Gina Lee Ferenzi
Retouch and Lettering - Star Print Brokers
Production Artist - Michael Paolilli
Graphic Designer - Monalisa De Asis

Editor - Bryce P. Coleman
Digital Imaging Manager - Chris Buford
Pre-Production Supervisor - Erika Terriquez
Art Director - Anne Marie Horne
Production Manager - Elisabeth Brizzi
Managing Editor - Vy Nguyen
VP of Production - Ron Klamert
Editor-in-Chief - Rob Tokar
Publisher - Mike Kiley
President and C.O.O. - John Parker
C.E.O. and Chief Creative Officer - Stuart Levy

A  Manga

TOKYOPOP and ⦿ are trademarks or registered trademarks of TOKYOPOP Inc.

TOKYOPOP Inc.
5900 Wilshire Blvd. Suite 2000
Los Angeles, CA 90036

E-mail: info@TOKYOPOP.com
Come visit us online at www.TOKYOPOP.com

My-HiME © 2005 SUNRISE © 2005 KIMURA Noboru / SATO Ken-etsu All rights reserved. First published in Japan in 2005 by Akita Publishing Co., Ltd., Tokyo. English translation rights in the U.S.A. and Canada arranged by Akita Publishing Co., Ltd. through Tuttle-Mori Agency, Inc., Tokyo English text copyright © 2007 TOKYOPOP Inc. All rights reserved. No portion of this book may be reproduced or transmitted in any form or by any means without written permission from the copyright holders. This manga is a work of fiction. Any resemblance to actual events or locales or persons, living or dead, is entirely coincidental.

ISBN: 978-1-59816-652-1

First TOKYOPOP printing: March 2007
10 9 8 7 6 5 4 3 2
Printed in the USA

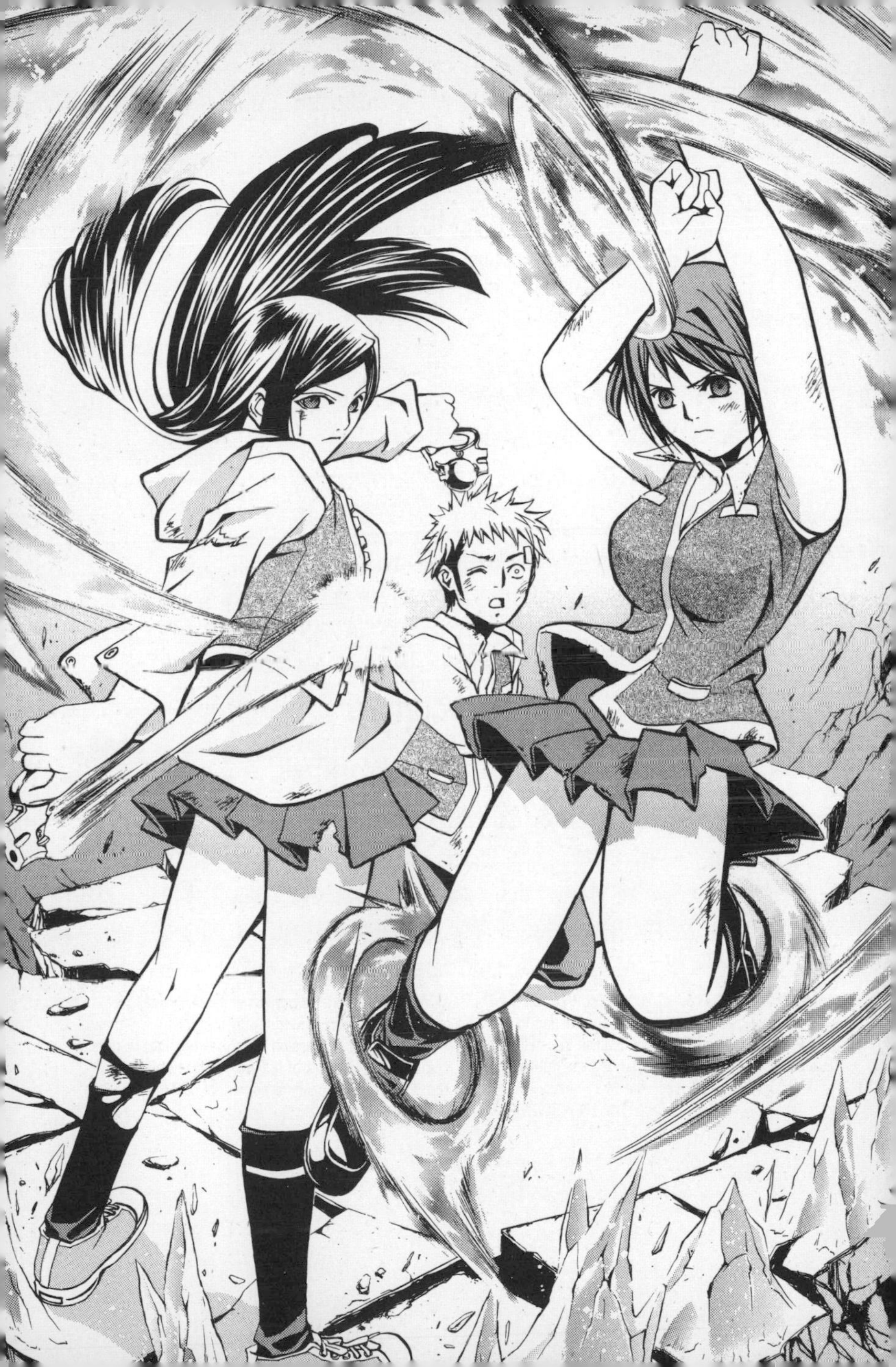

Previously in

My-HIME

When former kendo star Yuuichi Tate first arrived at Fuka Academy, his head was filled with big dreams of a Co-Ed "fateful encounter." But one should always be mindful of what they ask for...

It seems that Yuuichi's new school is home for a group of super-powered female students, known as "HIMEs." Soon, Yuuichi's path intersects two of Fuka's most volatile, competing HIMEs, Mai and Natsuki. When Yuuichi triggers Mai's "Child," and realizes that he's her "Key," a full-scale battle ensues, with poor Yuuichi caught in the middle! Both Mai and Natsuki lay claim to the hapless Yuuichi, which results in lots of structural damage to the school. Thinking that more healthy competition will help focus the students, Natsuki is assigned to the Ori-HIME squad (basically, the HIME A-Team). Meanwhile, a seductress named Nao is sent to use her feminine wiles on Yuuichi in order to bring him over to the side of the Ori-HIMEs.

My-HiME

2

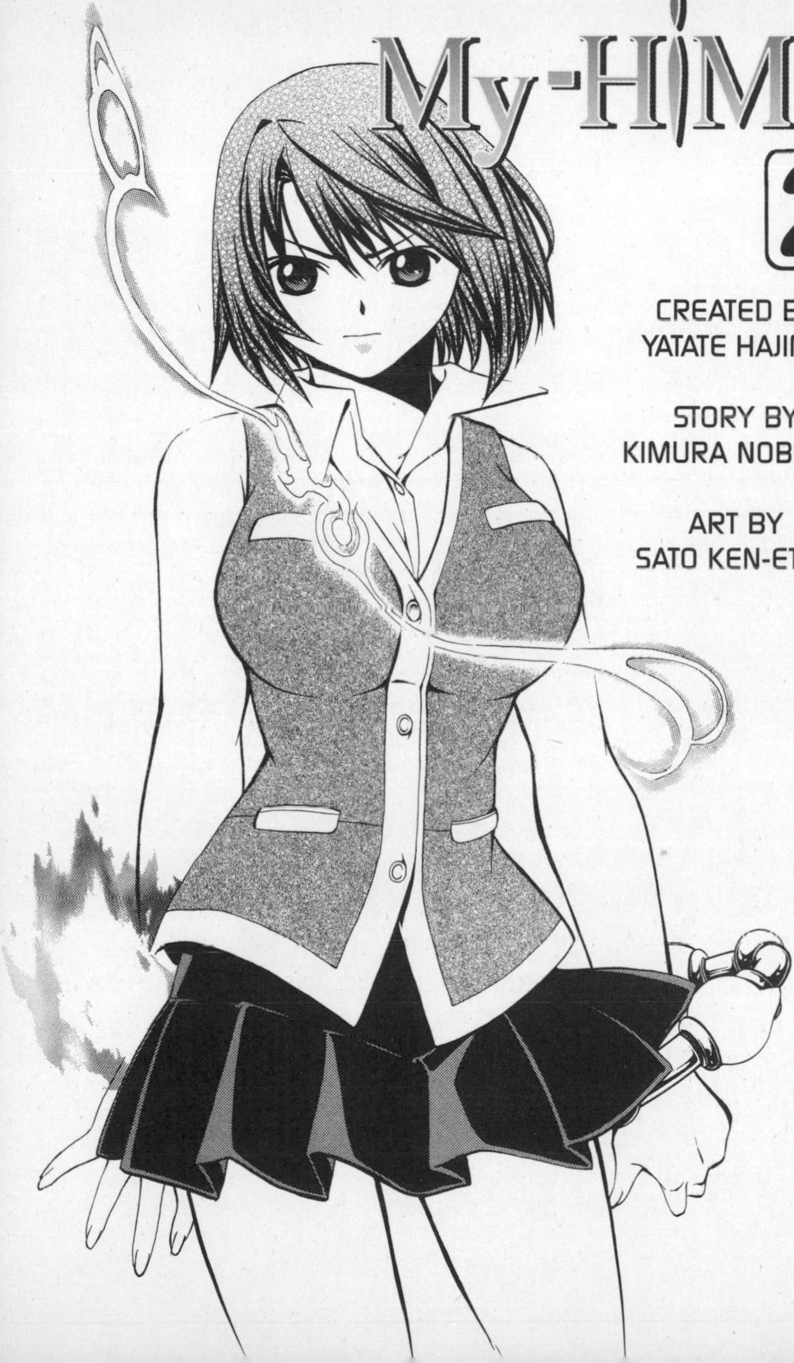

CREATED BY
YATATE HAJIME

STORY BY
KIMURA NOBORU

ART BY
SATO KEN-ETSU

My-HIME

CONTENTS

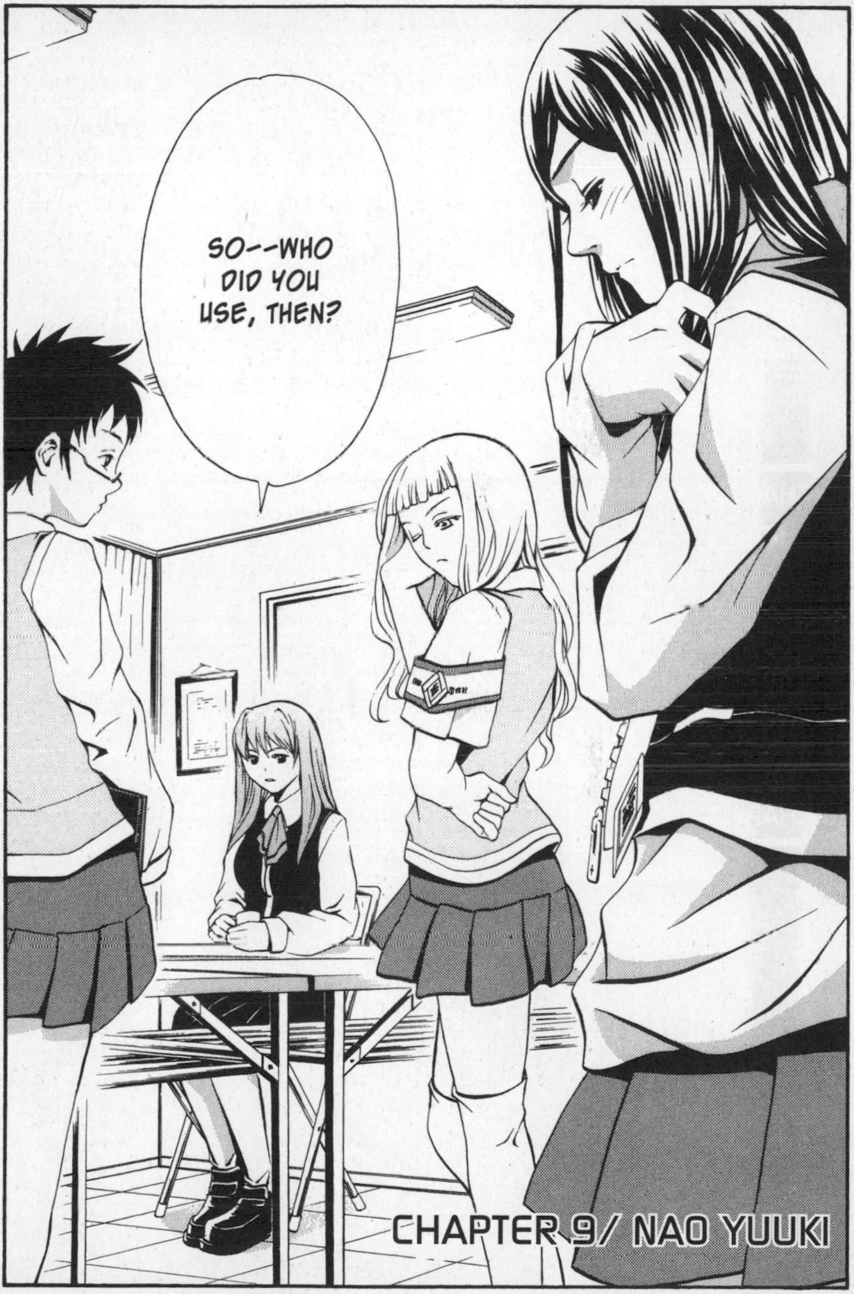
SO--WHO DID YOU USE, THEN?
CHAPTER 9/ NAO YUUKI

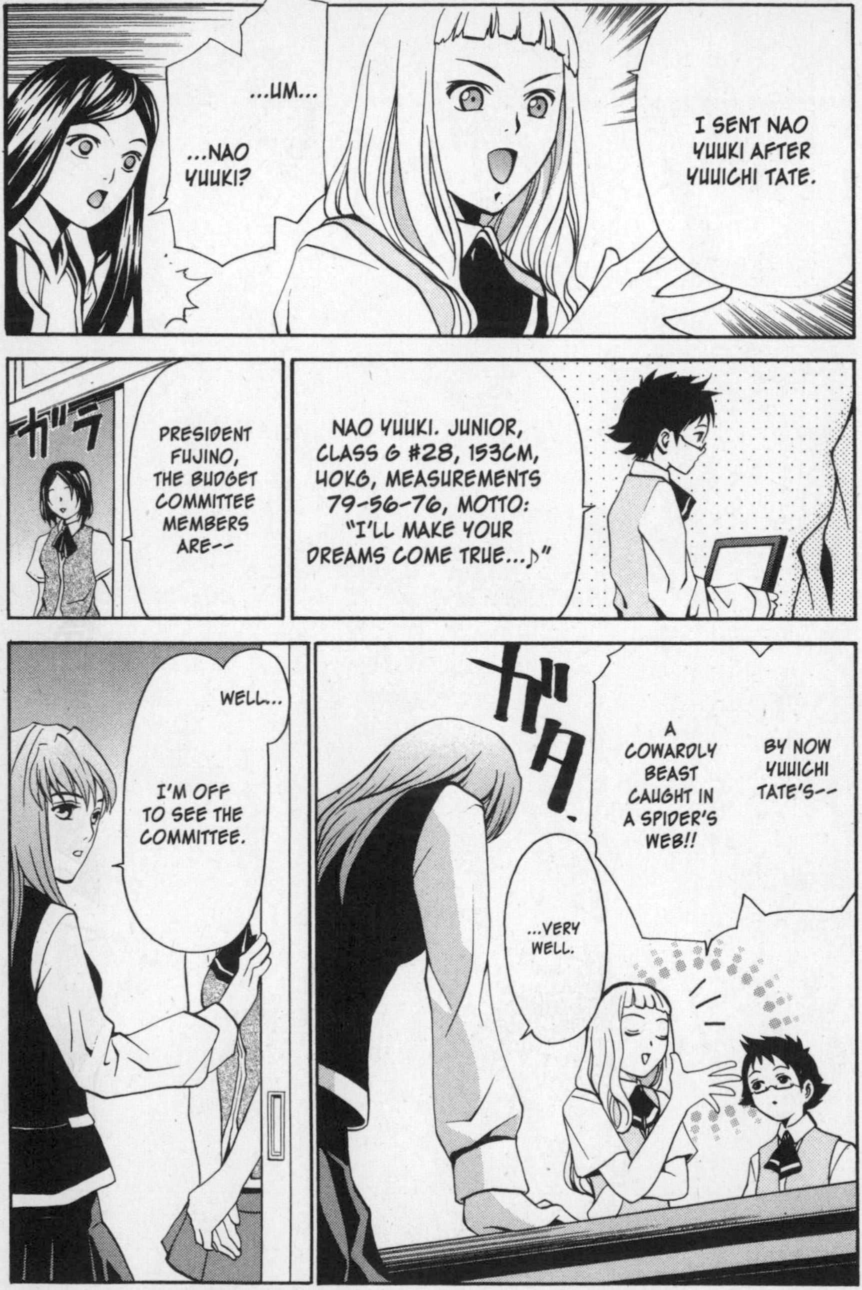
I SENT NAO YUUKI AFTER YUUICHI TATE.
...UM...
...NAO YUUKI?
NAO YUUKI. JUNIOR, CLASS 6 #28, 153CM, 40KG, MEASUREMENTS 79-56-76, MOTTO: "I'LL MAKE YOUR DREAMS COME TRUE...♪"
PRESIDENT FUJINO, THE BUDGET COMMITTEE MEMBERS ARE--
ガラ
BY NOW YUUICHI TATE'S--
A COWARDLY BEAST CAUGHT IN A SPIDER'S WEB!!
ガタ
...VERY WELL.
WELL...
I'M OFF TO SEE THE COMMITTEE.

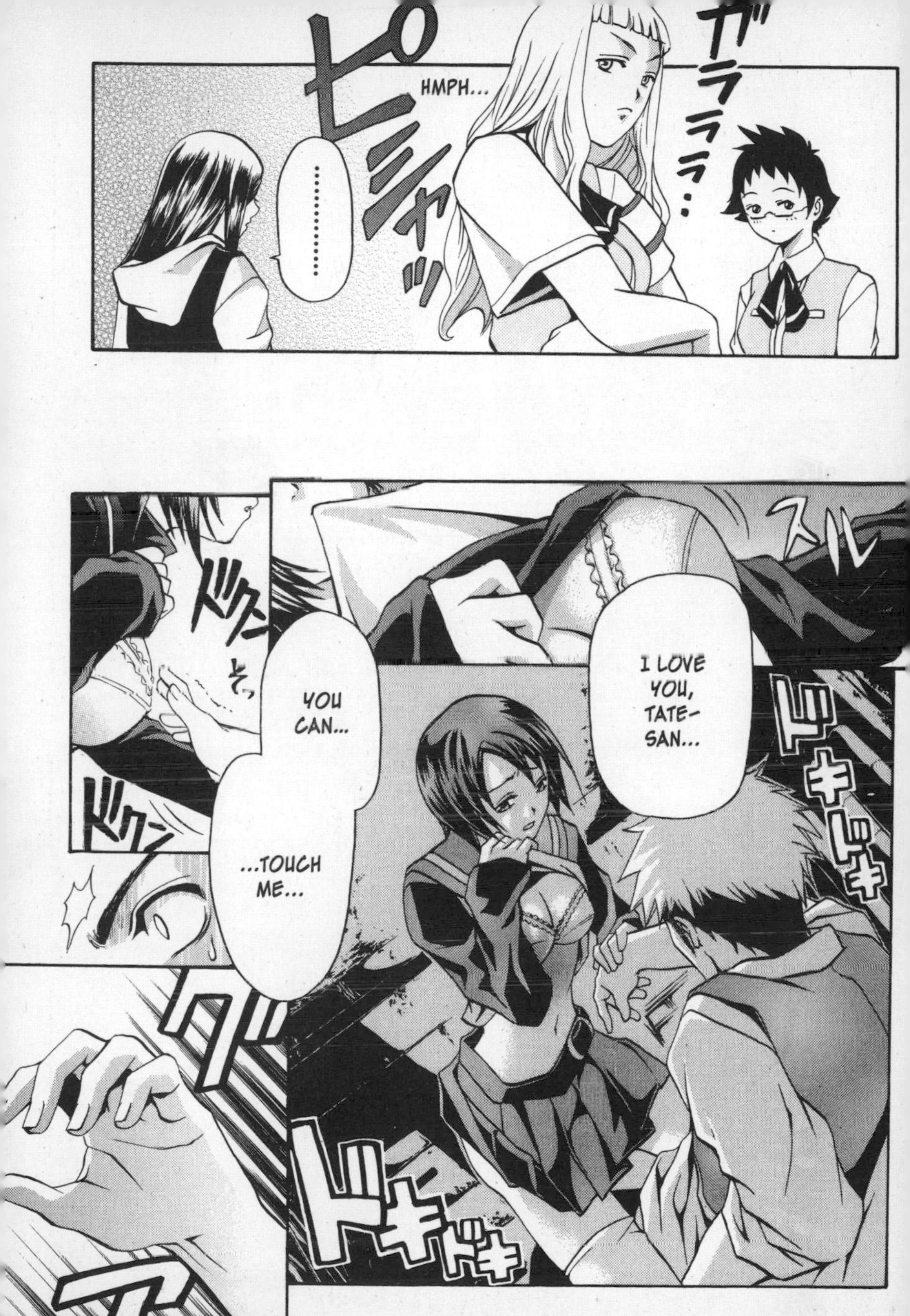
ガラララ‥
HMPH...
ピシャッ
......
スル
I LOVE YOU, TATE-SAN...
YOU CAN...
...TOUCH ME...
ドキドキ
ドクン
そっ
ドクン

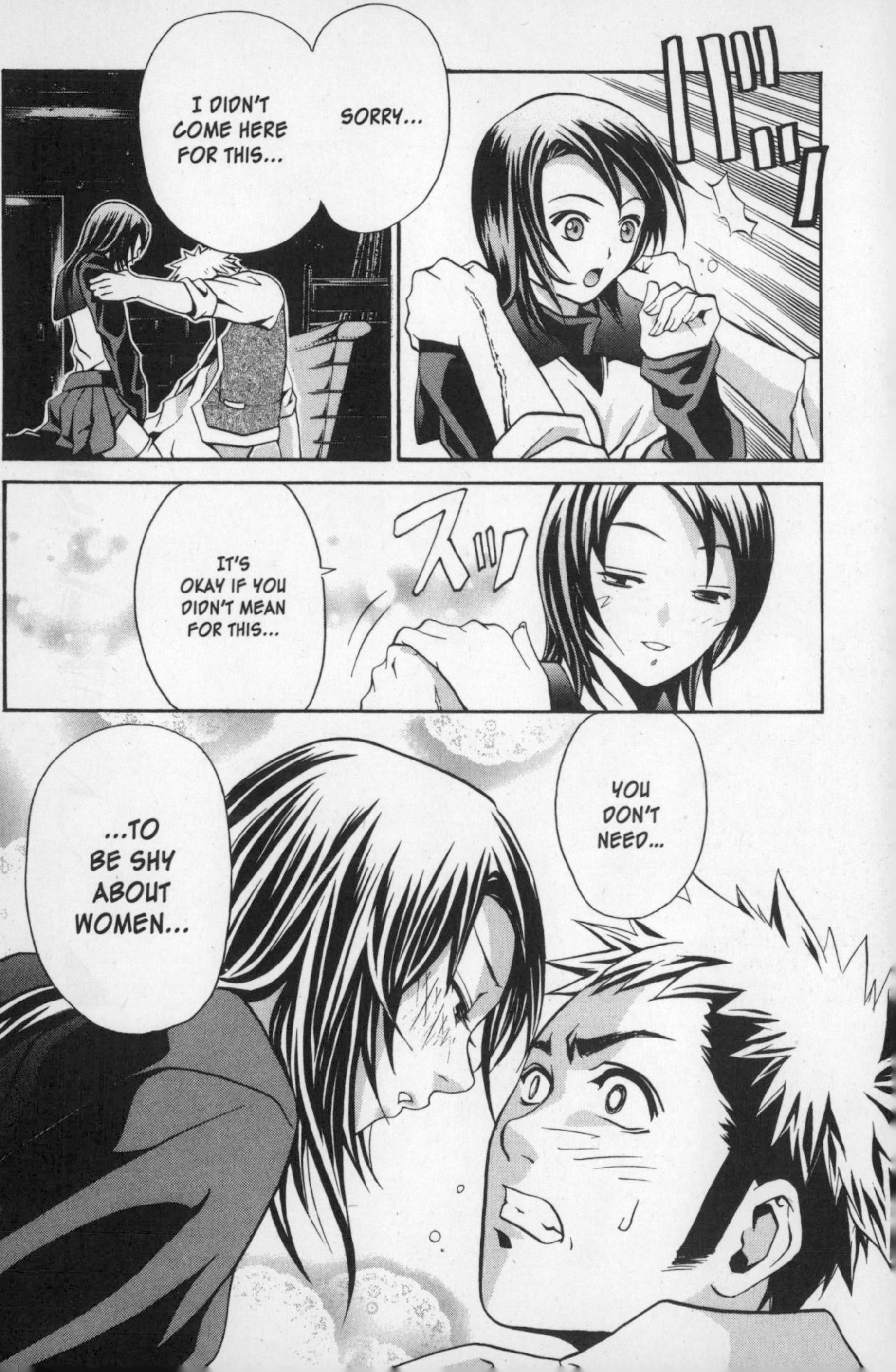
SORRY...
I DIDN'T COME HERE FOR THIS...
IT'S OKAY IF YOU DIDN'T MEAN FOR THIS...
YOU DON'T NEED...
...TO BE SHY ABOUT WOMEN...

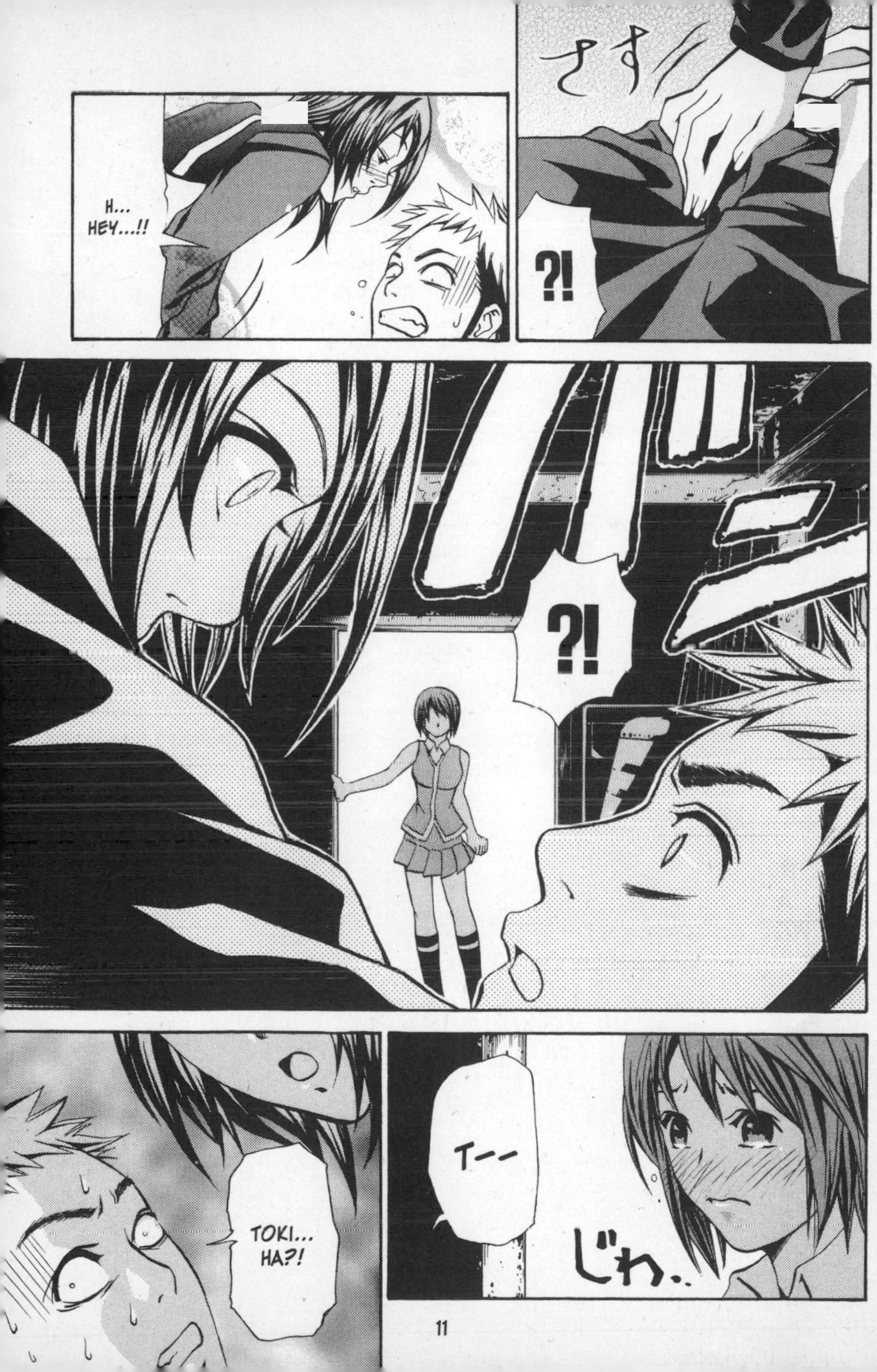
さす
?!
H... HEY...!!
?!
T--
じわ..
TOKI... HA?!

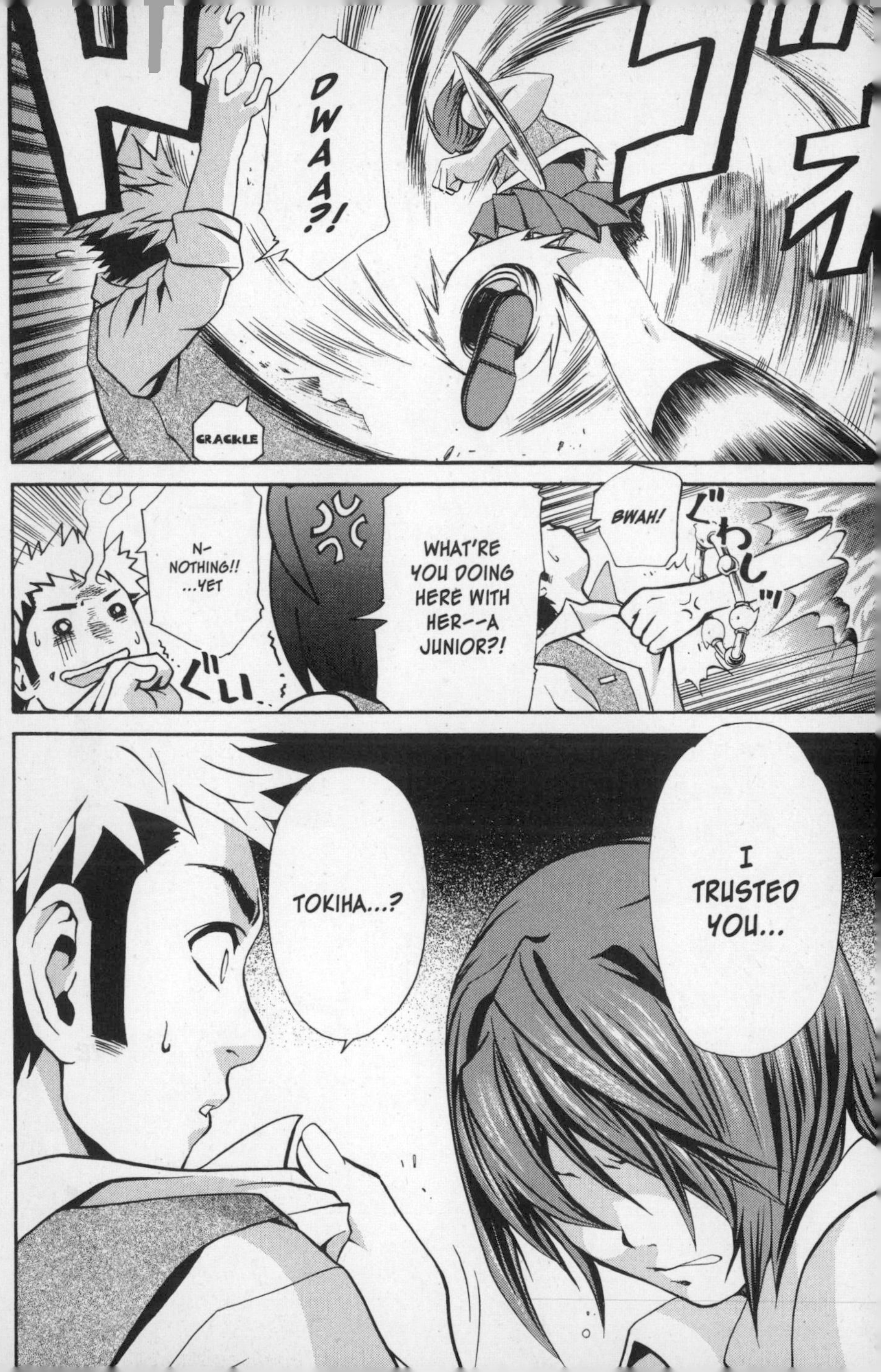
DWAAA?!
CRACKLE
BWAH!
ぐわし
WHAT'RE YOU DOING HERE WITH HER--A JUNIOR?!
N-NOTHING!! ...YET
ぐい
I TRUSTED YOU...
TOKIHA...?

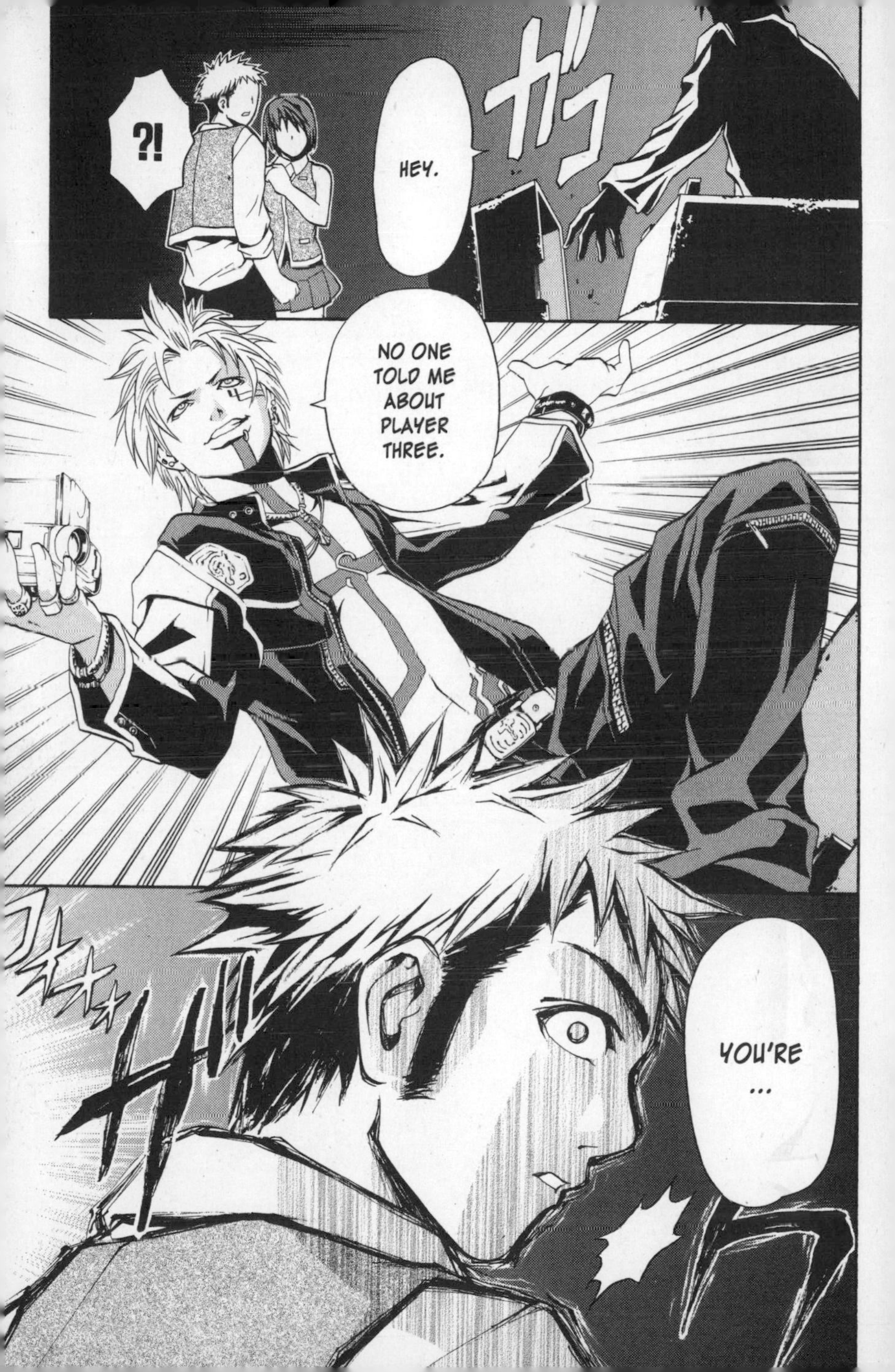
ガコ
HEY.
?!
NO ONE TOLD ME ABOUT PLAYER THREE.
YOU'RE ...

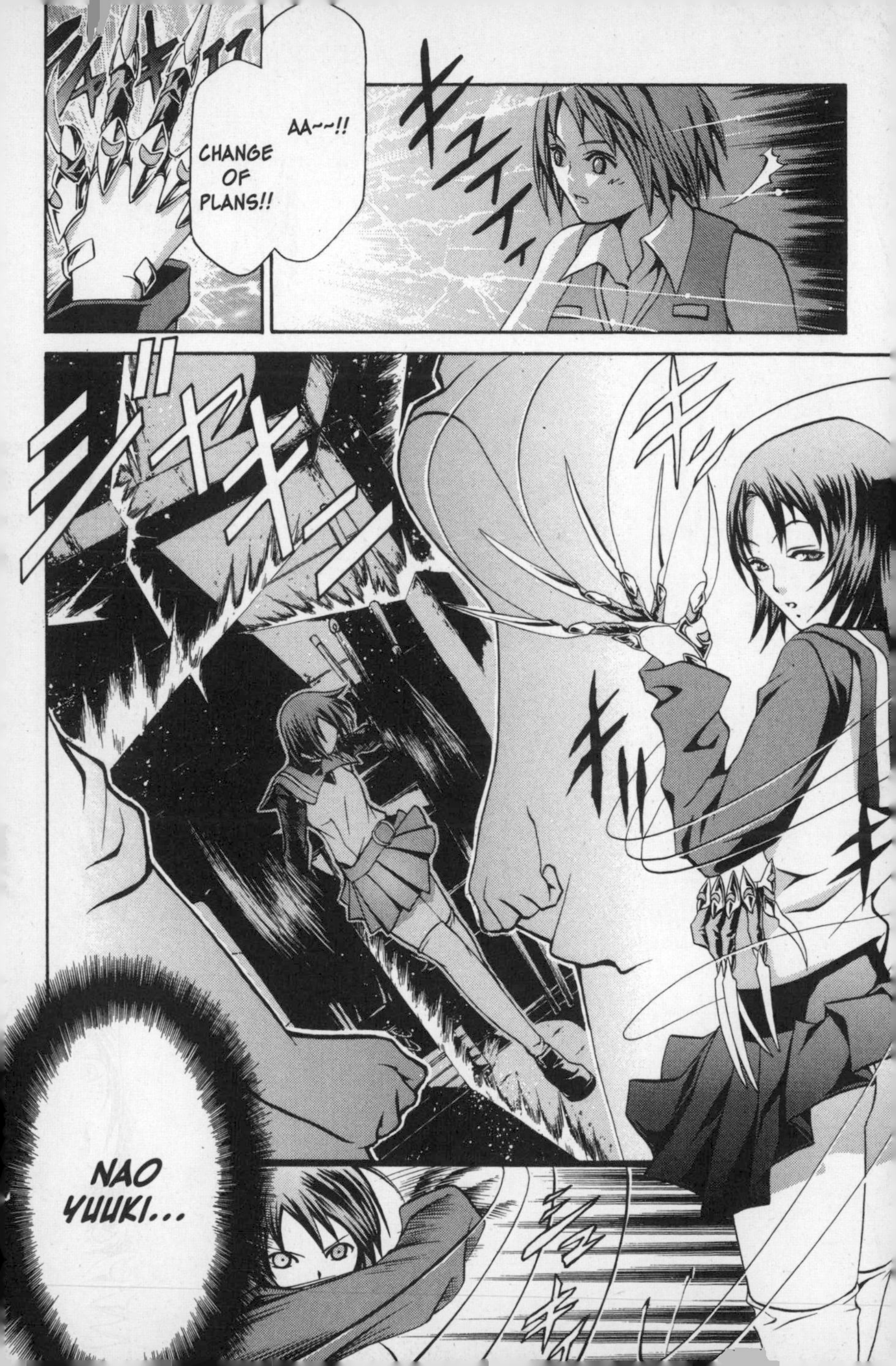

AA~~!!
CHANGE OF PLANS!!
NAO YUUKI...

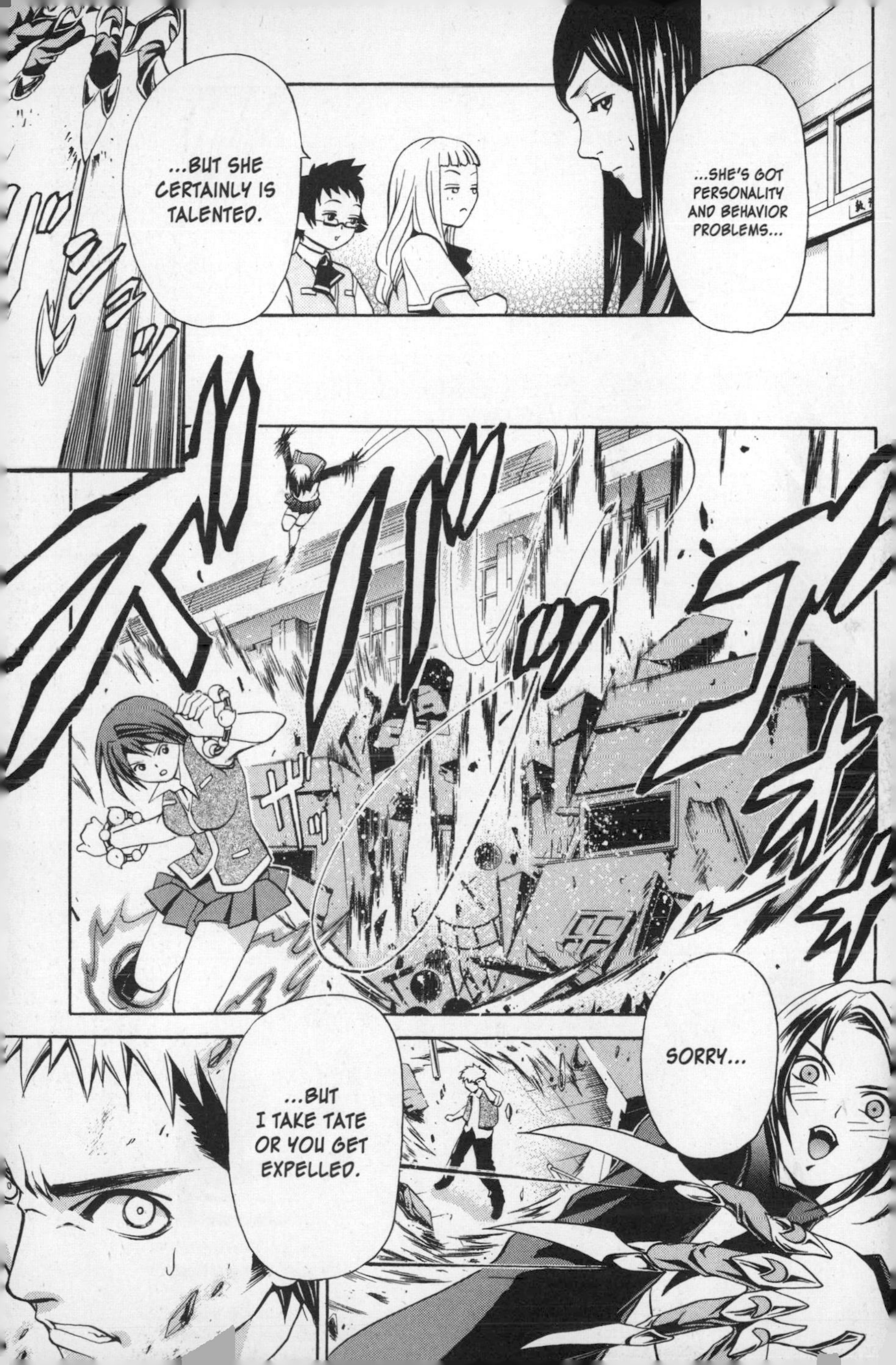
...SHE'S GOT PERSONALITY AND BEHAVIOR PROBLEMS...
...BUT SHE CERTAINLY IS TALENTED.
SORRY...
...BUT I TAKE TATE OR YOU GET EXPELLED.

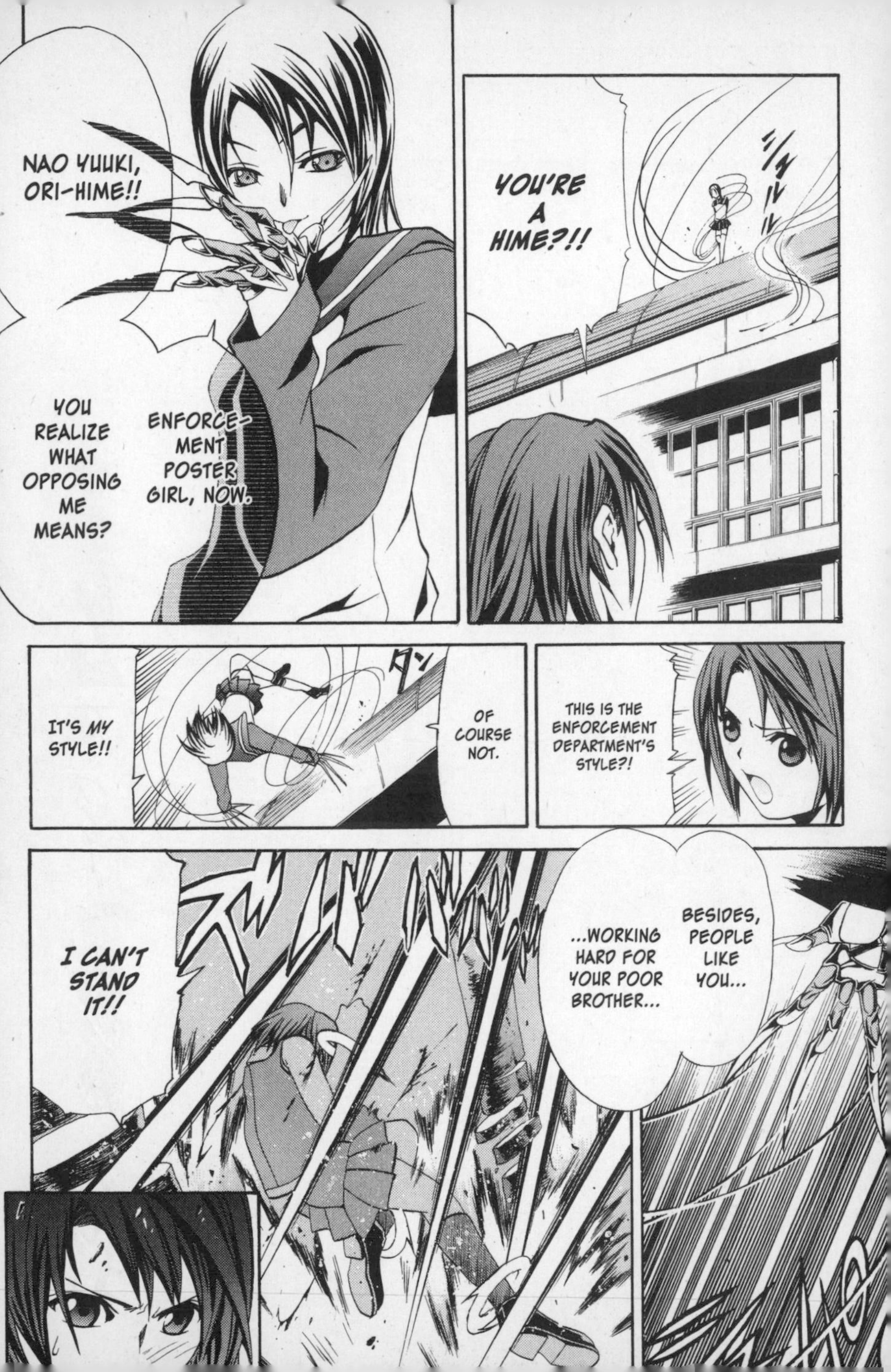
YOU'RE A HIME?!!
NAO YUUKI, ORI-HIME!!
ENFORCE-MENT POSTER GIRL, NOW.
YOU REALIZE WHAT OPPOSING ME MEANS?
THIS IS THE ENFORCEMENT DEPARTMENT'S STYLE?!
OF COURSE NOT.
IT'S MY STYLE!!
BESIDES, PEOPLE LIKE YOU...
...WORKING HARD FOR YOUR POOR BROTHER...
I CAN'T STAND IT!!

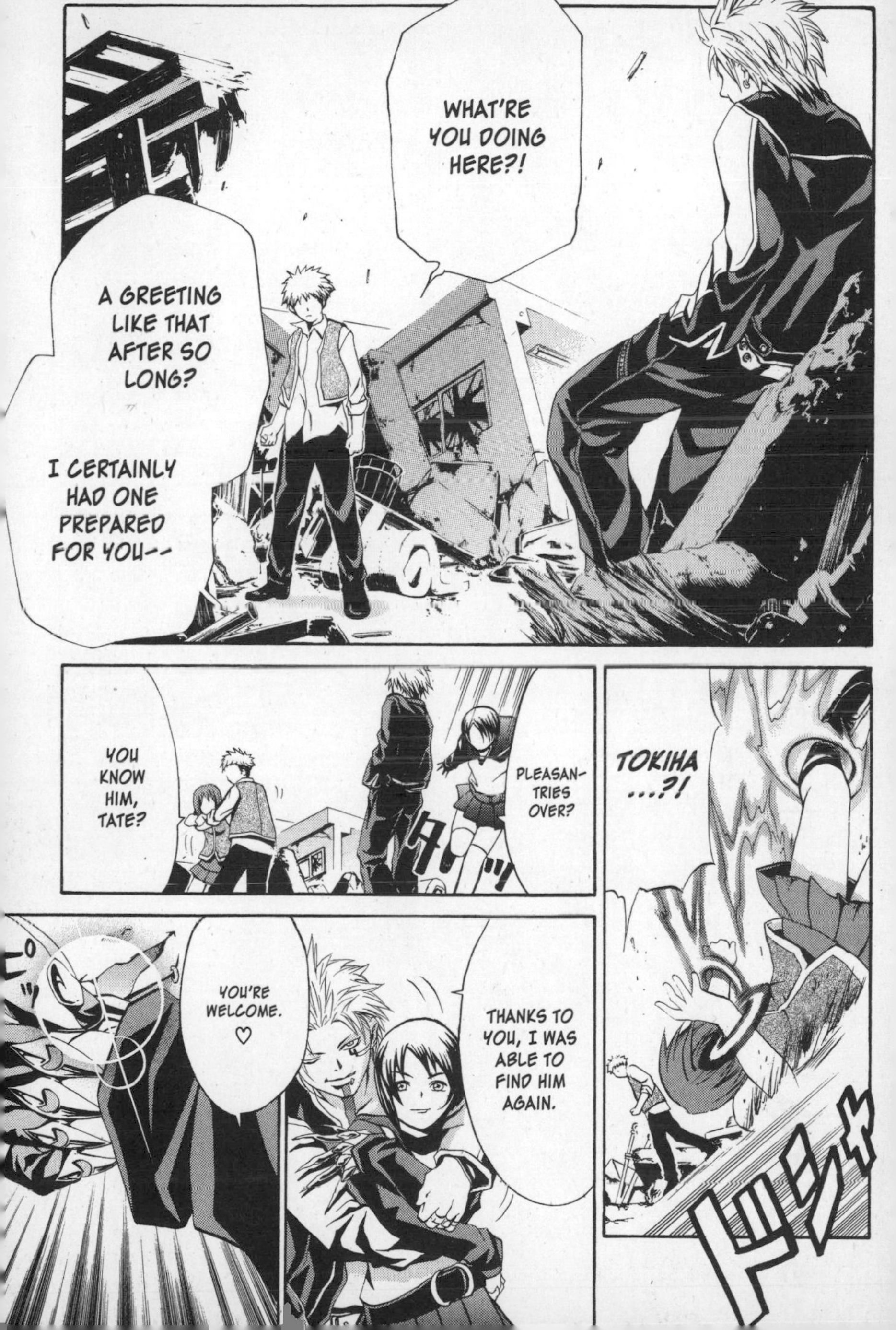
WHAT'RE YOU DOING HERE?!
A GREETING LIKE THAT AFTER SO LONG?
I CERTAINLY HAD ONE PREPARED FOR YOU--
TOKIHA...?!
PLEASAN-TRIES OVER?
YOU KNOW HIM, TATE?
THANKS TO YOU, I WAS ABLE TO FIND HIM AGAIN.
YOU'RE WELCOME. ♡

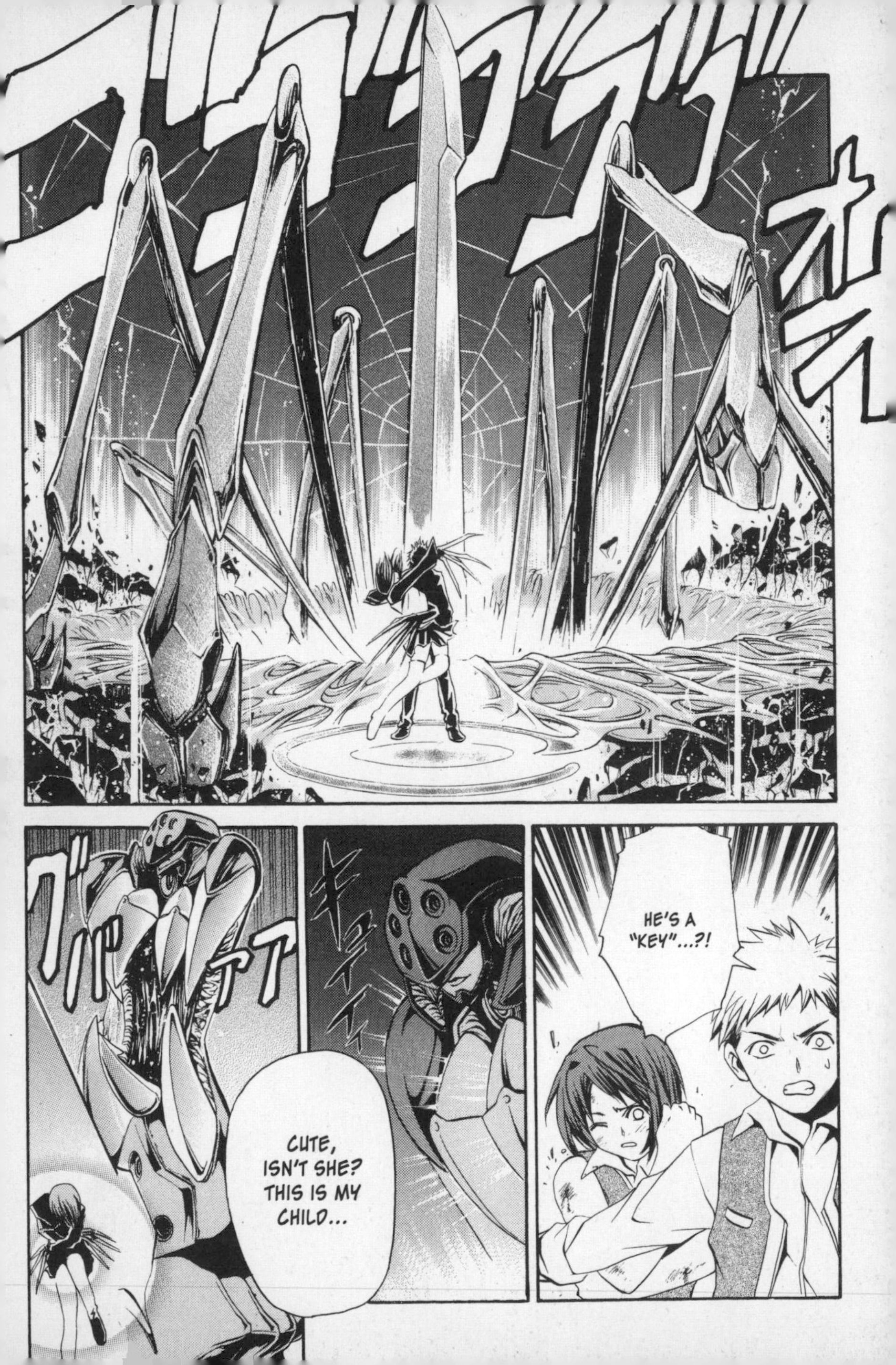
HE'S A "KEY"...?!
CUTE, ISN'T SHE? THIS IS MY CHILD...

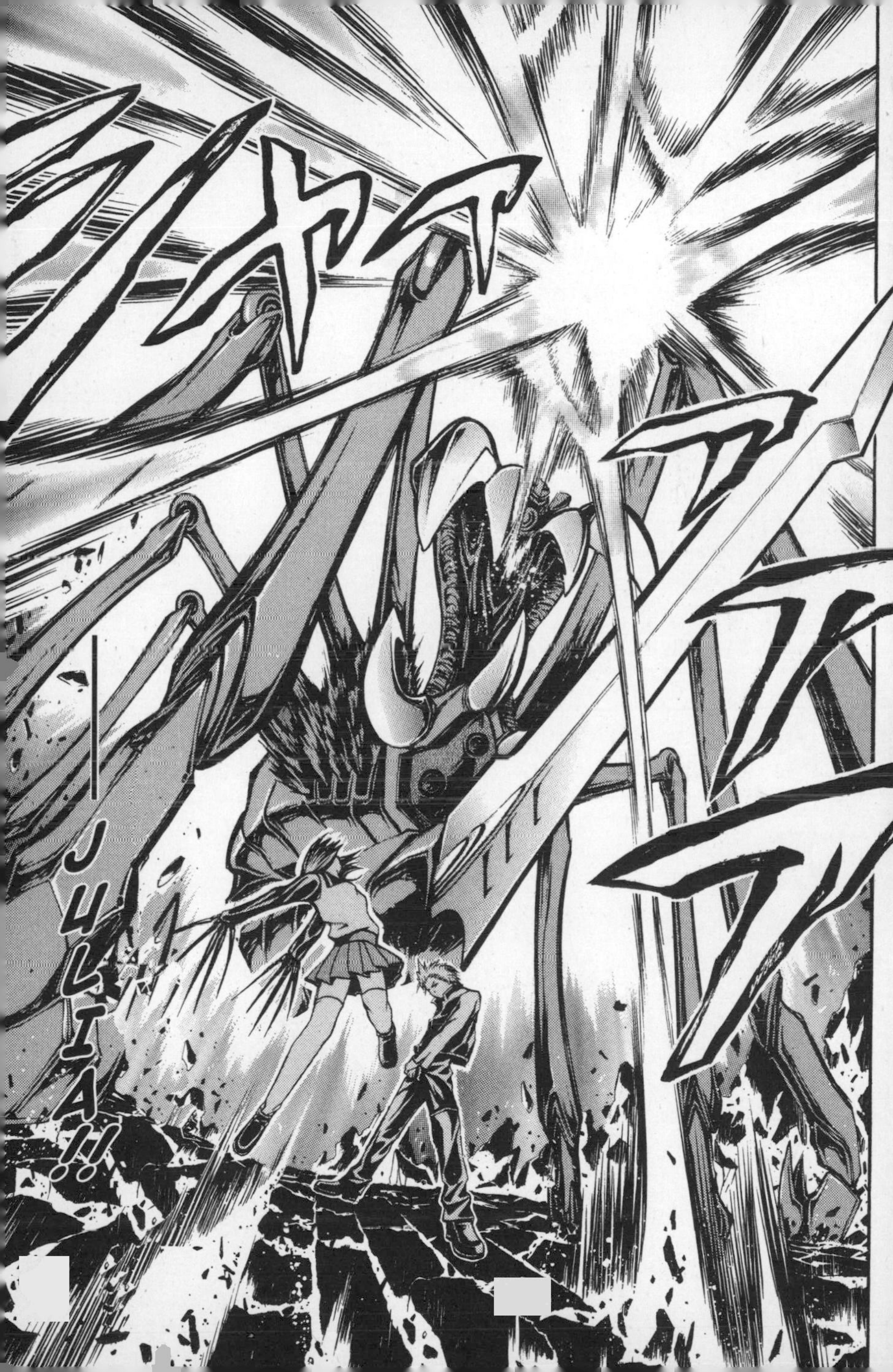
——JULIA!!

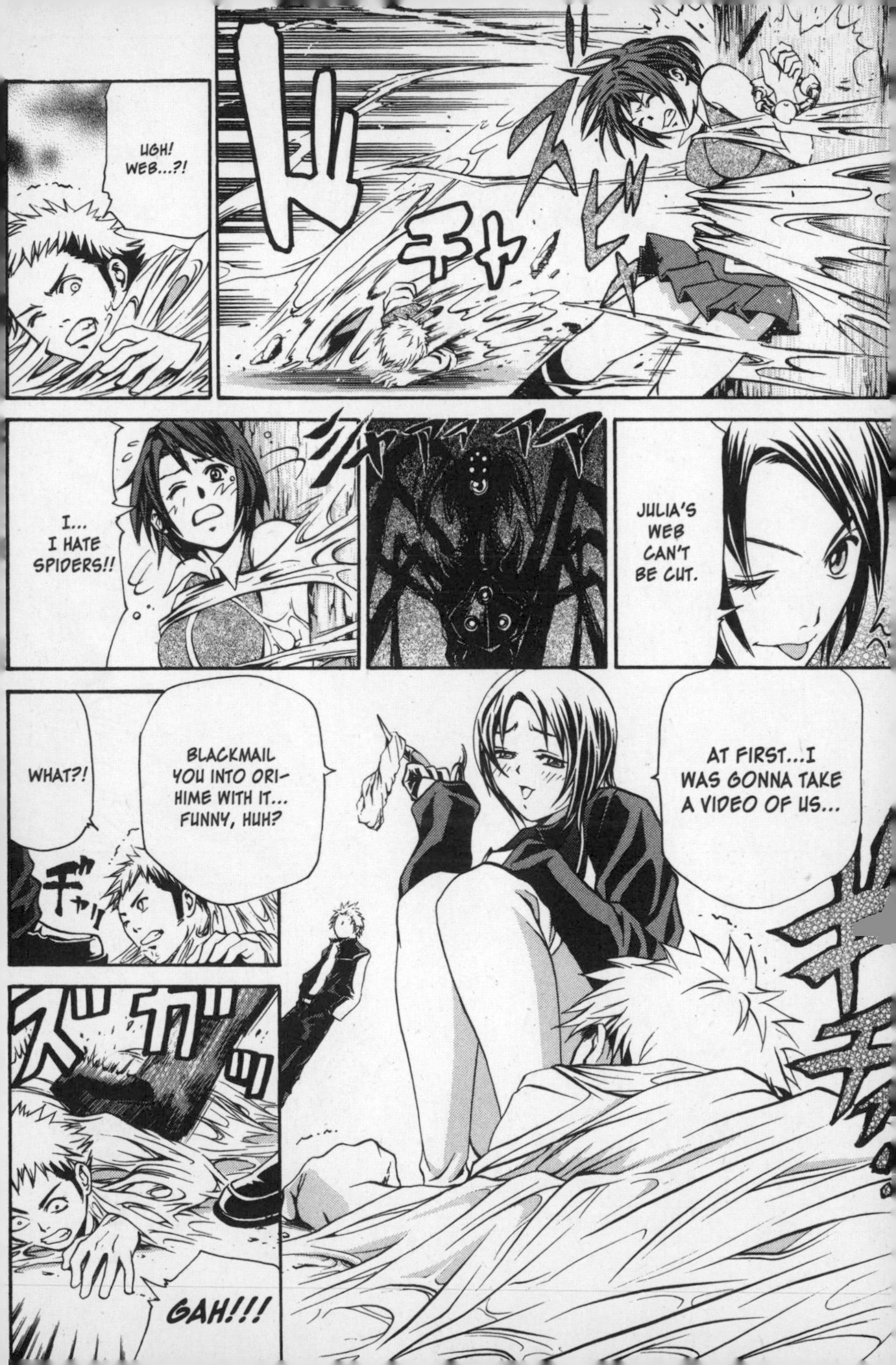
UGH! WEB...?!
JULIA'S WEB CAN'T BE CUT.
I... I HATE SPIDERS!!
AT FIRST...I WAS GONNA TAKE A VIDEO OF US...
BLACKMAIL YOU INTO ORI-HIME WITH IT... FUNNY, HUH?
WHAT?!
GAH!!!

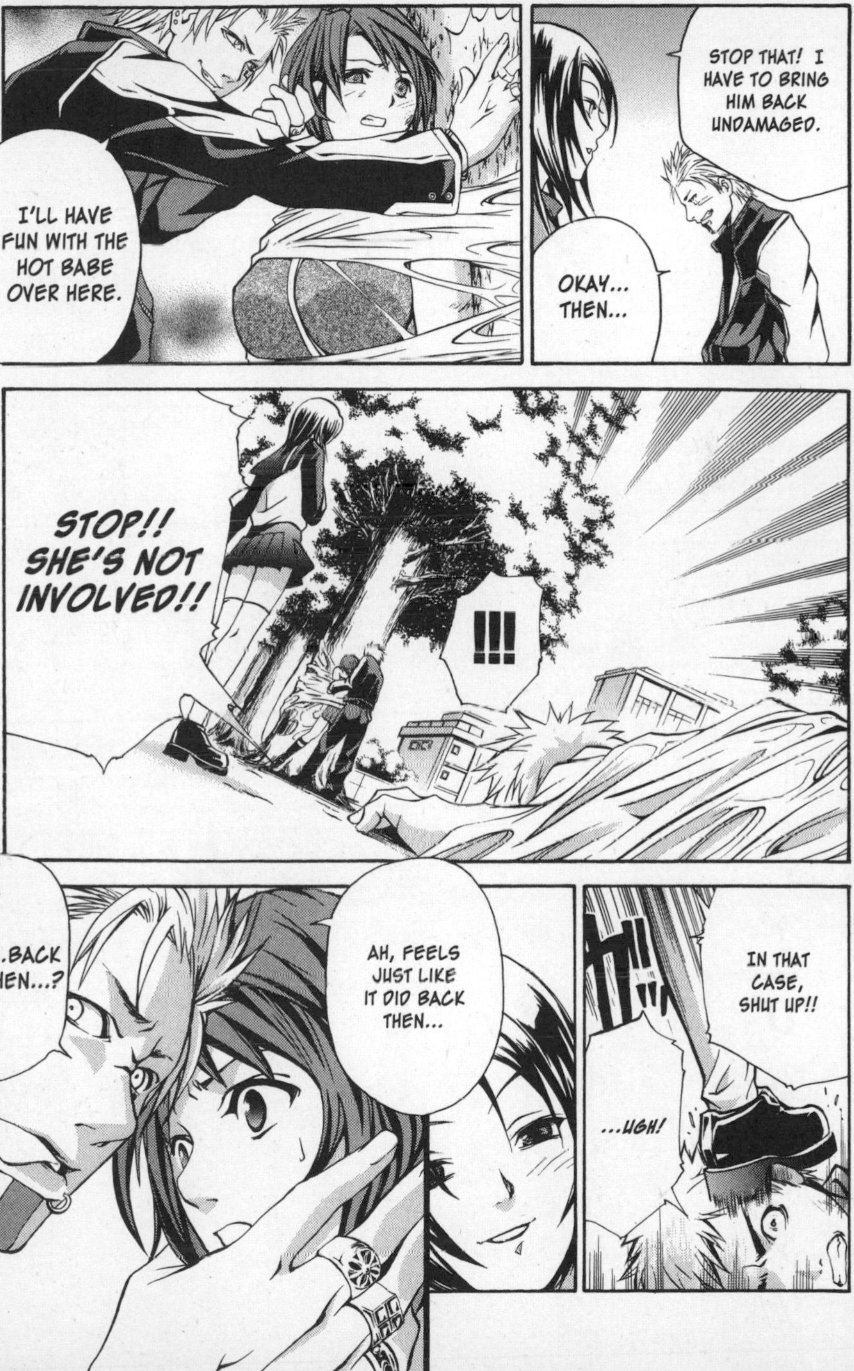
STOP THAT! I HAVE TO BRING HIM BACK UNDAMAGED.
OKAY... THEN...
I'LL HAVE FUN WITH THE HOT BABE OVER HERE.
STOP!! SHE'S NOT INVOLVED!!
!!!
IN THAT CASE, SHUT UP!!
...UGH!
AH, FEELS JUST LIKE IT DID BACK THEN...
...BACK THEN...?

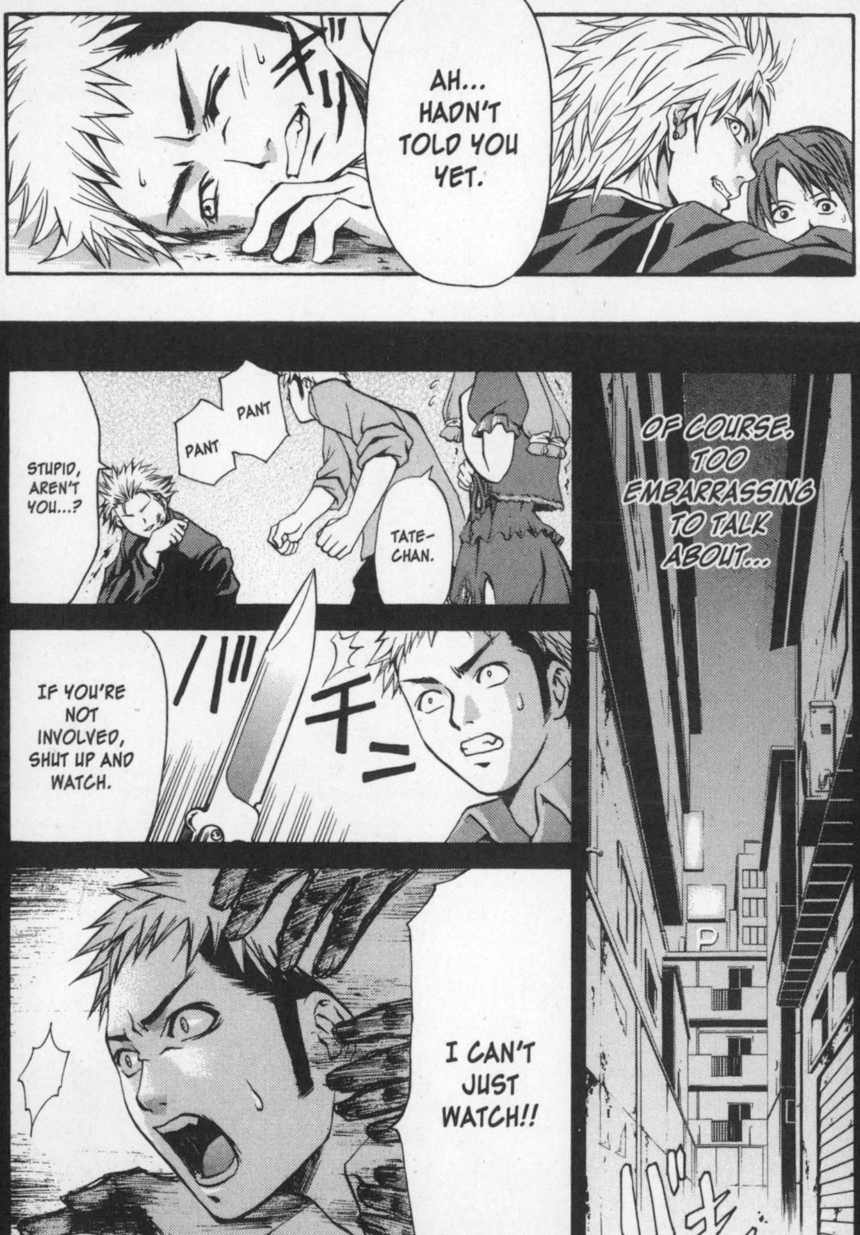
AH... HADN'T TOLD YOU YET.
ギリ
OF COURSE. TOO EMBARRASSING TO TALK ABOUT...
バキィ
TATE-CHAN.
PANT
PANT
STUPID, AREN'T YOU...?
IF YOU'RE NOT INVOLVED, SHUT UP AND WATCH.
I CAN'T JUST WATCH!!

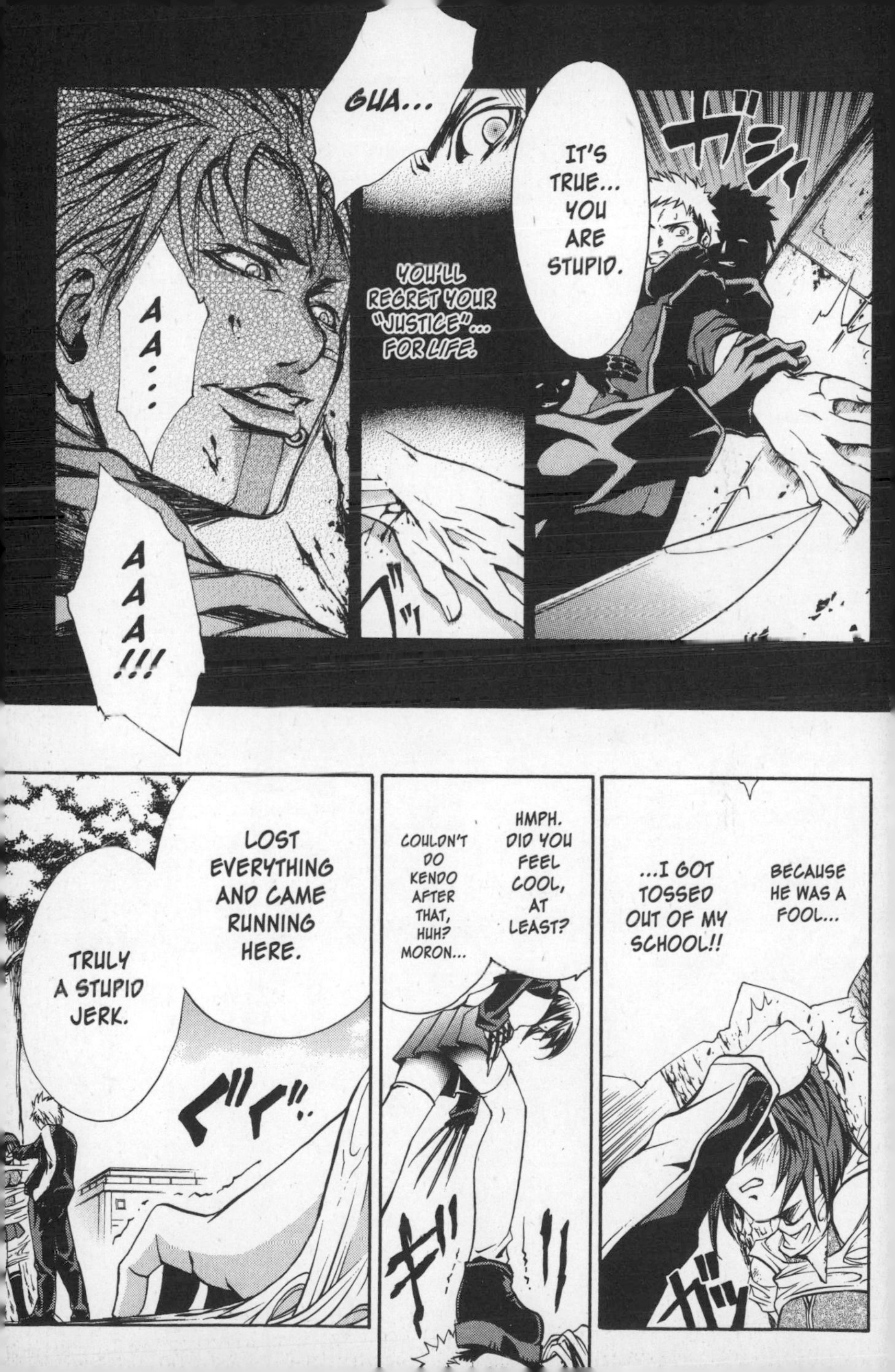

IT'S TRUE... YOU ARE STUPID.
GUA...
YOU'LL REGRET YOUR "JUSTICE"... FOR LIFE.
AA...
AAAA!!!
BECAUSE HE WAS A FOOL...
...I GOT TOSSED OUT OF MY SCHOOL!!
HMPH. DID YOU FEEL COOL, AT LEAST?
COULDN'T DO KENDO AFTER THAT, HUH? MORON...
LOST EVERYTHING AND CAME RUNNING HERE.
TRULY A STUPID JERK.

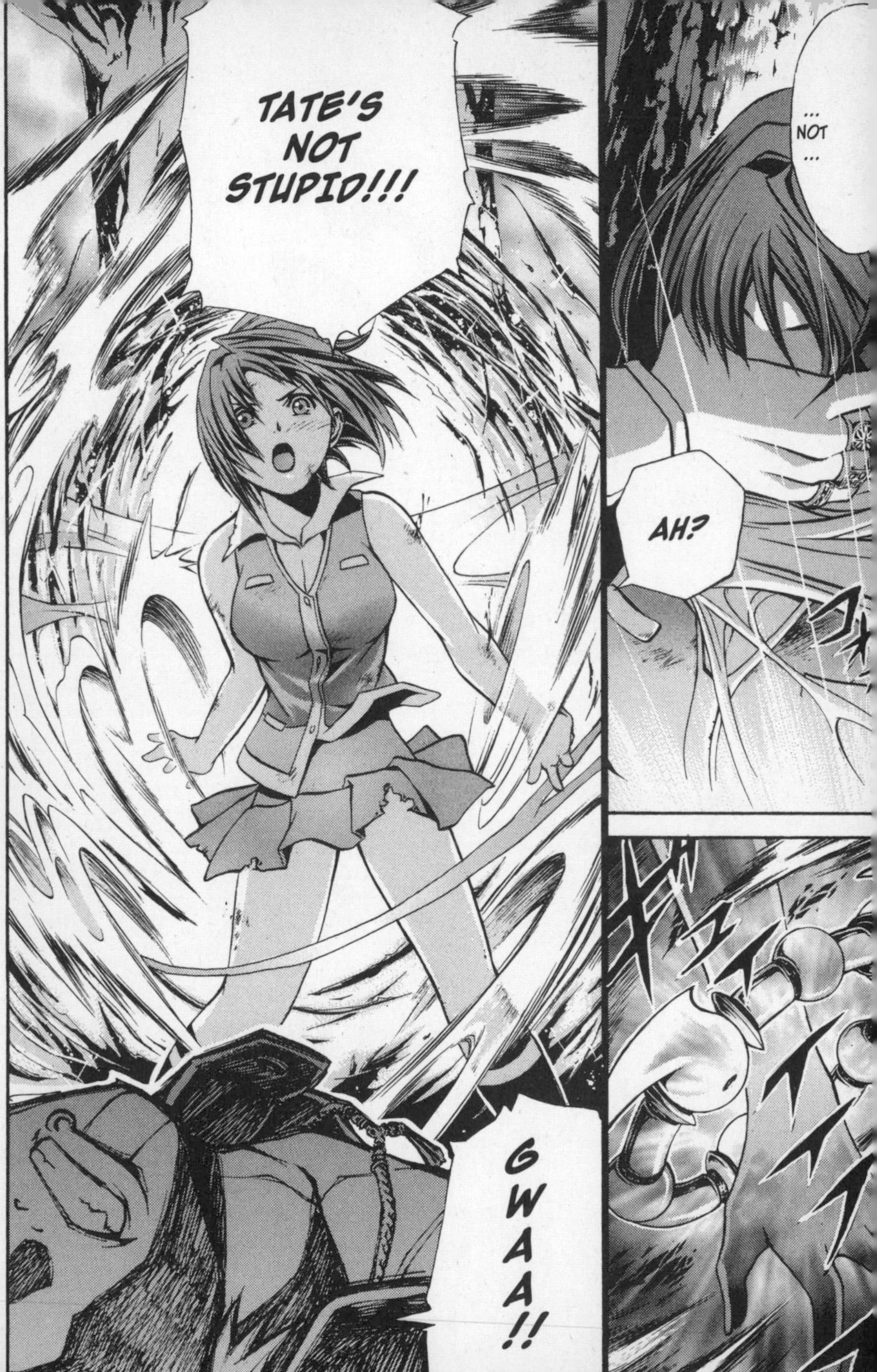
... NOT ...
AH?
TATE'S NOT STUPID!!!
GWAA!!

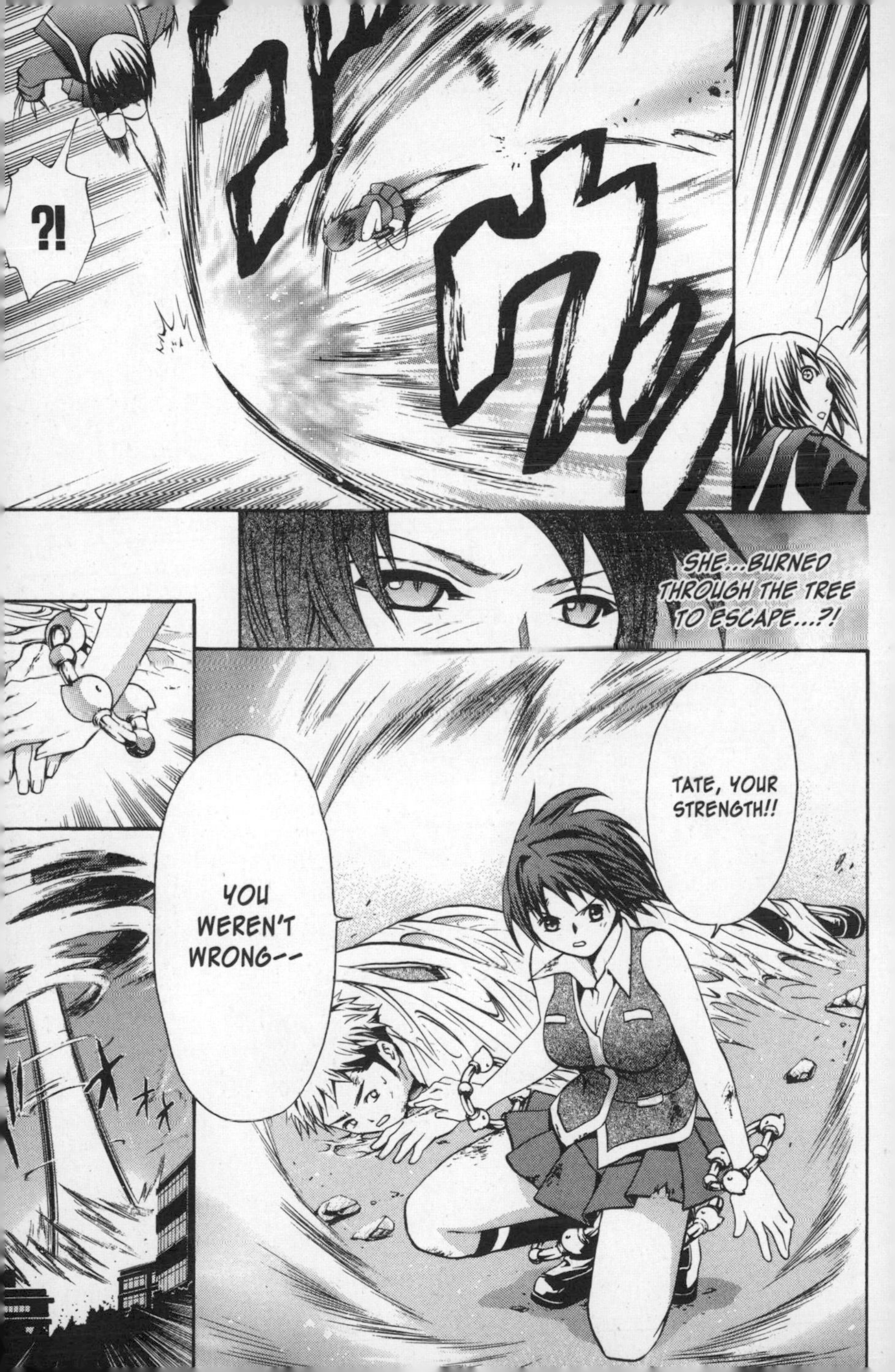
?!
SHE...BURNED THROUGH THE TREE TO ESCAPE...?!
TATE, YOUR STRENGTH!!
YOU WEREN'T WRONG--

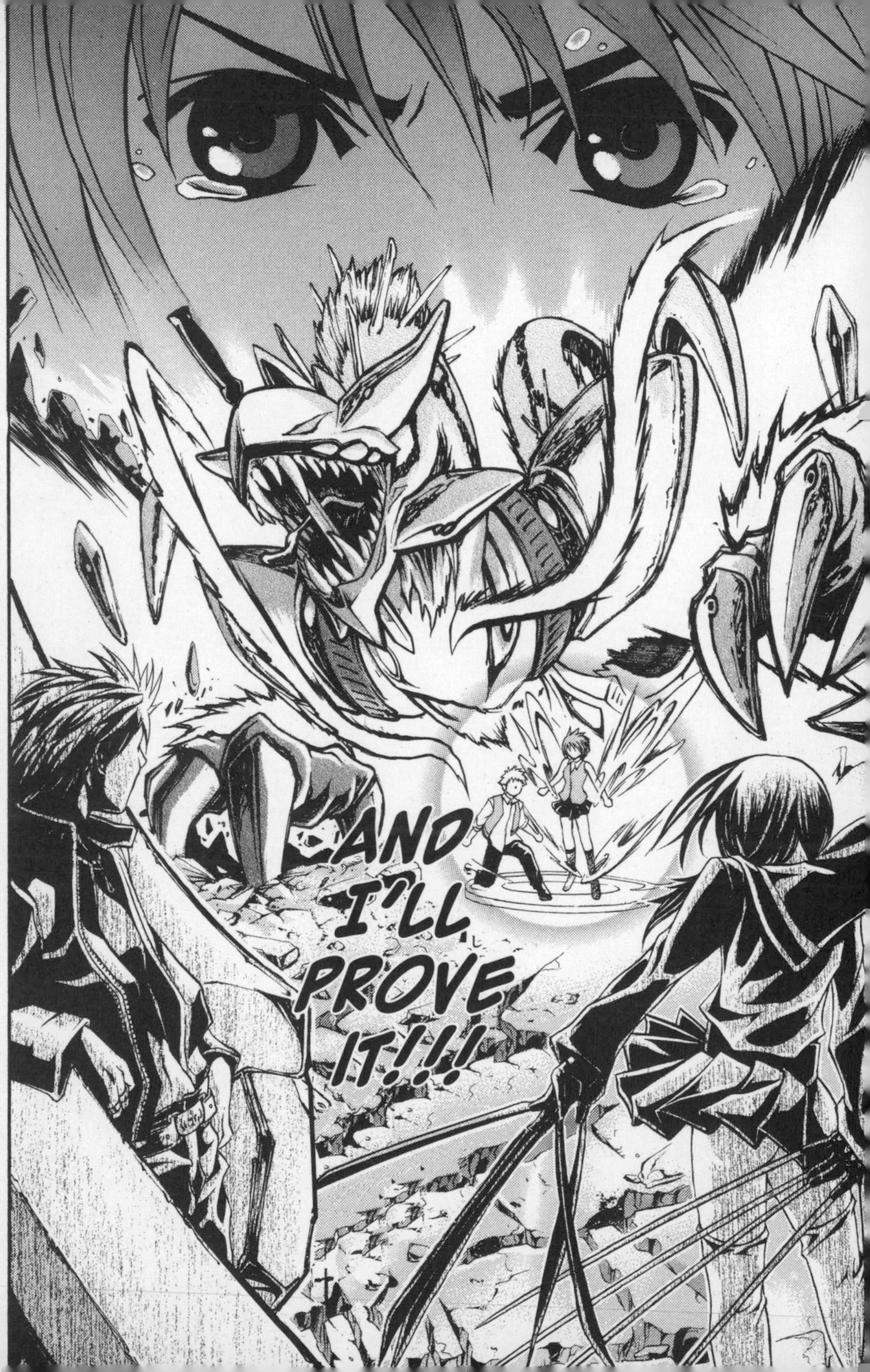
AND I'LL PROVE IT!!!!

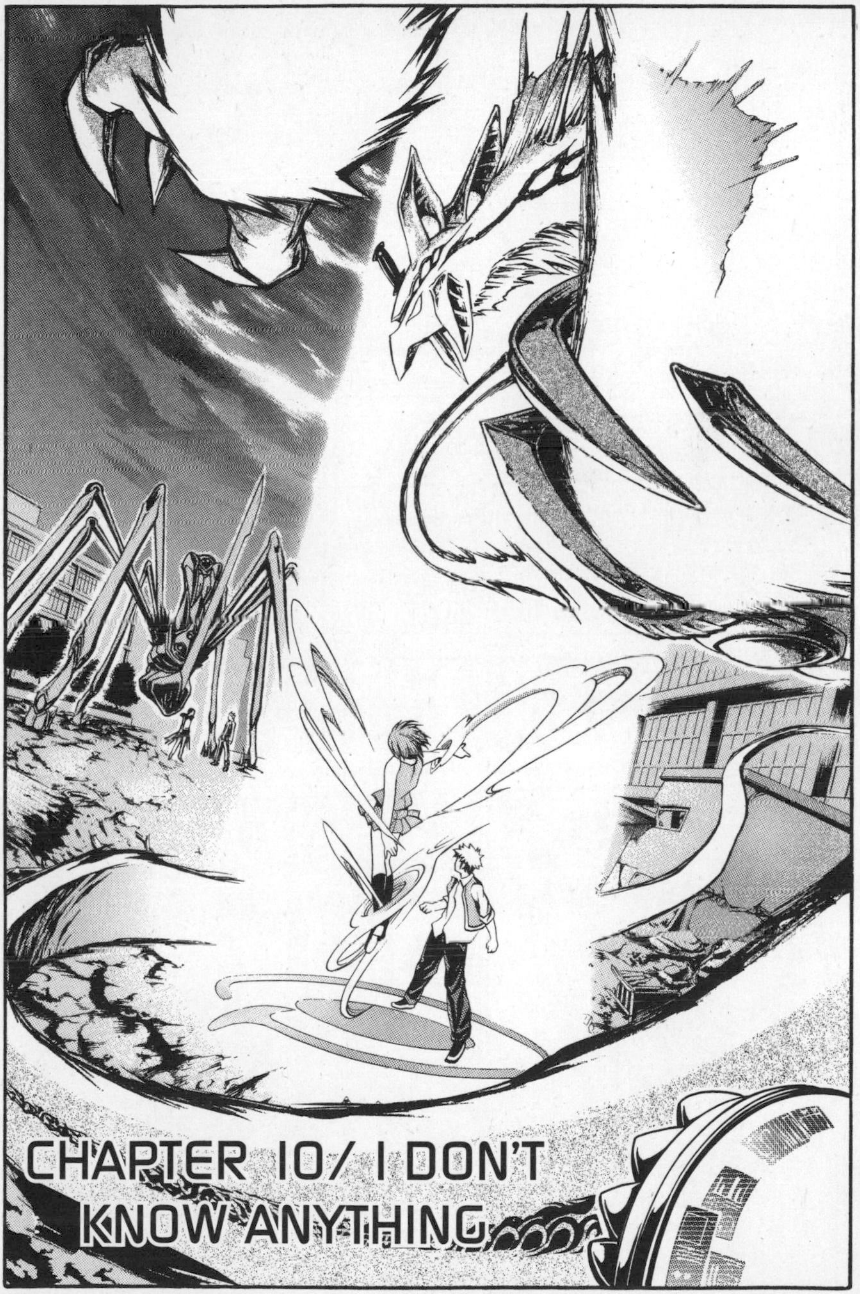
CHAPTER 10/ I DON'T
KNOW ANYTHING

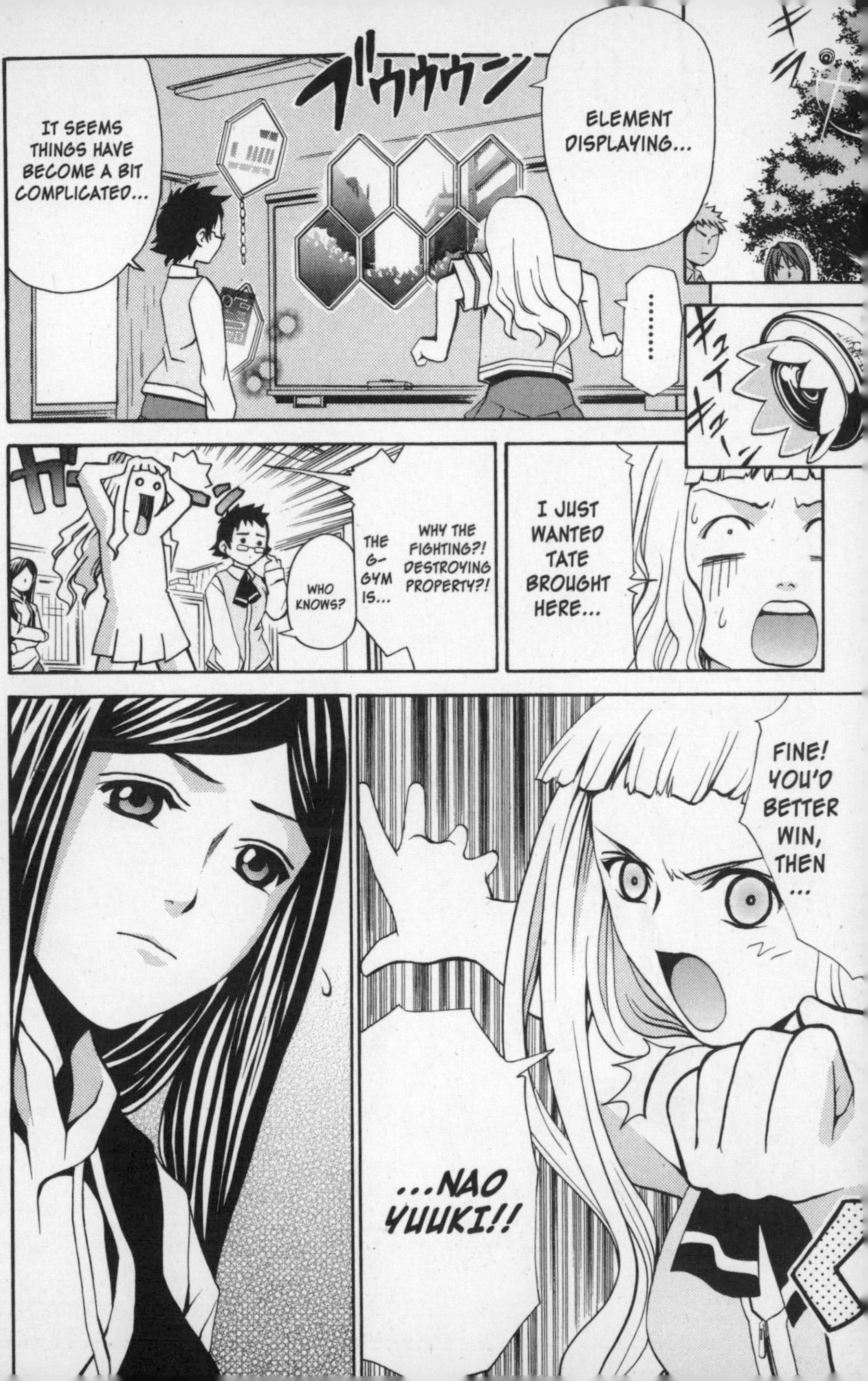
ELEMENT DISPLAYING...
......
ブゥウウン
IT SEEMS THINGS HAVE BECOME A BIT COMPLICATED...
I JUST WANTED TATE BROUGHT HERE...
WHY THE FIGHTING?! DESTROYING PROPERTY?!
THE G-GYM IS...
WHO KNOWS?
FINE! YOU'D BETTER WIN, THEN ...
...NAO YUUKI!!

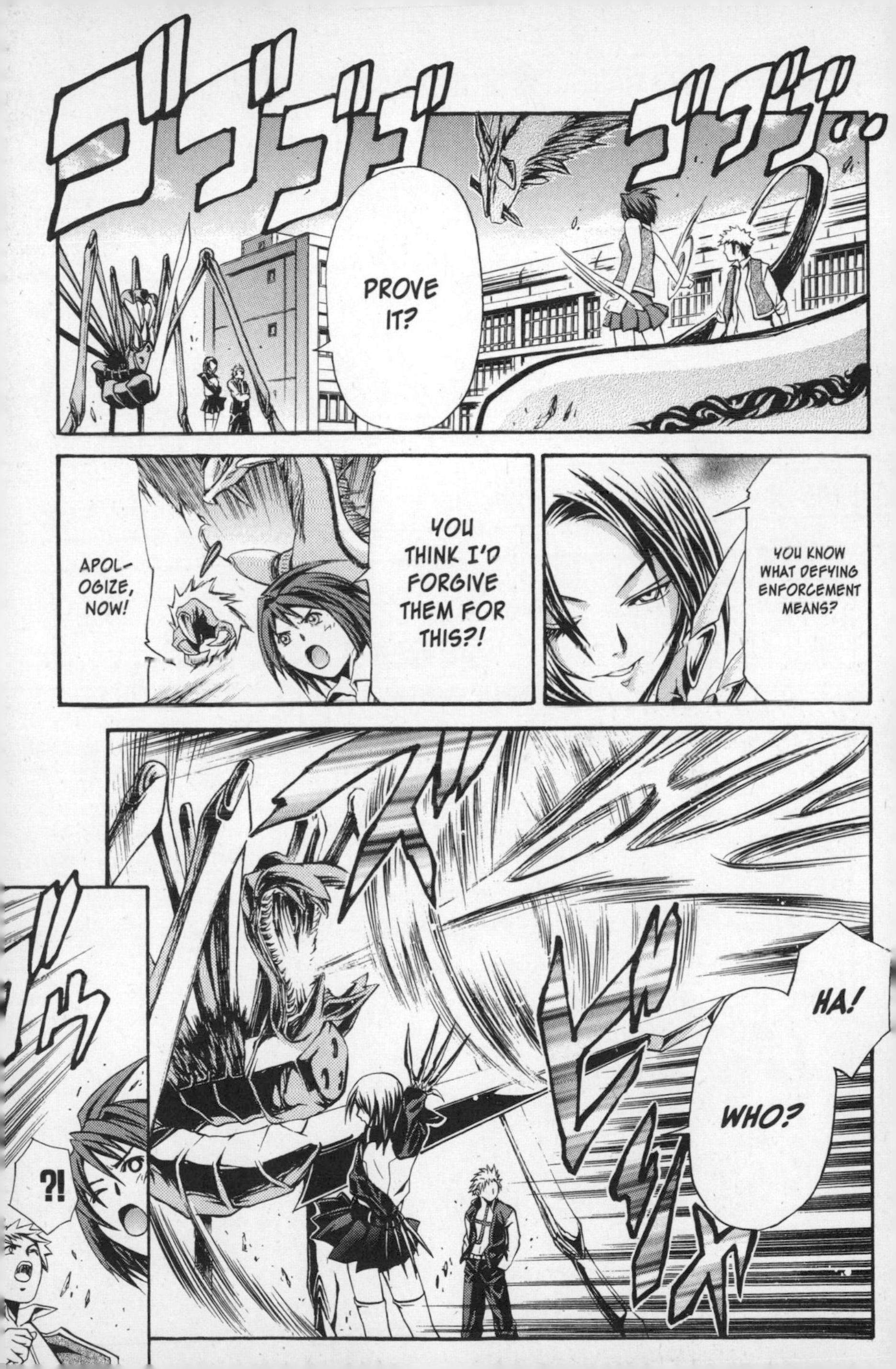
PROVE IT?
YOU KNOW WHAT DEFYING ENFORCEMENT MEANS?
YOU THINK I'D FORGIVE THEM FOR THIS?!
APOLOGIZE, NOW!
HA!
WHO?
?!

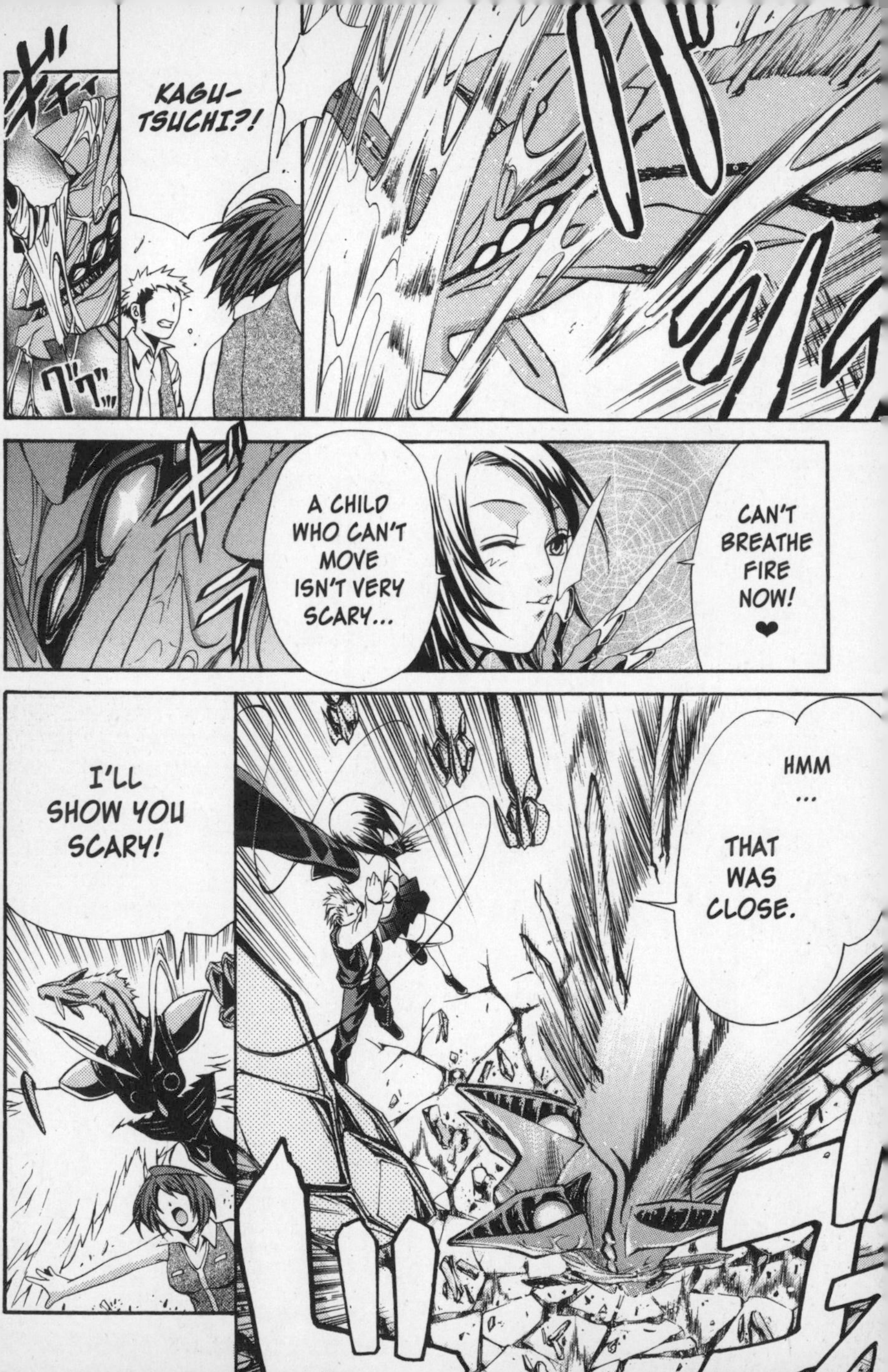
KAGU-TSUCHI?!
CAN'T BREATHE FIRE NOW! ❤
A CHILD WHO CAN'T MOVE ISN'T VERY SCARY...
HMM ... THAT WAS CLOSE.
I'LL SHOW YOU SCARY!

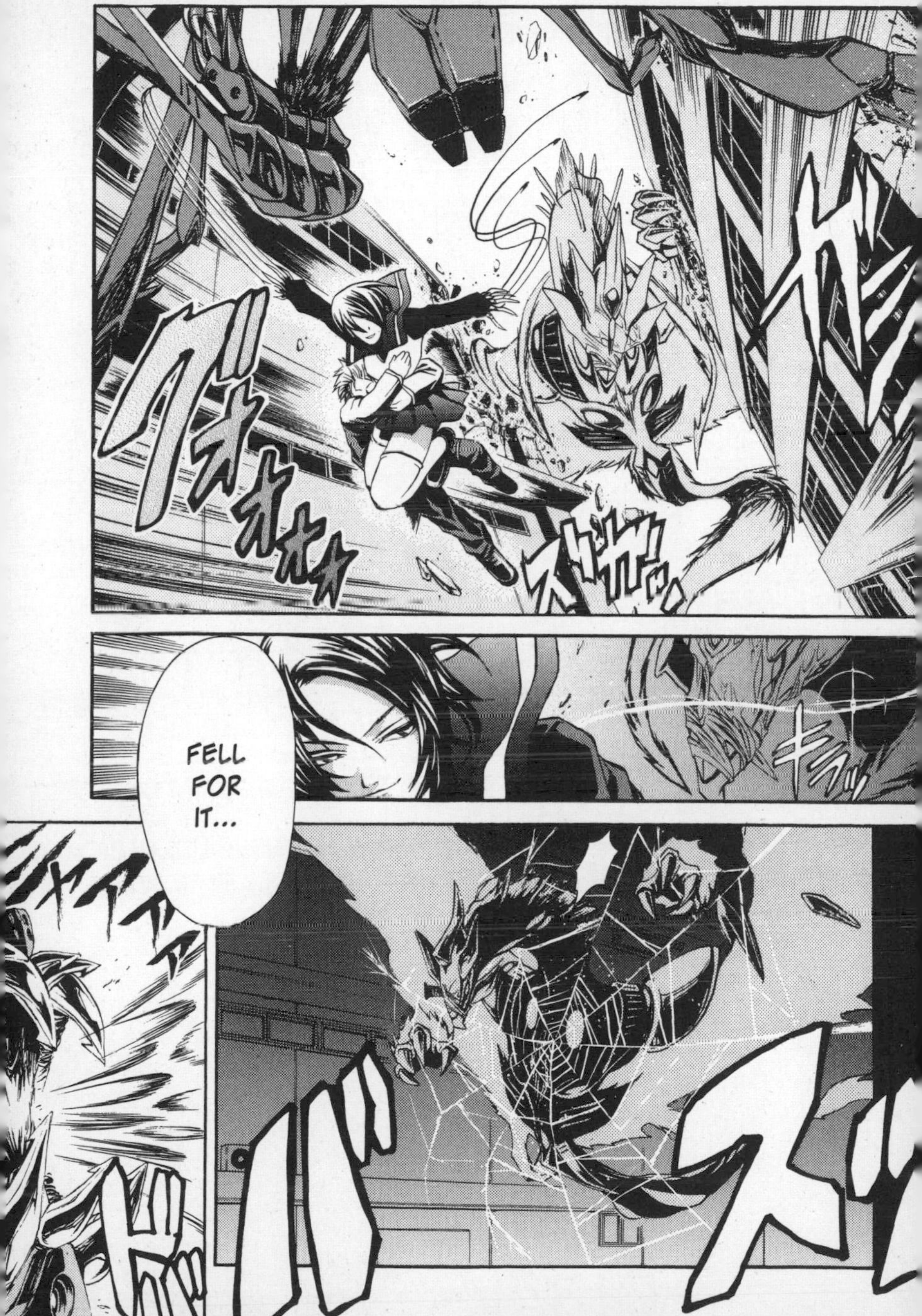
FELL FOR IT...

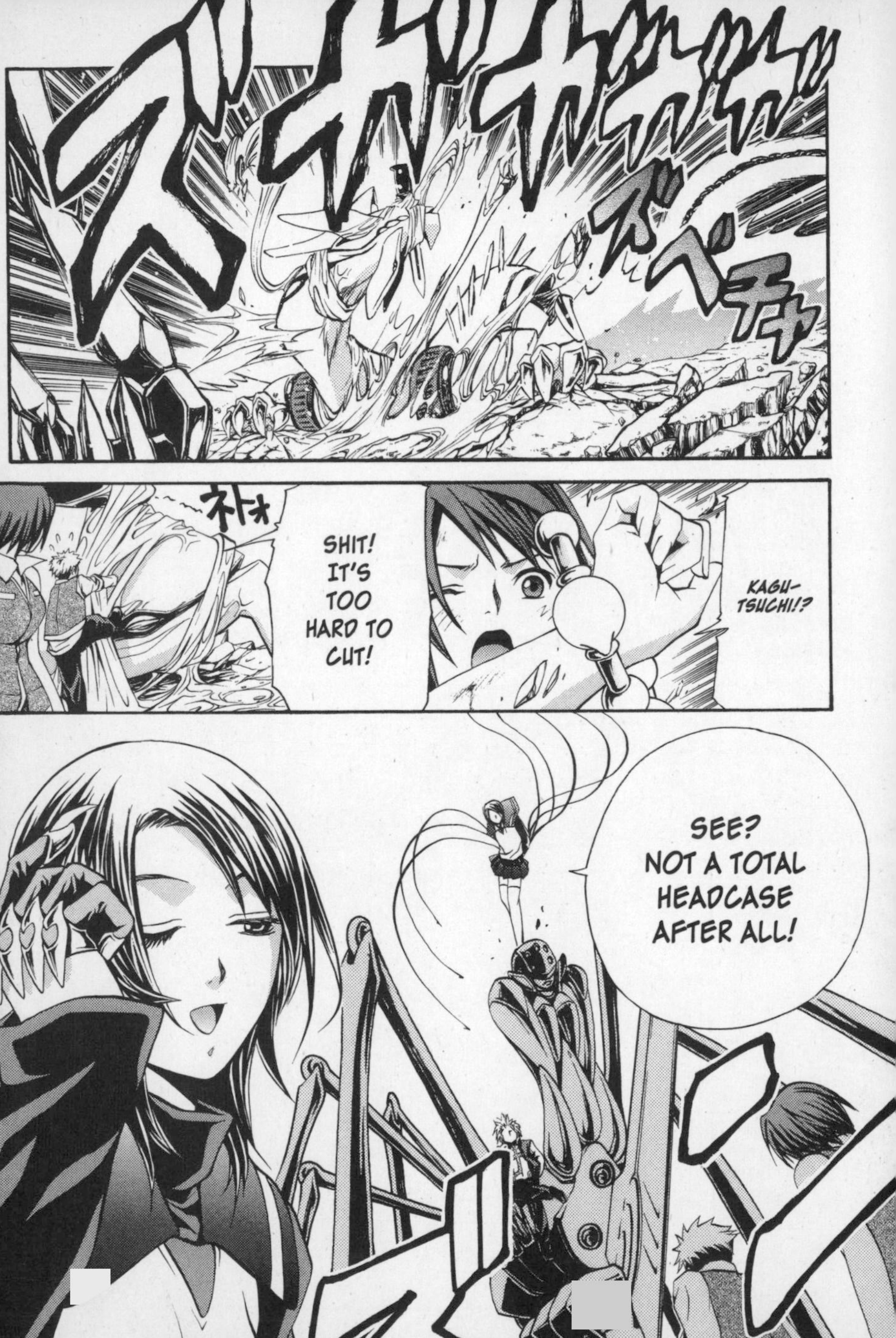
ズベチャ
KAGU-TSUCHI!?
SHIT! IT'S TOO HARD TO CUT!
ネトォ
SEE? NOT A TOTAL HEADCASE AFTER ALL!

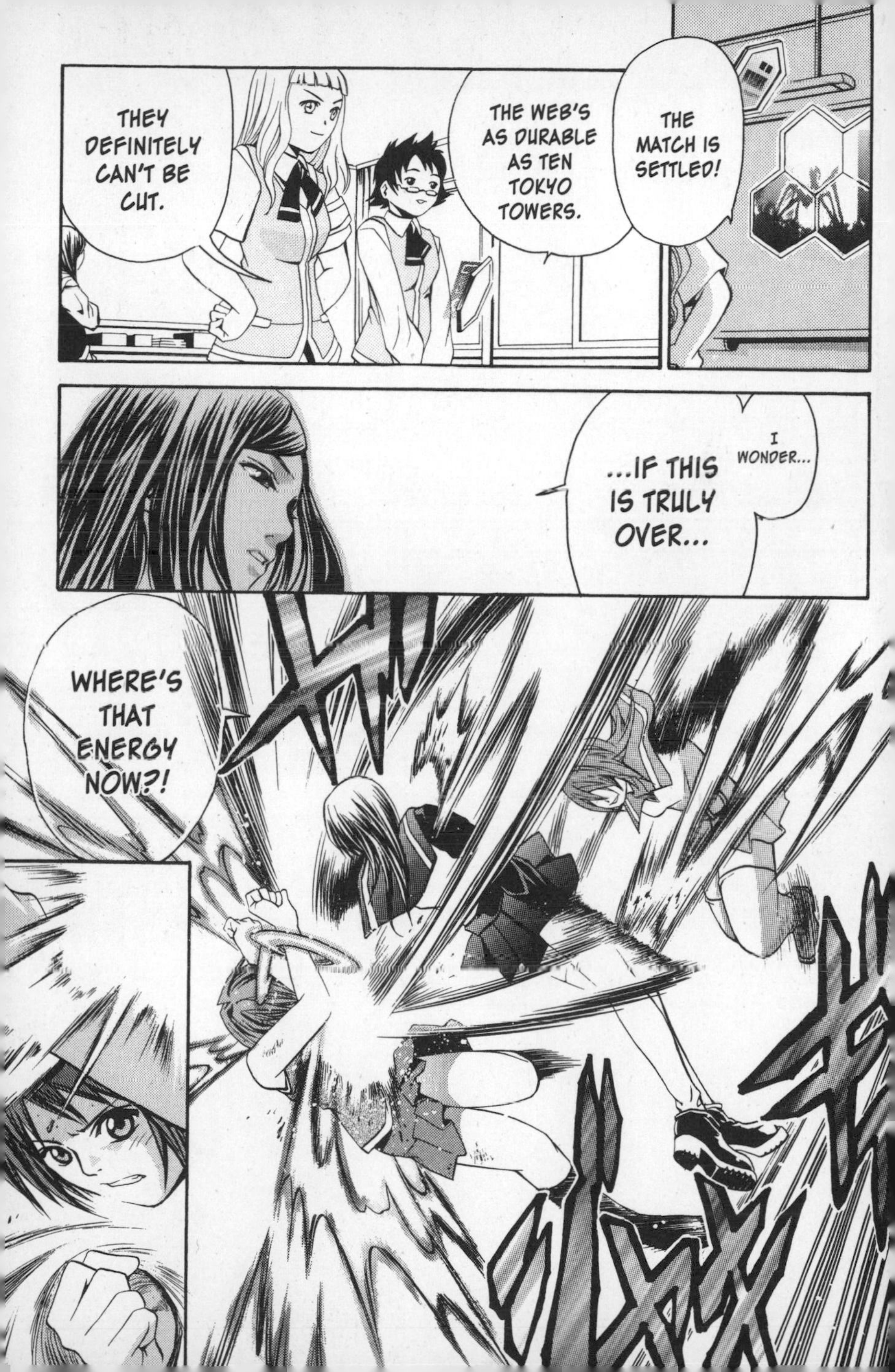
THE MATCH IS SETTLED!
THE WEB'S AS DURABLE AS TEN TOKYO TOWERS.
THEY DEFINITELY CAN'T BE CUT.
I WONDER...
...IF THIS IS TRULY OVER...
WHERE'S THAT ENERGY NOW?!

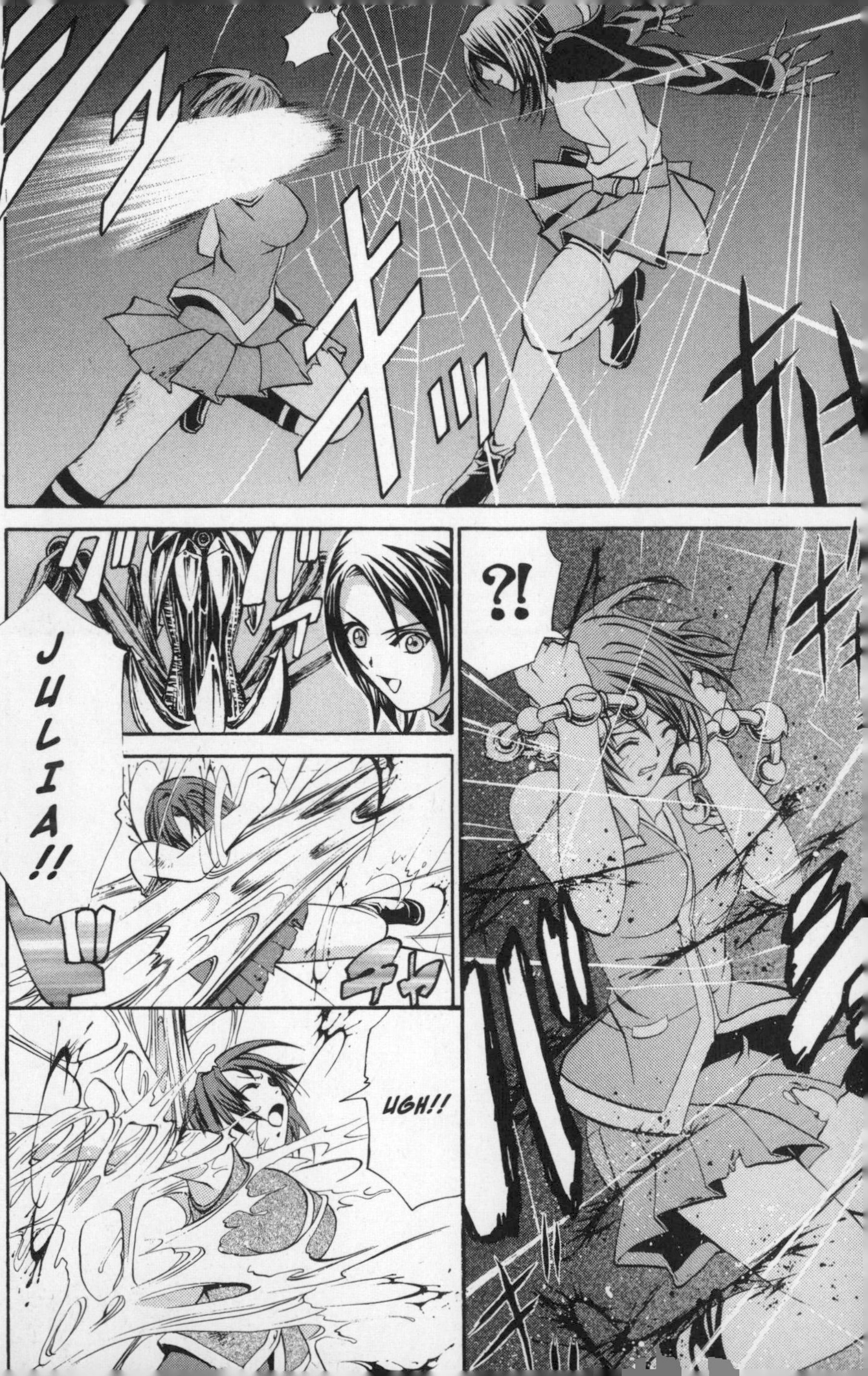
?!
JULIA!!
UGH!!

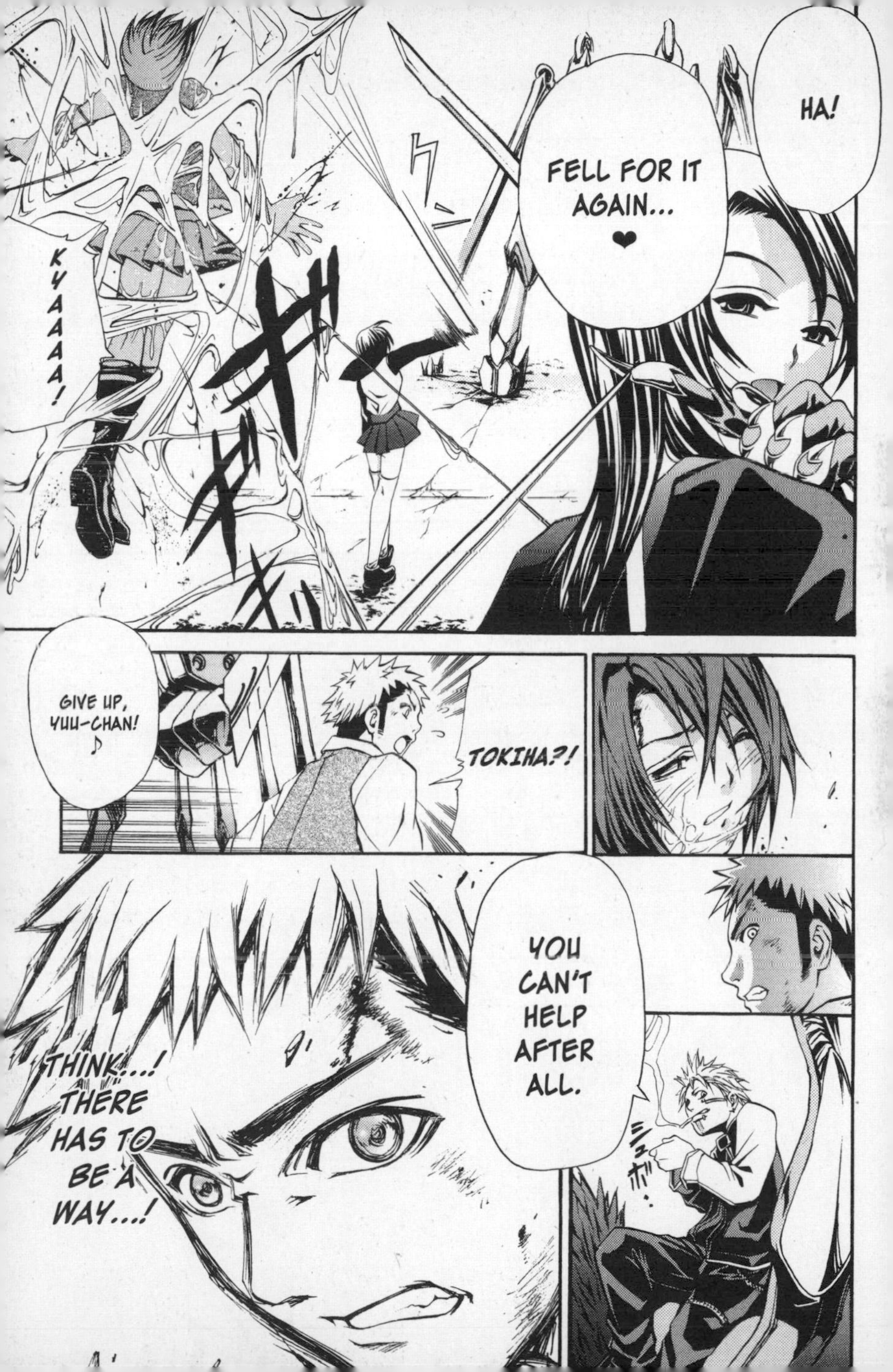

HA!
FELL FOR IT AGAIN... ❤
KYAAAAA!
TOKIHA?!
GIVE UP, YUU-CHAN! ♪
YOU CAN'T HELP AFTER ALL.
THINK...! THERE HAS TO BE A WAY...!

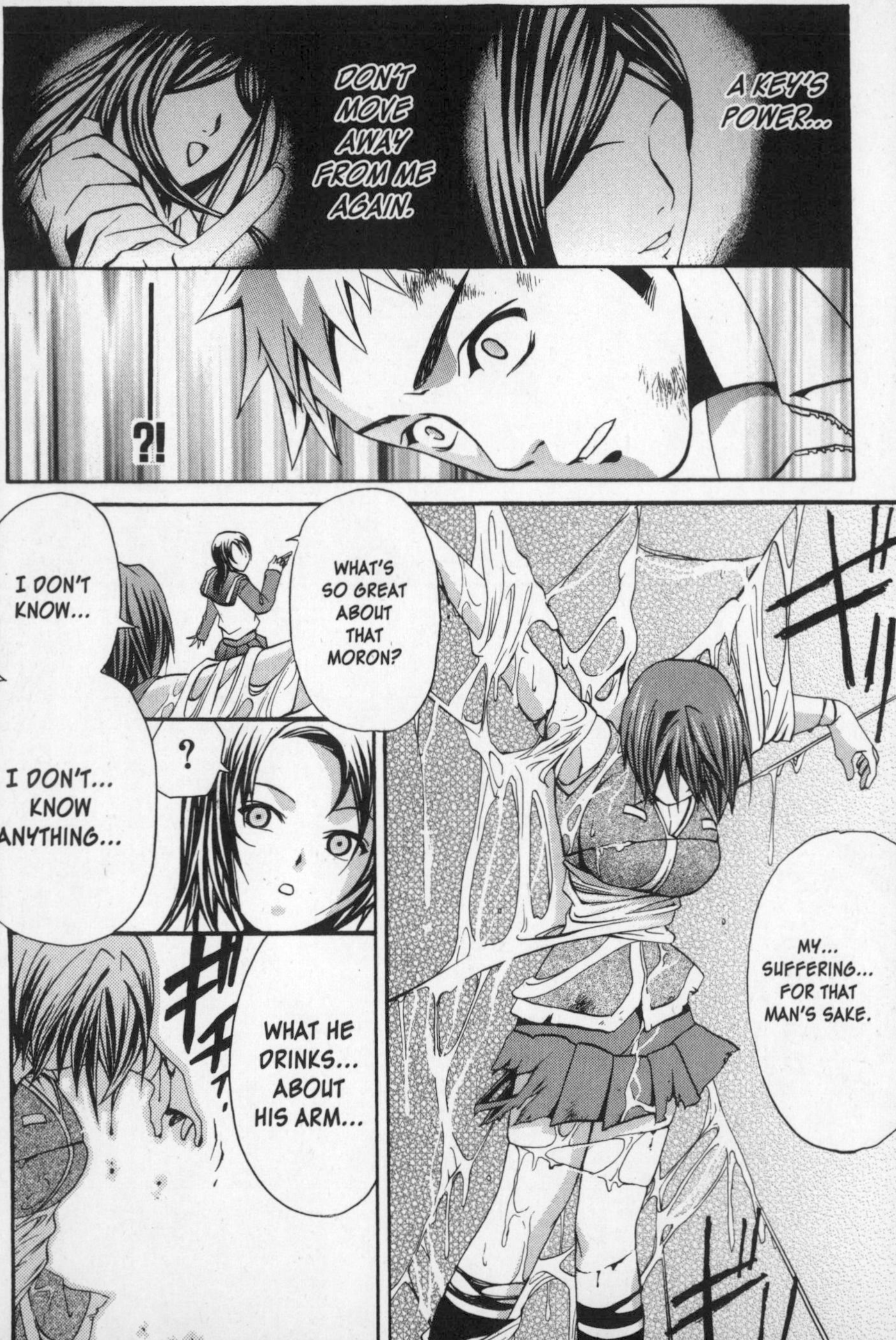
A KEY'S POWER...
DON'T MOVE AWAY FROM ME AGAIN.
?!
MY... SUFFERING... FOR THAT MAN'S SAKE.
WHAT'S SO GREAT ABOUT THAT MORON?
I DON'T KNOW...
?
I DON'T... KNOW ANYTHING...
WHAT HE DRINKS... ABOUT HIS ARM...

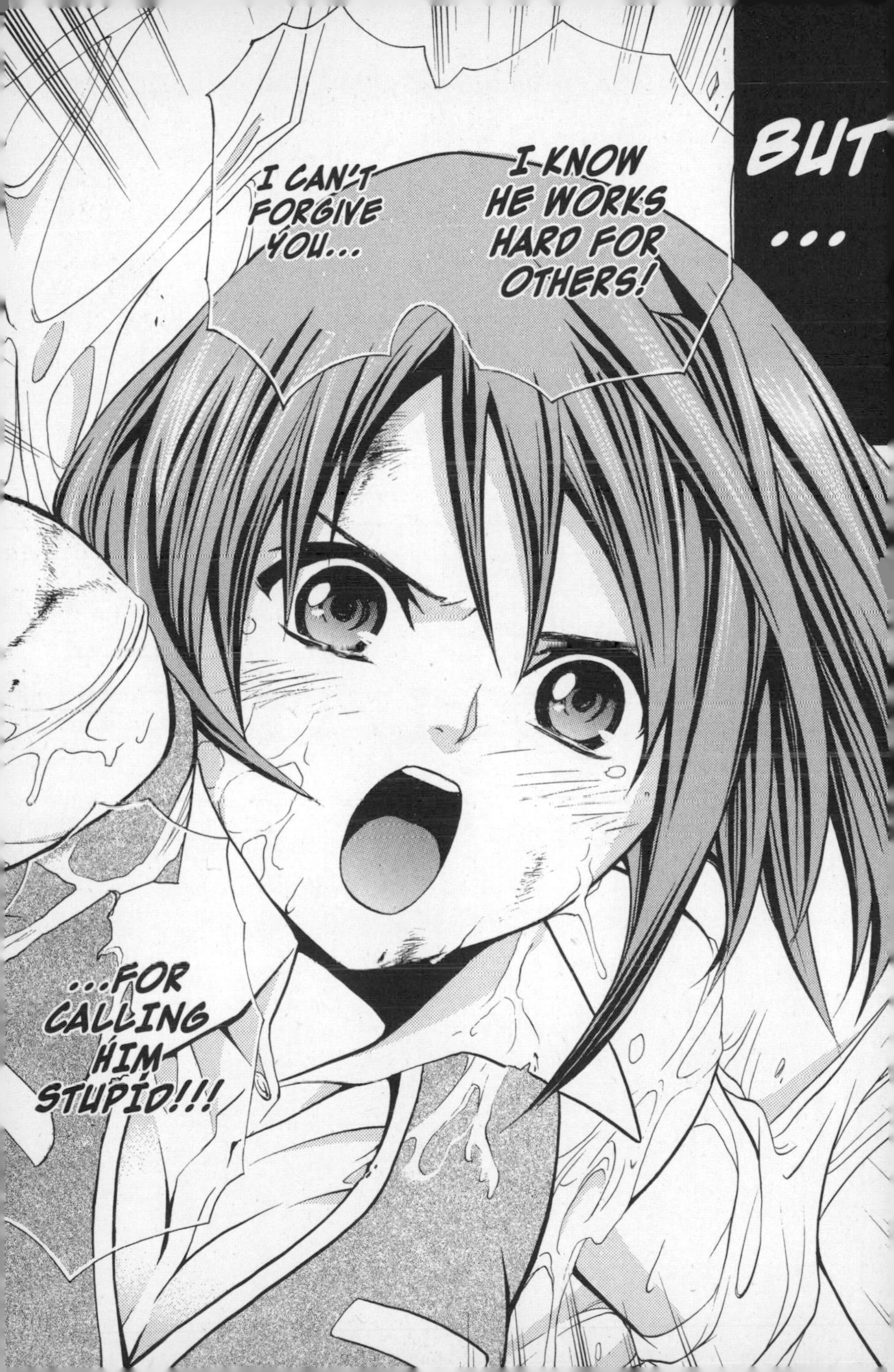
BUT...
I KNOW HE WORKS HARD FOR OTHERS!
I CAN'T FORGIVE YOU...
...FOR CALLING HIM STUPID!!!

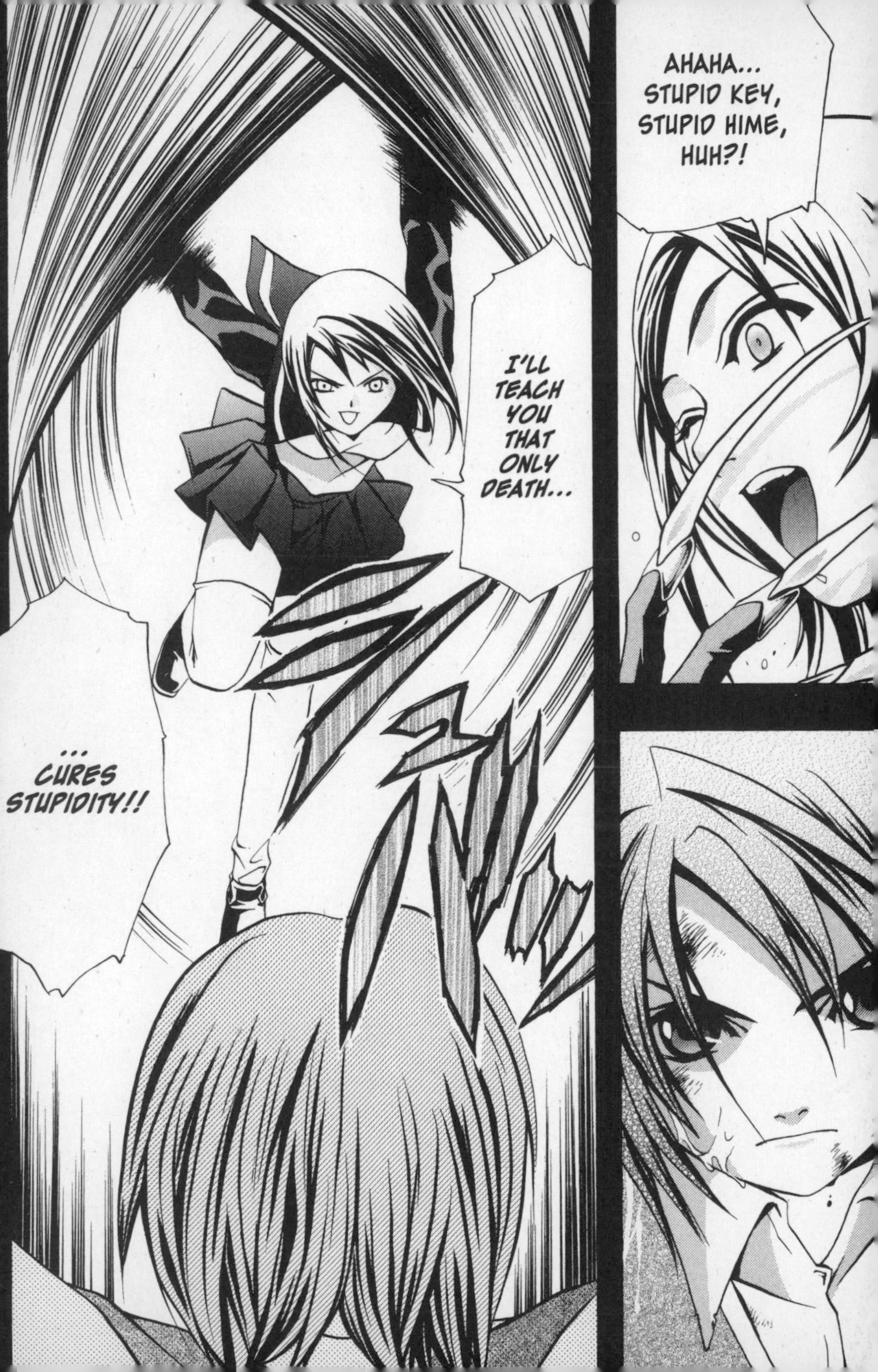
AHAHA... STUPID KEY, STUPID HIME, HUH?!
I'LL TEACH YOU THAT ONLY DEATH...
...CURES STUPIDITY!!

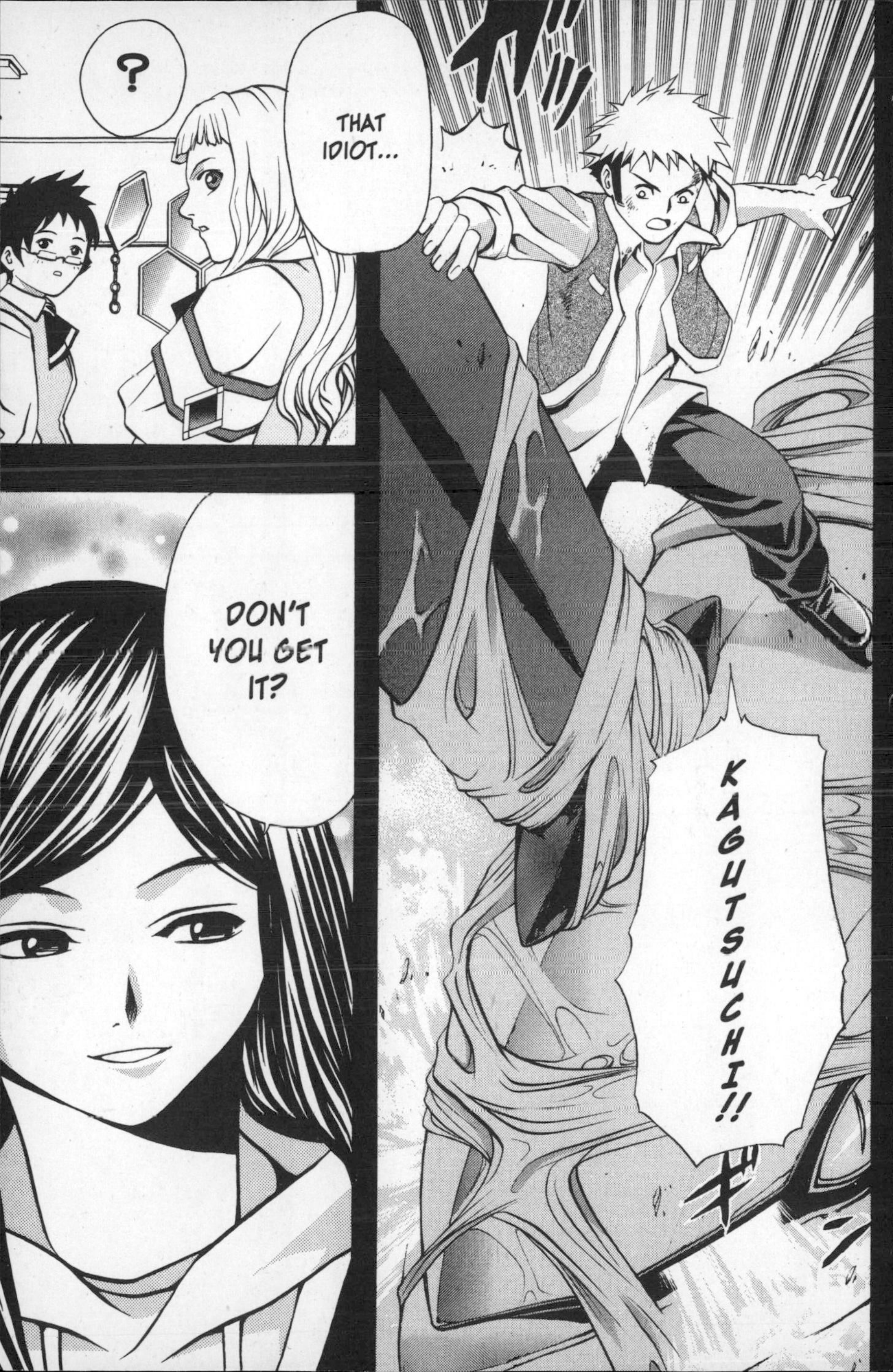
KAGUTSUCHI!!
THAT IDIOT...
?
DON'T YOU GET IT?

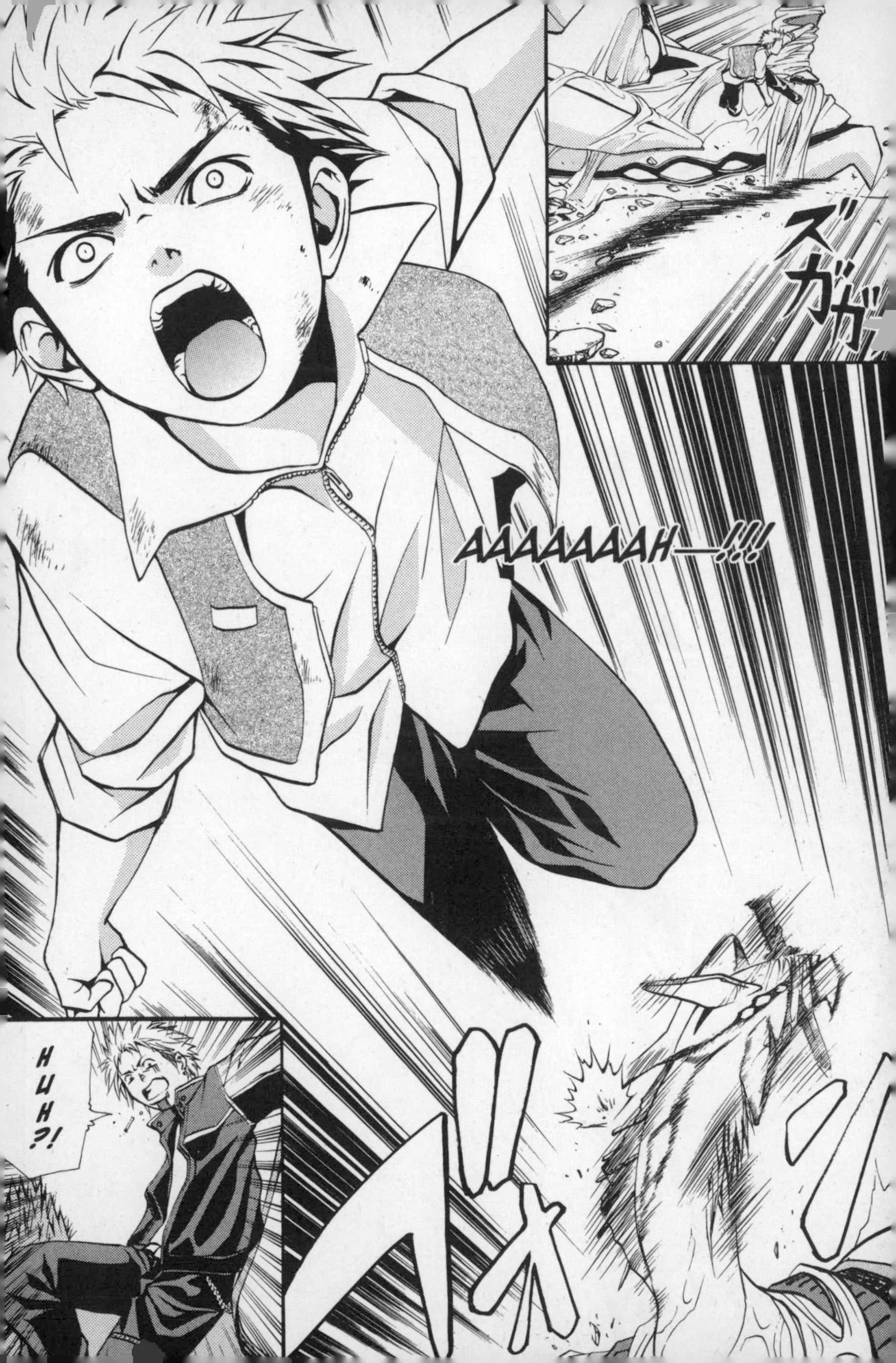
ズガガ
AAAAAAAH—!!!
HUH?!

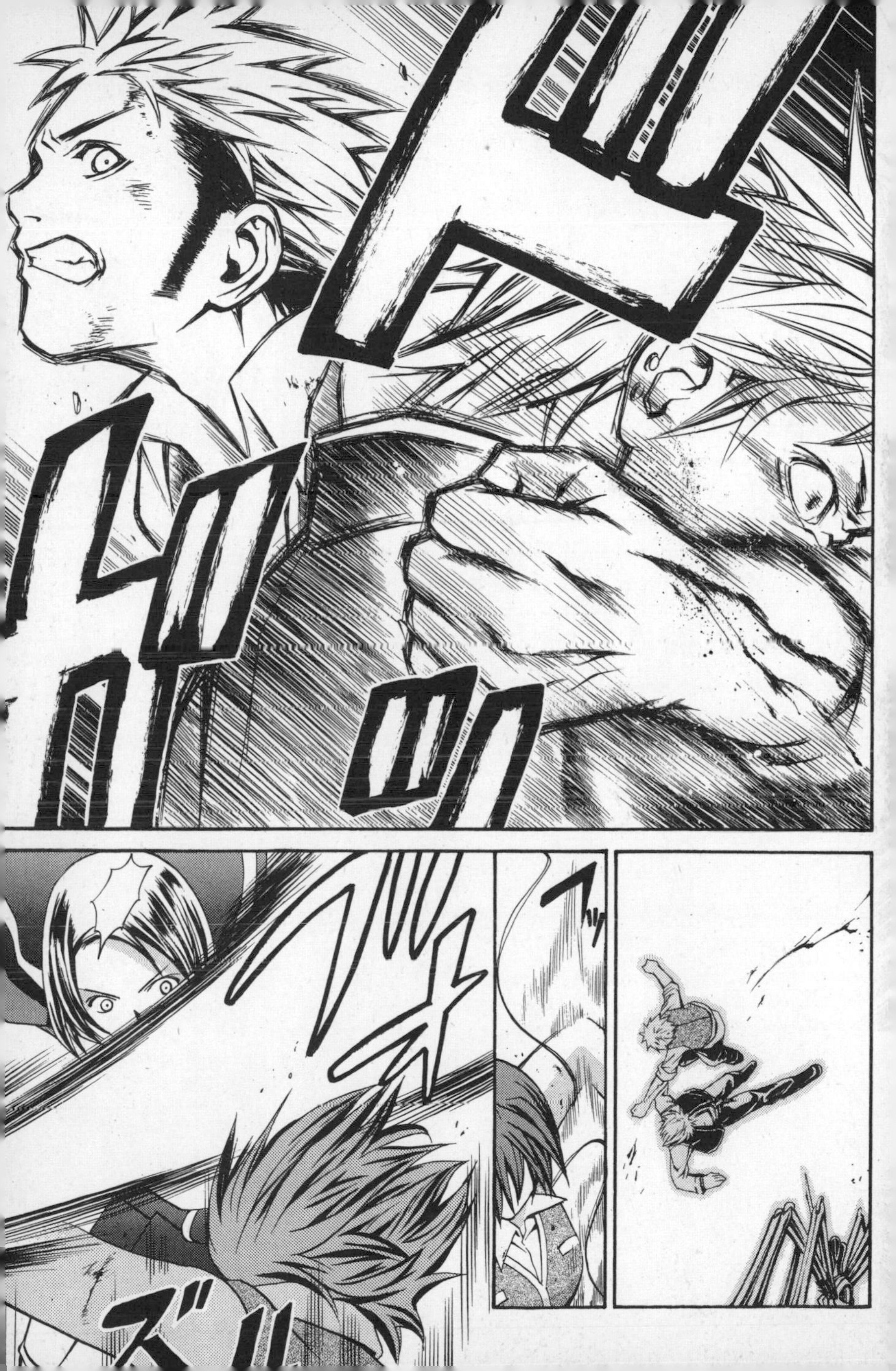

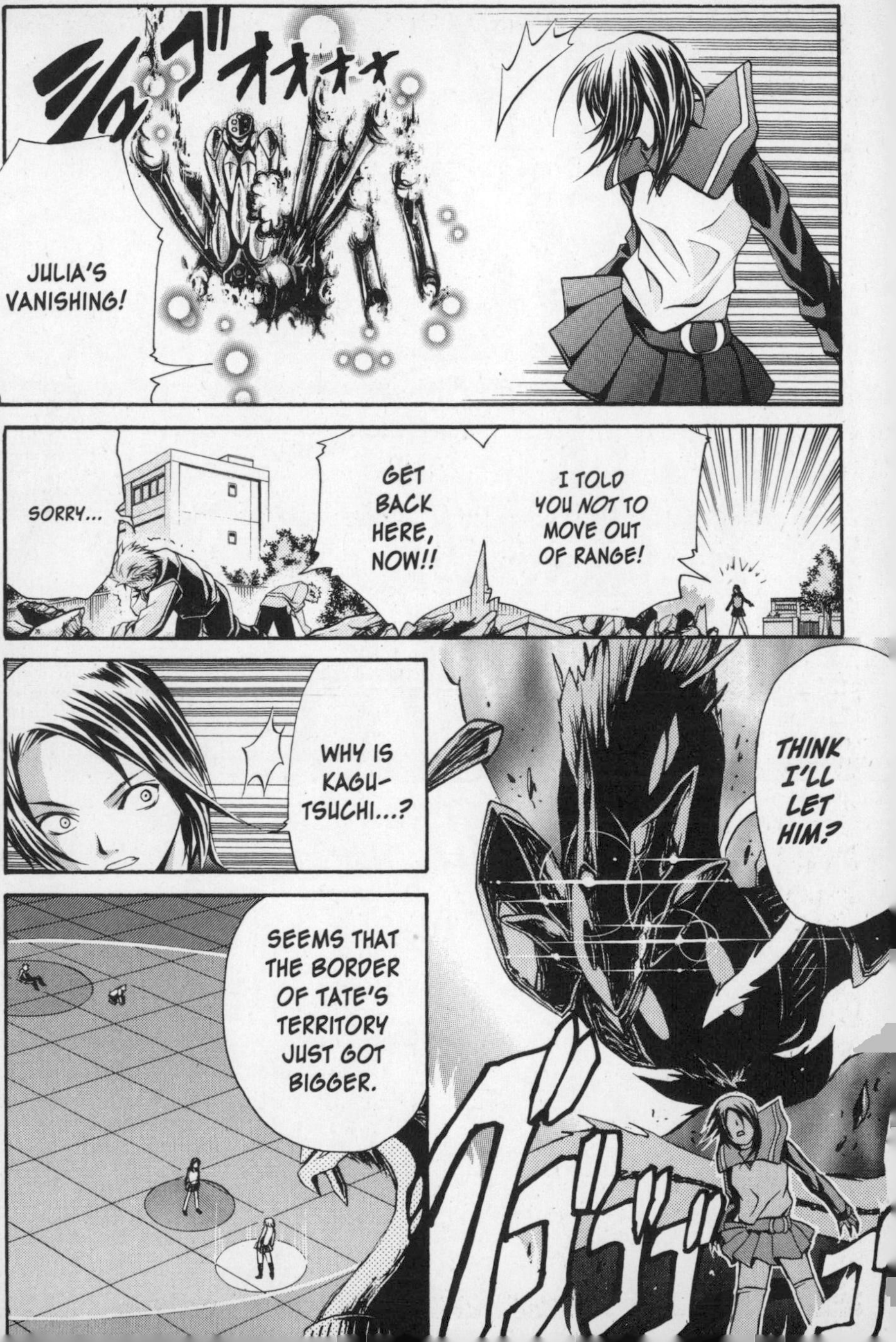

JULIA'S VANISHING!
I TOLD YOU *NOT* TO MOVE OUT OF RANGE!
GET BACK HERE, NOW!!
SORRY...
THINK I'LL LET HIM?
WHY IS KAGU-TSUCHI...?
SEEMS THAT THE BORDER OF TATE'S TERRITORY JUST GOT BIGGER.

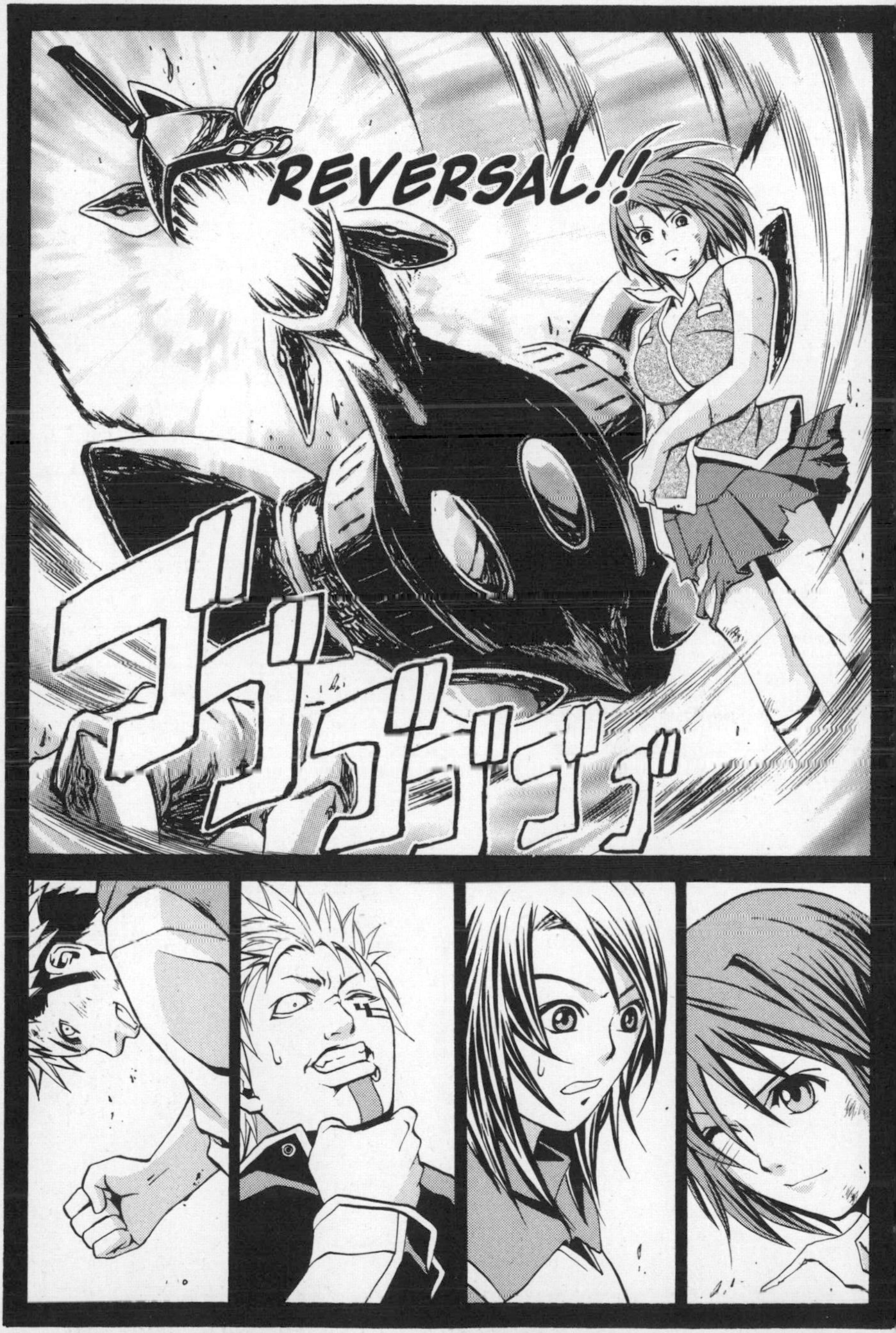
REVERSAL!!

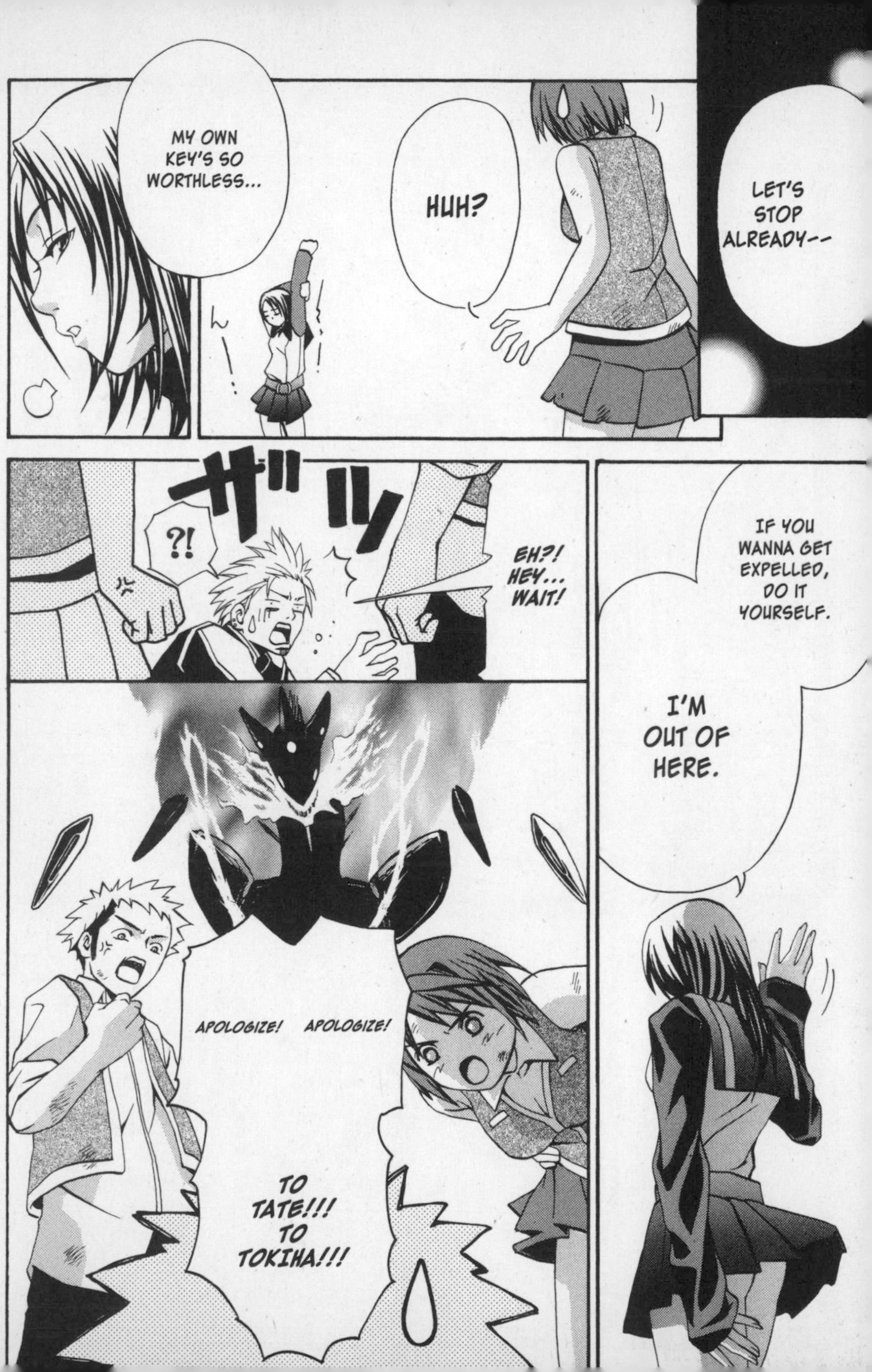
LET'S STOP ALREADY--
HUH?
MY OWN KEY'S SO WORTHLESS...
IF YOU WANNA GET EXPELLED, DO IT YOURSELF.
I'M OUT OF HERE.
ザッ
?!
EH?! HEY... WAIT!
APOLOGIZE! APOLOGIZE!
TO TATE!!! TO TOKIHA!!!

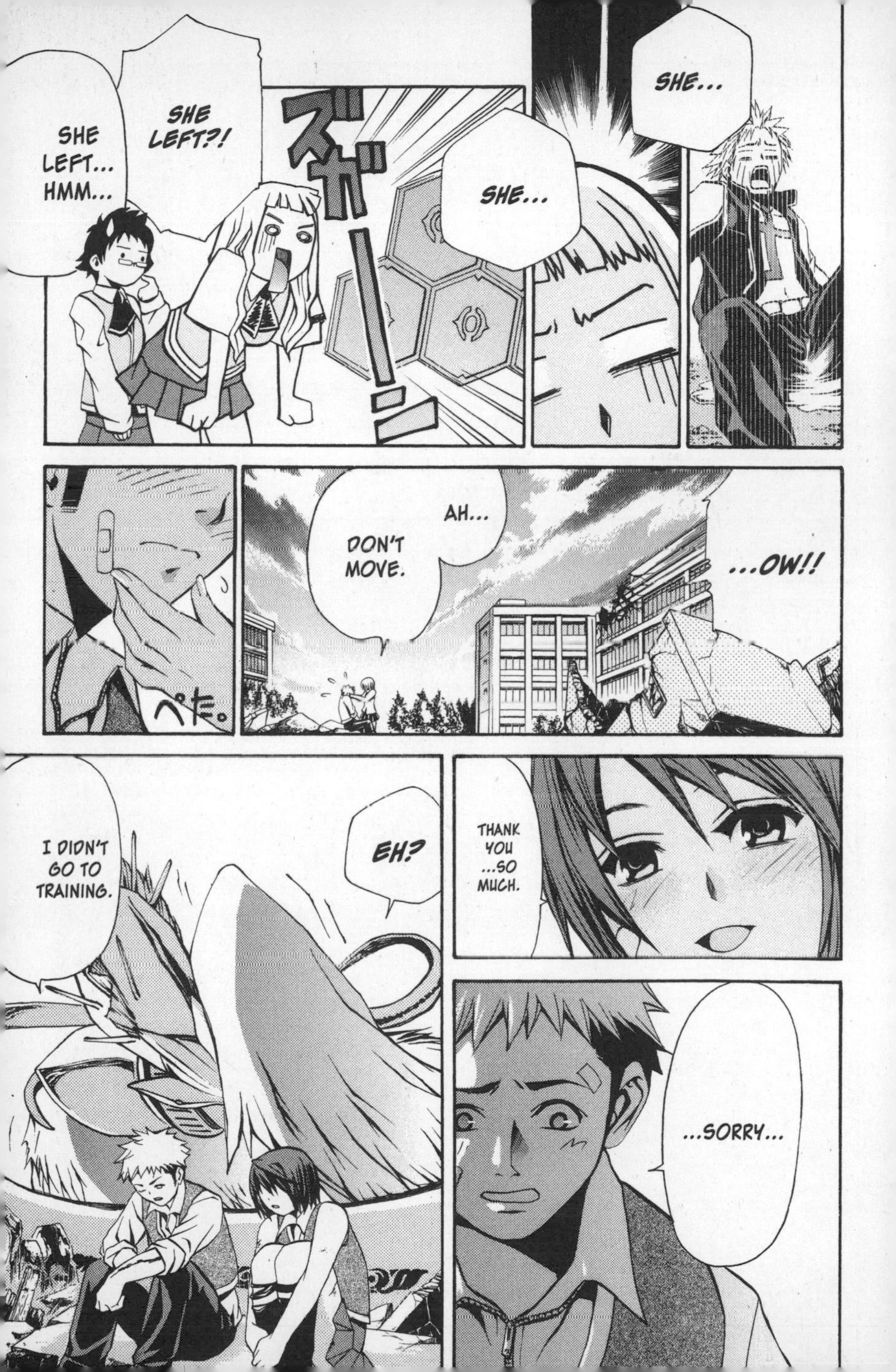
SHE...
SHE...
ズガー!!
SHE LEFT?!
SHE LEFT... HMM...
...OW!!
AH... DON'T MOVE.
ぺた。
THANK YOU ...SO MUCH.
...SORRY...
EH?
I DIDN'T GO TO TRAINING.

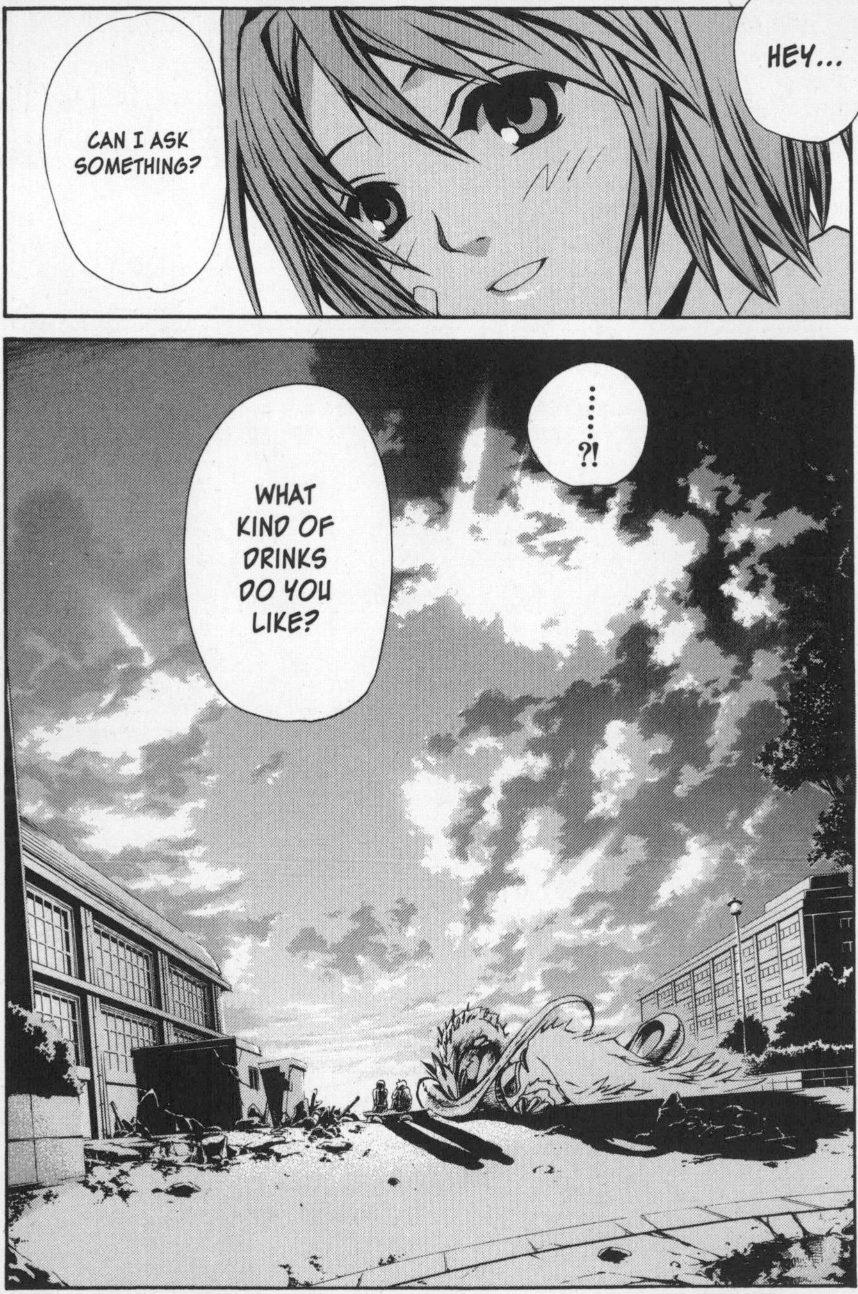
HEY...
CAN I ASK SOMETHING?
......?!
WHAT KIND OF DRINKS DO YOU LIKE?

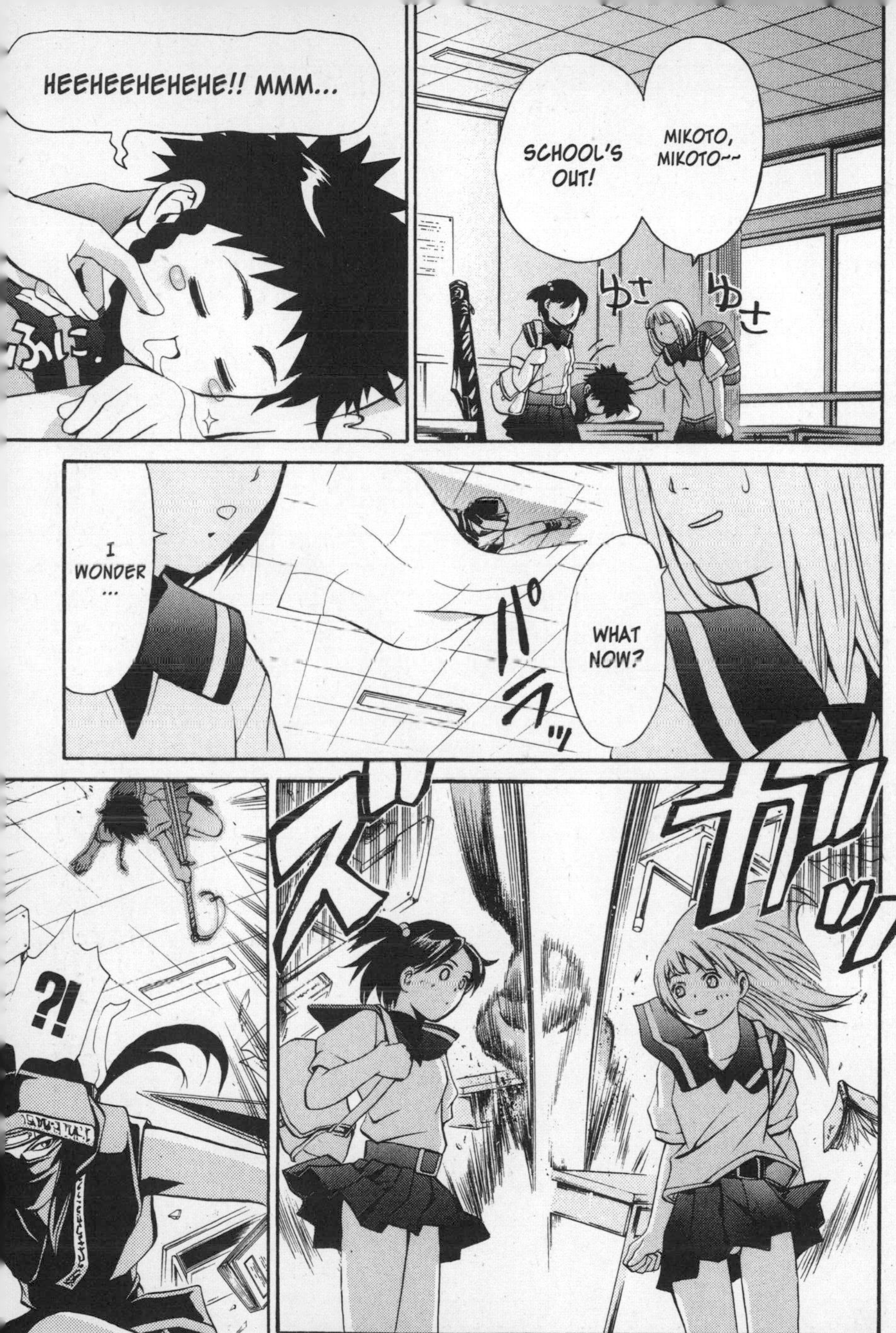

MIKOTO, MIKOTO~~
SCHOOL'S OUT!
ゆさ
ゆさ
HEEHEEHEHEHE!! MMM...
ふに
WHAT NOW?
パラッ
I WONDER ...
ガッ
ズ
?!

CHAPTER 11 / MIKOTO MINAGI

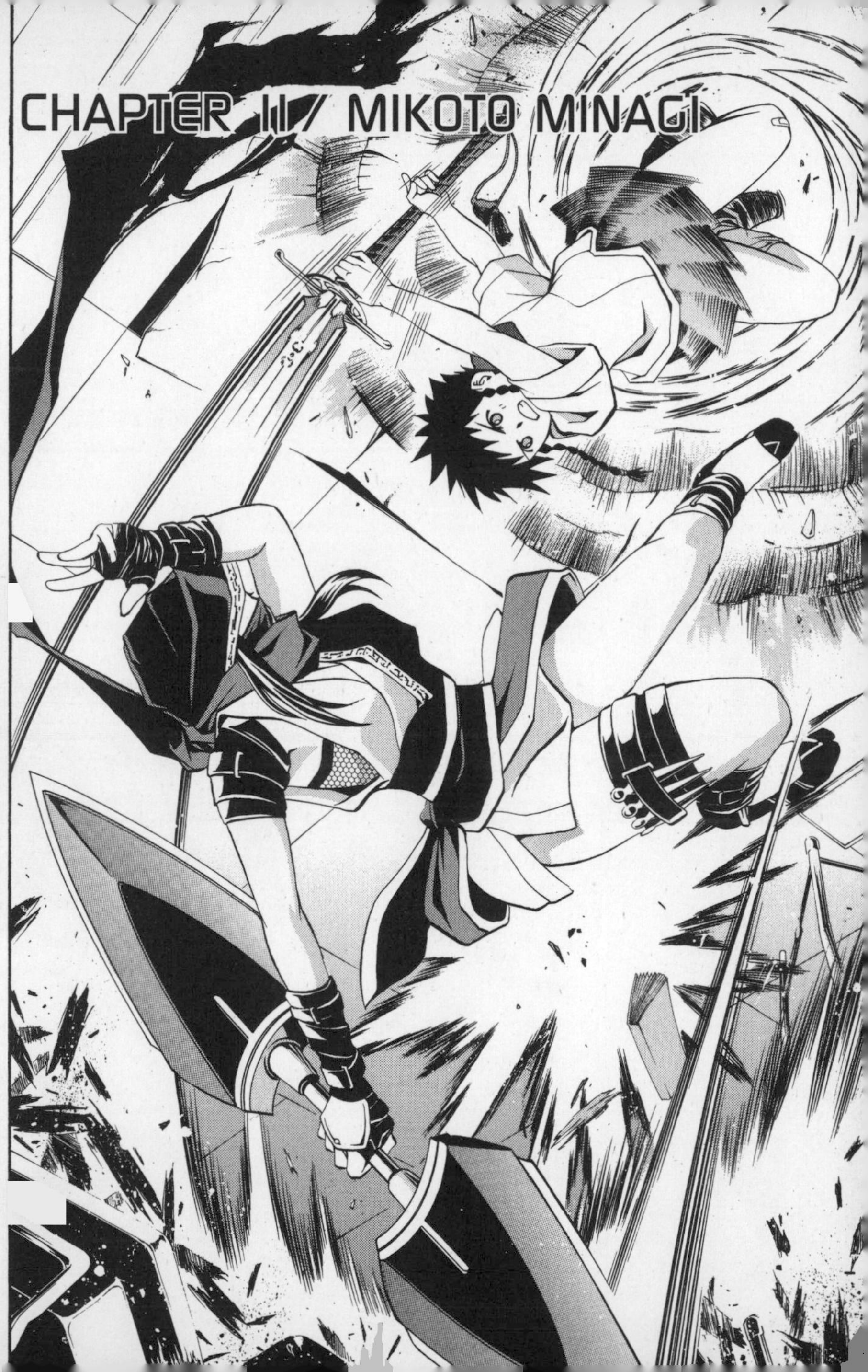
CHAPTER 11 / MIKOTO MINAGI

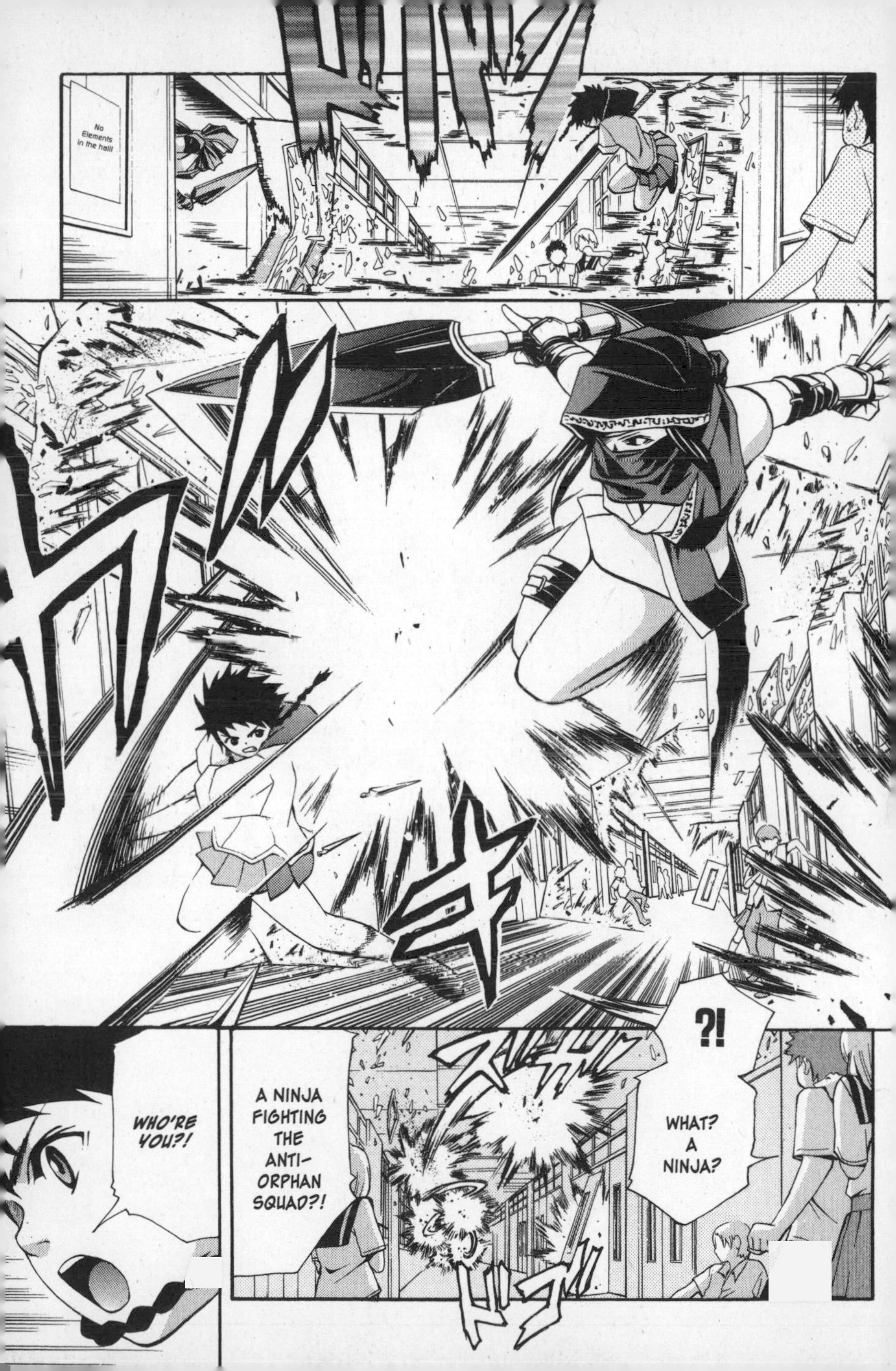
No Elements in the hall!
?!
WHAT? A NINJA?
A NINJA FIGHTING THE ANTI-ORPHAN SQUAD?!
WHO'RE YOU?!

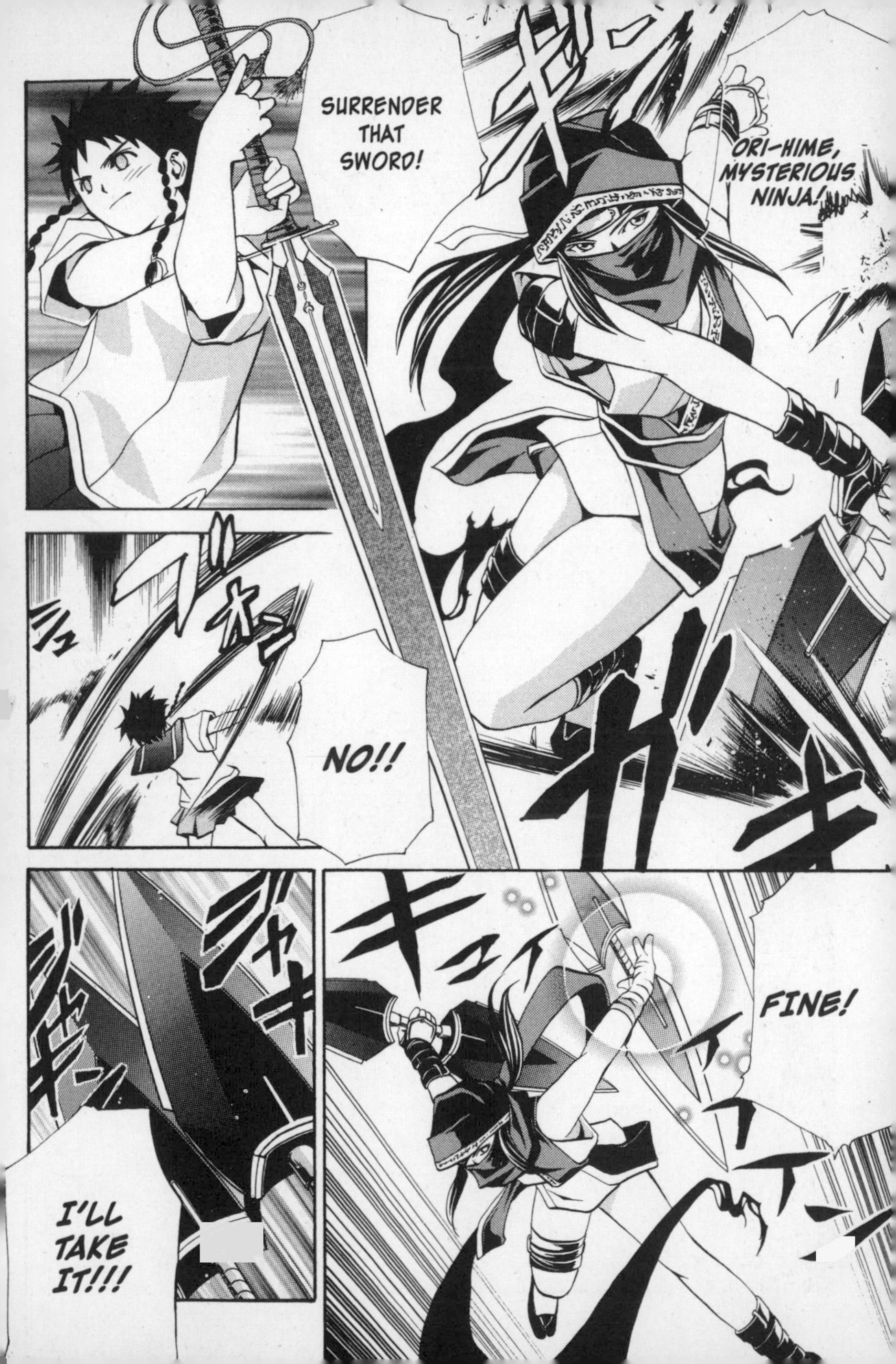
ORI-HIME, MYSTERIOUS NINJA!
SURRENDER THAT SWORD!
NO!!
FINE!
I'LL TAKE IT!!!

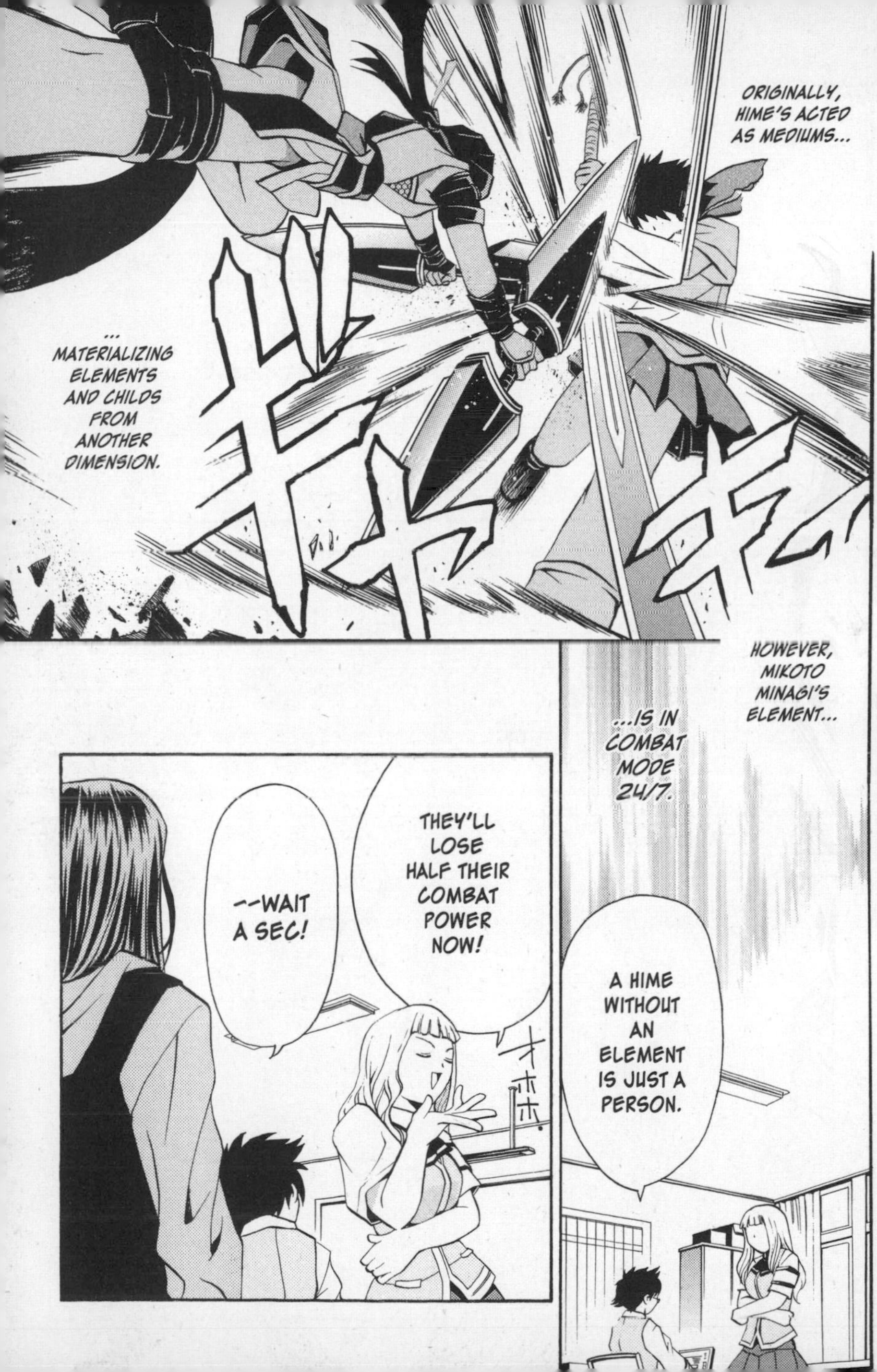
ORIGINALLY, HIME'S ACTED AS MEDIUMS...
...MATERIALIZING ELEMENTS AND CHILDS FROM ANOTHER DIMENSION.
HOWEVER, MIKOTO MINAGI'S ELEMENT...
...IS IN COMBAT MODE 24/7.
A HIME WITHOUT AN ELEMENT IS JUST A PERSON.
THEY'LL LOSE HALF THEIR COMBAT POWER NOW!
--WAIT A SEC!
オホホ

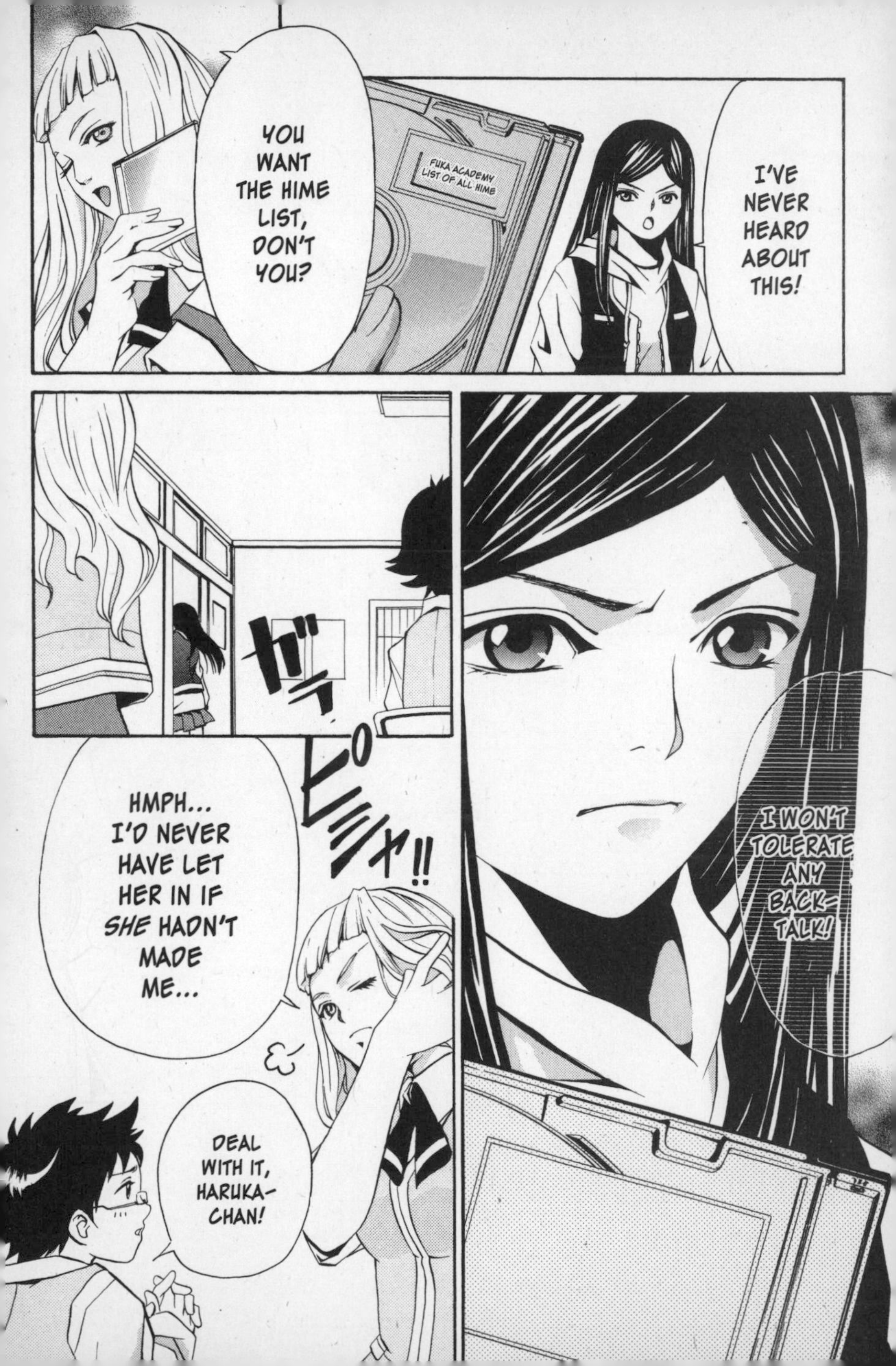
I'VE NEVER HEARD ABOUT THIS!
FUKA ACADEMY LIST OF ALL HIME
YOU WANT THE HIME LIST, DON'T YOU?
I WON'T TOLERATE ANY BACK-TALK!
ガラ
ピシャ!!
HMPH... I'D NEVER HAVE LET HER IN IF *SHE* HADN'T MADE ME...
DEAL WITH IT, HARUKA-CHAN!

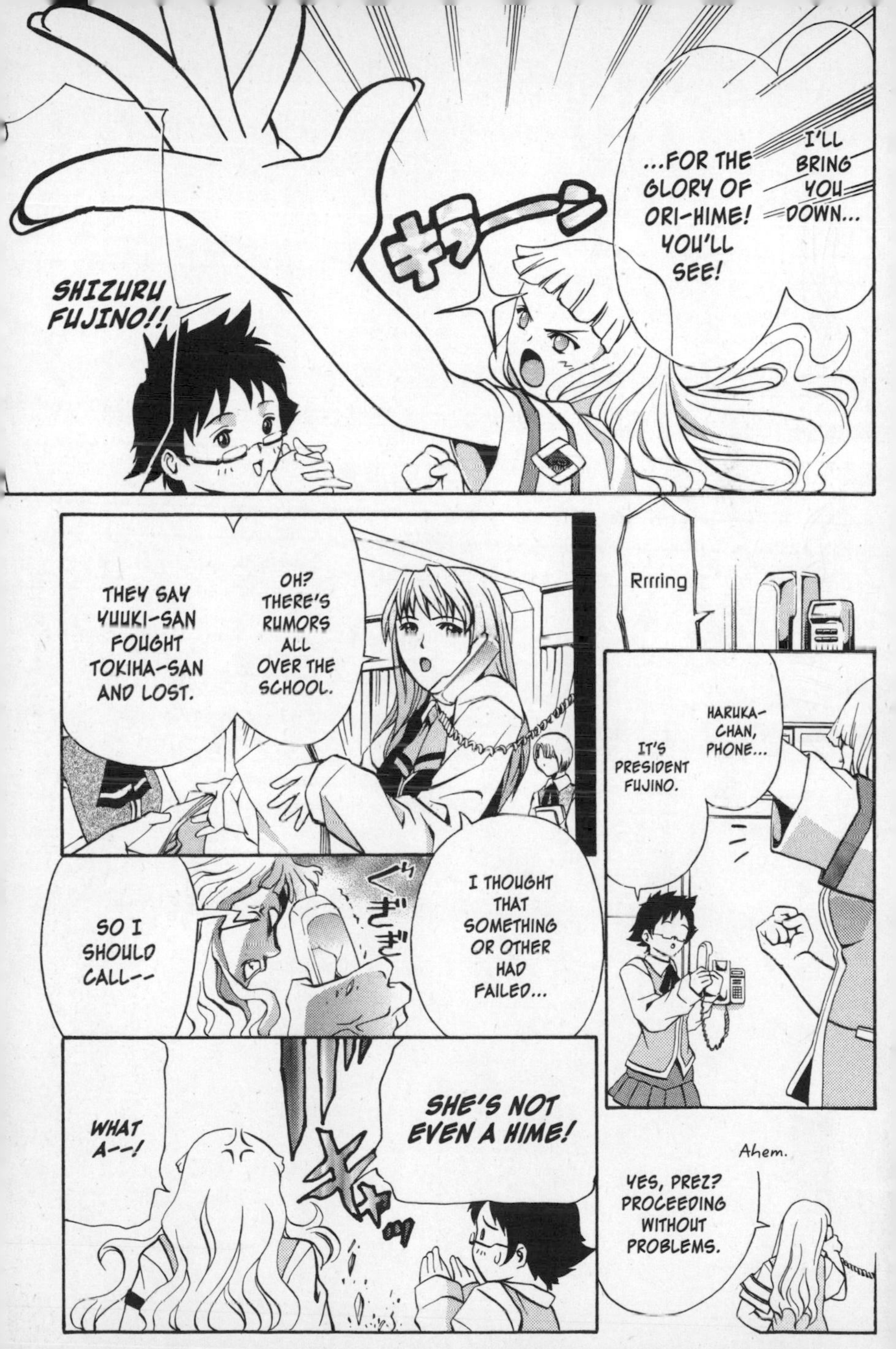
I'LL BRING YOU DOWN...
...FOR THE GLORY OF ORI-HIME! YOU'LL SEE!
キラーン
SHIZURU FUJINO!!
Rrrring
HARUKA-CHAN, PHONE...
IT'S PRESIDENT FUJINO.
Ahem.
YES, PREZ? PROCEEDING WITHOUT PROBLEMS.
OH? THERE'S RUMORS ALL OVER THE SCHOOL.
THEY SAY YUUKI-SAN FOUGHT TOKIHA-SAN AND LOST.
I THOUGHT THAT SOMETHING OR OTHER HAD FAILED...
ぐぎぎ
SO I SHOULD CALL--
SHE'S NOT EVEN A HIME!
WHAT A--!

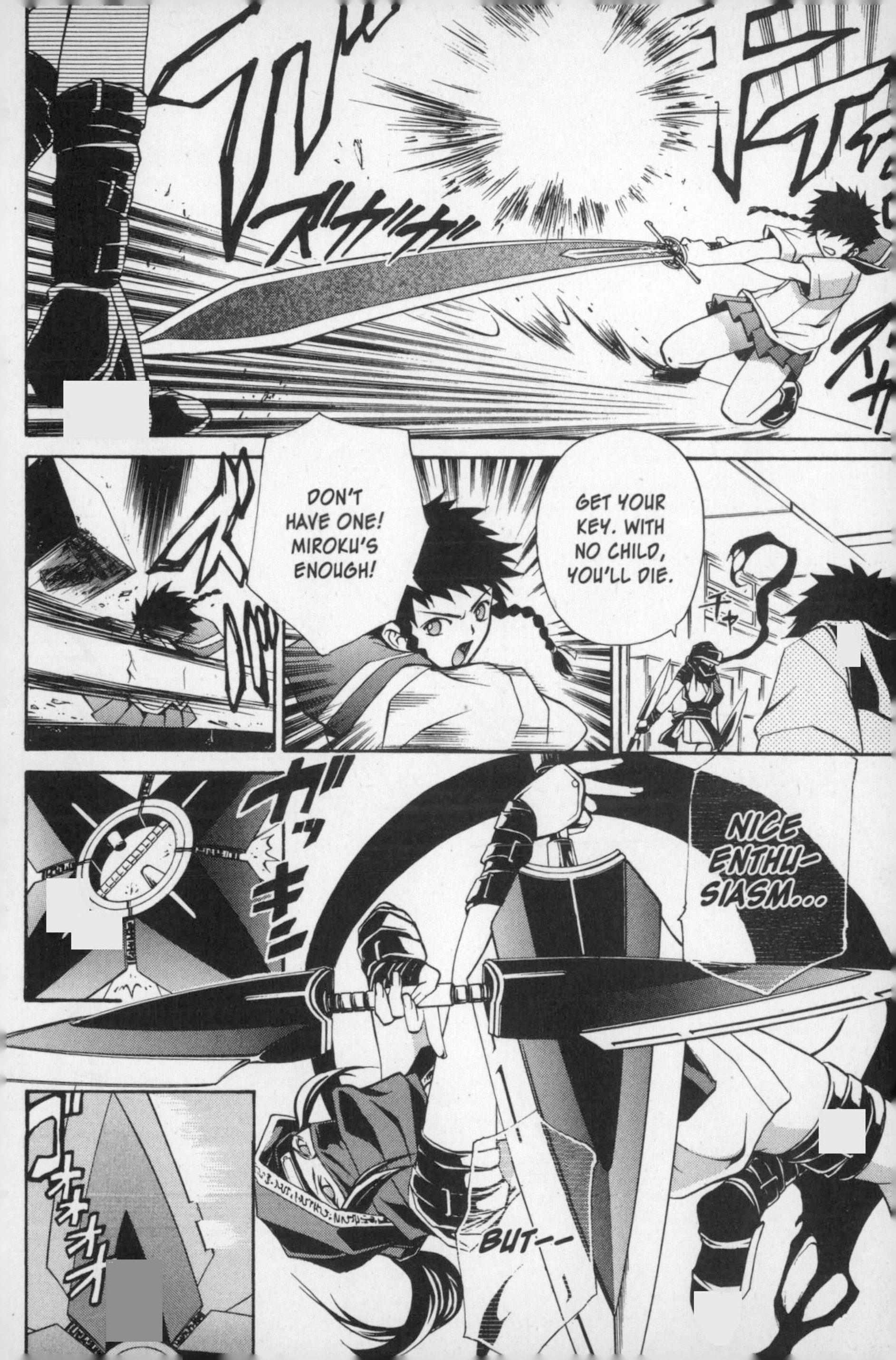
GET YOUR KEY. WITH NO CHILD, YOU'LL DIE.
DON'T HAVE ONE! MIROKU'S ENOUGH!
NICE ENTHU-SIASM...
BUT--

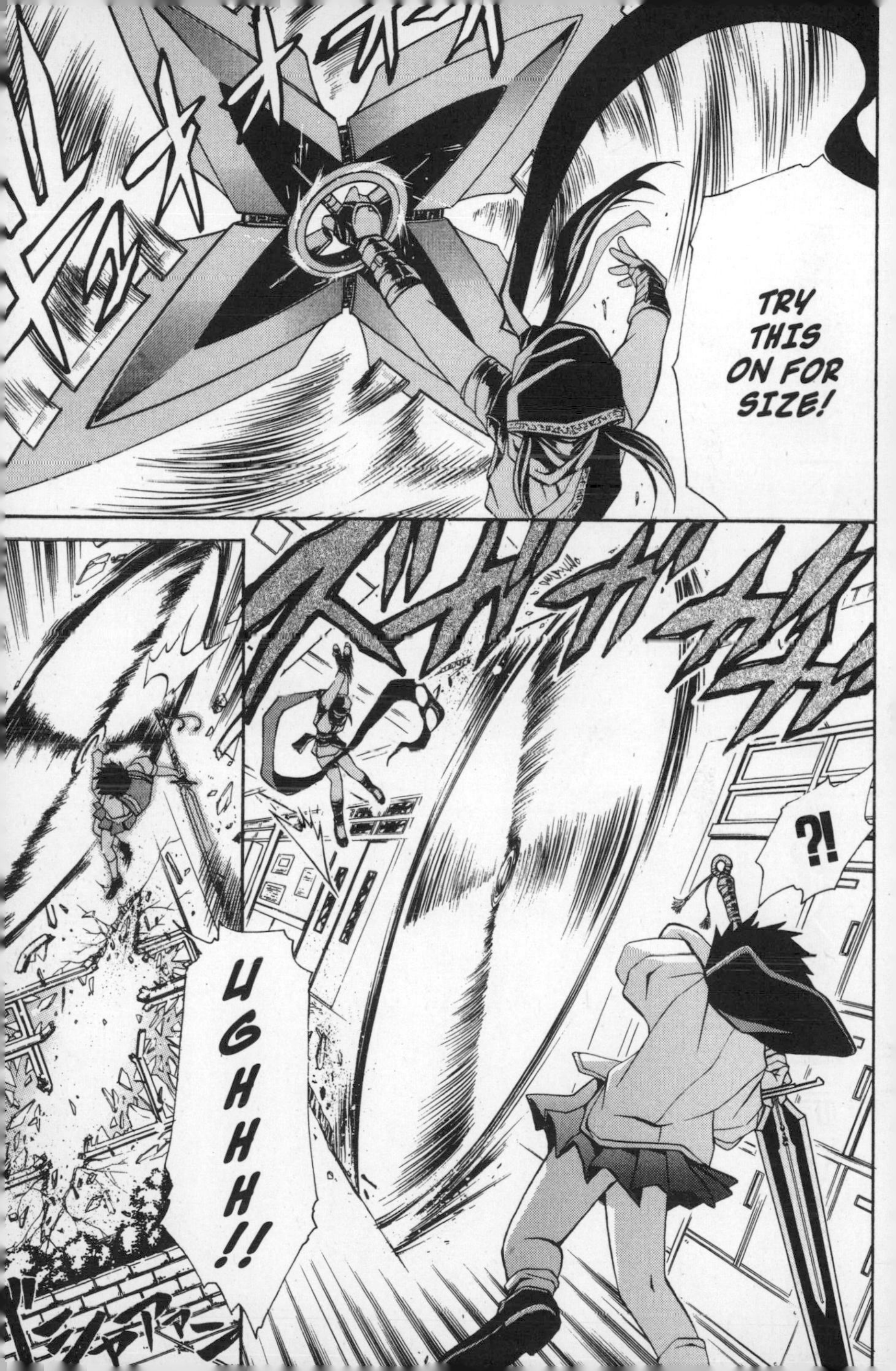
TRY THIS ON FOR SIZE!
?!
UGHHH!!

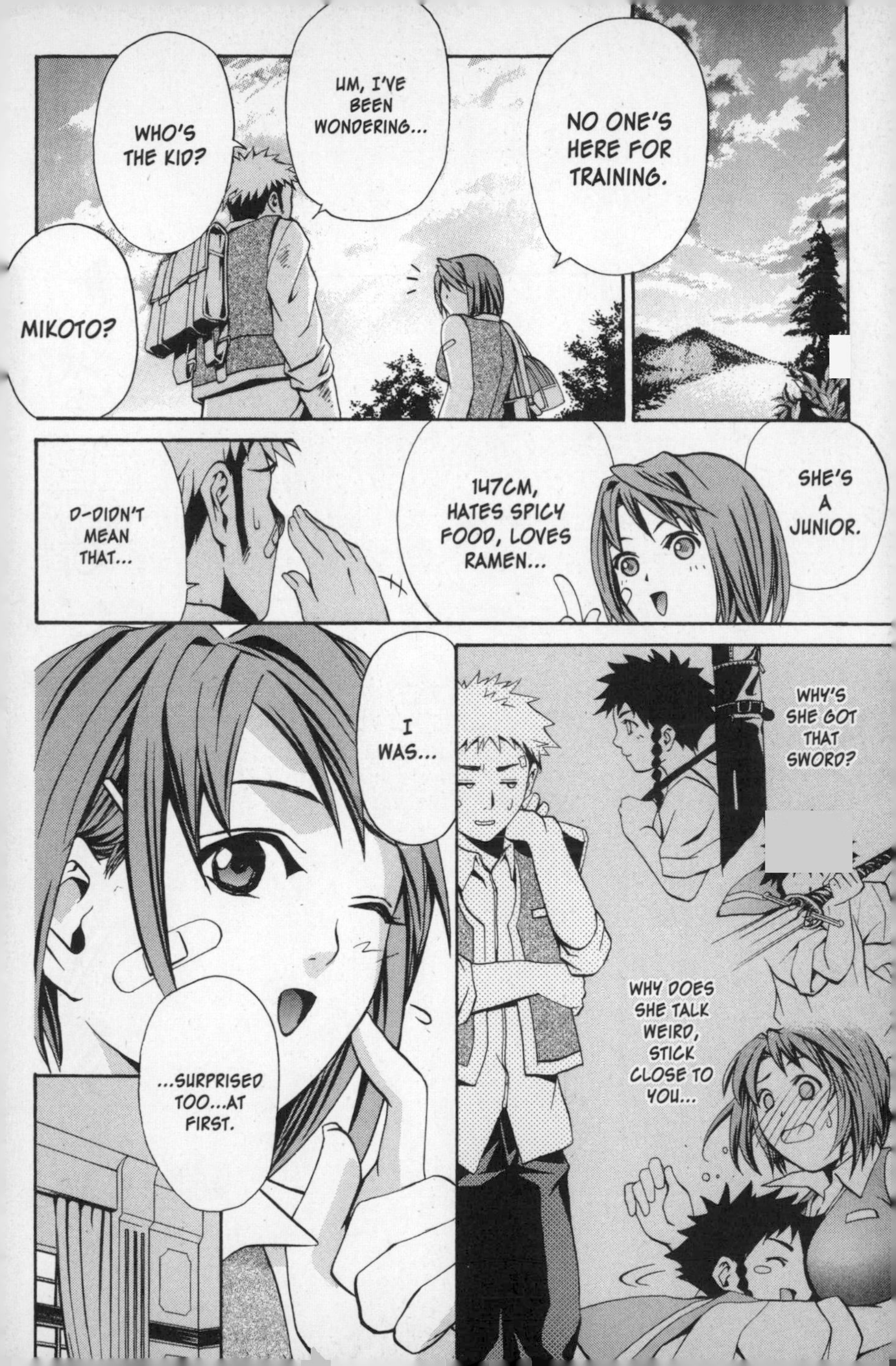
NO ONE'S HERE FOR TRAINING.
UM, I'VE BEEN WONDERING...
WHO'S THE KID?
MIKOTO?
SHE'S A JUNIOR.
147CM, HATES SPICY FOOD, LOVES RAMEN...
D-DIDN'T MEAN THAT...
WHY'S SHE GOT THAT SWORD?
WHY DOES SHE TALK WEIRD, STICK CLOSE TO YOU...
I WAS...
...SURPRISED TOO...AT FIRST.

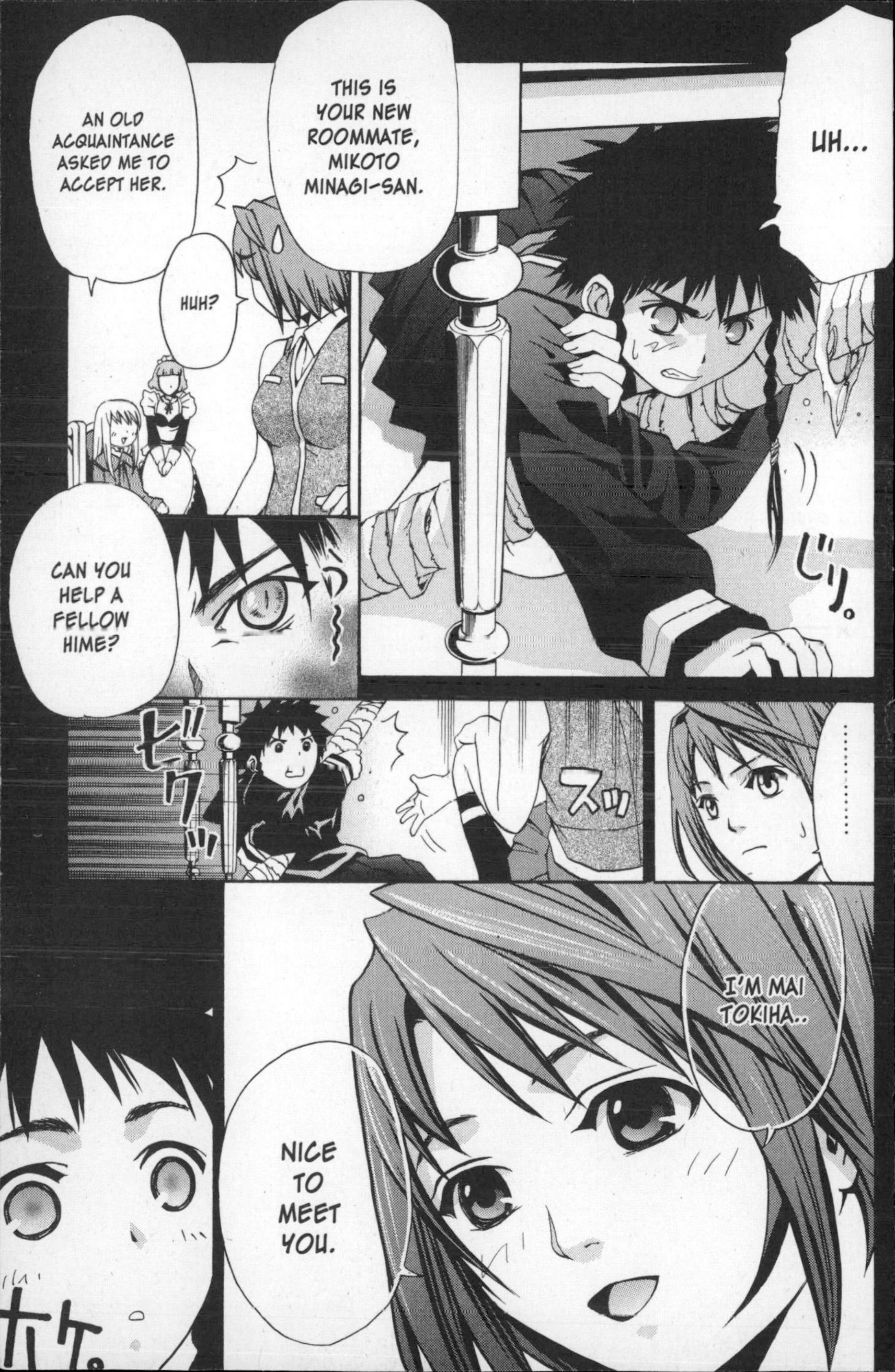
UH...
じり。
THIS IS YOUR NEW ROOMMATE, MIKOTO MINAGI-SAN.
HUH?
AN OLD ACQUAINTANCE ASKED ME TO ACCEPT HER.
CAN YOU HELP A FELLOW HIME?
......
スッ
ビクッ
I'M MAI TOKIHA..
NICE TO MEET YOU.
ホケ。

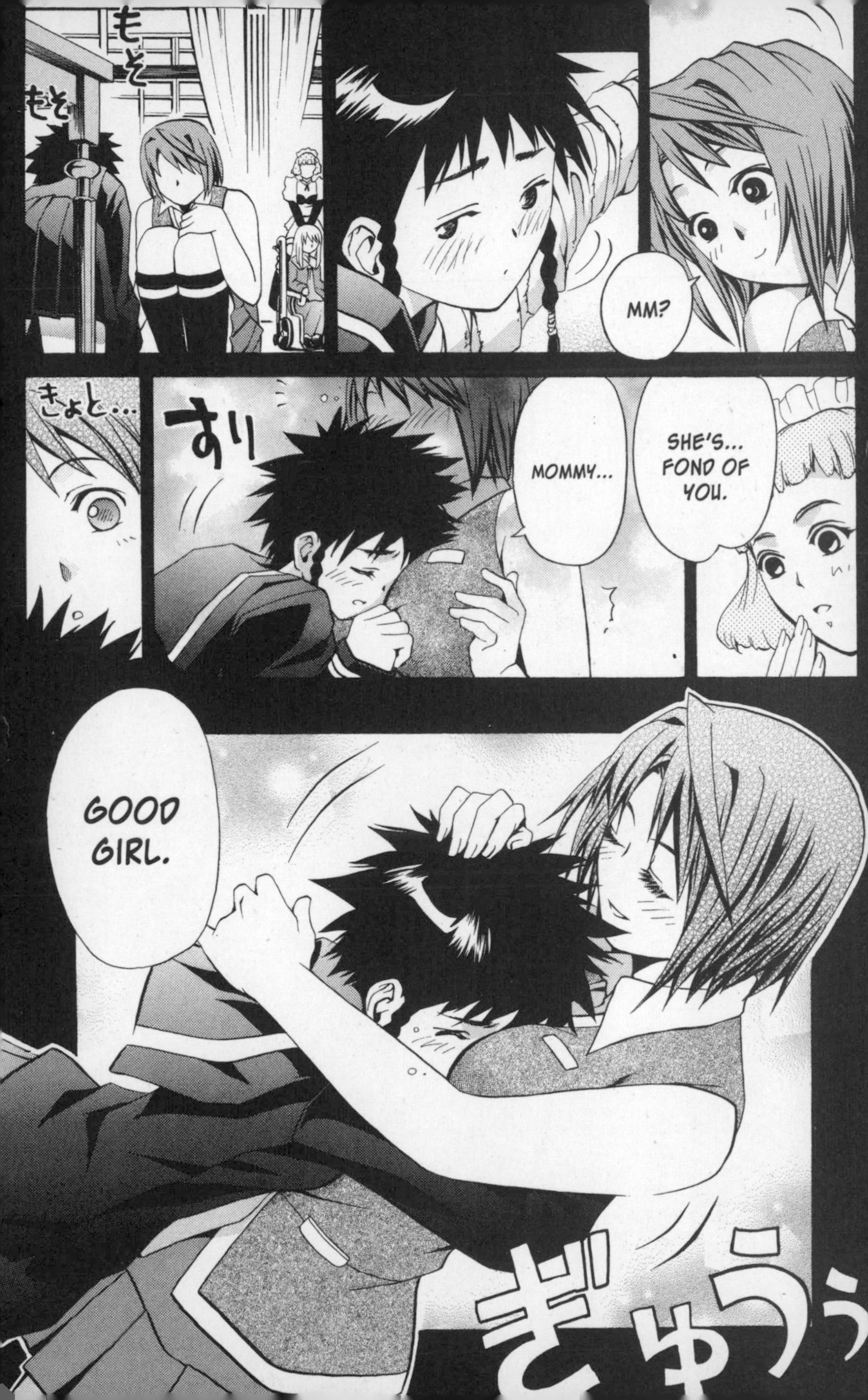
MM?
もぞ
もぞ
SHE'S... FOND OF YOU.
MOMMY...
すり
きょと...
GOOD GIRL.
ぎゅうう.

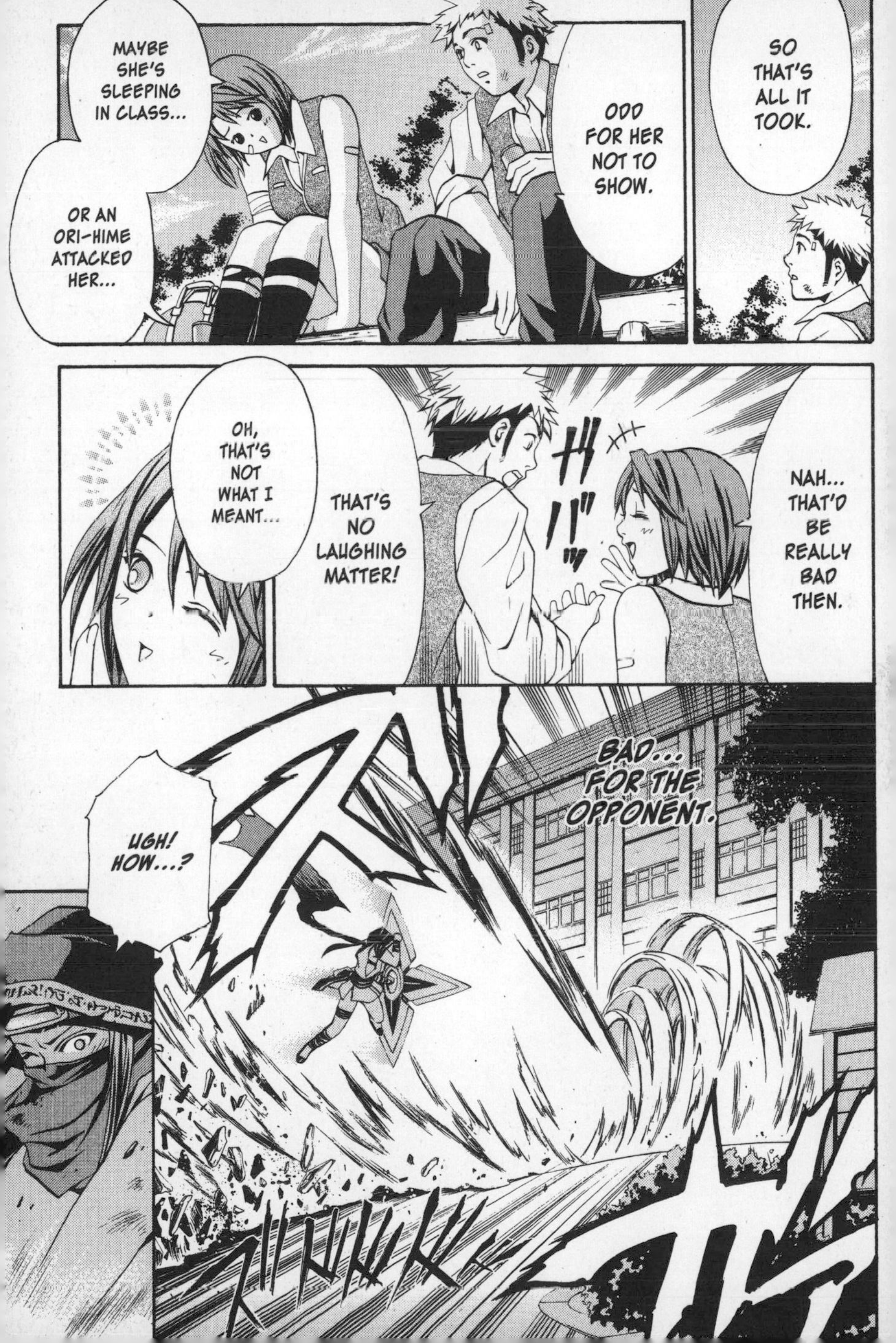
SO THAT'S ALL IT TOOK.
ODD FOR HER NOT TO SHOW.
MAYBE SHE'S SLEEPING IN CLASS...
OR AN ORI-HIME ATTACKED HER...
NAH... THAT'D BE REALLY BAD THEN.
THAT'S NO LAUGHING MATTER!
OH, THAT'S NOT WHAT I MEANT...
BAD... FOR THE OPPONENT.
UGH! HOW...?

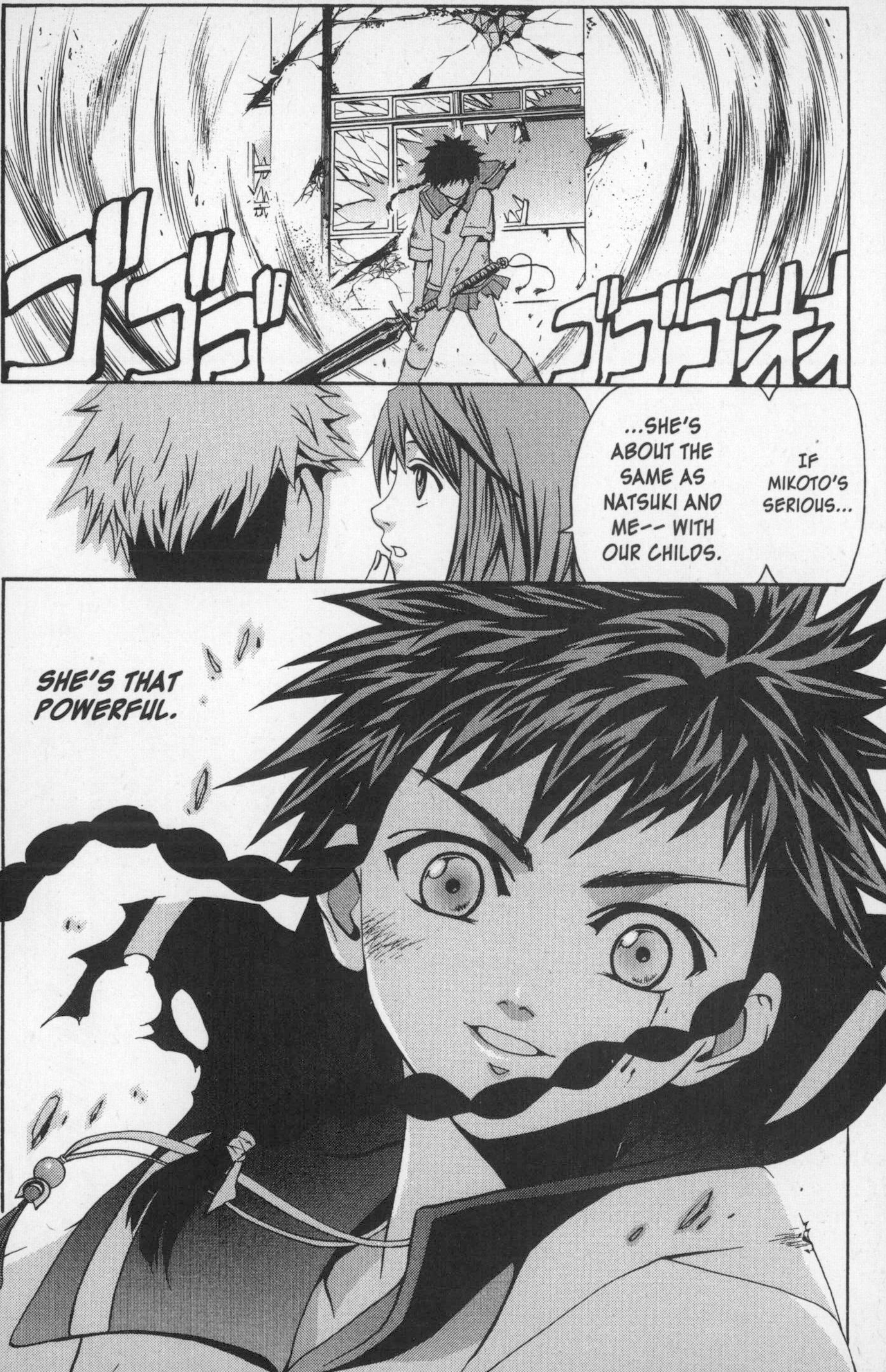
IF MIKOTO'S SERIOUS...
...SHE'S ABOUT THE SAME AS NATSUKI AND ME-- WITH OUR CHILDS.
SHE'S THAT POWERFUL.

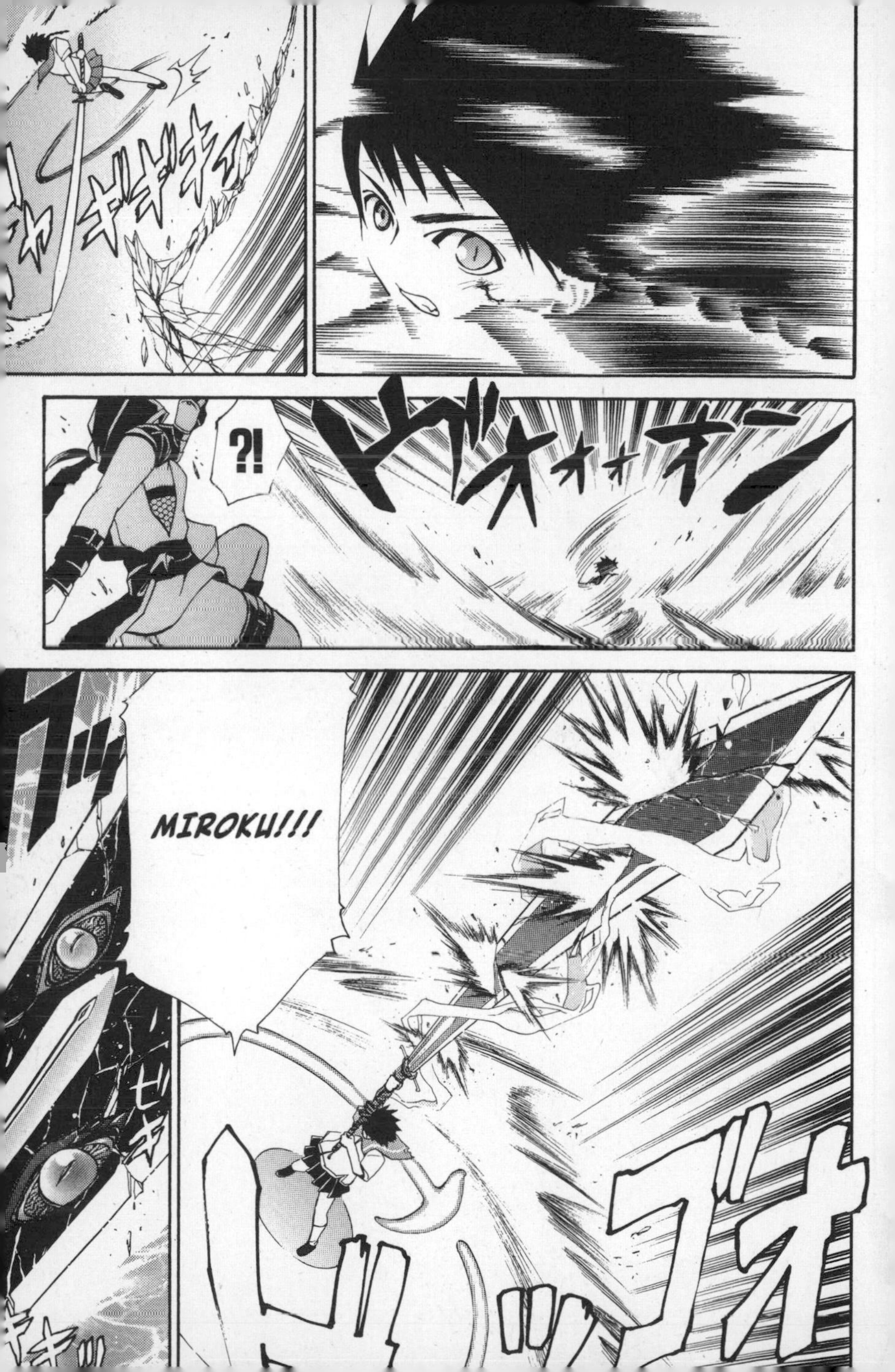
?!
MIROKU!!!

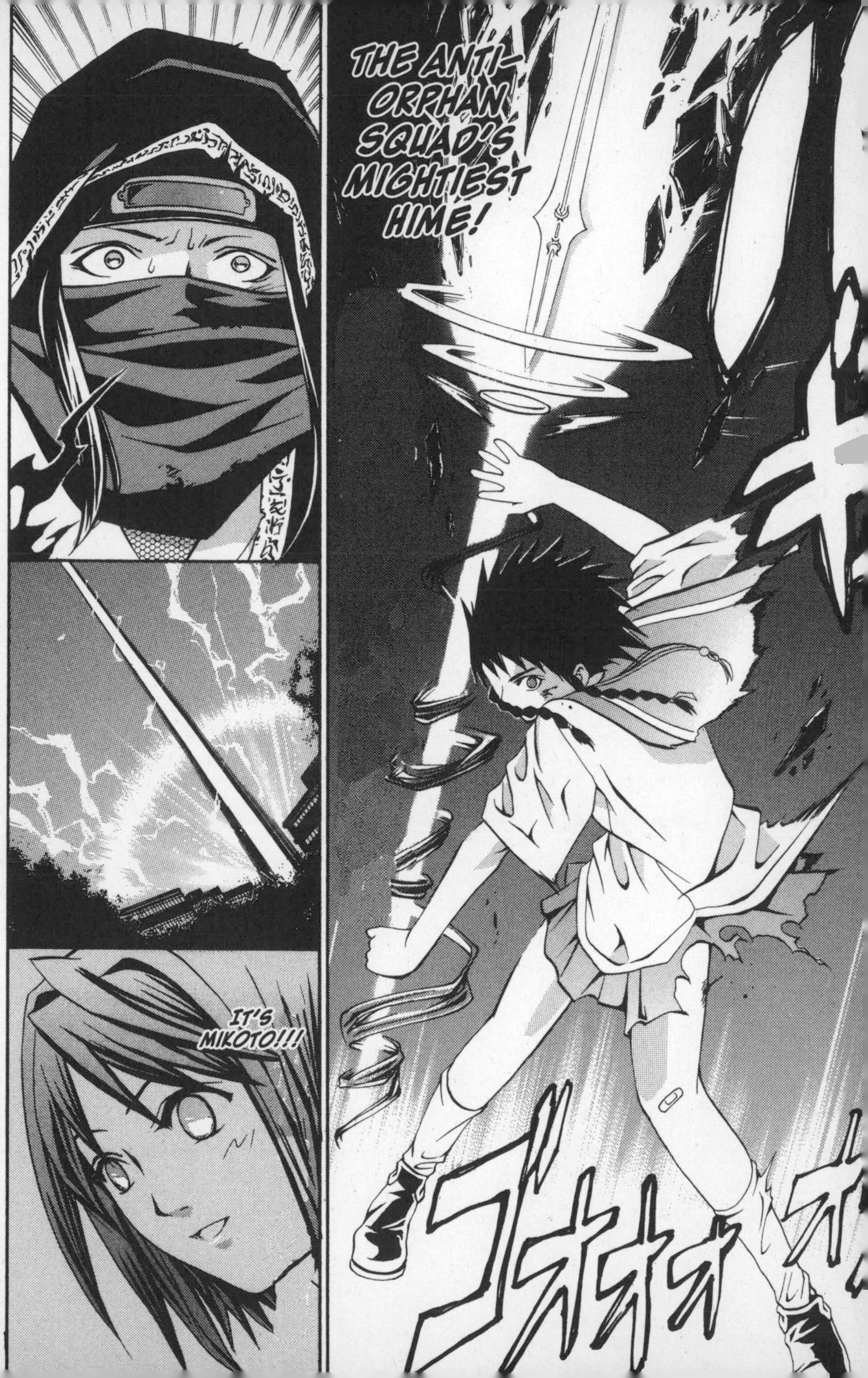
THE ANTI-ORPHAN SQUAD'S MIGHTIEST HIME!
ゴオオオ
IT'S MIKOTO!!!

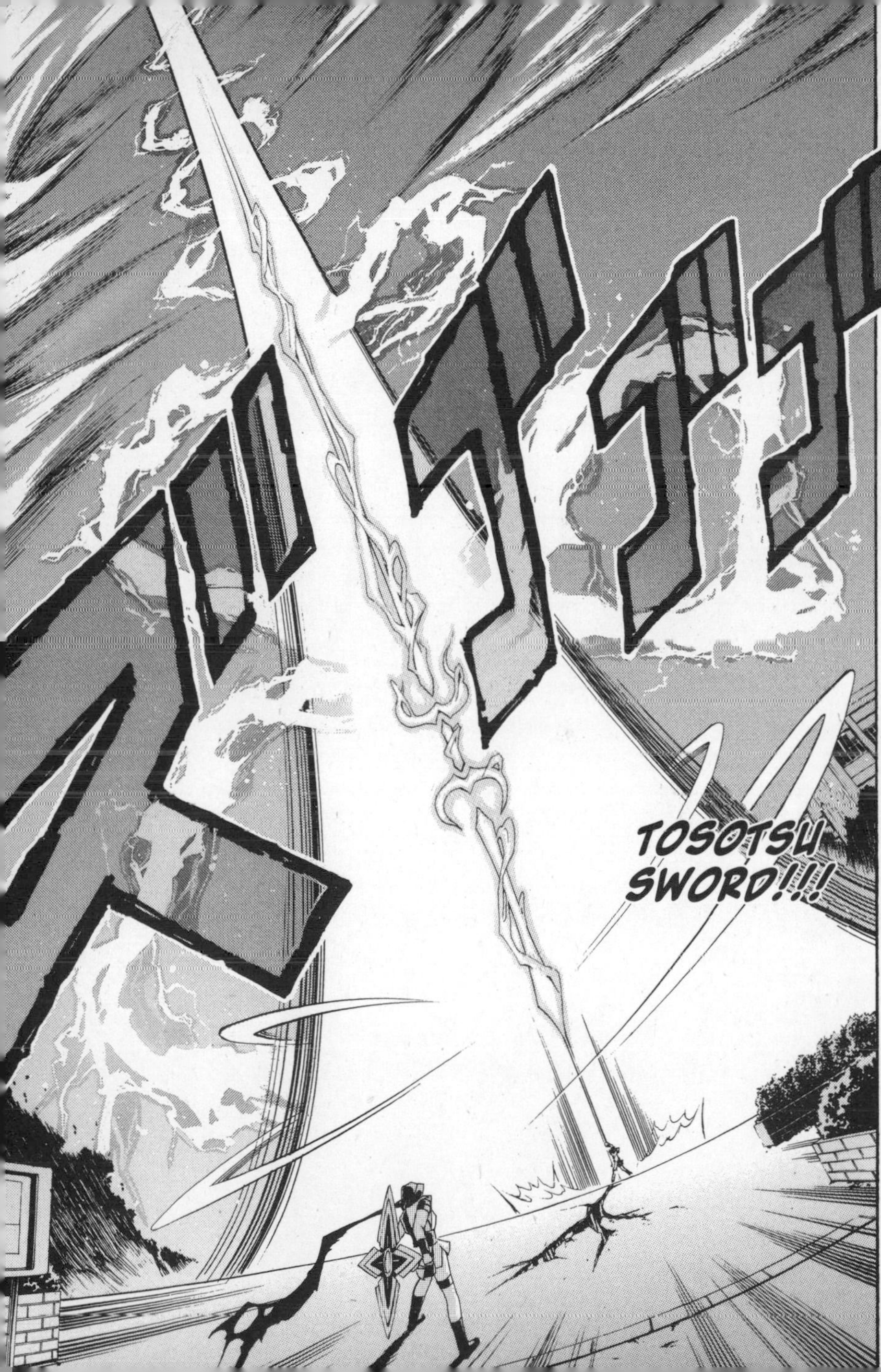
TOSOTSU SWORD!!!

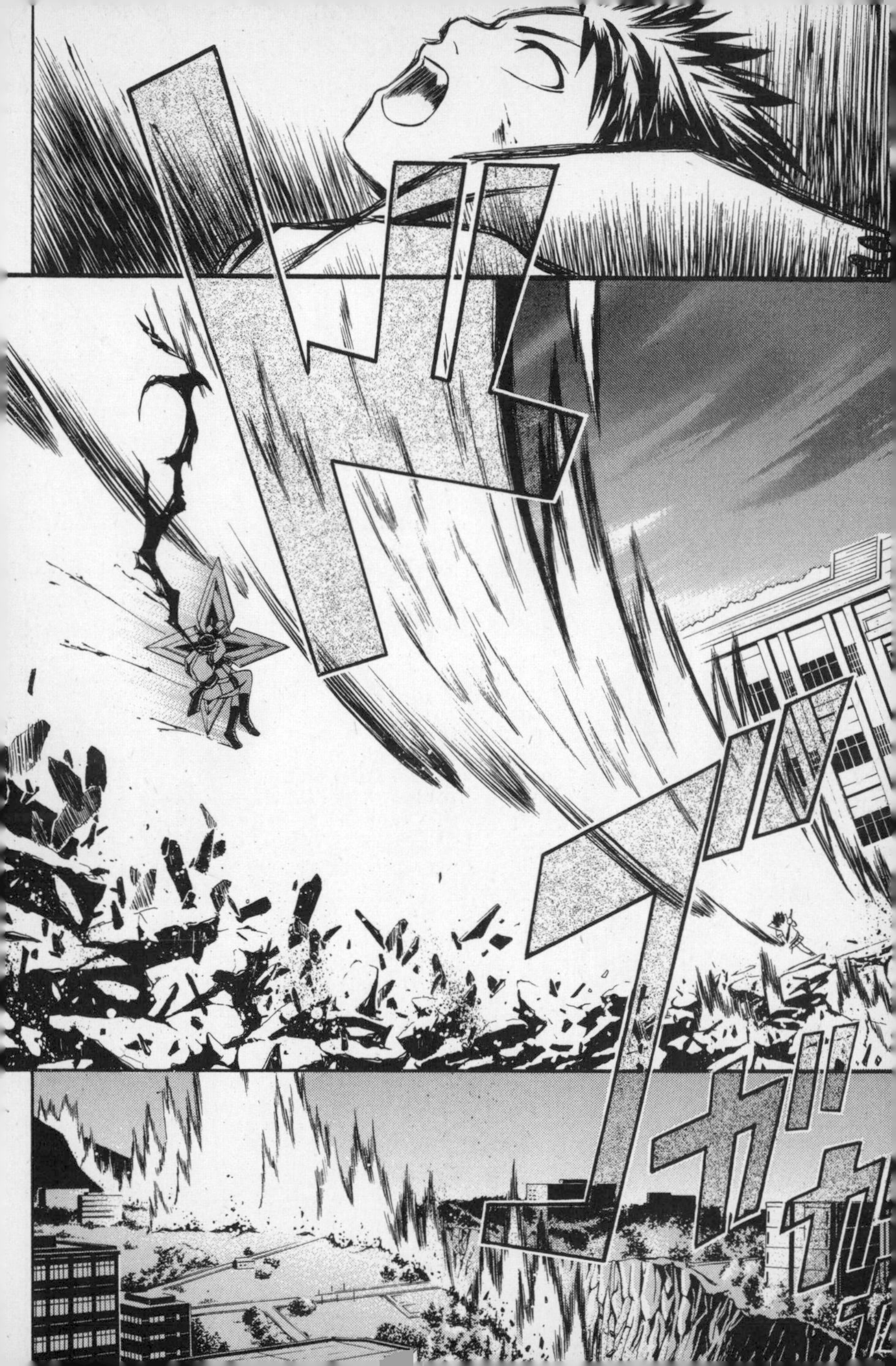

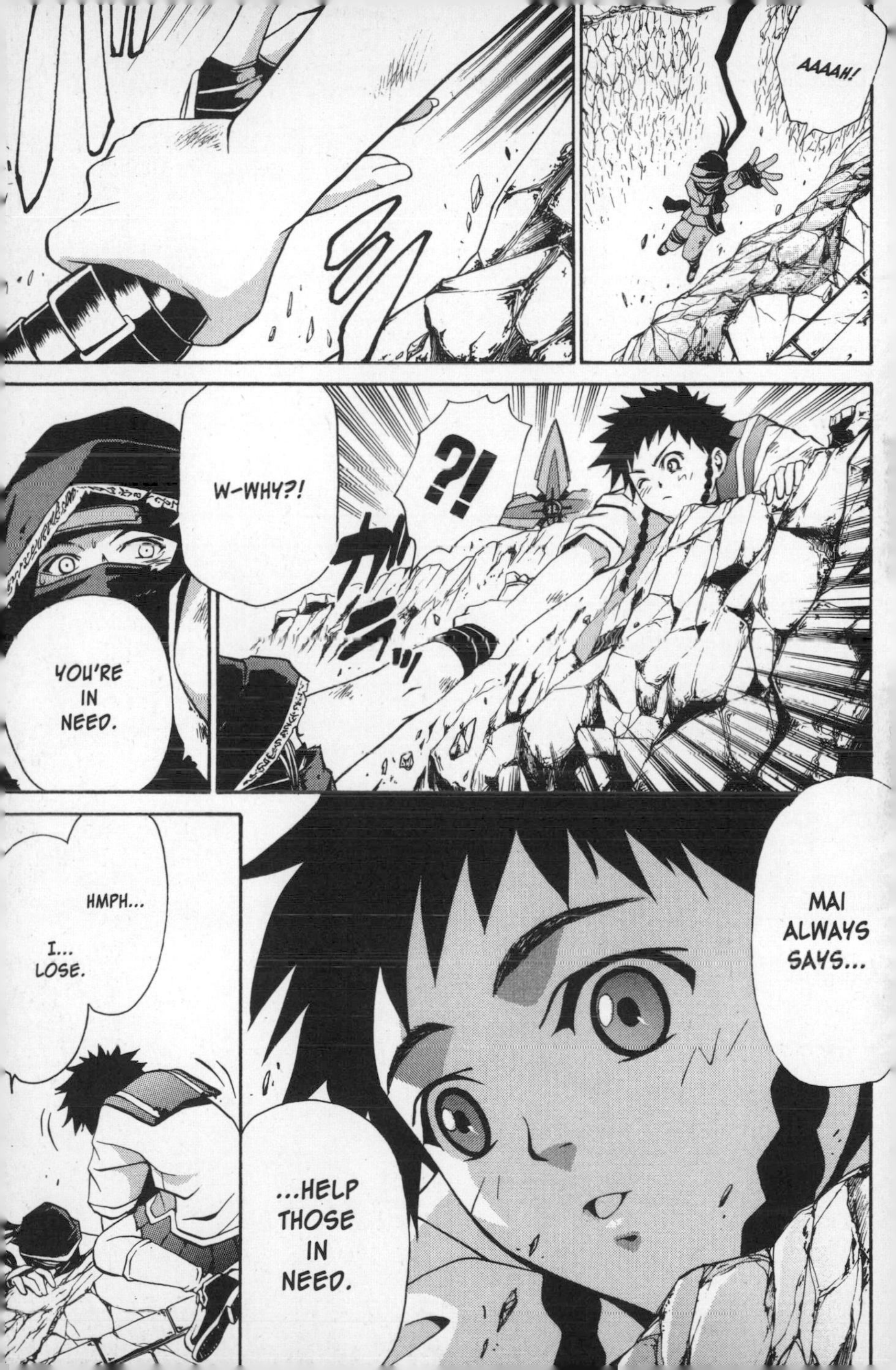
AAAAH!
?!
W-WHY?!
YOU'RE IN NEED.
MAI ALWAYS SAYS...
...HELP THOSE IN NEED.
HMPH...
I... LOSE.

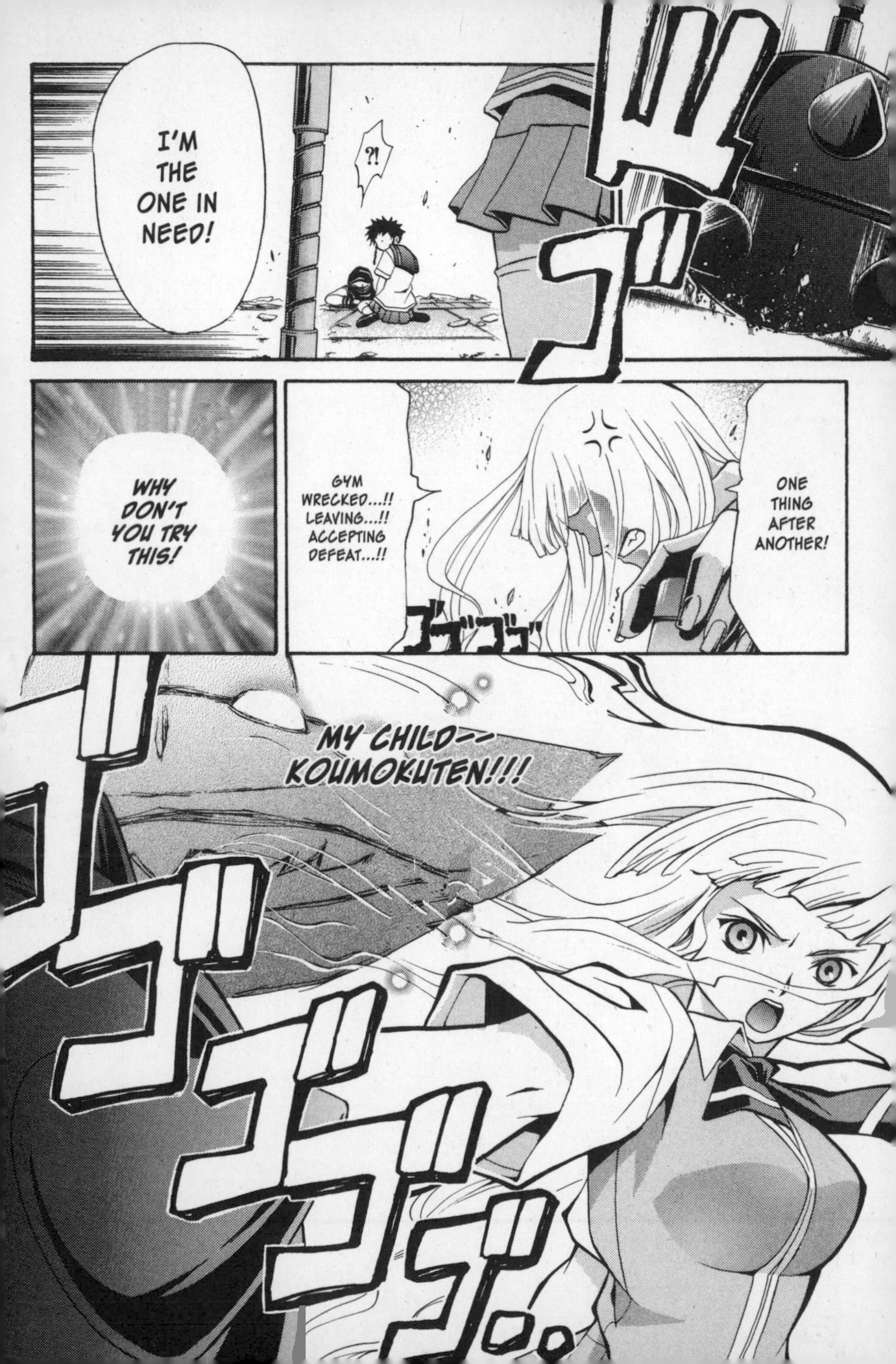
?!
I'M THE ONE IN NEED!
ONE THING AFTER ANOTHER!
GYM WRECKED...!! LEAVING...!! ACCEPTING DEFEAT...!!
WHY DON'T YOU TRY THIS!
MY CHILD-- KOUMOKUTEN!!!

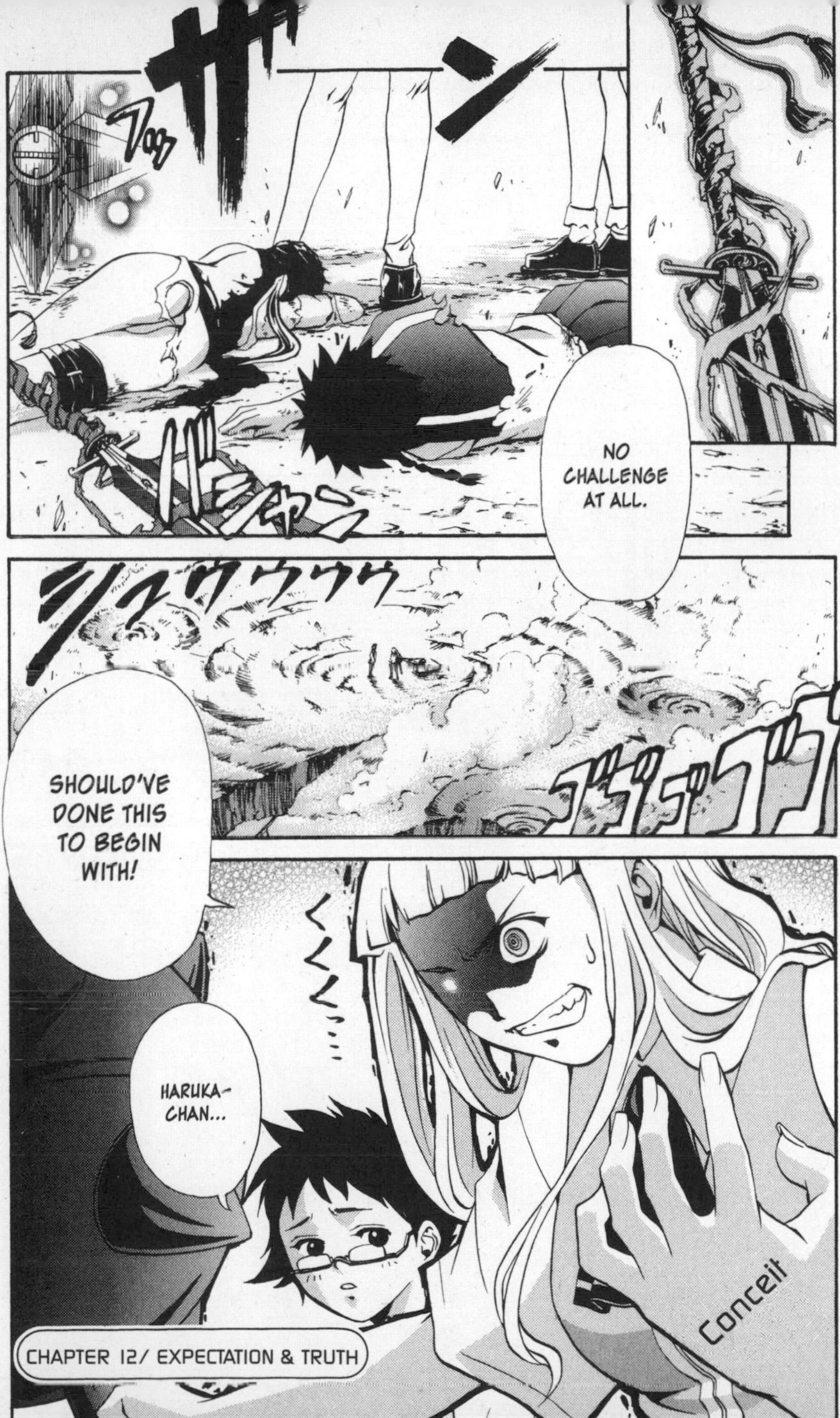

ザザン
シャン
NO CHALLENGE AT ALL.
シュウウウウ
SHOULD'VE DONE THIS TO BEGIN WITH!
くくくっ…
HARUKA-CHAN...
Conceit
CHAPTER 12/ EXPECTATION & TRUTH

CHAPTER 12/ EXPECTATION & TRUTH

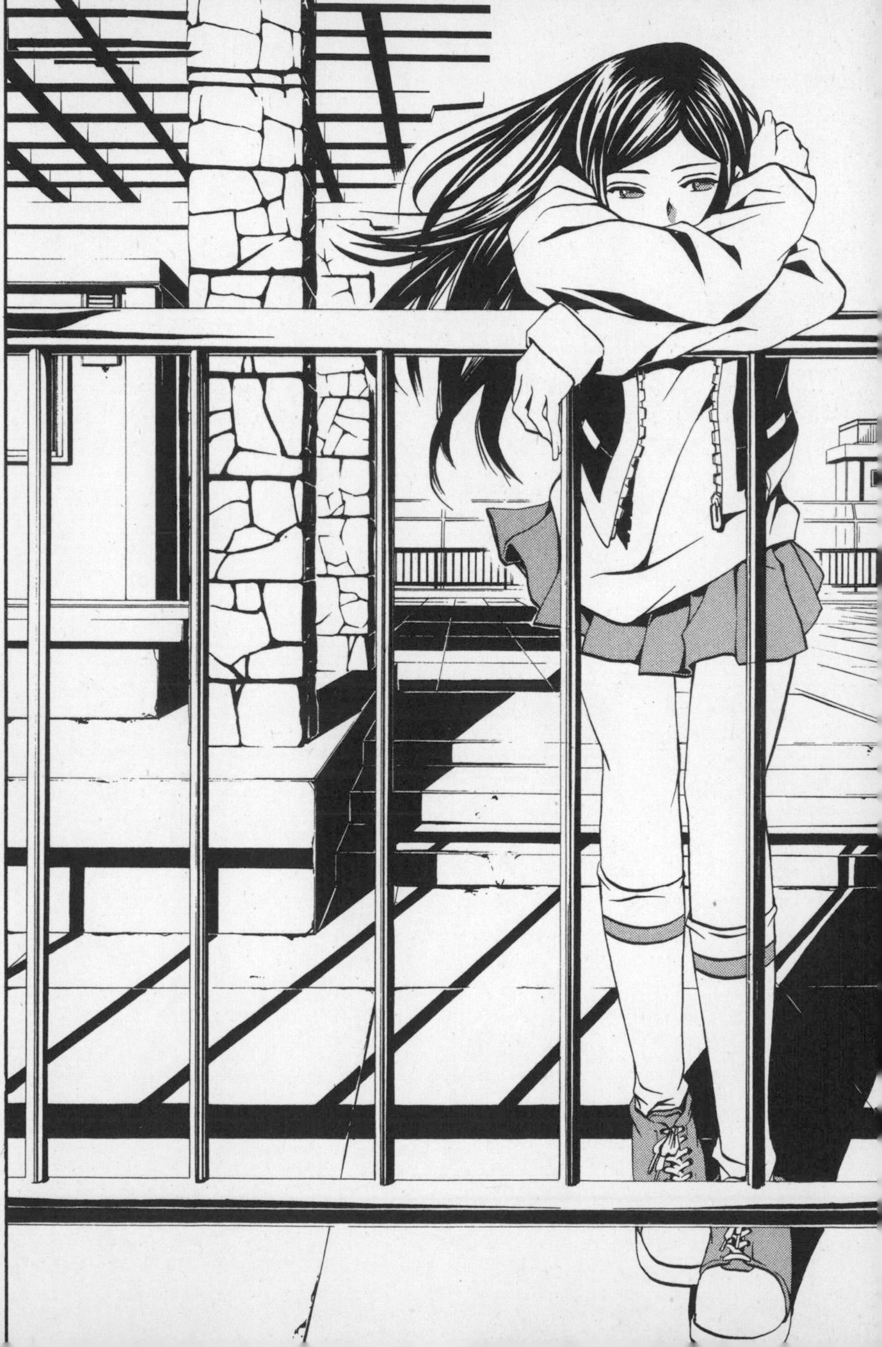

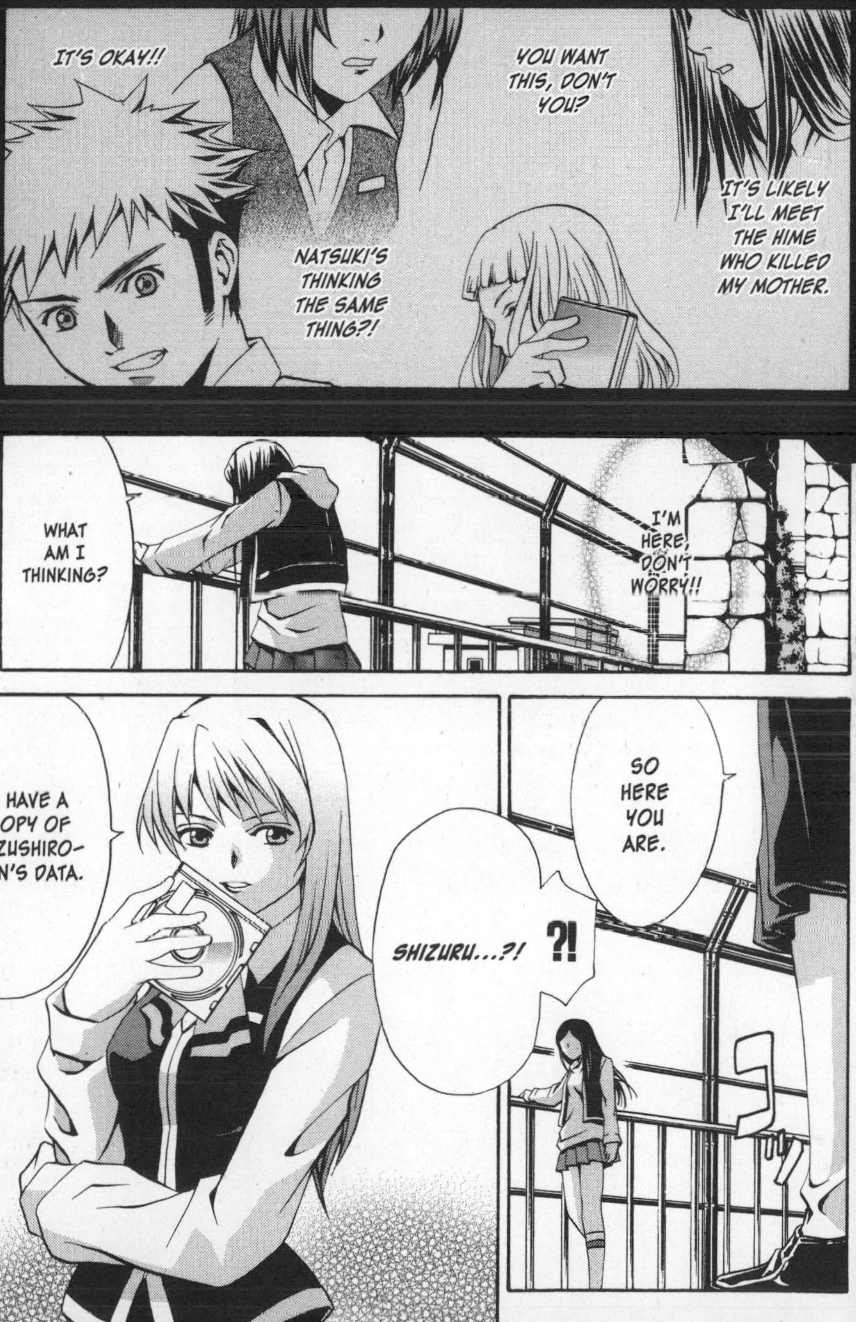
IT'S LIKELY I'LL MEET THE HIME WHO KILLED MY MOTHER.
YOU WANT THIS, DON'T YOU?
NATSUKI'S THINKING THE SAME THING?!
IT'S OKAY!!
I'M HERE, DON'T WORRY!!
WHAT AM I THINKING?
SO HERE YOU ARE.
?!
SHIZURU...?!
I HAVE A COPY OF SUZUSHIRO-SAN'S DATA.

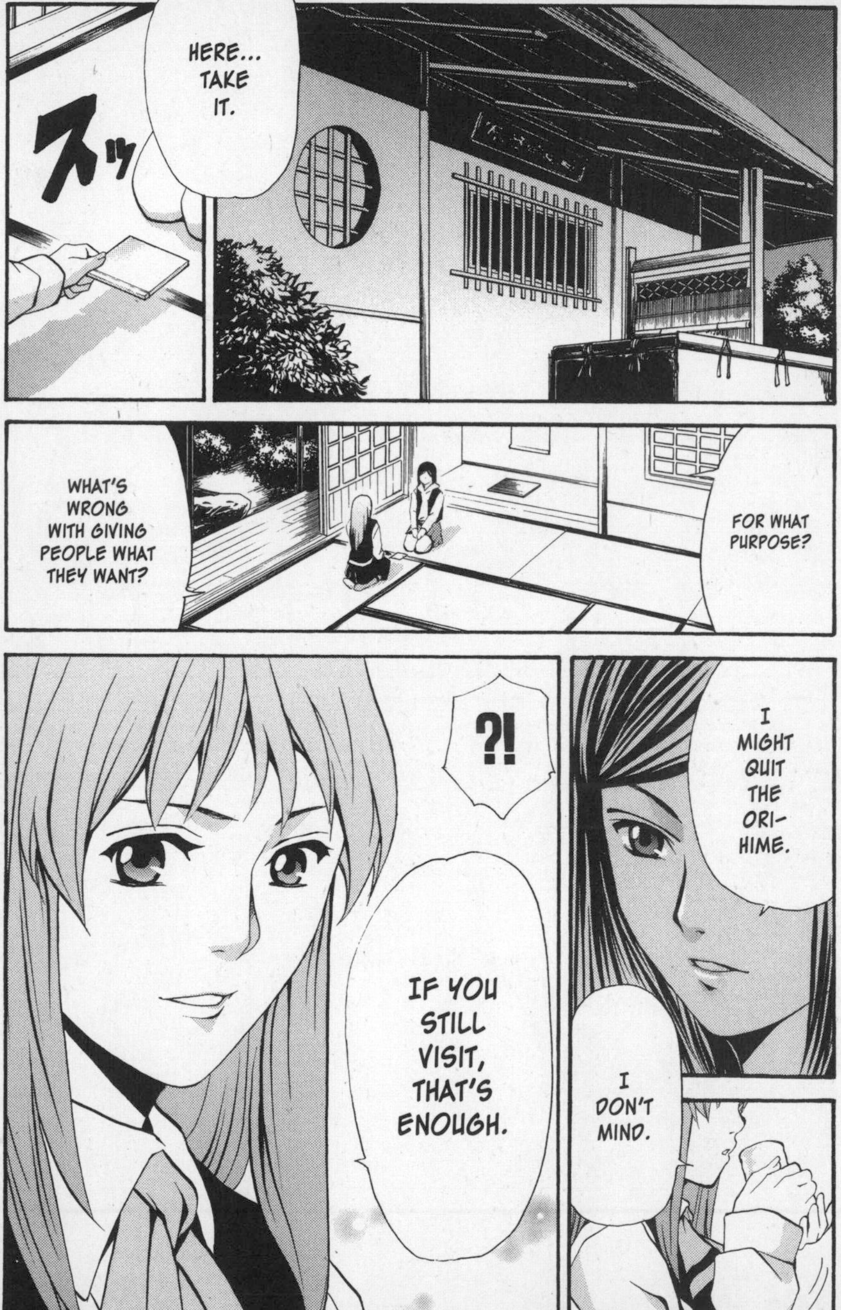
HERE... TAKE IT.
スッ
FOR WHAT PURPOSE?
WHAT'S WRONG WITH GIVING PEOPLE WHAT THEY WANT?
I MIGHT QUIT THE ORI-HIME.
I DON'T MIND.
?!
IF YOU STILL VISIT, THAT'S ENOUGH.

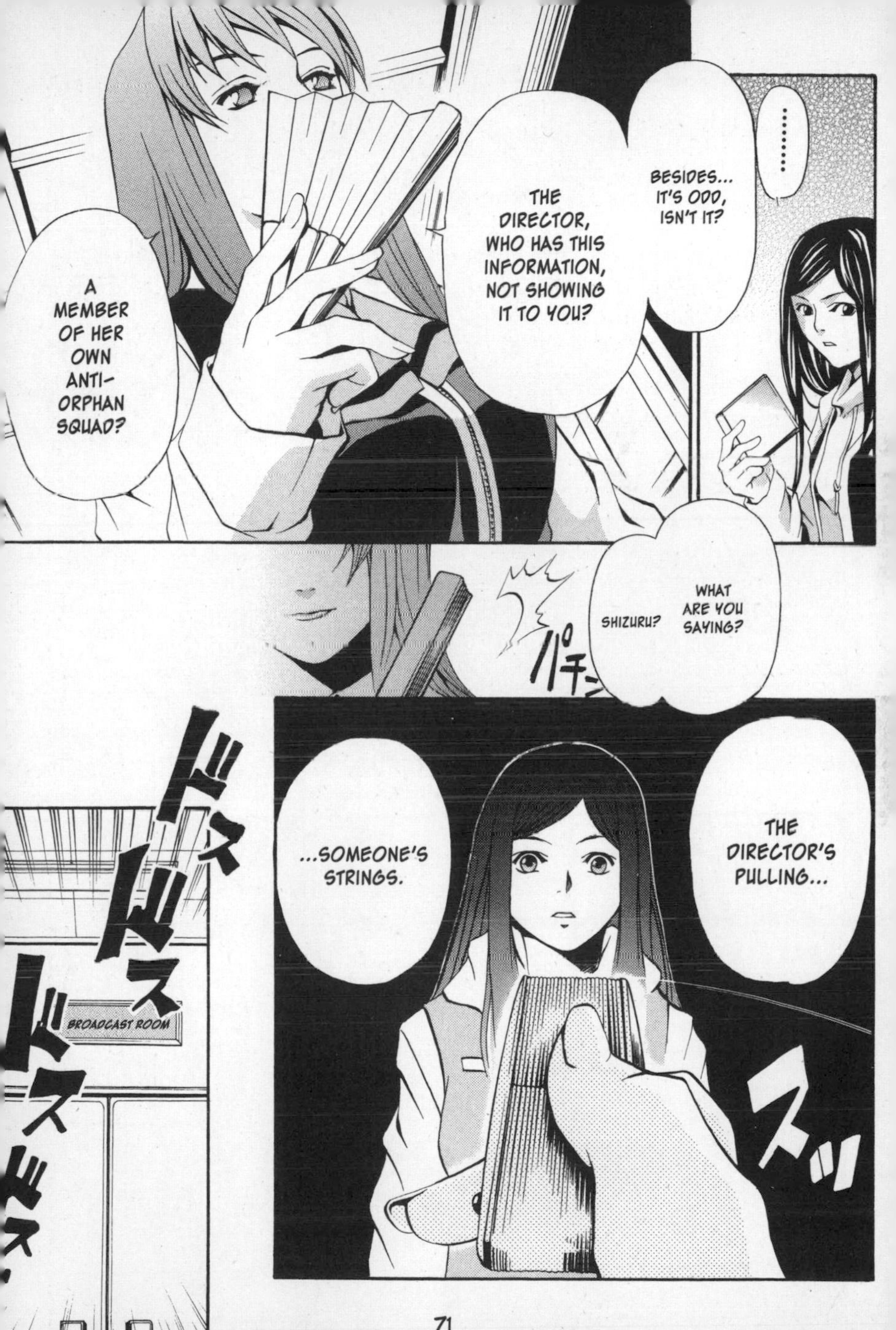
......
BESIDES... IT'S ODD, ISN'T IT?
THE DIRECTOR, WHO HAS THIS INFORMATION, NOT SHOWING IT TO YOU?
A MEMBER OF HER OWN ANTI-ORPHAN SQUAD?
WHAT ARE YOU SAYING?
SHIZURU?
THE DIRECTOR'S PULLING...
...SOMEONE'S STRINGS.
スッ
BROADCAST ROOM

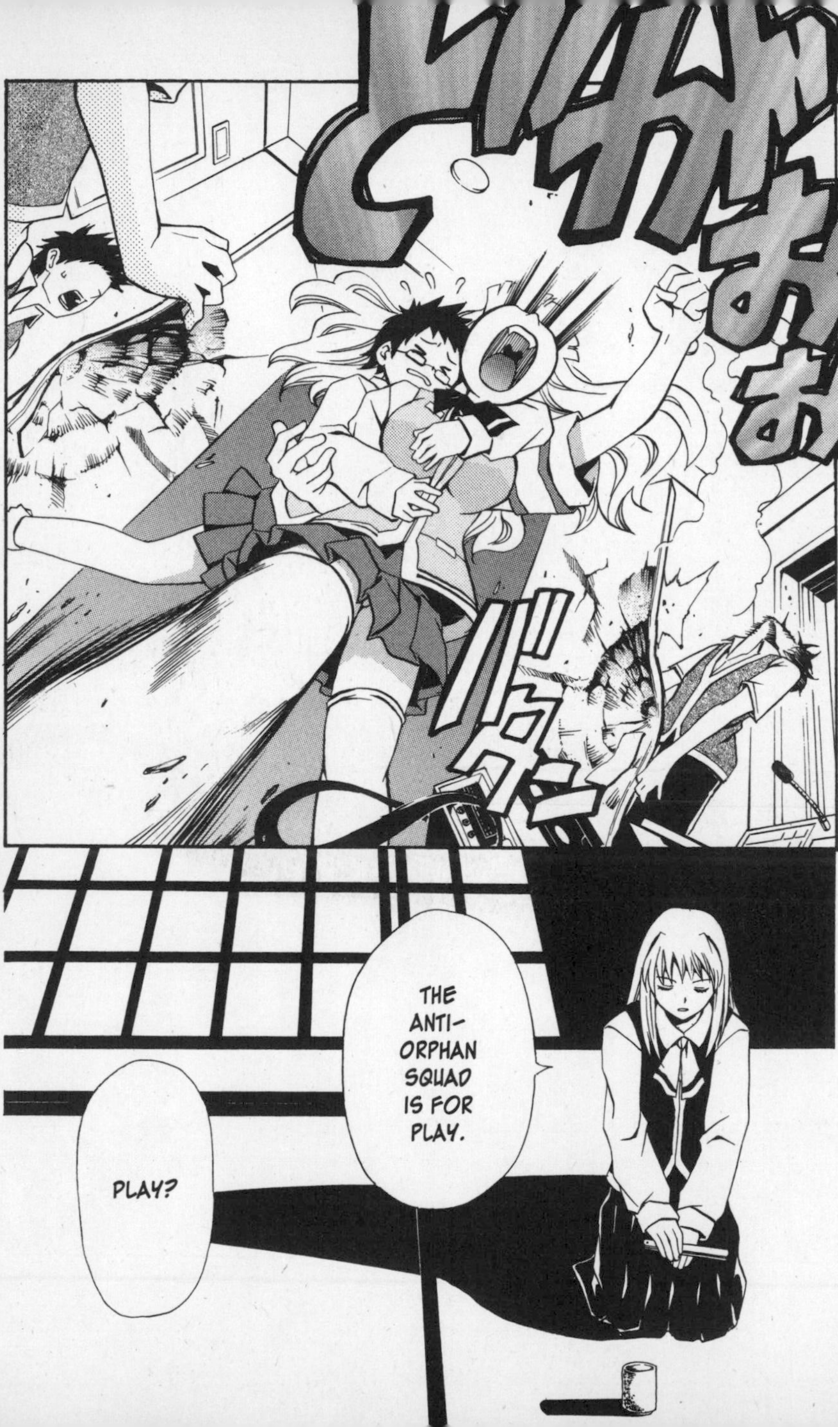
THE ANTI-ORPHAN SQUAD IS FOR PLAY.
PLAY?

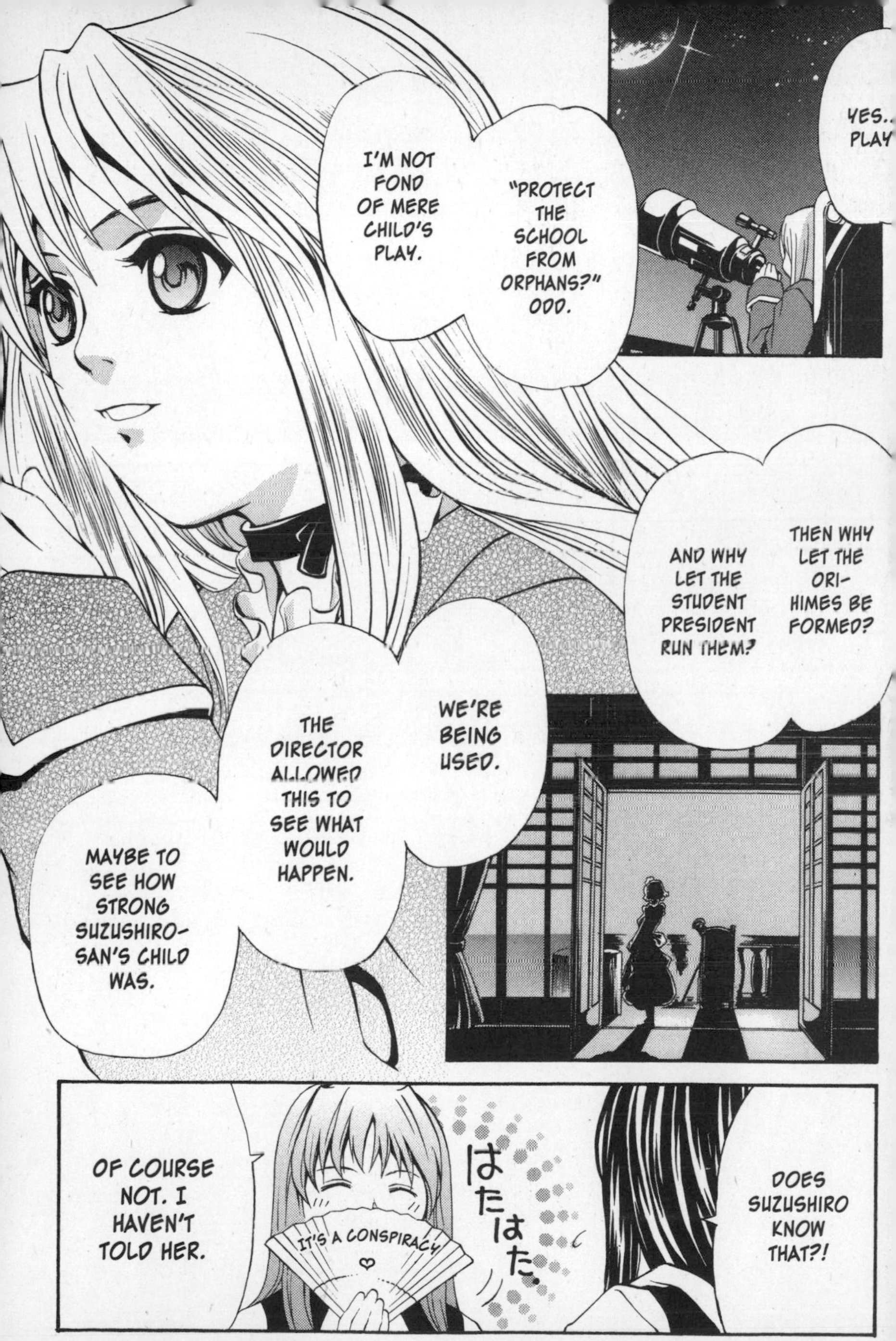
YES.. PLAY
"PROTECT THE SCHOOL FROM ORPHANS?" ODD.
I'M NOT FOND OF MERE CHILD'S PLAY.
THEN WHY LET THE ORI-HIMES BE FORMED?
AND WHY LET THE STUDENT PRESIDENT RUN THEM?
WE'RE BEING USED.
THE DIRECTOR ALLOWED THIS TO SEE WHAT WOULD HAPPEN.
MAYBE TO SEE HOW STRONG SUZUSHIRO-SAN'S CHILD WAS.
DOES SUZUSHIRO KNOW THAT?!
はたはた
OF COURSE NOT. I HAVEN'T TOLD HER.
IT'S A CONSPIRACY ♡

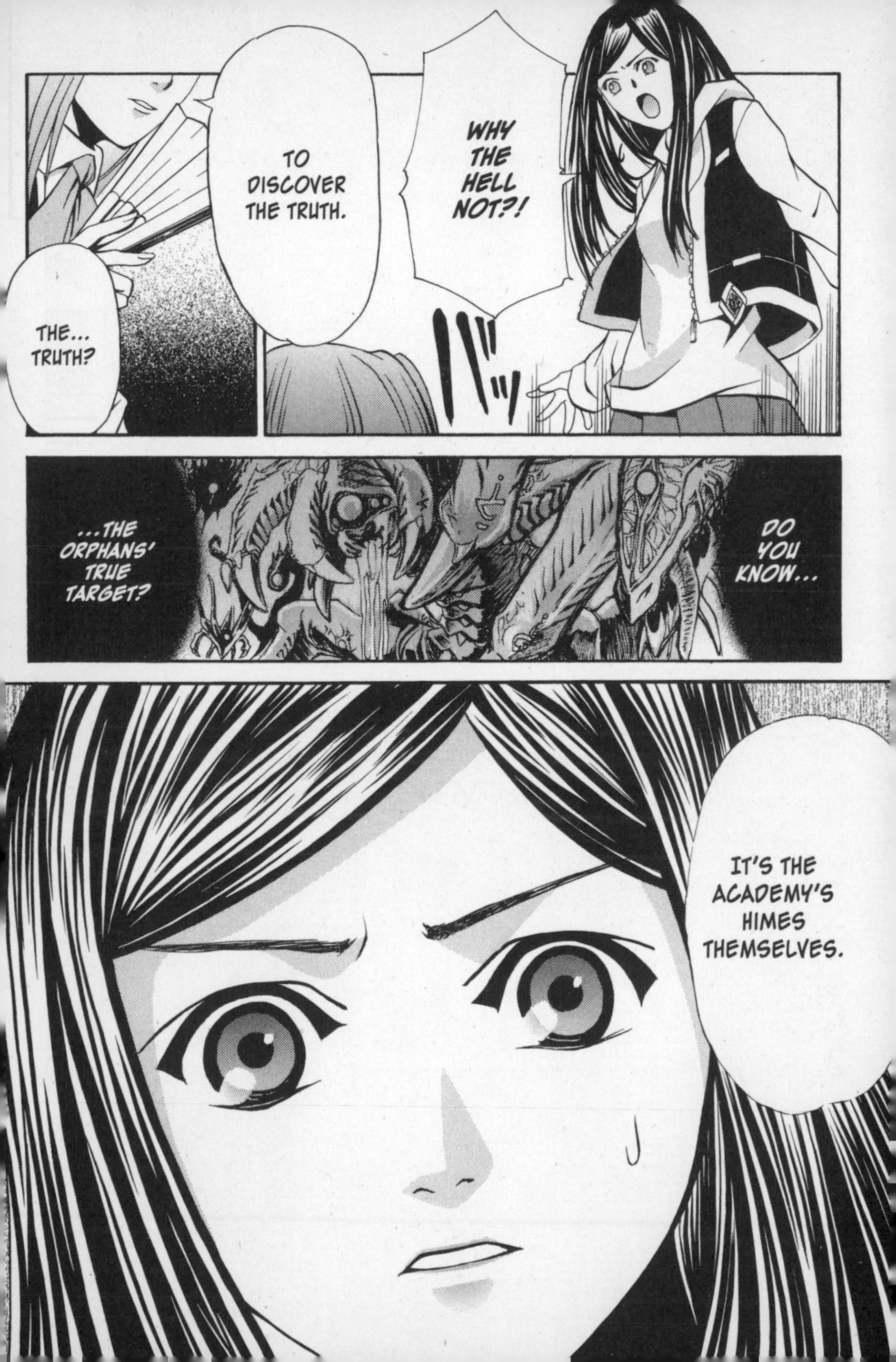
WHY THE HELL NOT?!
バッ
TO DISCOVER THE TRUTH.
THE... TRUTH?
DO YOU KNOW...
...THE ORPHANS' TRUE TARGET?
IT'S THE ACADEMY'S HIMES THEMSELVES.

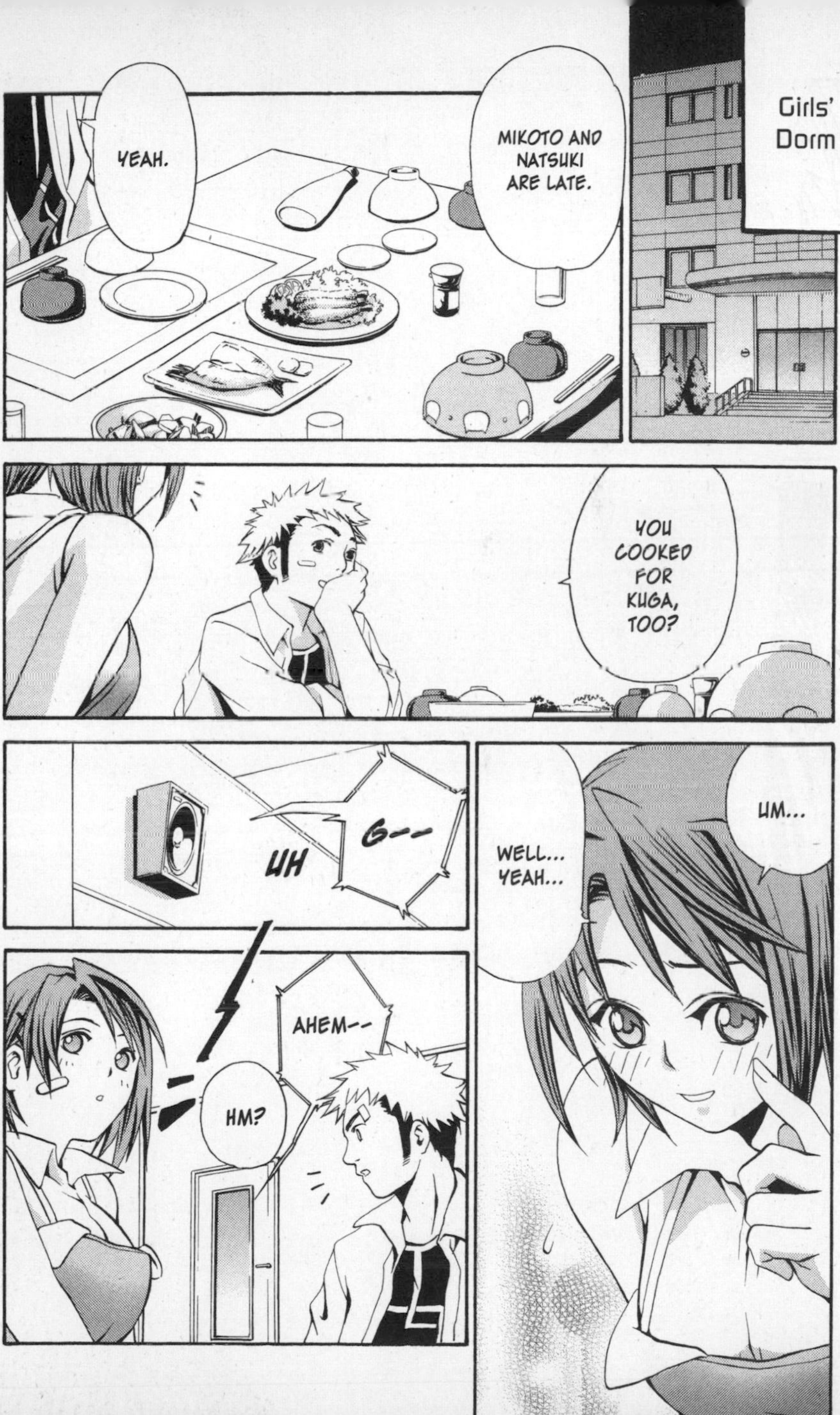
Girls' Dorm
MIKOTO AND NATSUKI ARE LATE.
YEAH.
YOU COOKED FOR KUGA, TOO?
UM...
WELL... YEAH...
G--
UH
AHEM--
HM?

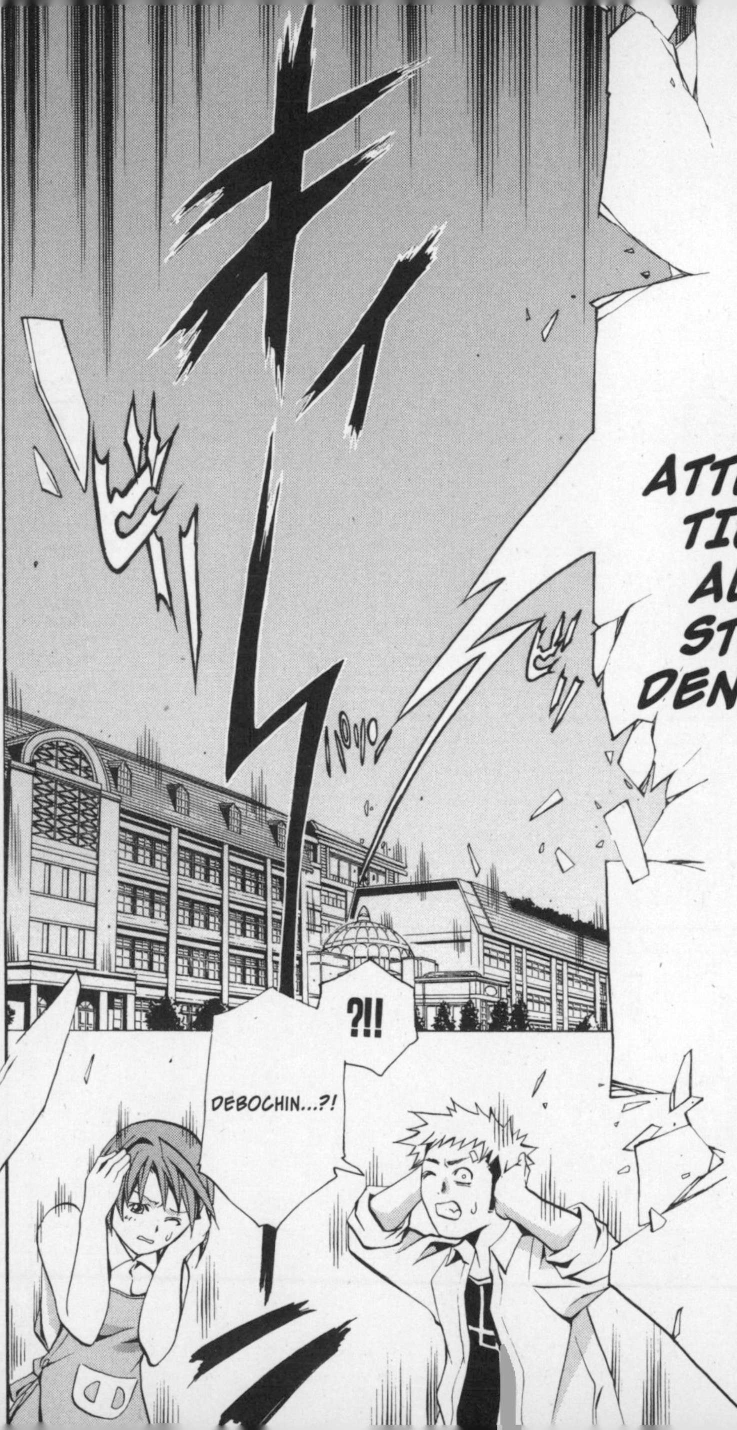
ATTEN-
TION
ALL
STU-
DENTS!!
?!!
DEBOCHIN...?!

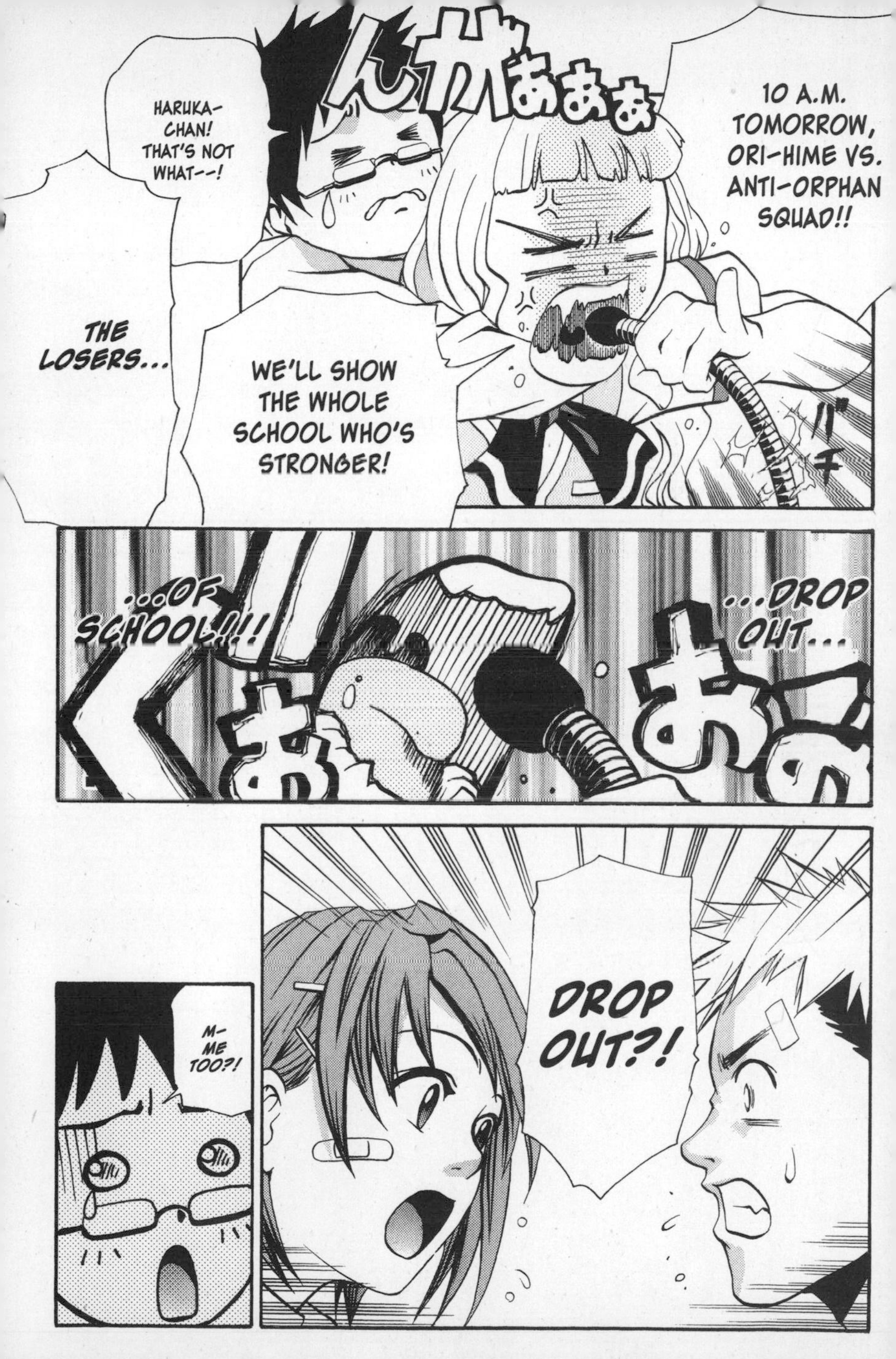
10 A.M. TOMORROW, ORI-HIME VS. ANTI-ORPHAN SQUAD!!
WE'LL SHOW THE WHOLE SCHOOL WHO'S STRONGER!
THE LOSERS...
HARUKA-CHAN! THAT'S NOT WHAT--!
...DROP OUT...
...OF SCHOOL!!!!
DROP OUT?!
M-ME TOO?!

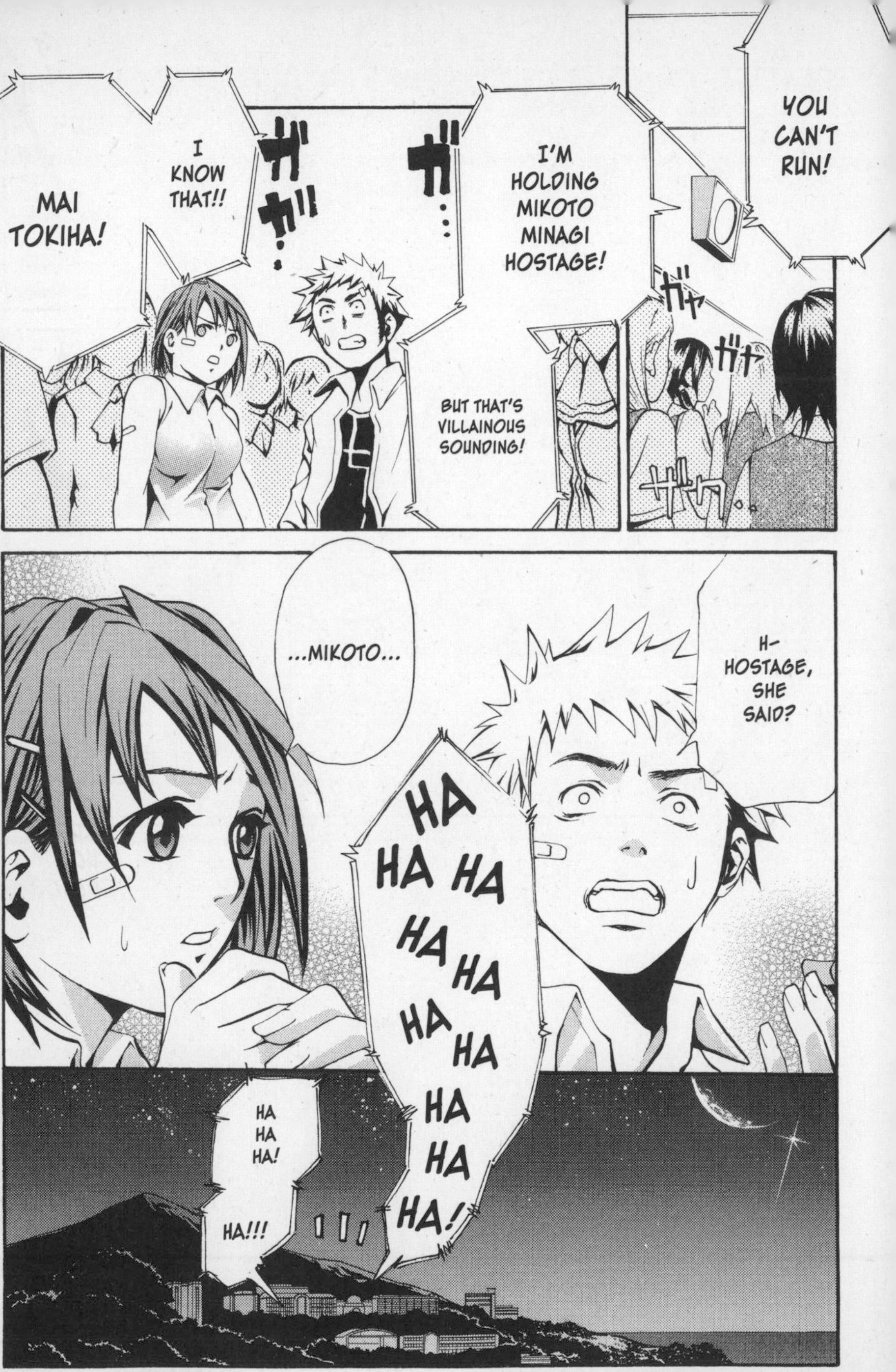
YOU CAN'T RUN!
ガヤ
ガヤ
ザワ。
I'M HOLDING MIKOTO MINAGI HOSTAGE!
BUT THAT'S VILLAINOUS SOUNDING!
ガ…
ガガ!
I KNOW THAT!!
MAI TOKIHA!
H-HOSTAGE, SHE SAID?
...MIKOTO...
HA HA HA HA HA HA HA HA HA HA HA HA!
HA HA HA!
HA!!!

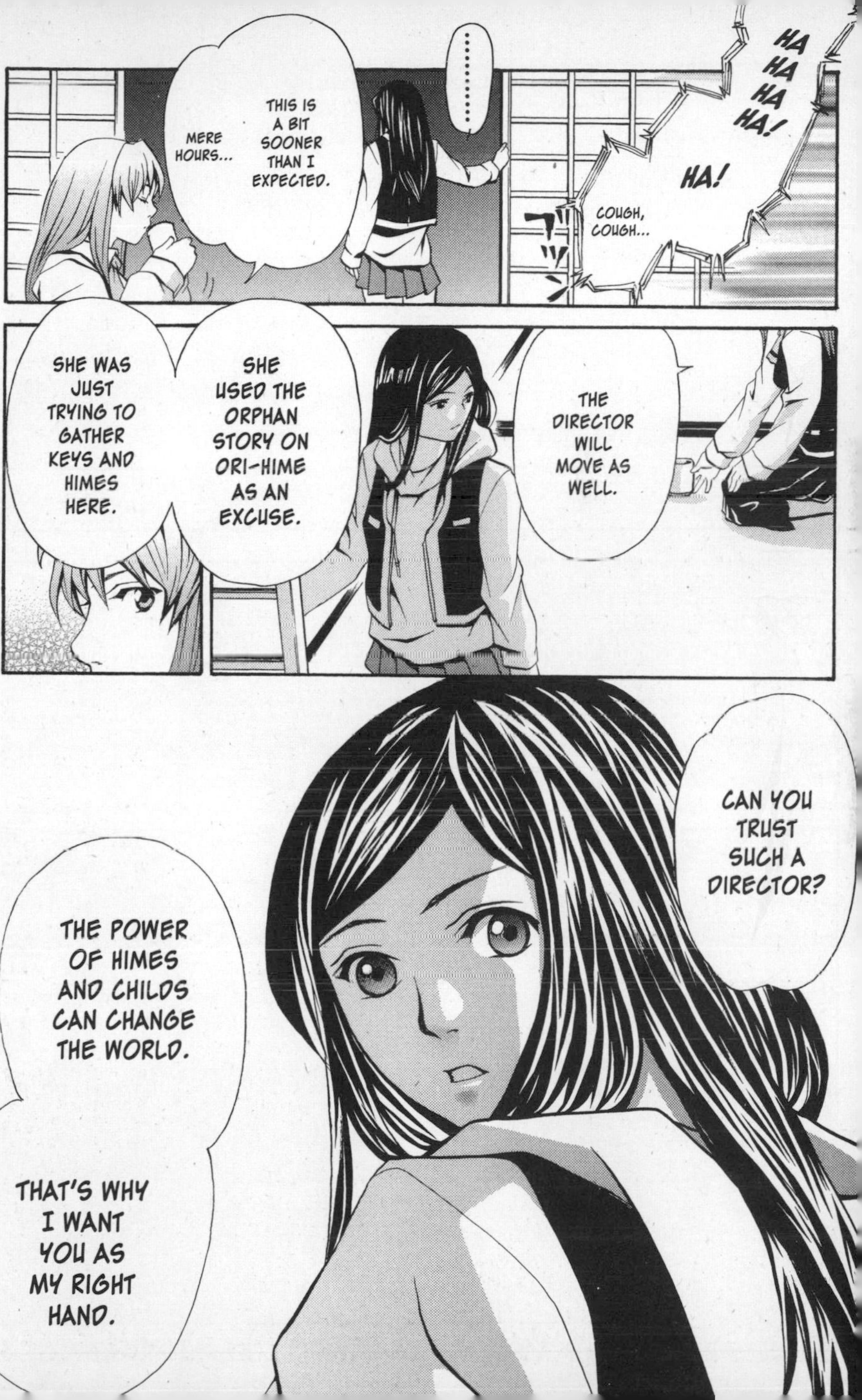
HA HA HA HA!
HA!
COUGH, COUGH...
......
THIS IS A BIT SOONER THAN I EXPECTED.
MERE HOURS...
THE DIRECTOR WILL MOVE AS WELL.
SHE USED THE ORPHAN STORY ON ORI-HIME AS AN EXCUSE.
SHE WAS JUST TRYING TO GATHER KEYS AND HIMES HERE.
CAN YOU TRUST SUCH A DIRECTOR?
THE POWER OF HIMES AND CHILDS CAN CHANGE THE WORLD.
THAT'S WHY I WANT YOU AS MY RIGHT HAND.

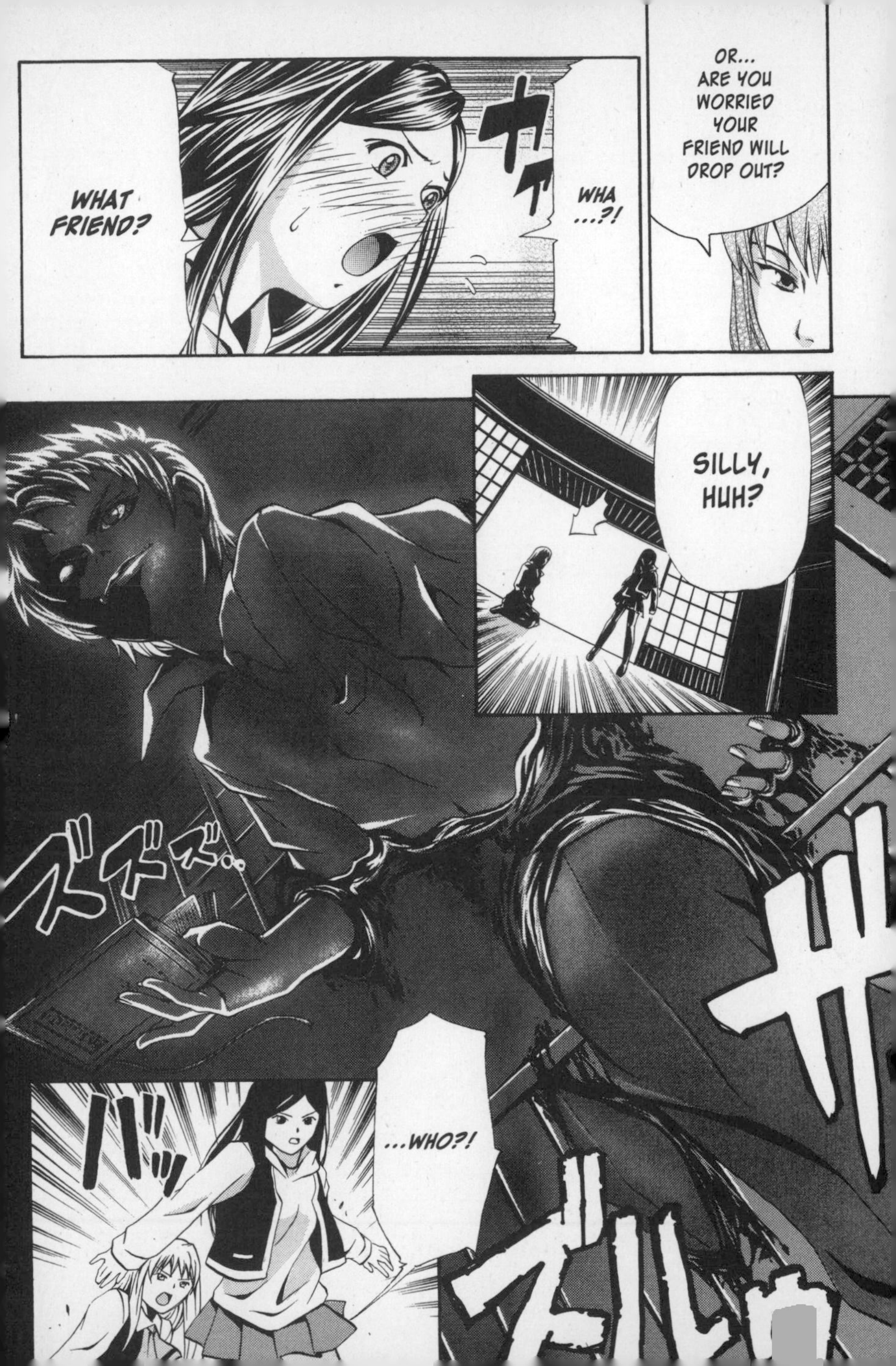
OR... ARE YOU WORRIED YOUR FRIEND WILL DROP OUT?
WHA ...?!
WHAT FRIEND?
SILLY, HUH?
...WHO?!

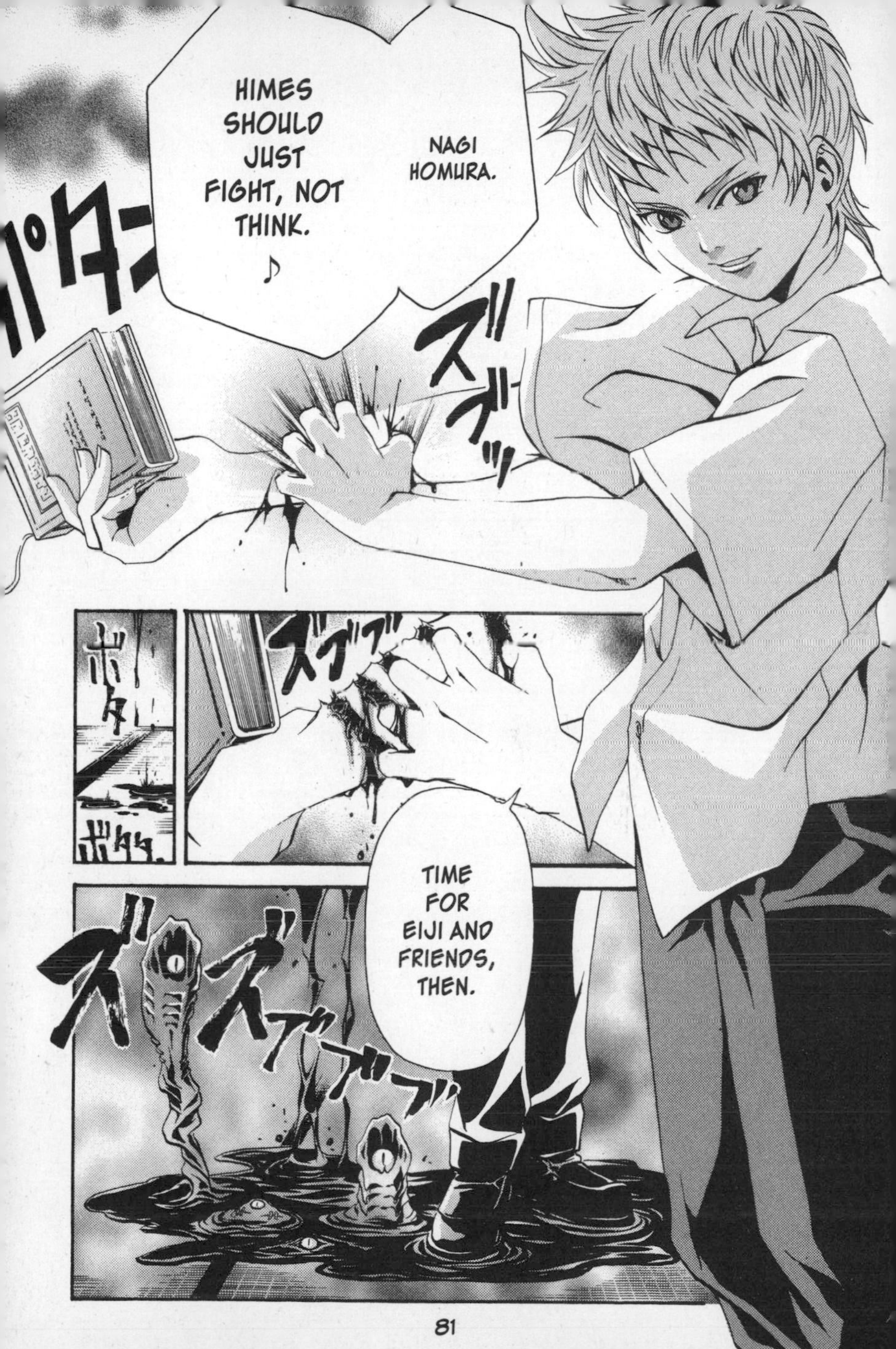
NAGI HOMURA.
HIMES SHOULD JUST FIGHT, NOT THINK. ♪
TIME FOR EIJI AND FRIENDS, THEN.

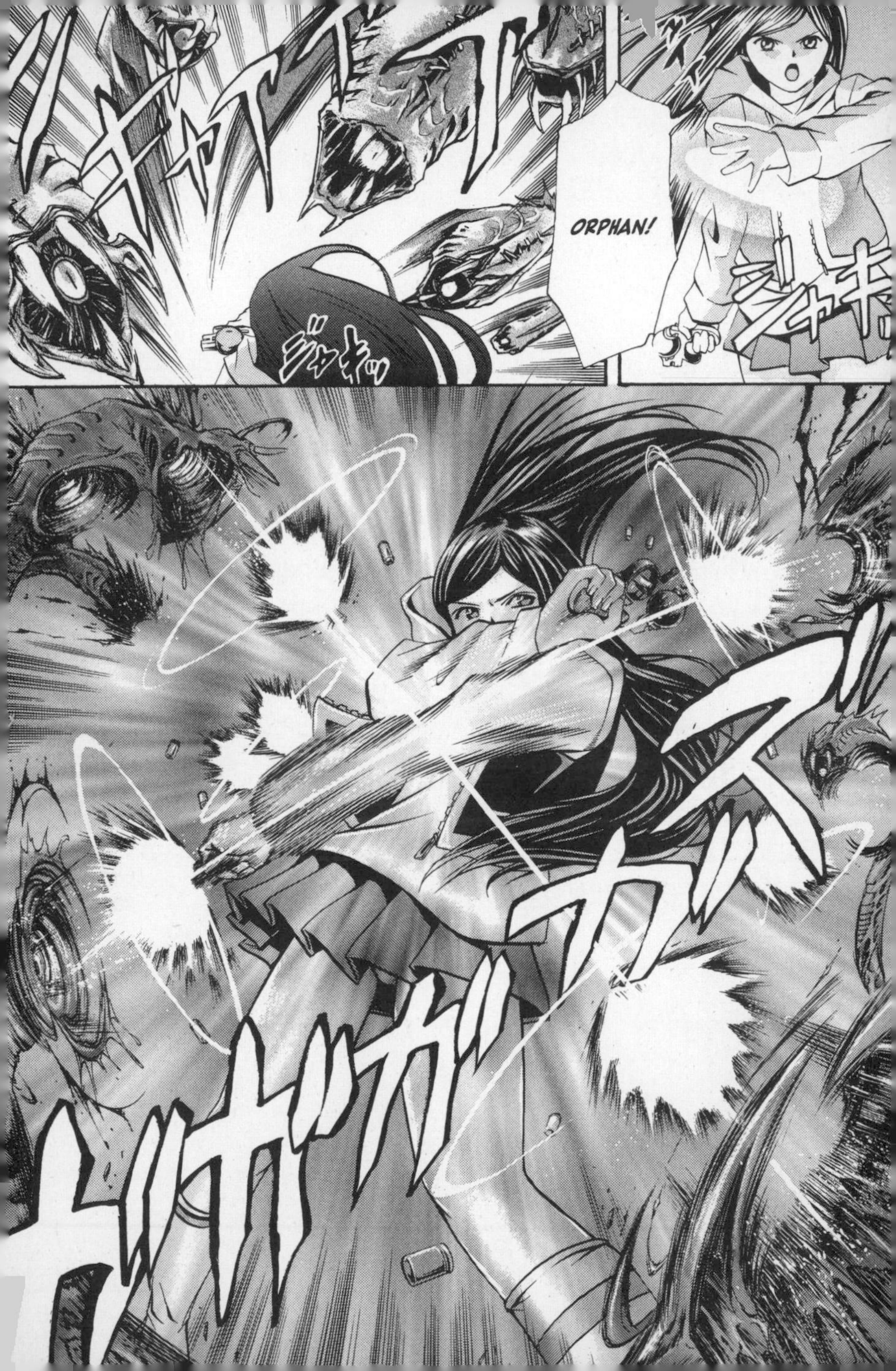
ORPHAN!
ジャキ
ジャキッ

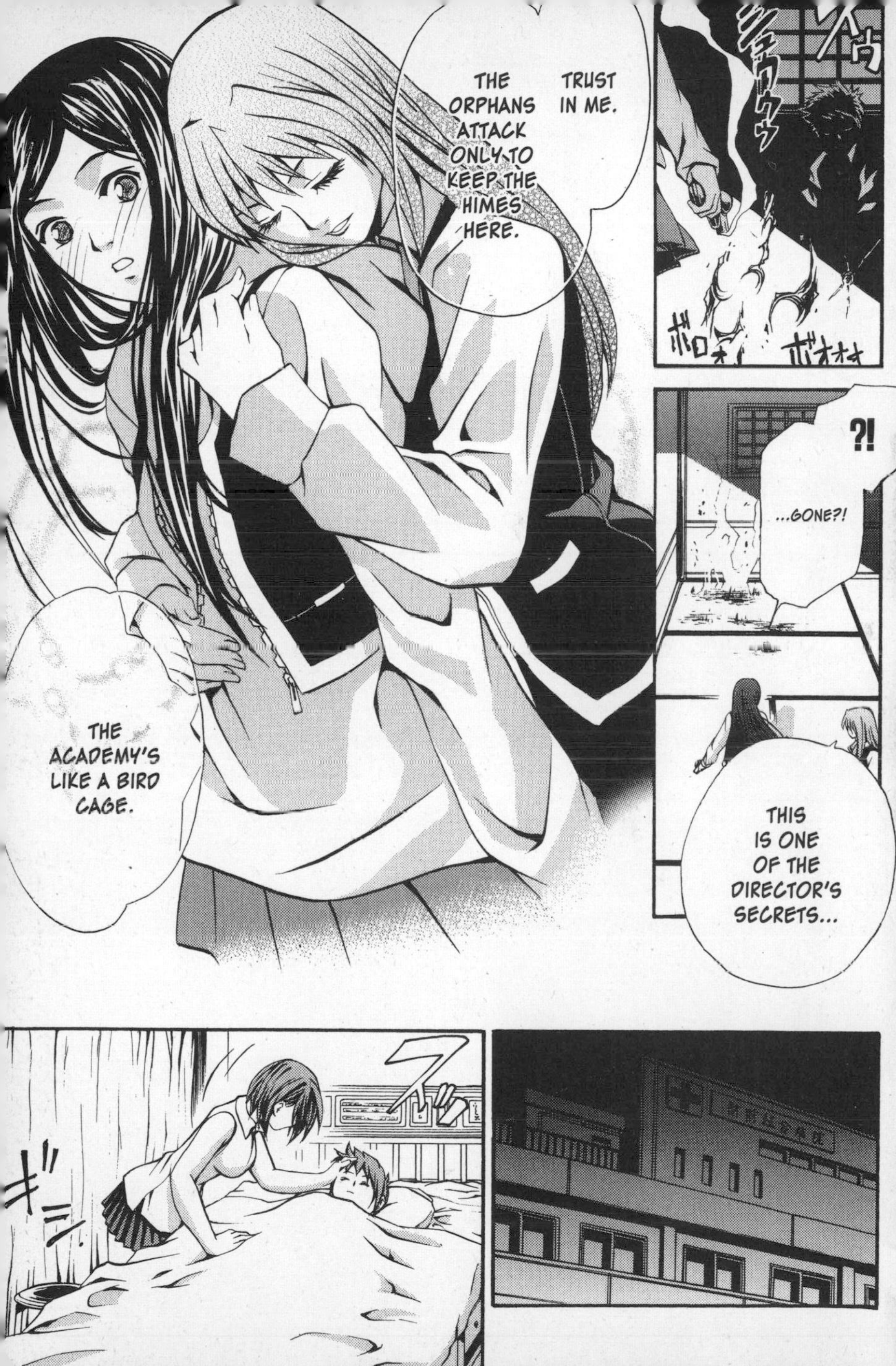
?!
...GONE?!
THIS IS ONE OF THE DIRECTOR'S SECRETS...
TRUST IN ME.
THE ORPHANS ATTACK ONLY TO KEEP THE HIMES HERE.
THE ACADEMY'S LIKE A BIRD CAGE.

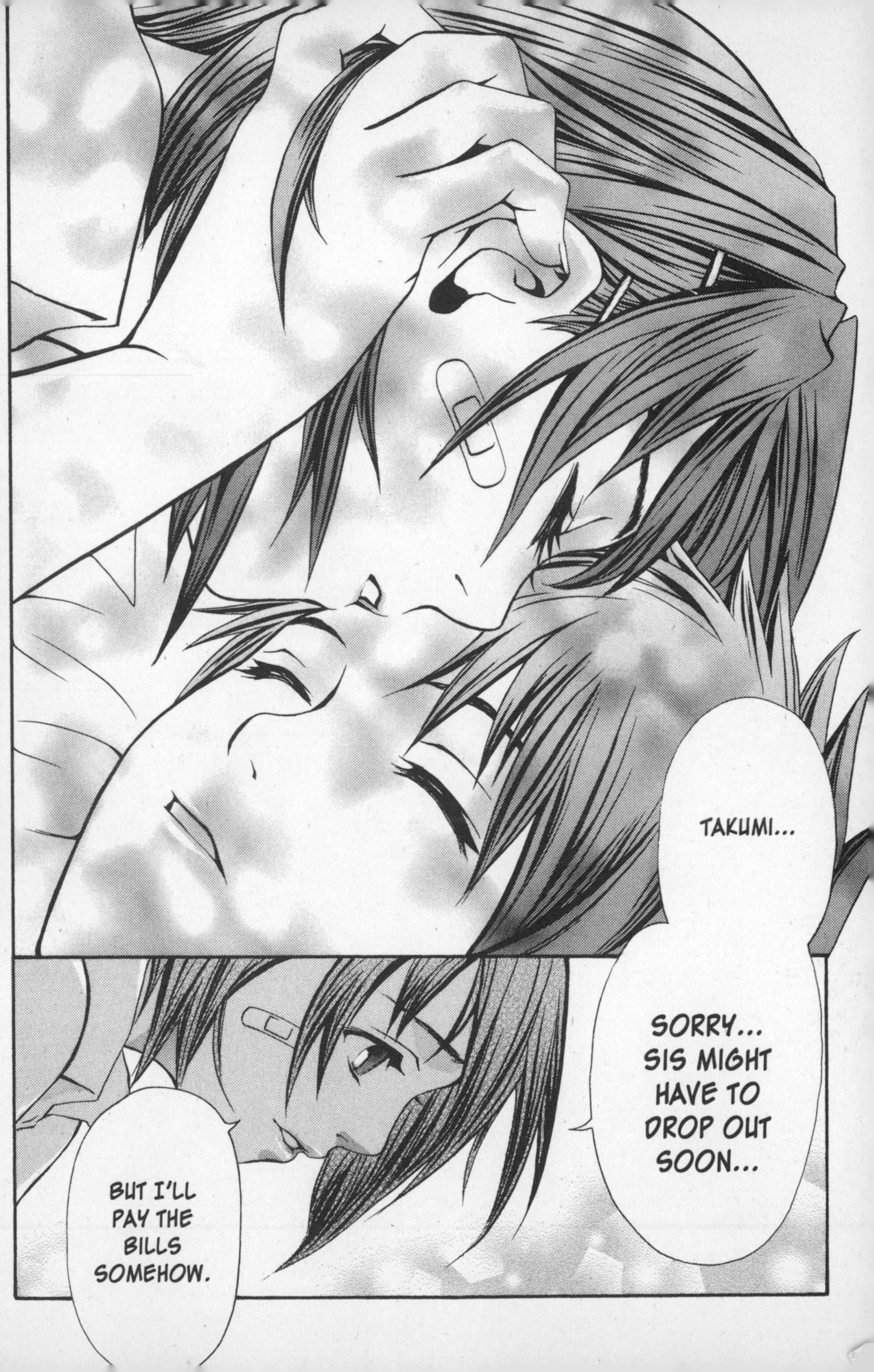
TAKUMI...
SORRY... SIS MIGHT HAVE TO DROP OUT SOON...
BUT I'LL PAY THE BILLS SOMEHOW.

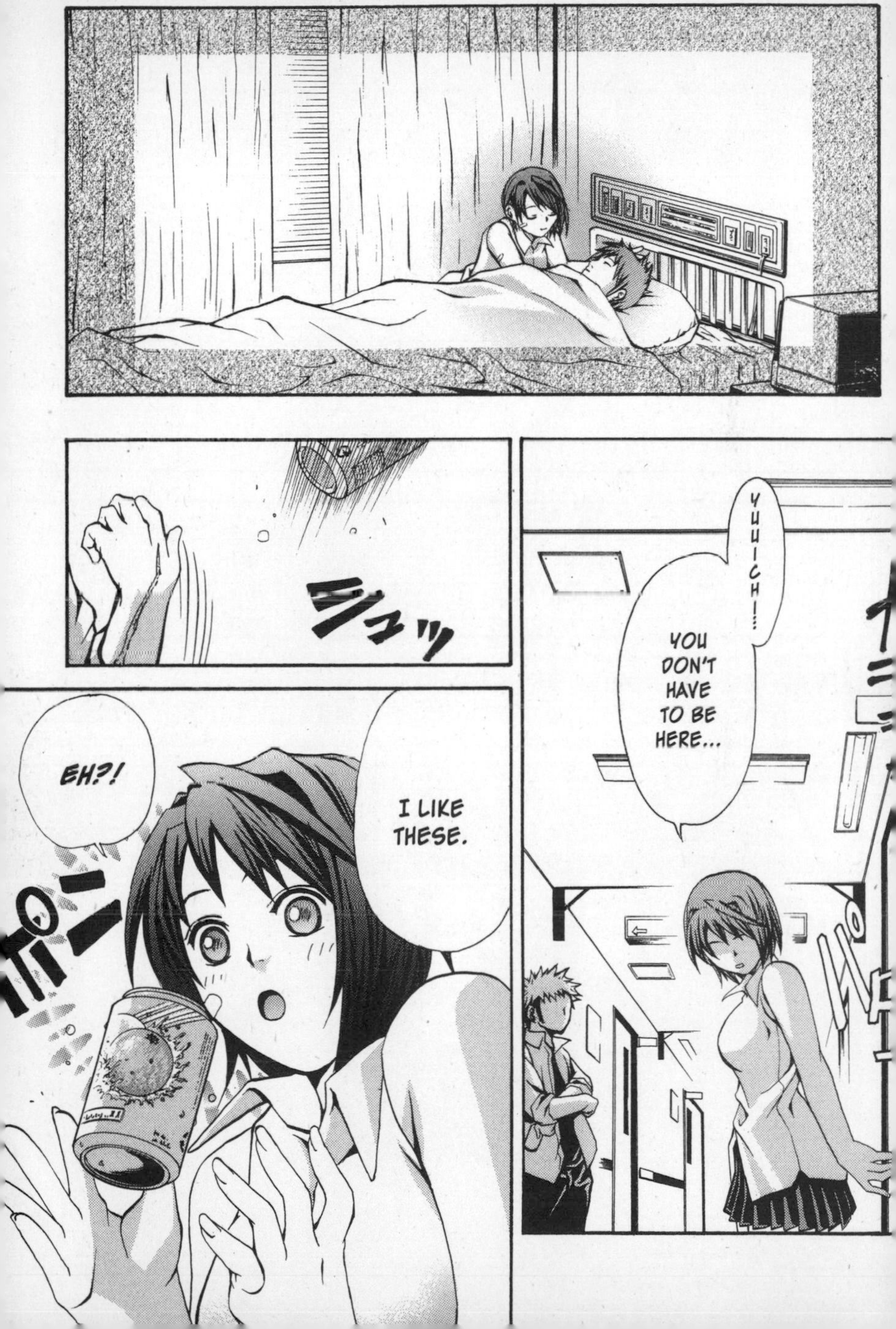
YUUICHI!!
YOU DON'T HAVE TO BE HERE...
シュッ
I LIKE THESE.
EH?!

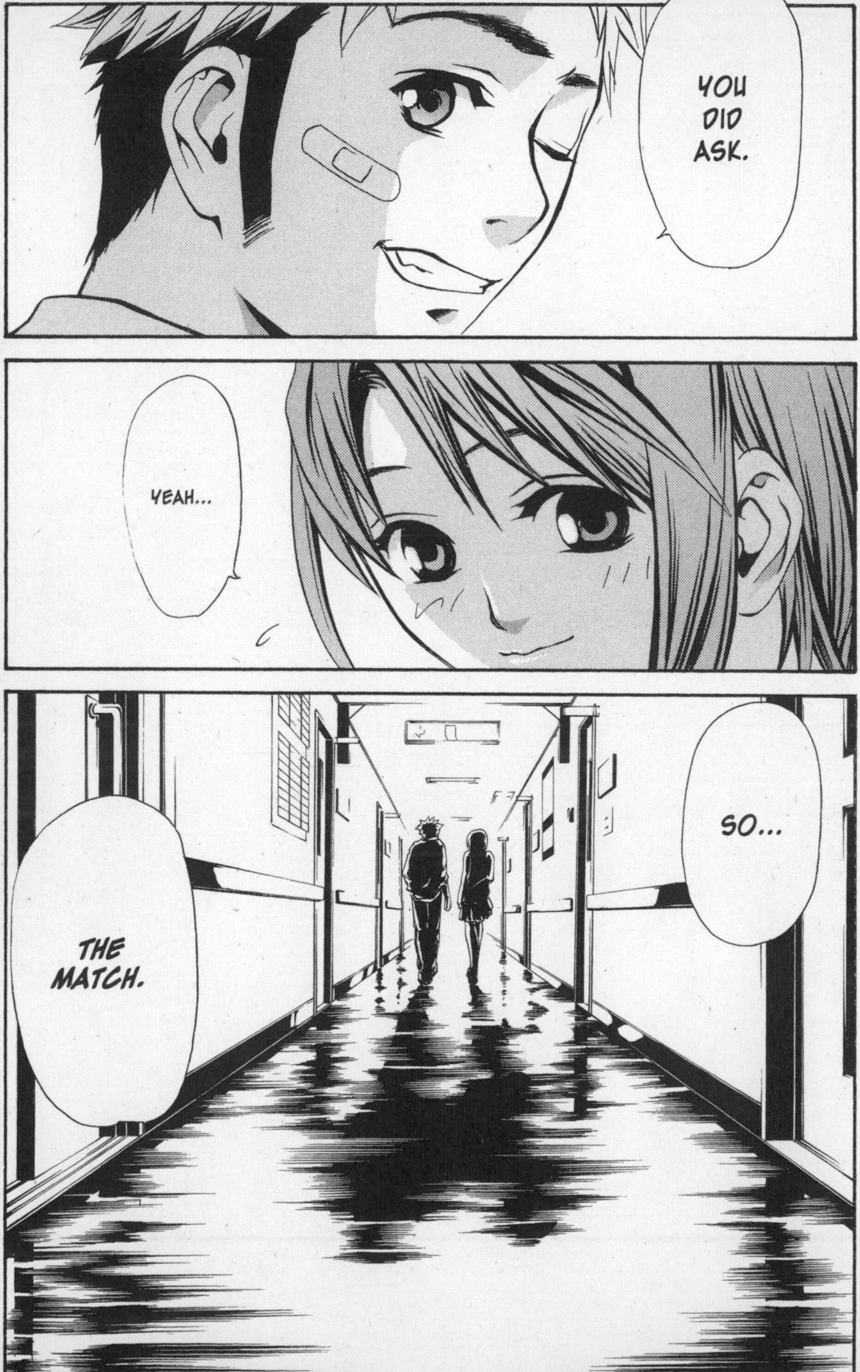
YOU DID ASK.
YEAH...
SO...
THE MATCH.

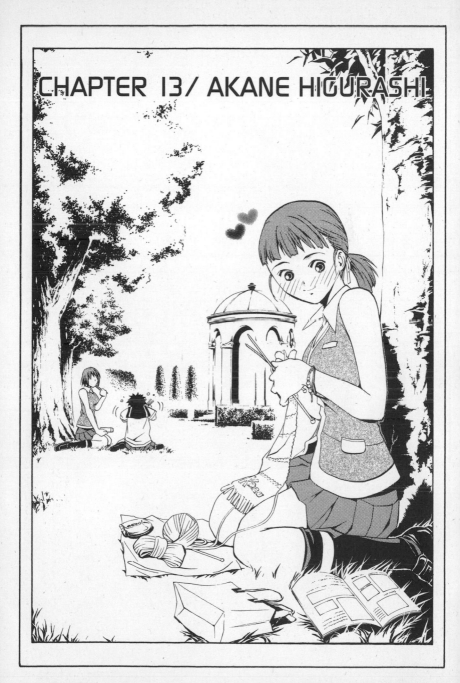

CHAPTER 13/ AKANE HIGURASHI

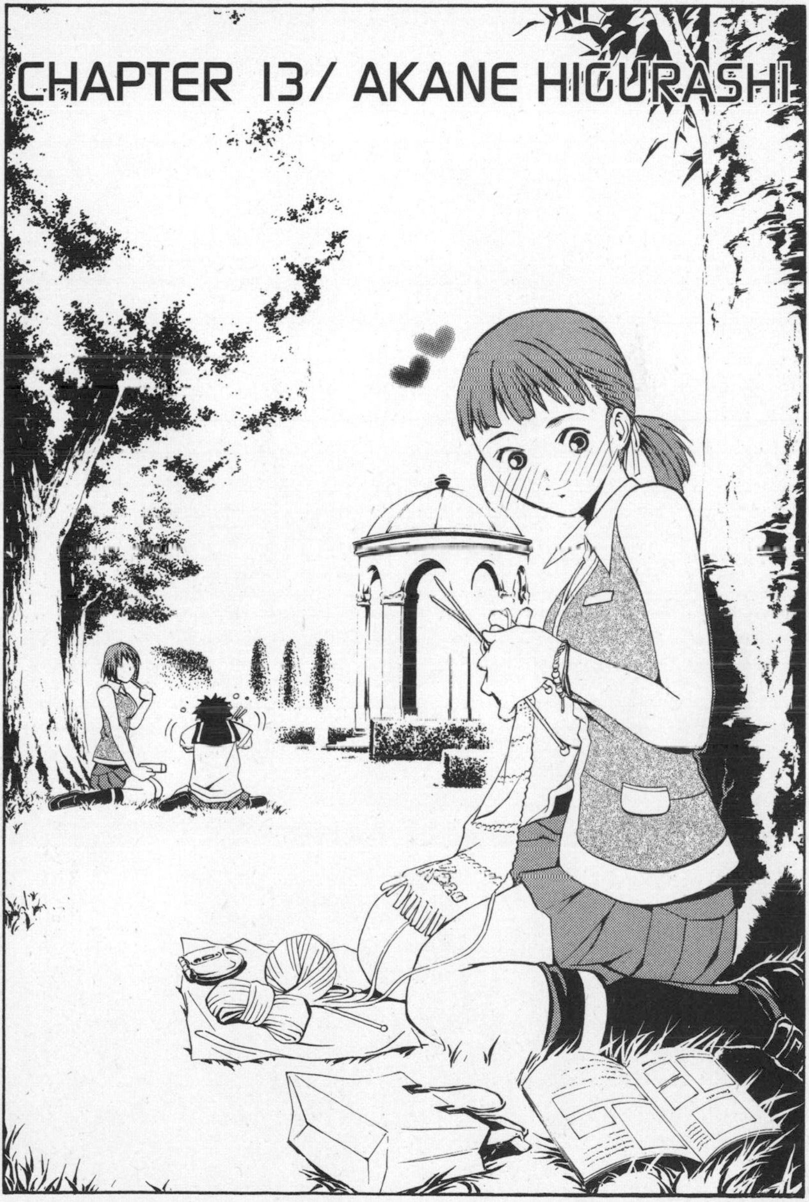

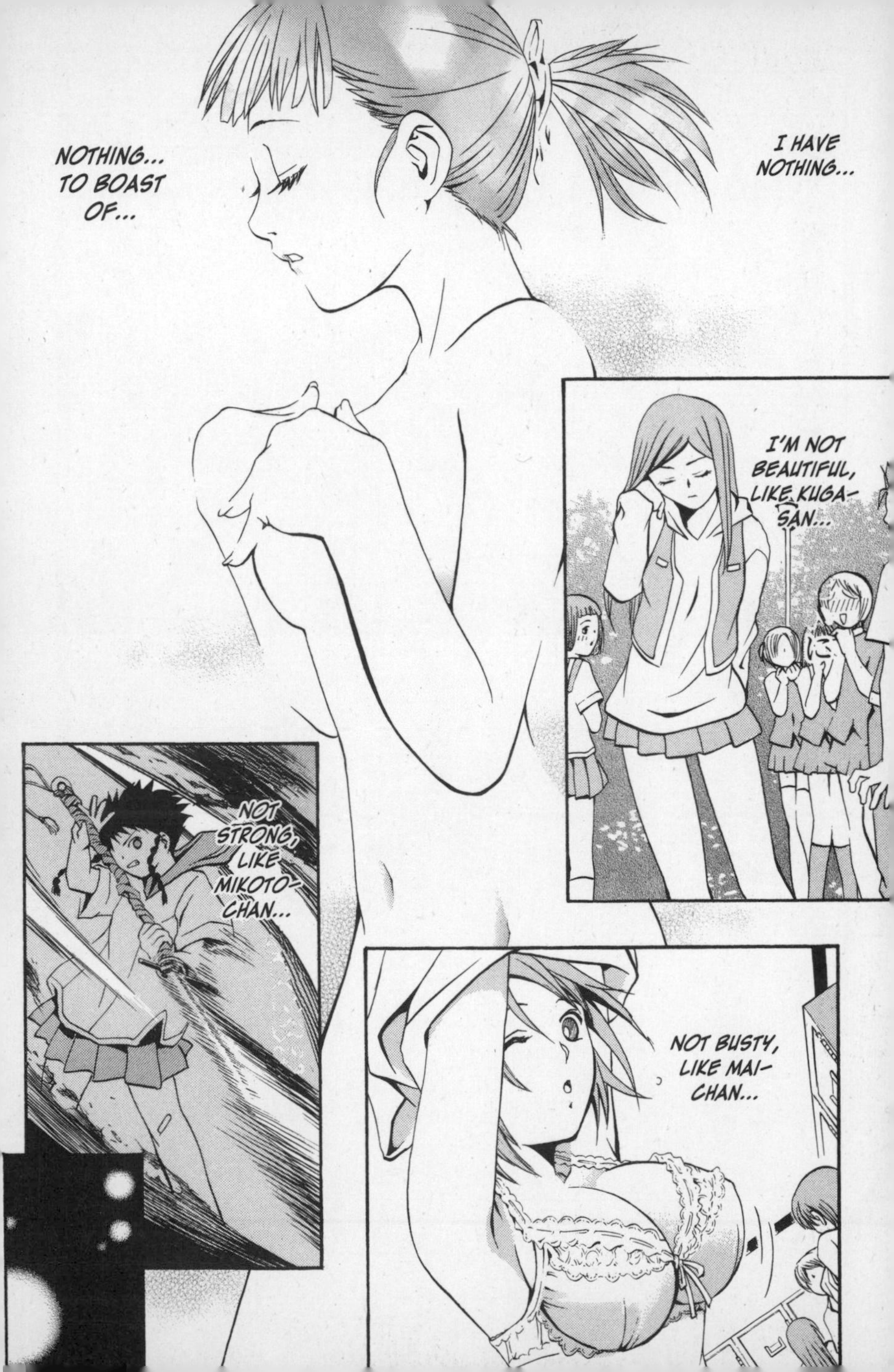
I HAVE NOTHING...
NOTHING... TO BOAST OF...
I'M NOT BEAUTIFUL, LIKE KUGA-SAN...
NOT STRONG, LIKE MIKOTO-CHAN...
NOT BUSTY, LIKE MAI-CHAN...

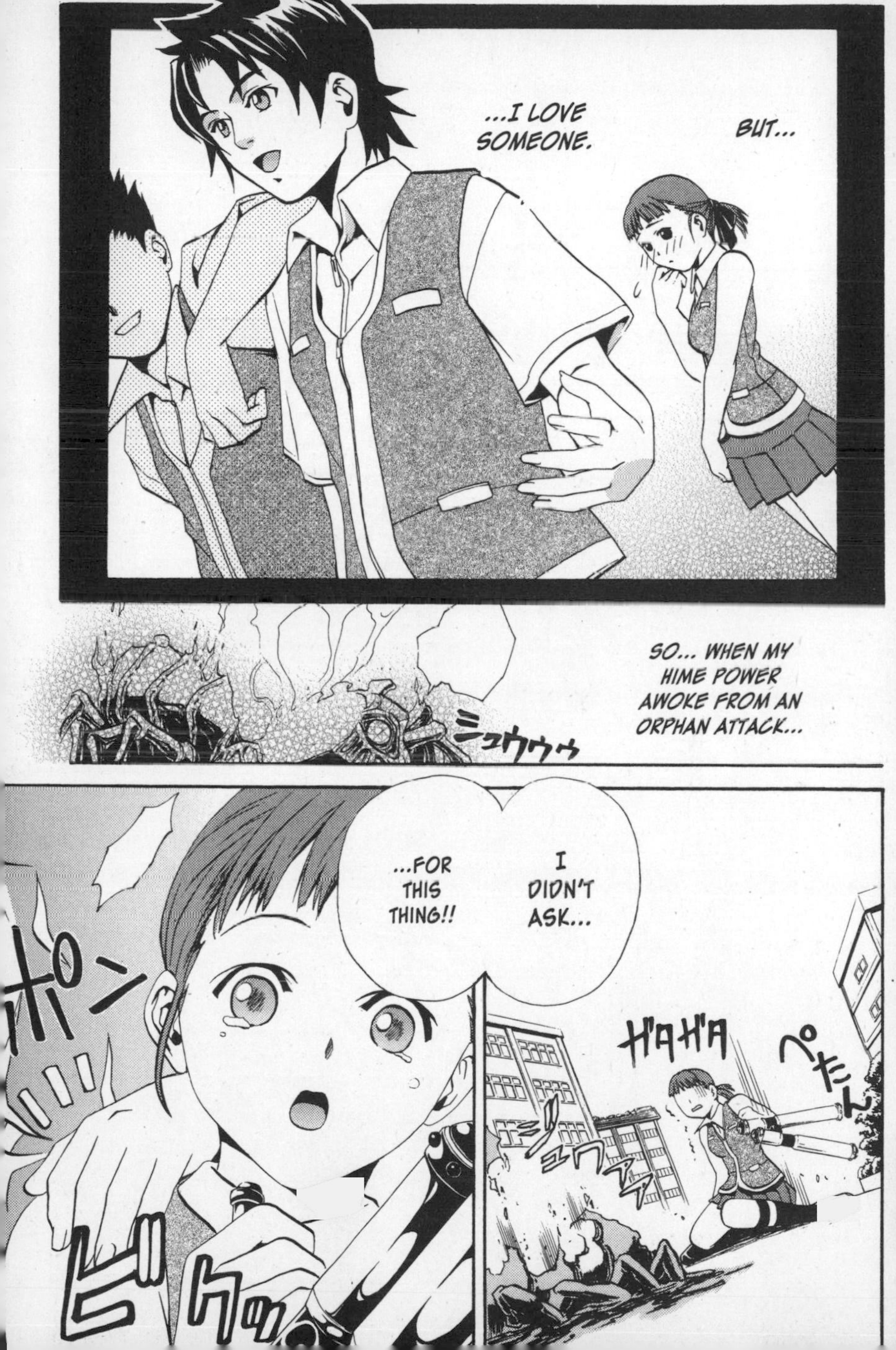
BUT...
...I LOVE SOMEONE.
SO... WHEN MY HIME POWER AWOKE FROM AN ORPHAN ATTACK...
シュウウウ
ぺたん
ガタガタ
ジュワァ
I DIDN'T ASK...
...FOR THIS THING!!
ポン
ビクッ

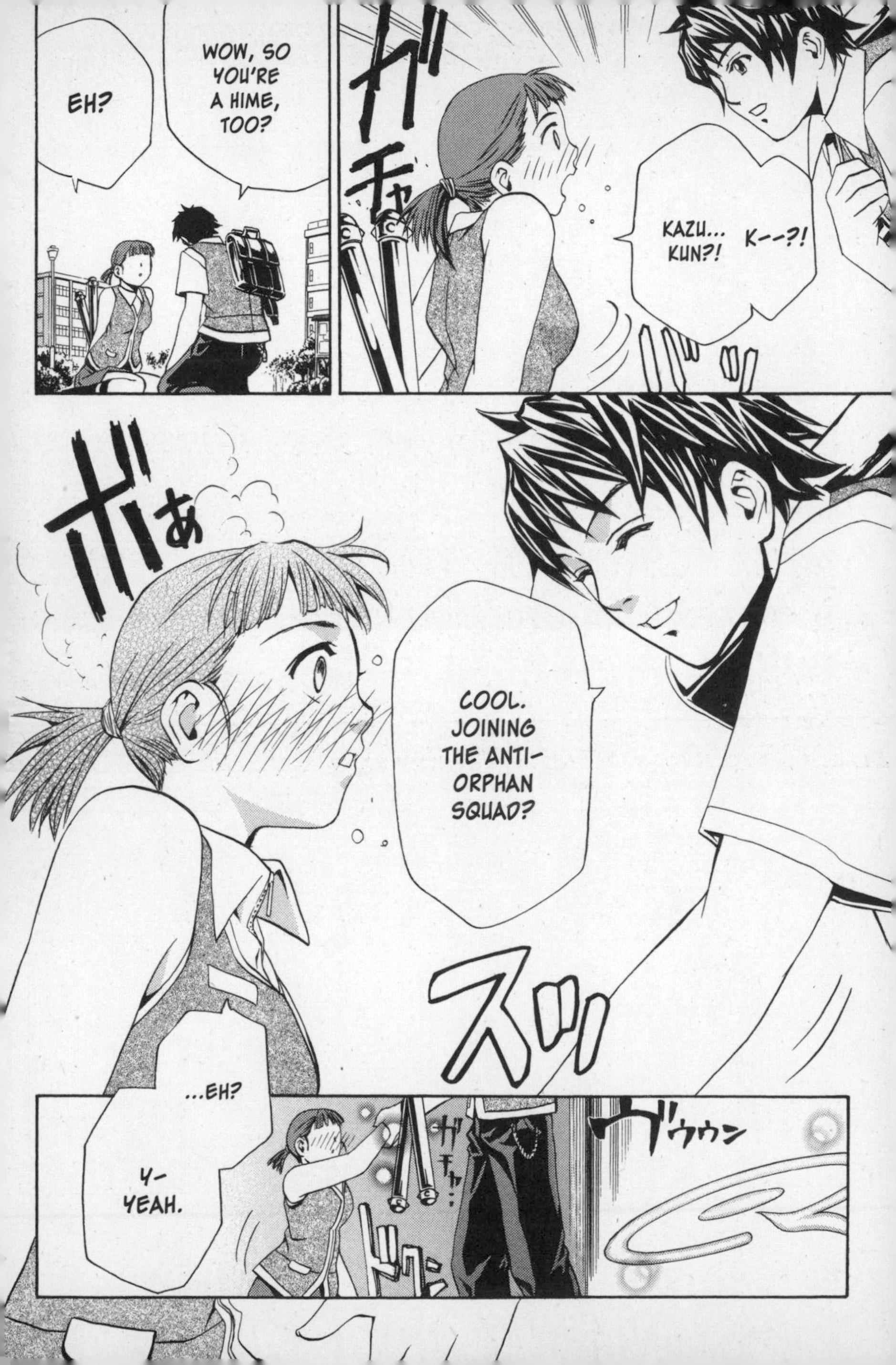
ガチャ
K--?!
KAZU... KUN?!
WOW, SO YOU'RE A HIME, TOO?
EH?
ボあ
COOL. JOINING THE ANTI-ORPHAN SQUAD?
スッ
ヴゥウン
...EH?
Y-YEAH.

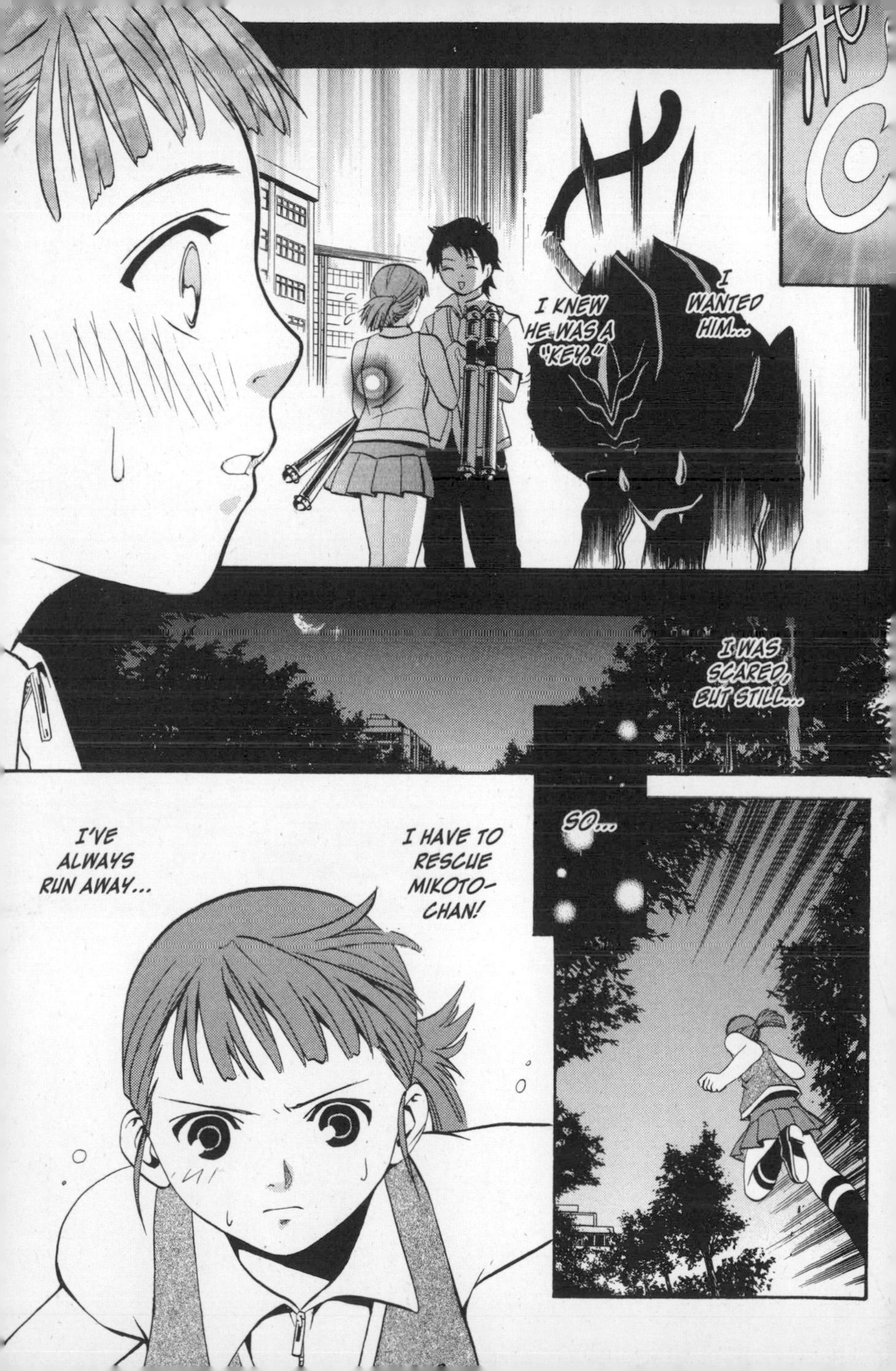
I WANTED HIM...
I KNEW HE WAS A "KEY."
I WAS SCARED, BUT STILL...
SO...
I HAVE TO RESCUE MIKOTO-CHAN!
I'VE ALWAYS RUN AWAY...

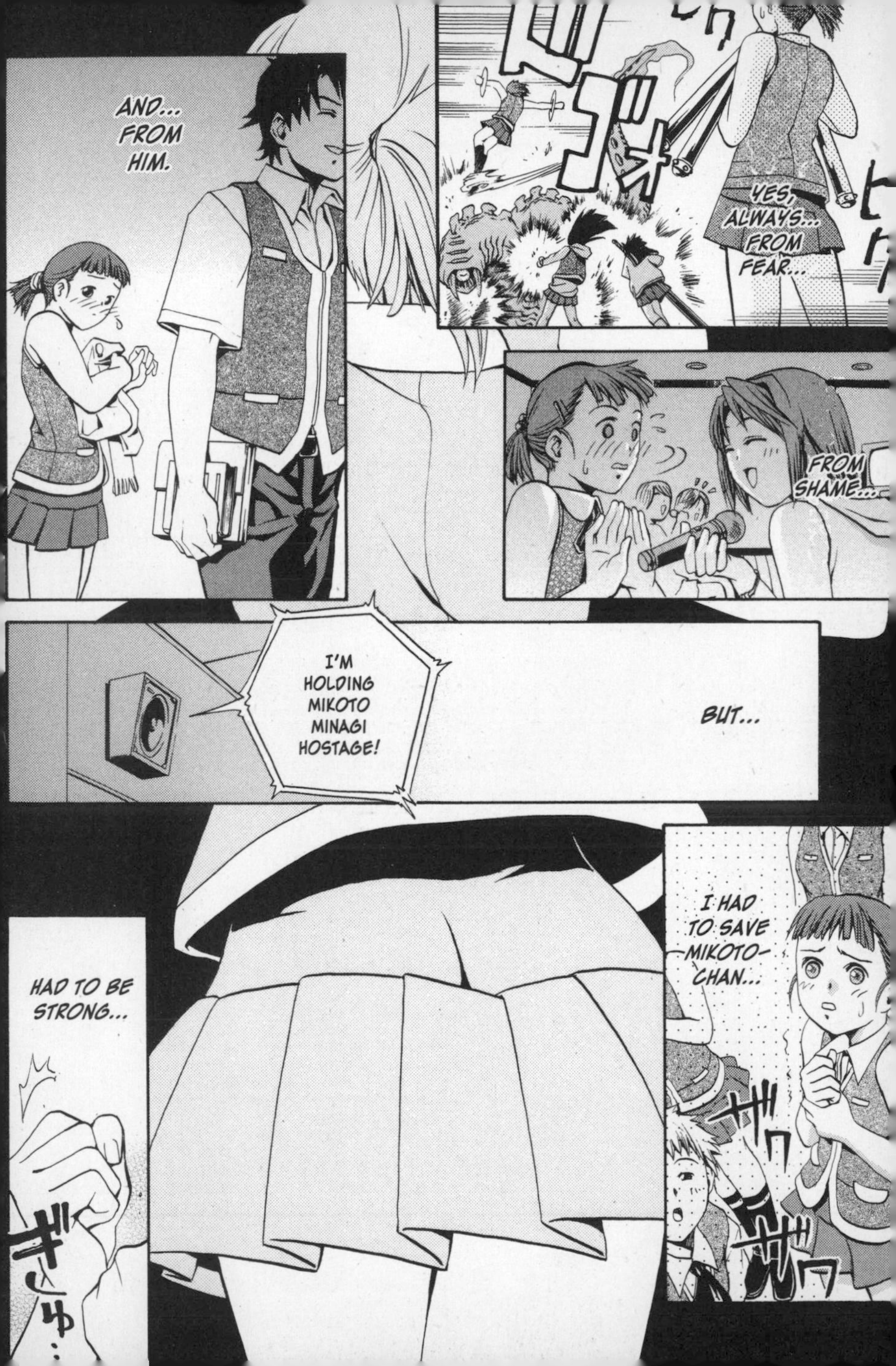
YES, ALWAYS... FROM FEAR...
FROM SHAME...
AND... FROM HIM.
BUT...
I'M HOLDING MIKOTO MINAGI HOSTAGE!
I HAD TO SAVE MIKOTO-CHAN...
HAD TO BE STRONG...

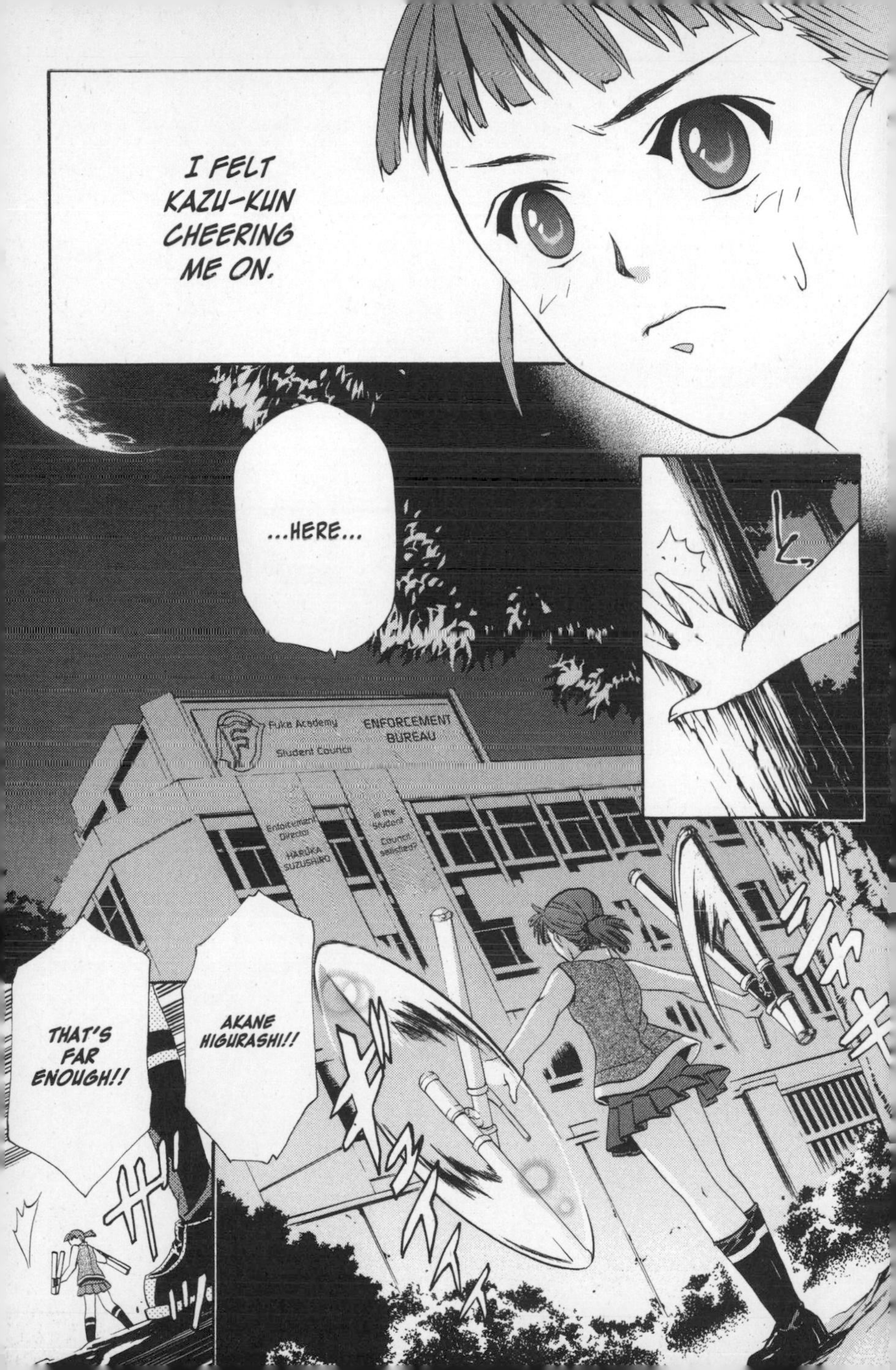
I FELT KAZU-KUN CHEERING ME ON.
...HERE...
Fuka Academy Student Council
ENFORCEMENT BUREAU
HARUKA SUZUSHIRO
AKANE HIGURASHI!!
THAT'S FAR ENOUGH!!

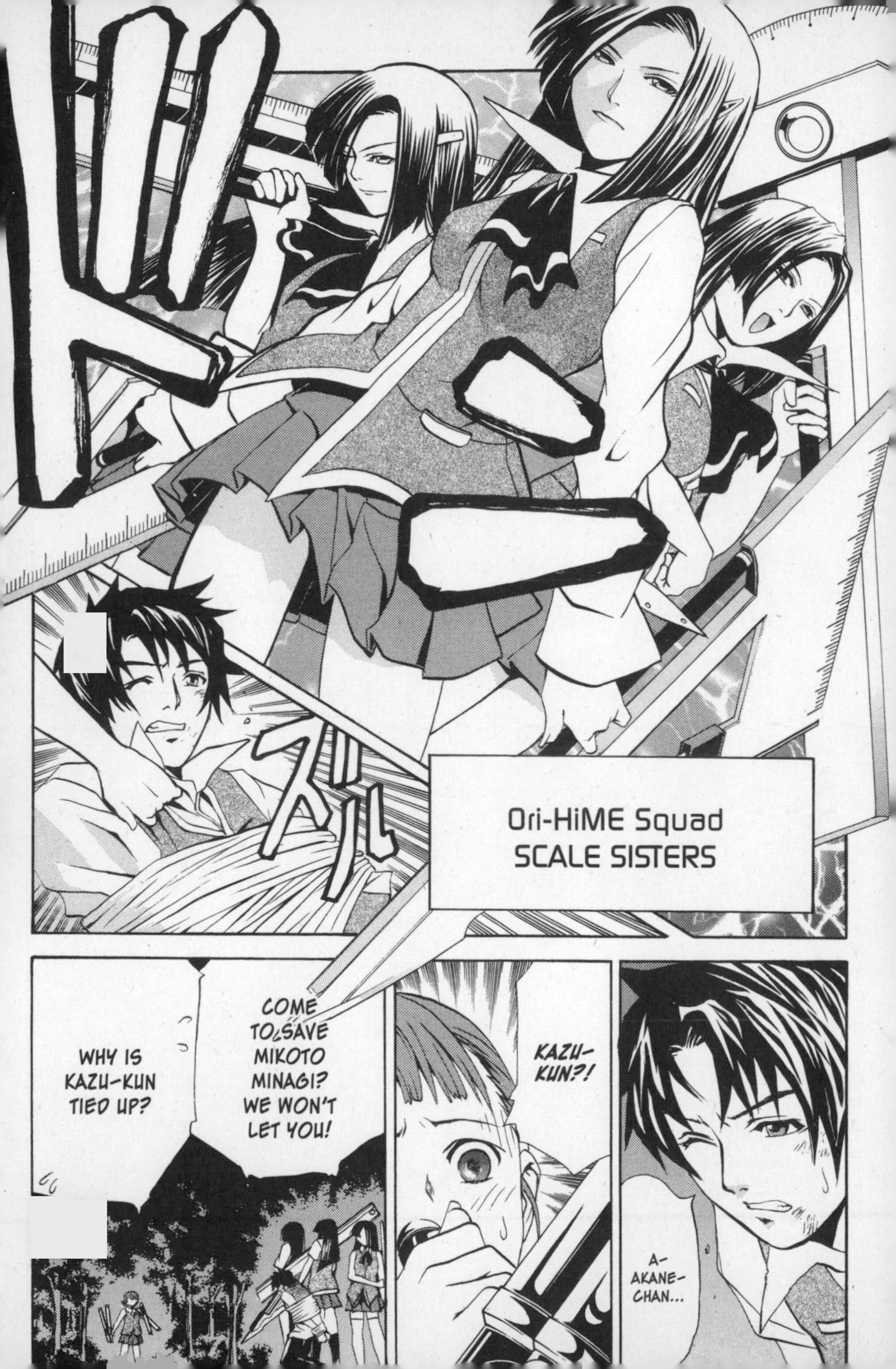
Ori-HiME Squad
SCALE SISTERS
A-AKANE-CHAN...
KAZU-KUN?!
COME TO SAVE MIKOTO MINAGI? WE WON'T LET YOU!
WHY IS KAZU-KUN TIED UP?

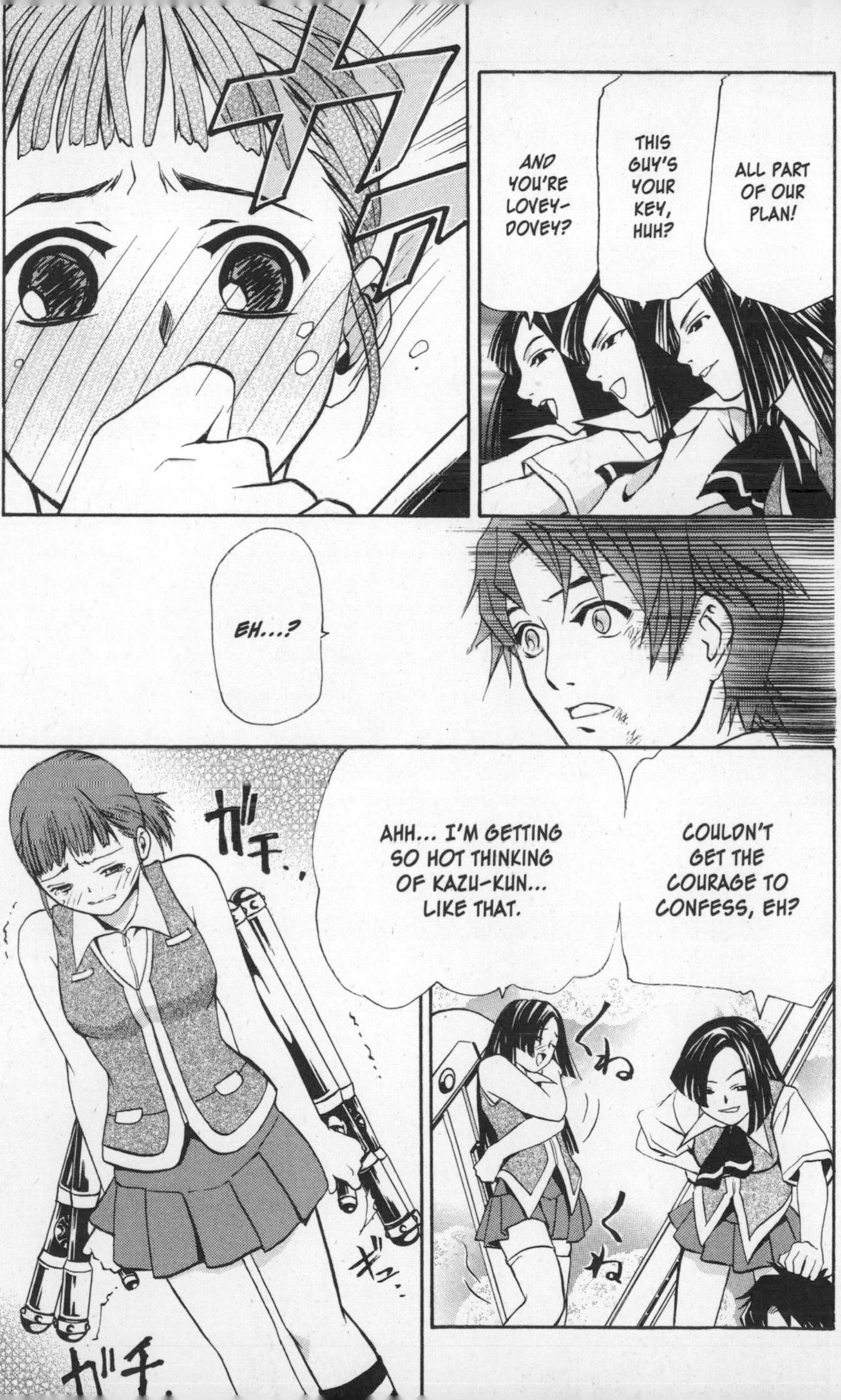
ALL PART OF OUR PLAN!
THIS GUY'S YOUR KEY, HUH?
AND YOU'RE LOVEY-DOVEY?
EH...?
COULDN'T GET THE COURAGE TO CONFESS, EH?
AHH... I'M GETTING SO HOT THINKING OF KAZU-KUN... LIKE THAT.

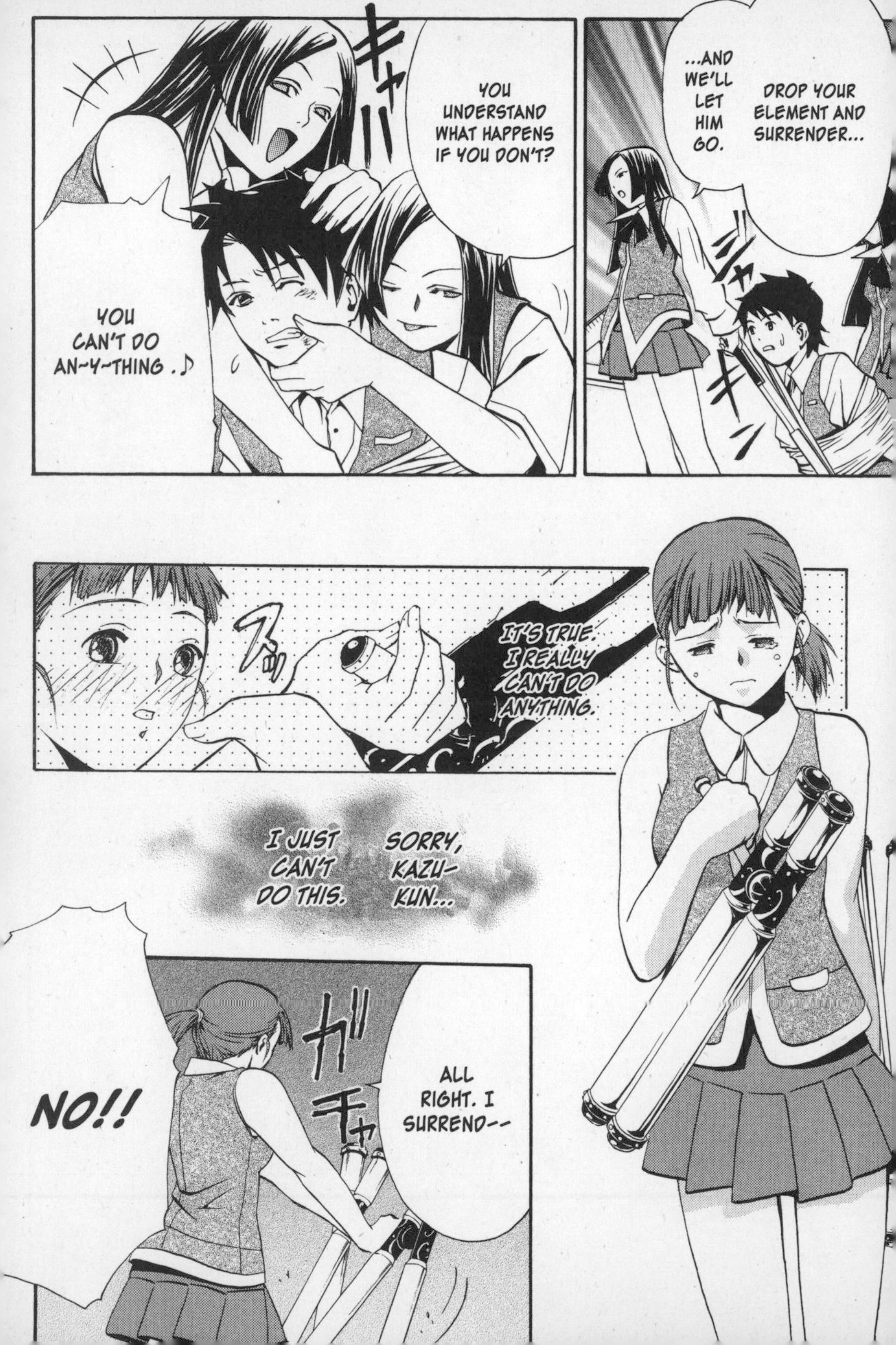
DROP YOUR ELEMENT AND SURRENDER...
...AND WE'LL LET HIM GO.
YOU UNDERSTAND WHAT HAPPENS IF YOU DON'T?
YOU CAN'T DO AN~Y~THING.♪
IT'S TRUE. I REALLY CAN'T DO ANYTHING.
SORRY, KAZU-KUN...
I JUST CAN'T DO THIS.
ALL RIGHT. I SURREND--
NO!!

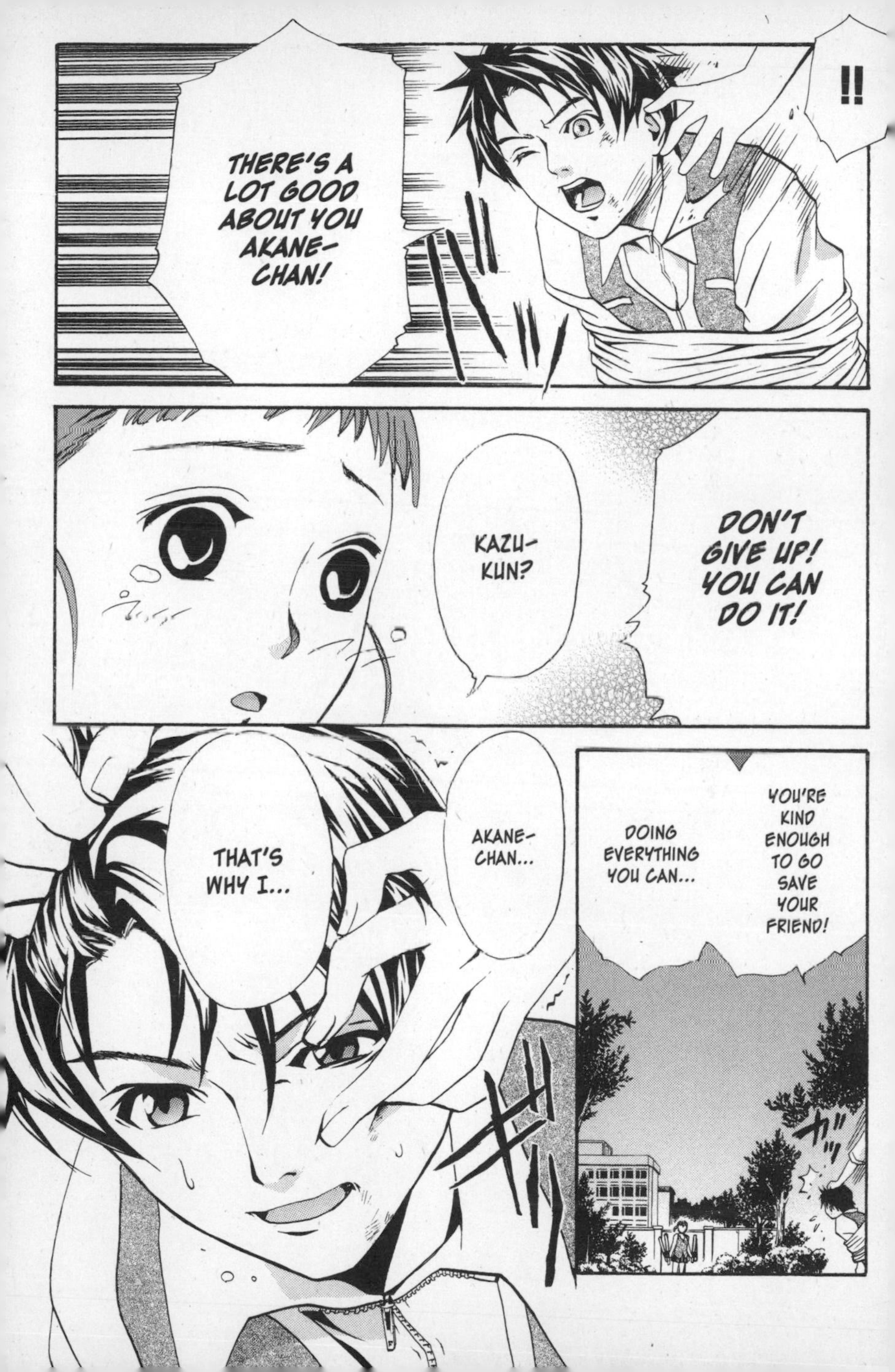
!!
THERE'S A LOT GOOD ABOUT YOU AKANE-CHAN!
DON'T GIVE UP! YOU CAN DO IT!
KAZU-KUN?
YOU'RE KIND ENOUGH TO GO SAVE YOUR FRIEND!
DOING EVERYTHING YOU CAN...
ガッ
AKANE-CHAN...
THAT'S WHY I...

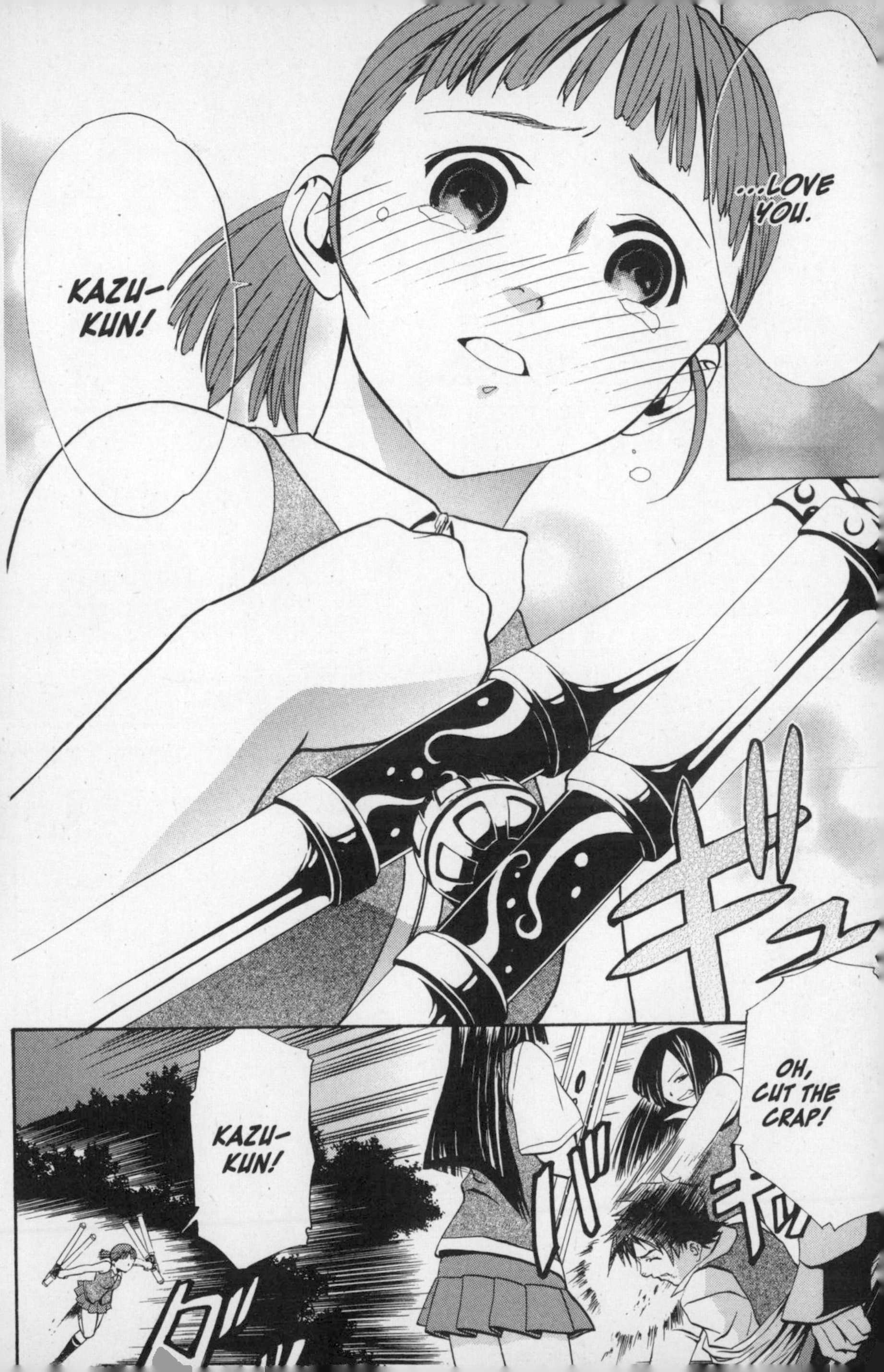
...LOVE YOU.
KAZU-KUN!
OH, CUT THE CRAP!
KAZU-KUN!

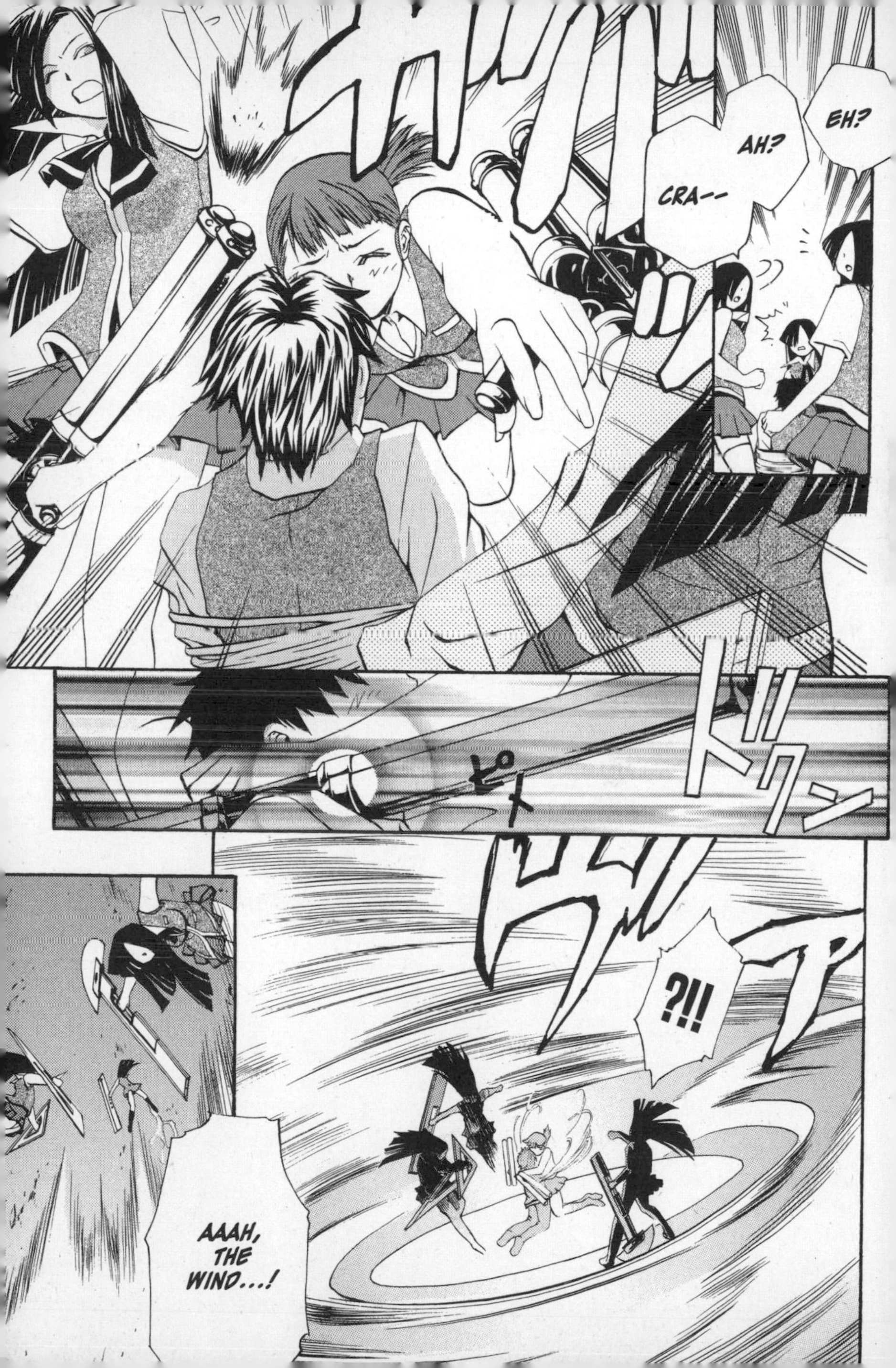
EH?
AH?
CRA--
ドクン
?!!
AAAH, THE WIND...!

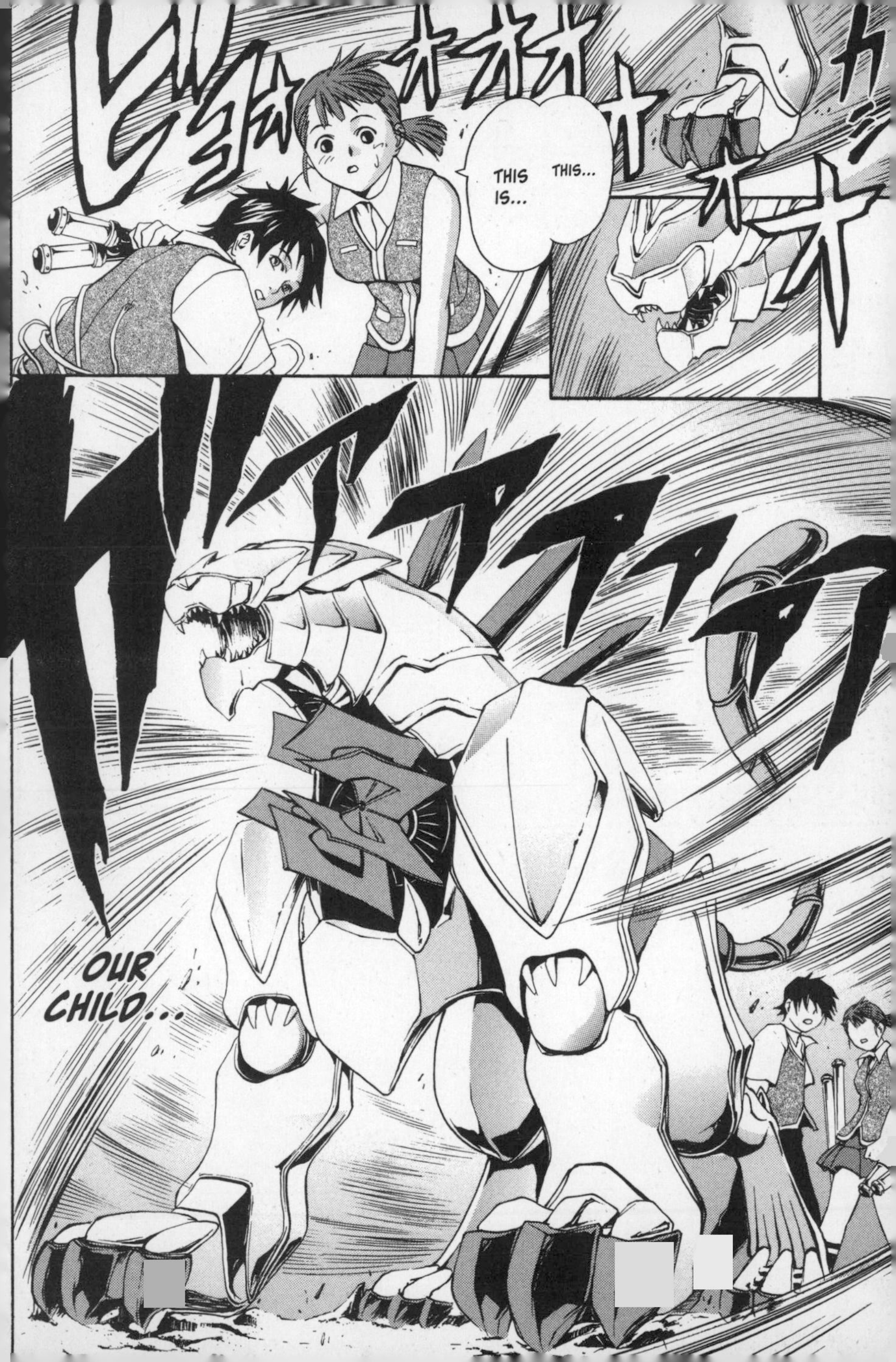
THIS...
THIS IS...
OUR CHILD...

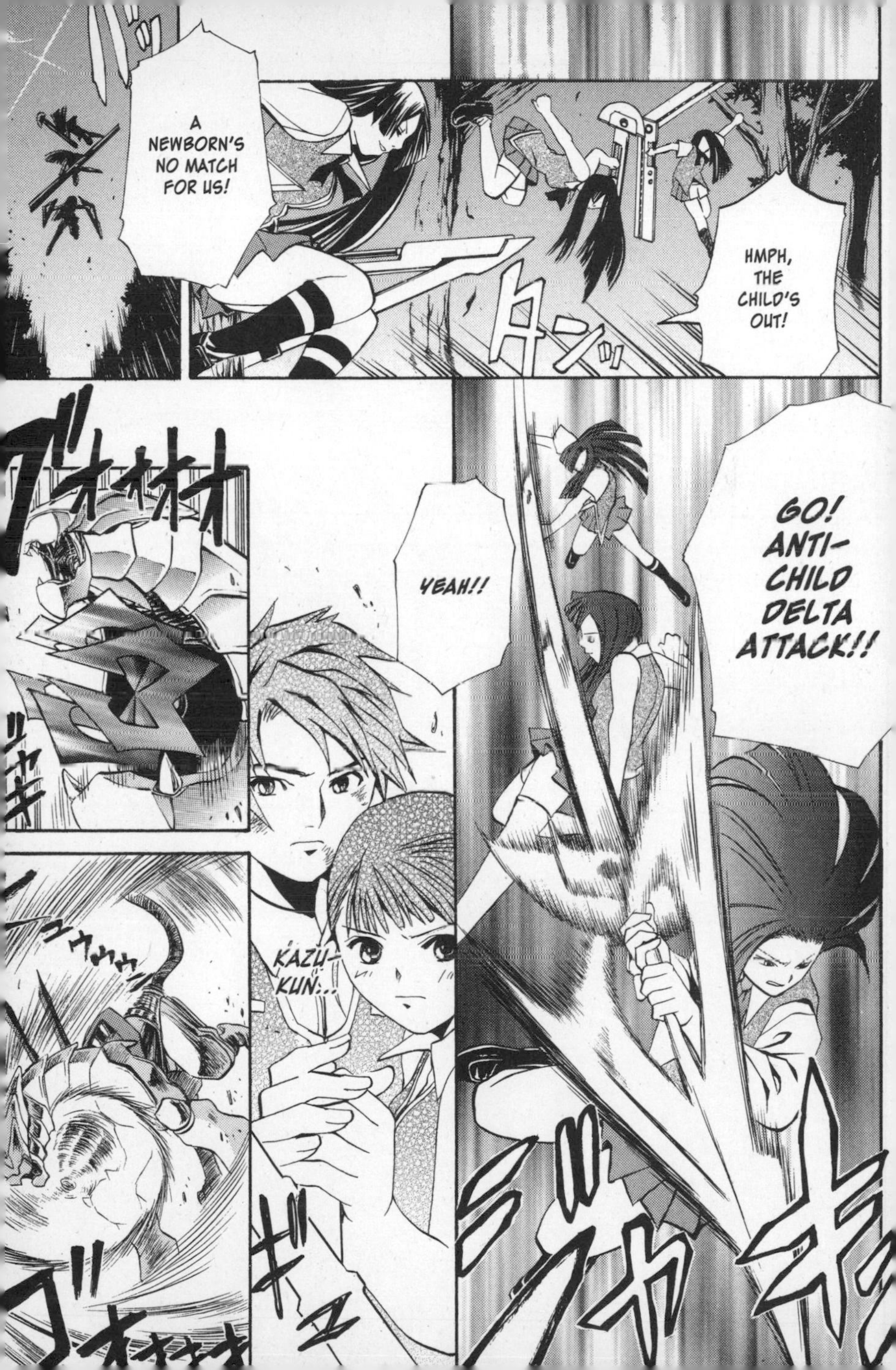
HMPH, THE CHILD'S OUT!
A NEWBORN'S NO MATCH FOR US!
GO! ANTI-CHILD DELTA ATTACK!!
YEAH!!
KAZU-KUN...

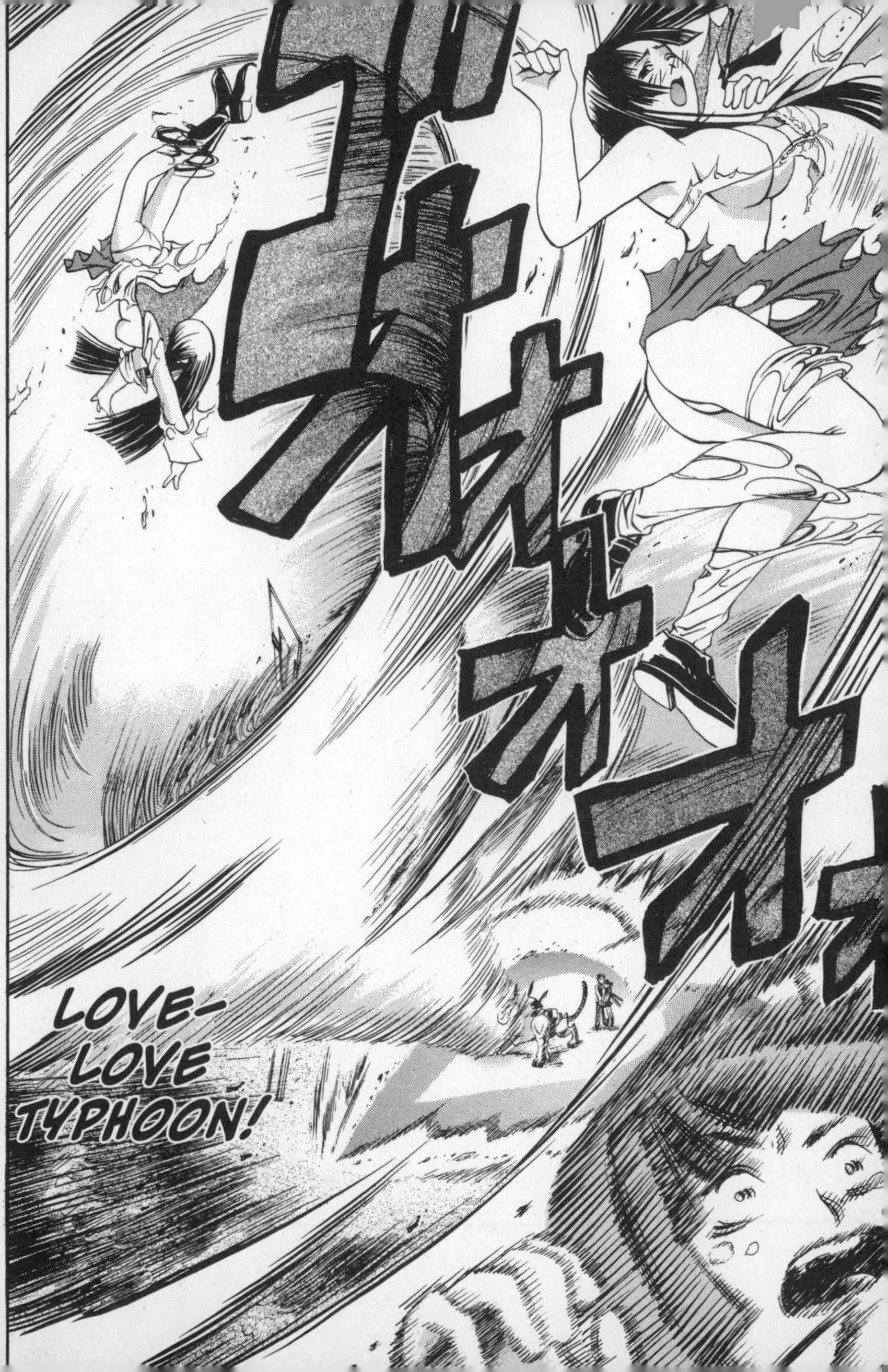
LOVE-LOVE TYPHOON!

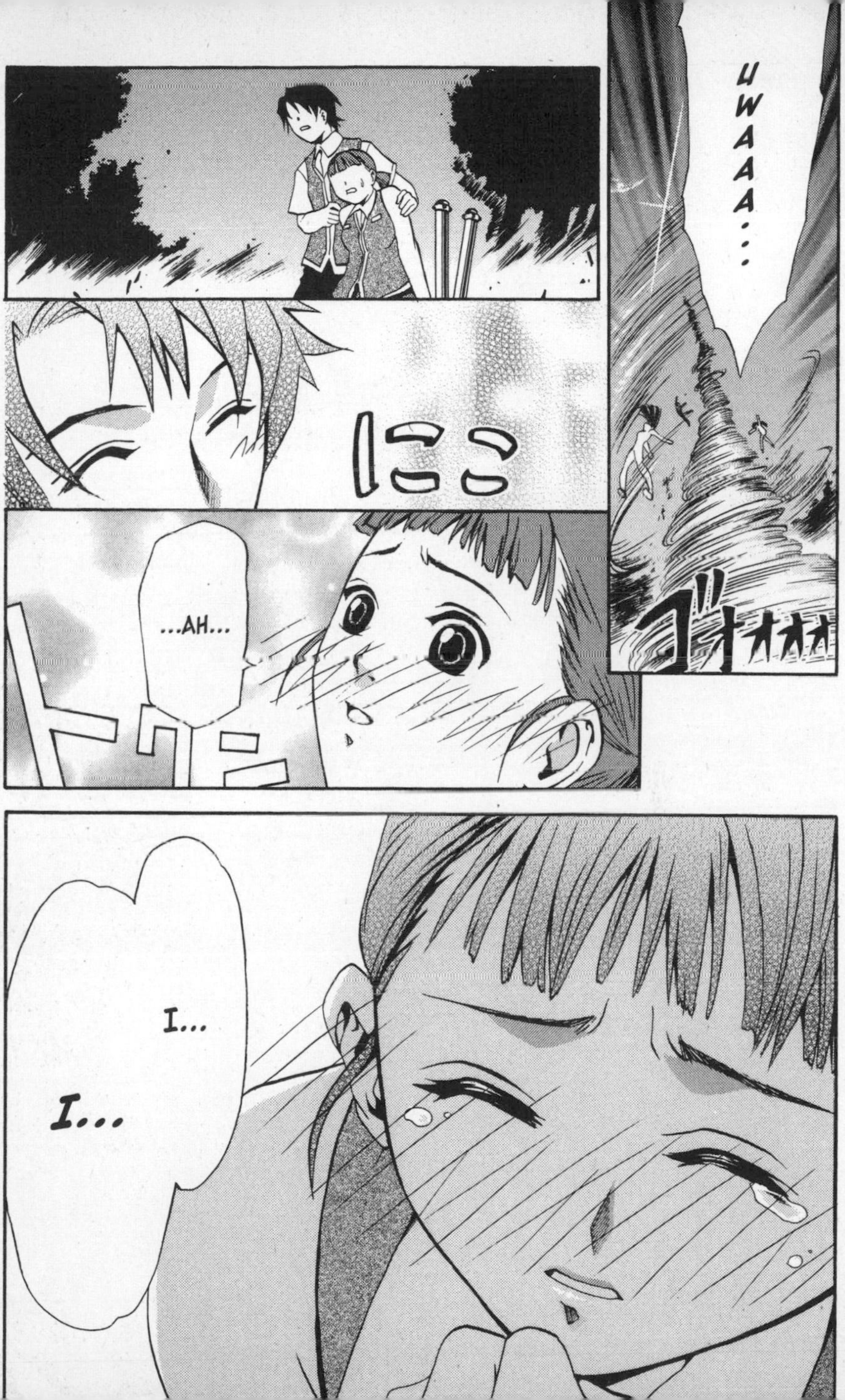
UWAAAA...
ゴオオオオ
にこ
...AH...
I...
I...

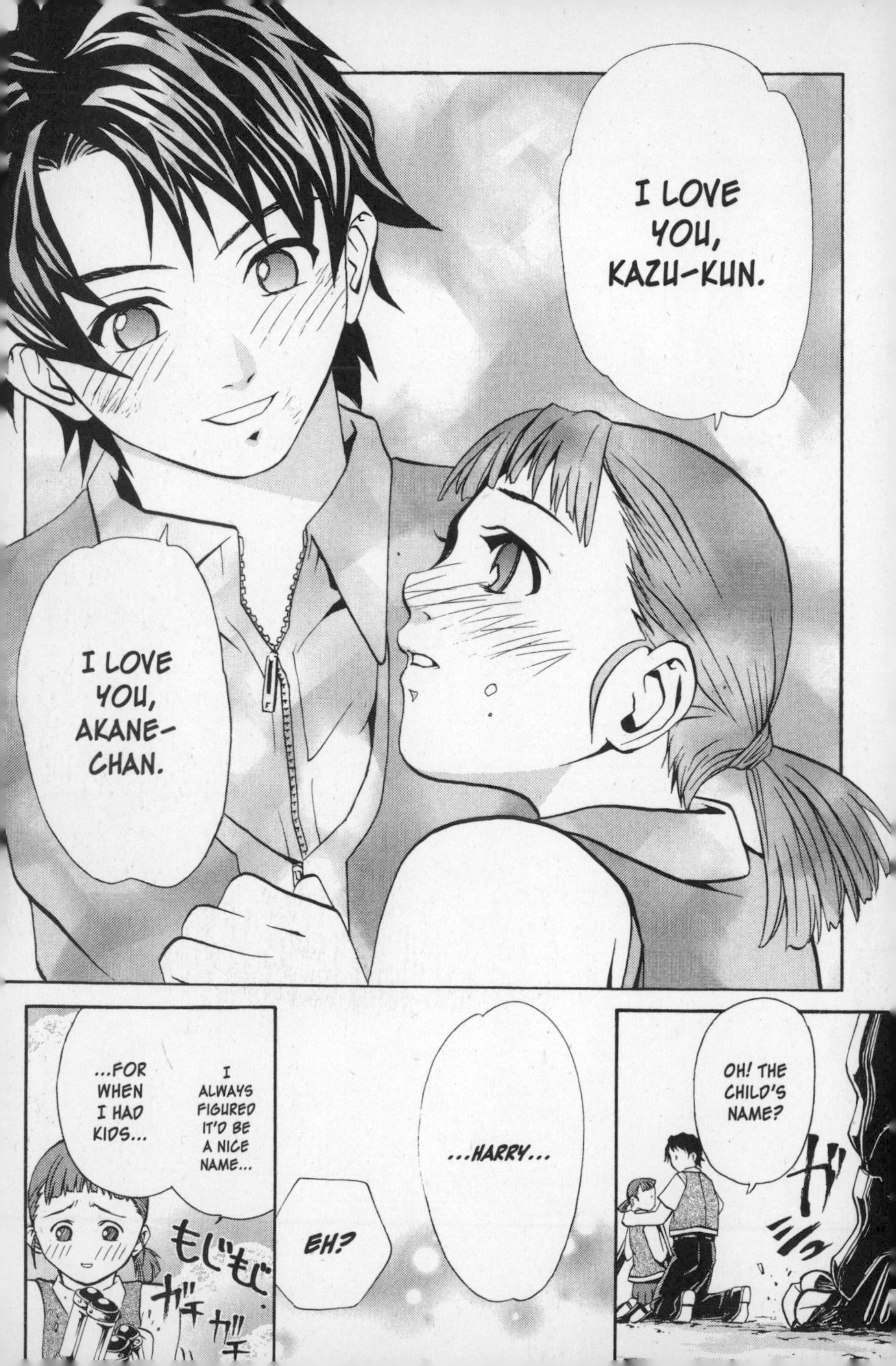
I LOVE YOU, KAZU-KUN.
I LOVE YOU, AKANE-CHAN.
OH! THE CHILD'S NAME?
...HARRY...
EH?
I ALWAYS FIGURED IT'D BE A NICE NAME...
...FOR WHEN I HAD KIDS...
もじもじ
ガチ ガチ

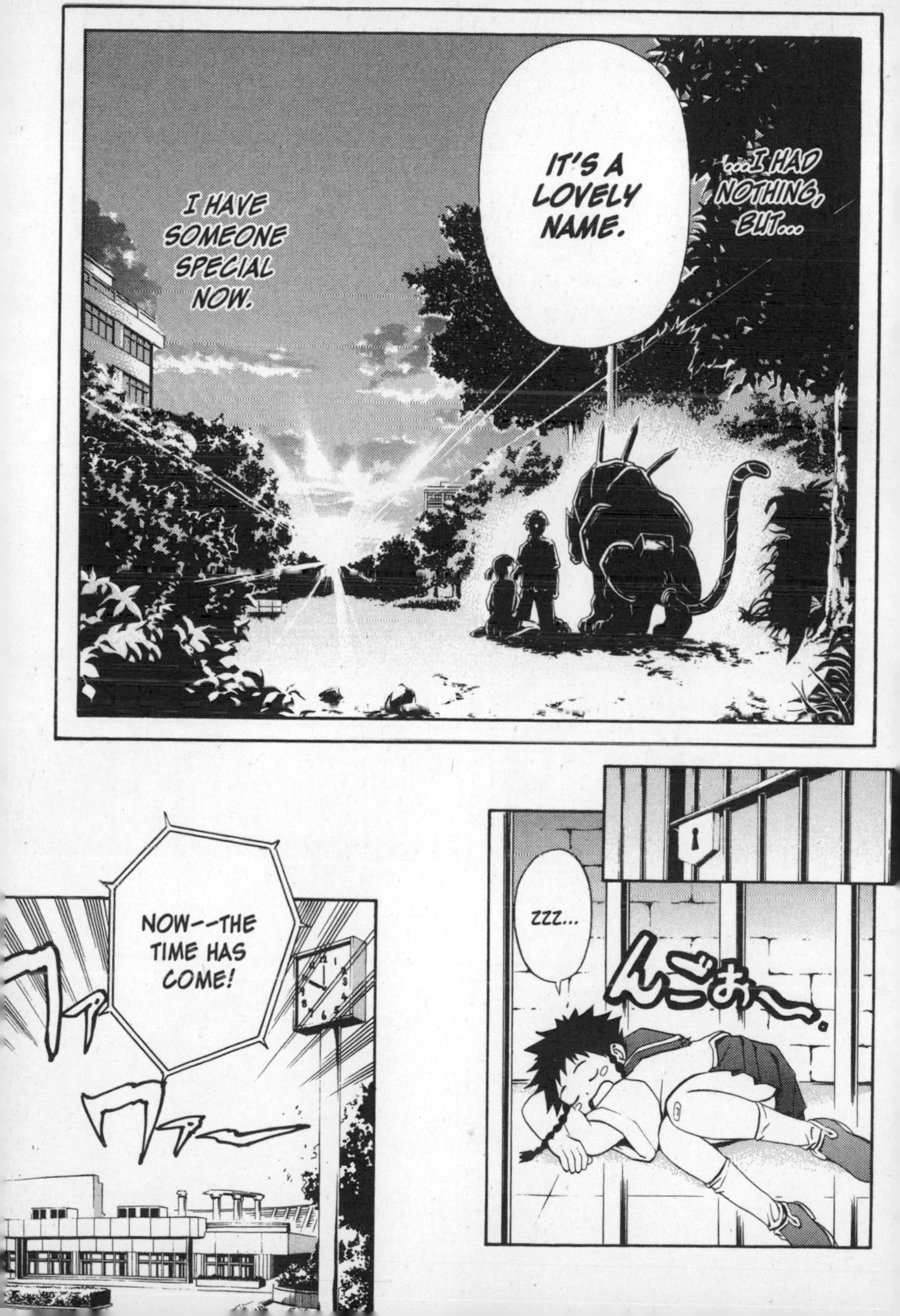
...I HAD NOTHING, BUT...
IT'S A LOVELY NAME.
I HAVE SOMEONE SPECIAL NOW.
ZZZ...
んごぉ～。
NOW--THE TIME HAS COME!
ワァ
ワァ～

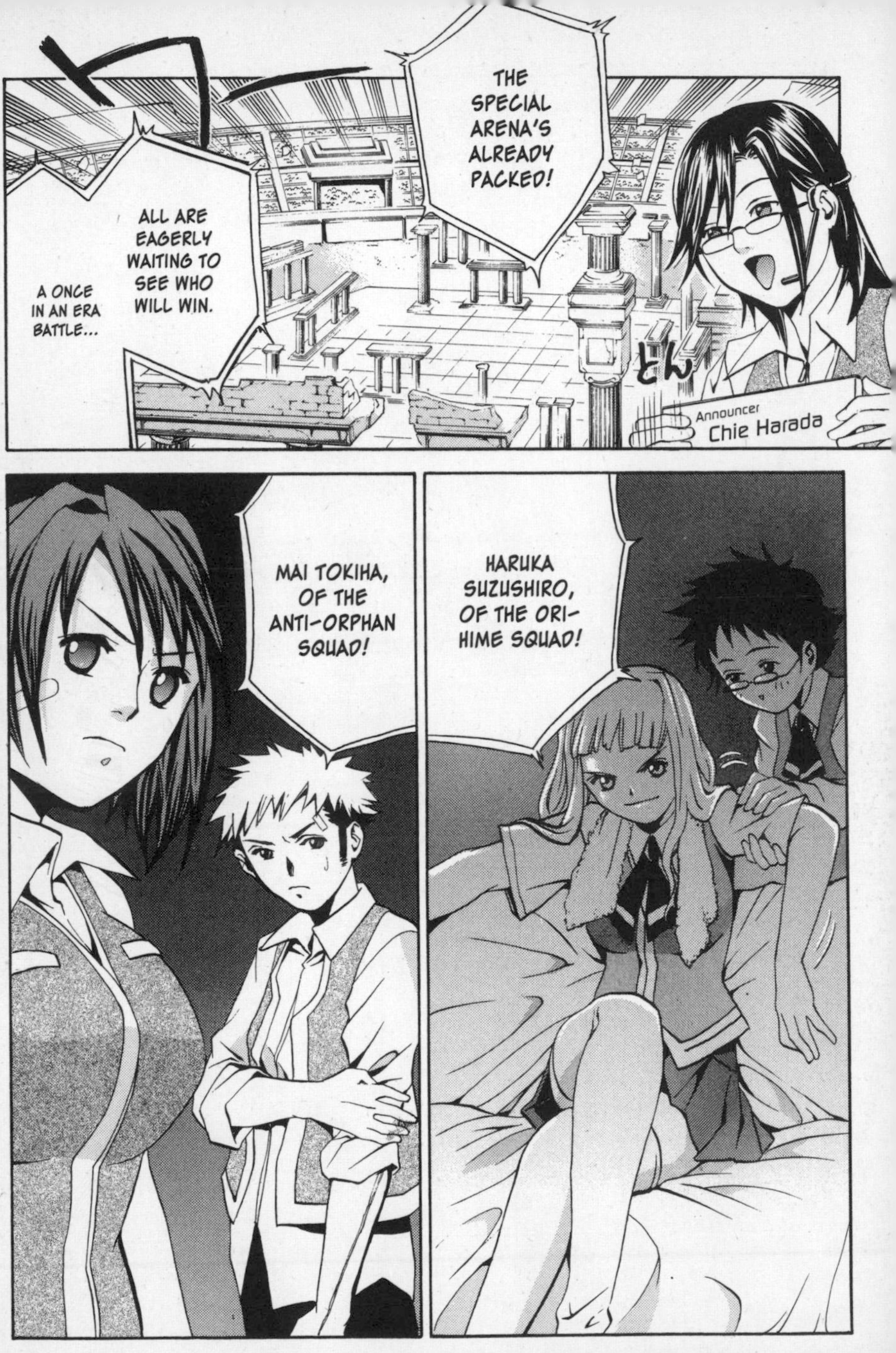
THE SPECIAL ARENA'S ALREADY PACKED!
ALL ARE EAGERLY WAITING TO SEE WHO WILL WIN.
A ONCE IN AN ERA BATTLE...
とん
Announcer
Chie Harada
HARUKA SUZUSHIRO, OF THE ORI-HIME SQUAD!
MAI TOKIHA, OF THE ANTI-ORPHAN SQUAD!

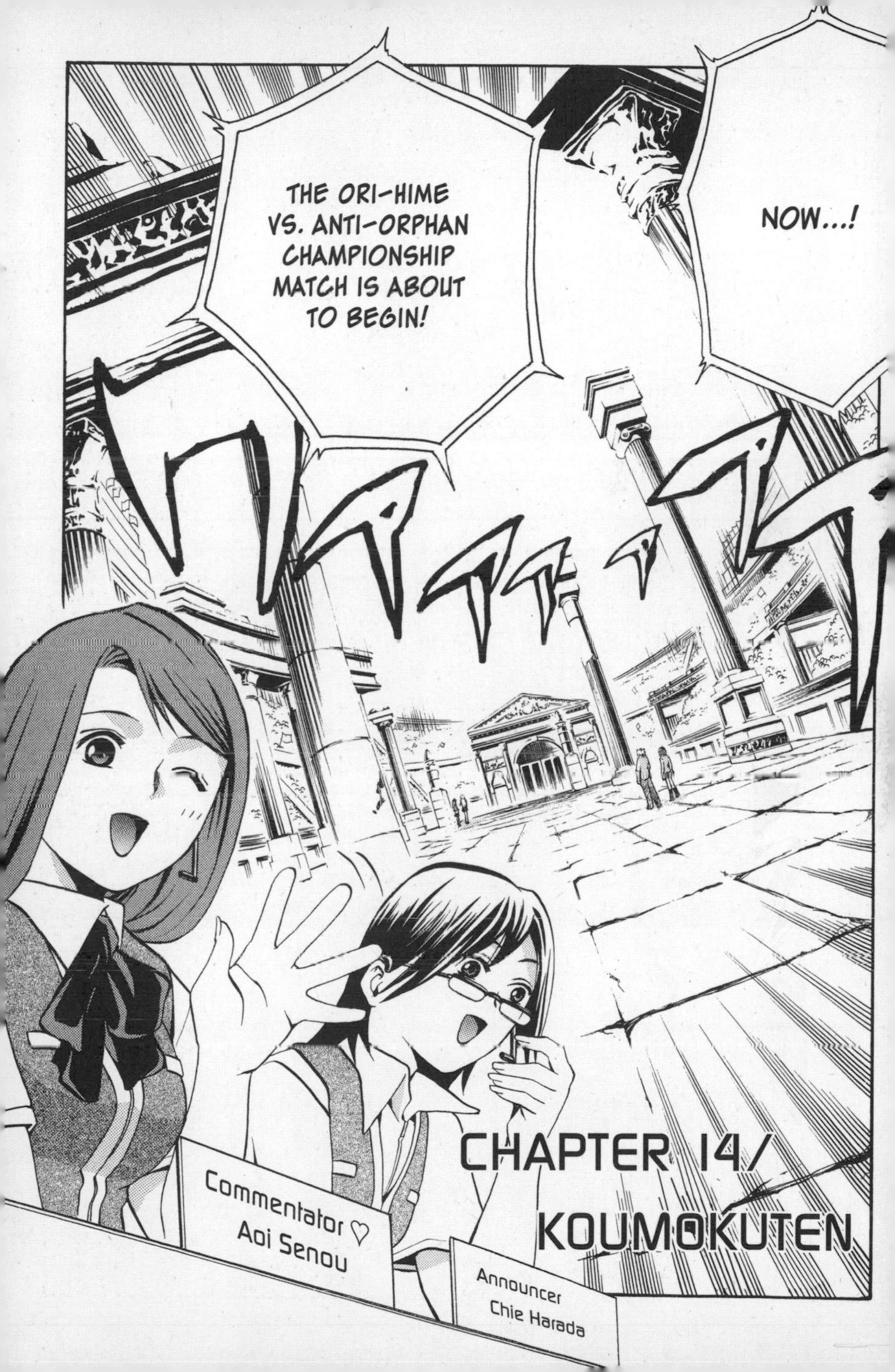
NOW...!
THE ORI-HIME VS. ANTI-ORPHAN CHAMPIONSHIP MATCH IS ABOUT TO BEGIN!
CHAPTER 14/ KOUMOKUTEN
Commentator ♡ Aoi Senou
Announcer Chie Harada

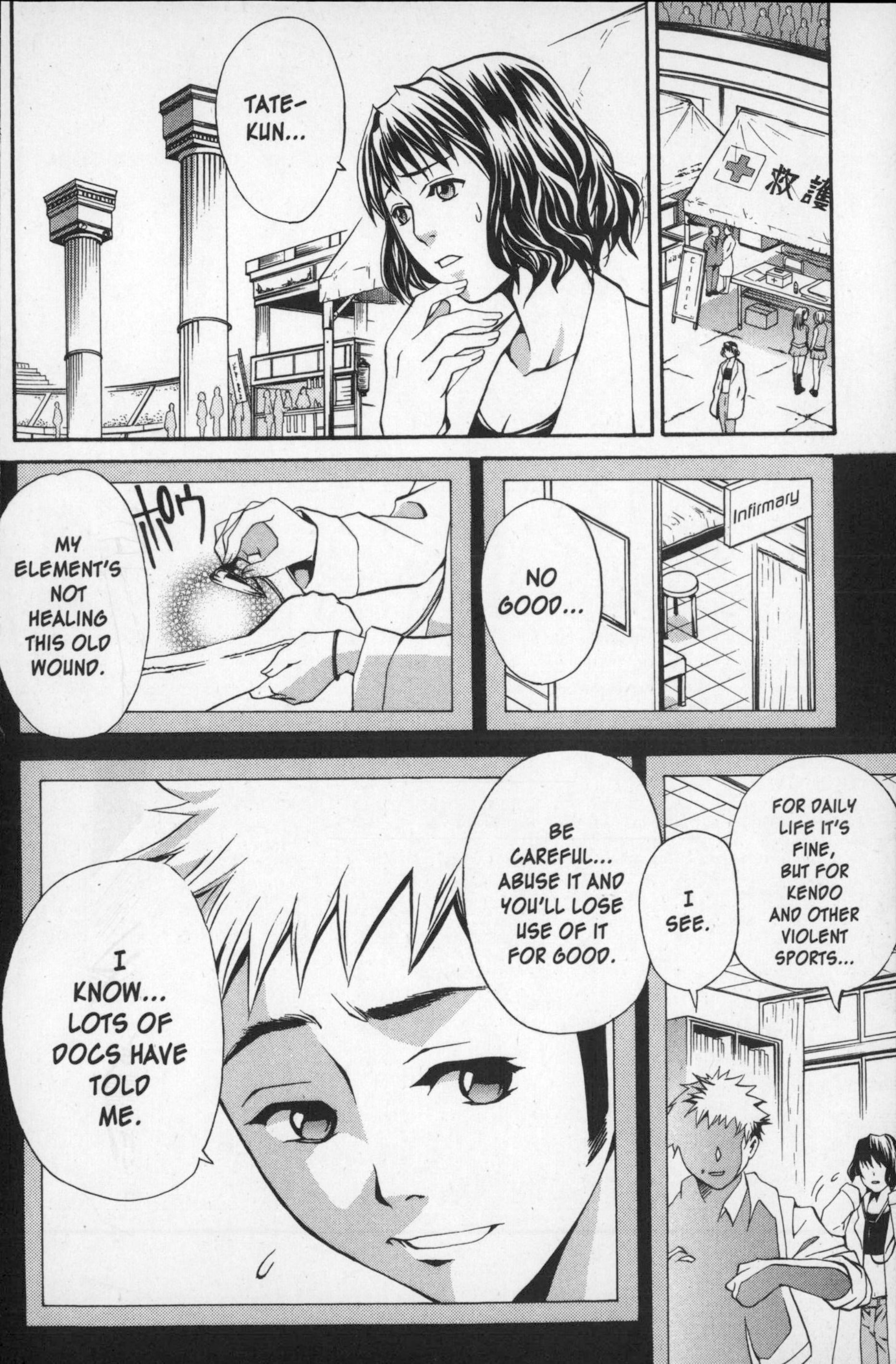
救護
Clinic
TATE-KUN...
Infirmary
NO GOOD...
MY ELEMENT'S NOT HEALING THIS OLD WOUND.
FOR DAILY LIFE IT'S FINE, BUT FOR KENDO AND OTHER VIOLENT SPORTS...
I SEE.
BE CAREFUL... ABUSE IT AND YOU'LL LOSE USE OF IT FOR GOOD.
I KNOW... LOTS OF DOCS HAVE TOLD ME.

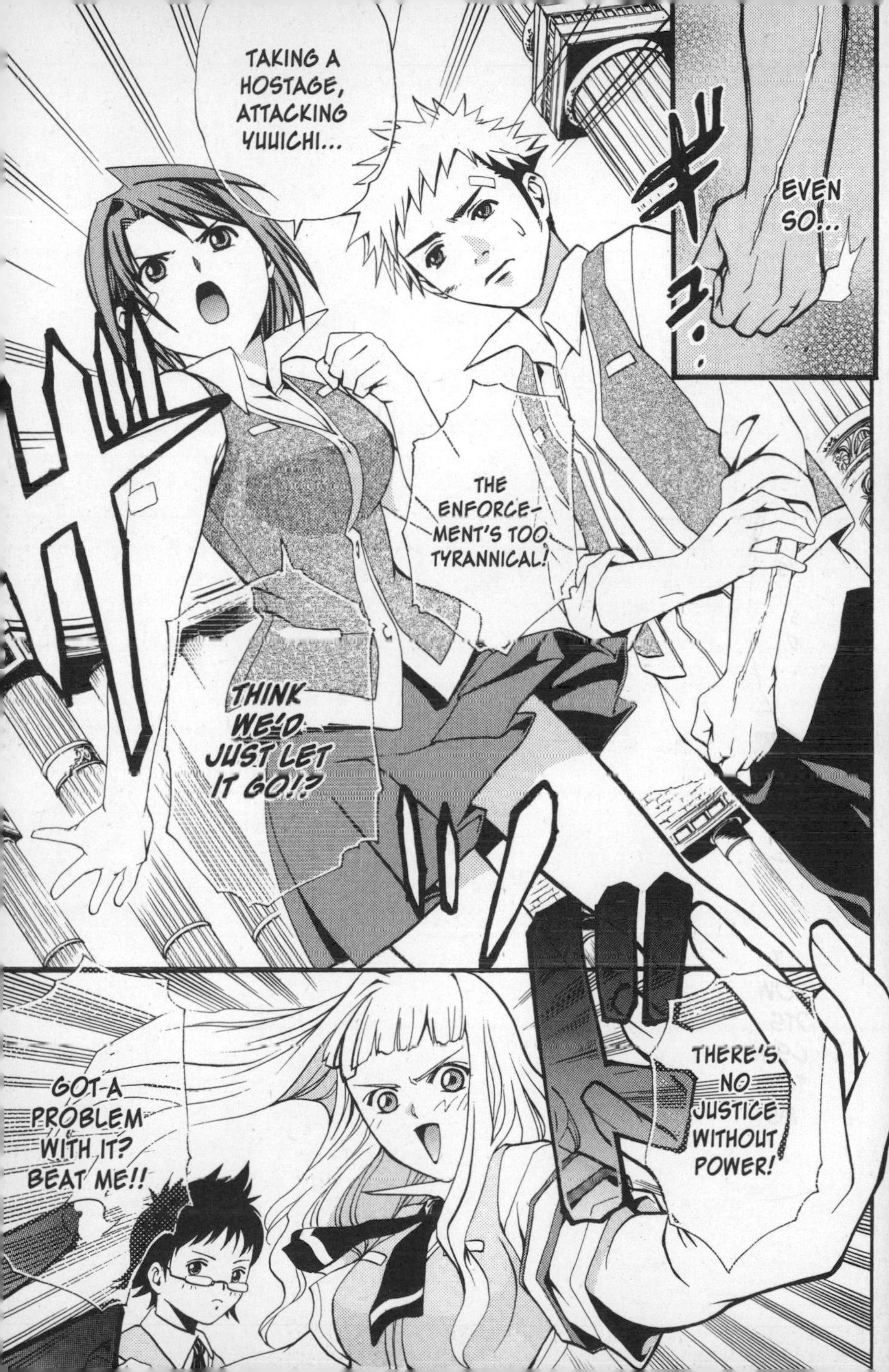
EVEN SO...
TAKING A HOSTAGE, ATTACKING YUUICHI...
THE ENFORCEMENT'S TOO TYRANNICAL!
THINK WE'D JUST LET IT GO!?
THERE'S NO JUSTICE WITHOUT POWER!
GOT A PROBLEM WITH IT? BEAT ME!!

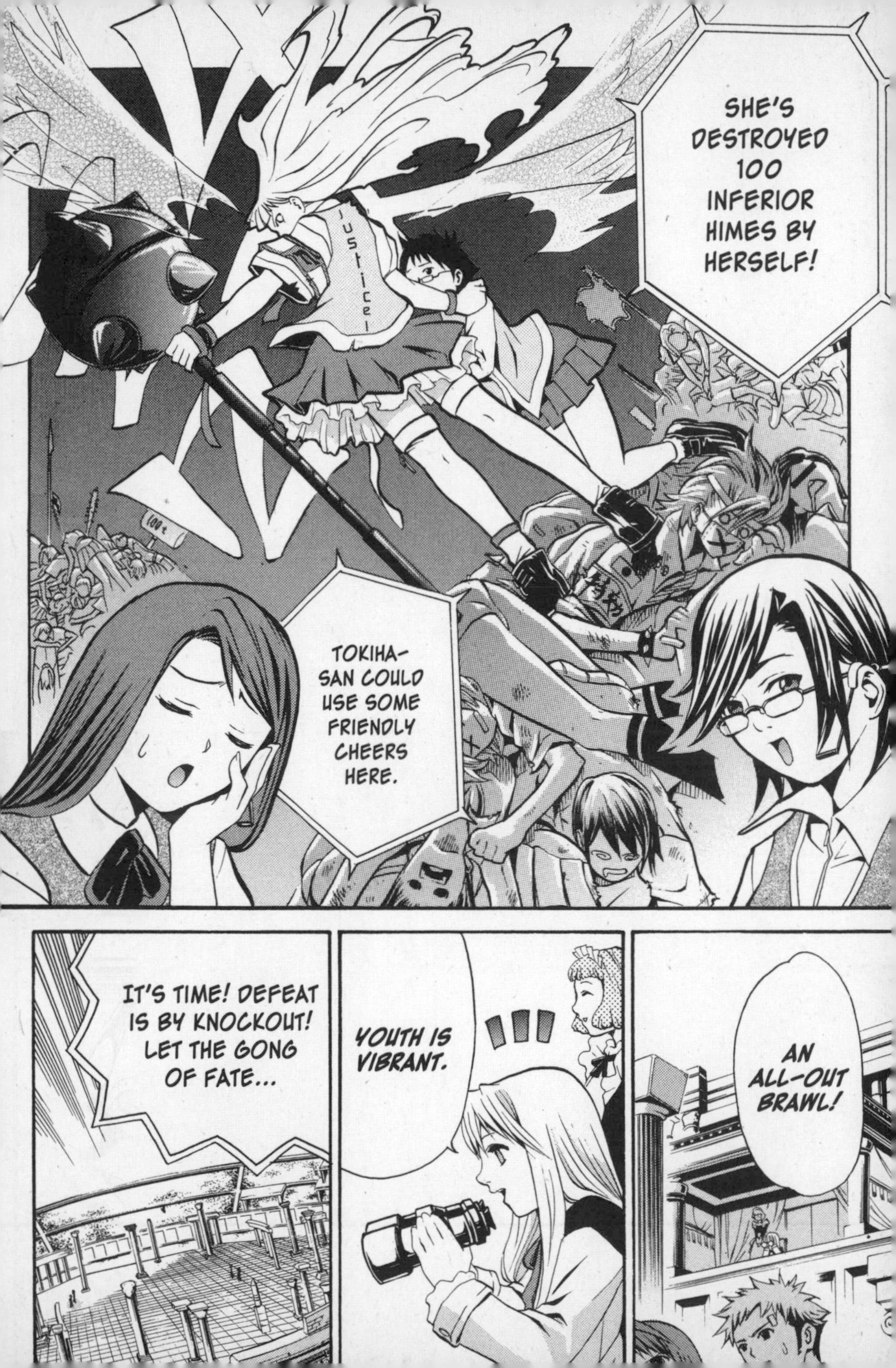
SHE'S DESTROYED 100 INFERIOR HIMES BY HERSELF!
Justice!
TOKIHA-SAN COULD USE SOME FRIENDLY CHEERS HERE.
AN ALL-OUT BRAWL!
YOUTH IS VIBRANT.
IT'S TIME! DEFEAT IS BY KNOCKOUT! LET THE GONG OF FATE...

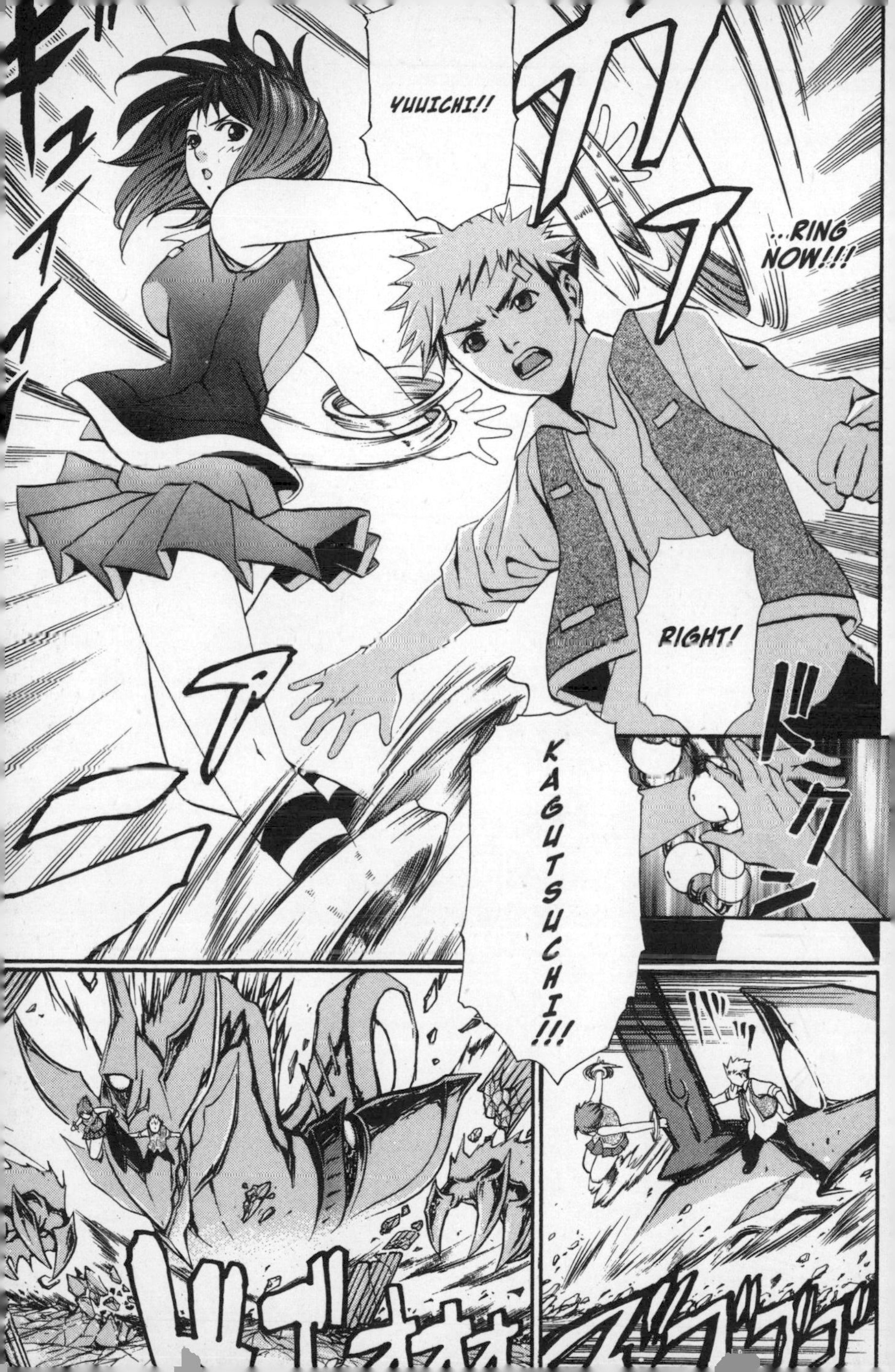
...RING NOW!!!
YUUICHI!!
RIGHT!
KAGUTSUCHI!!!

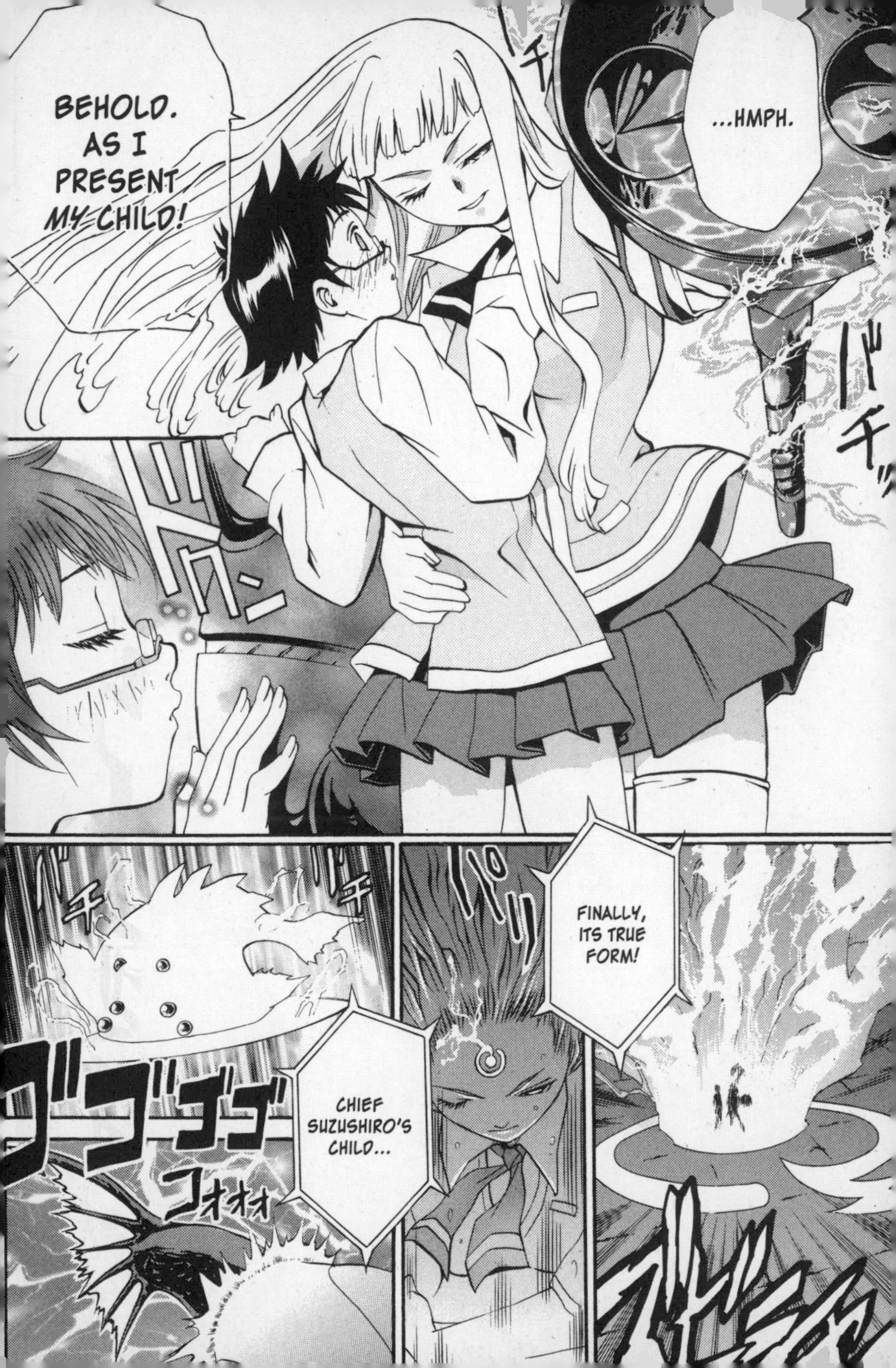
...HMPH.
BEHOLD. AS I PRESENT MY CHILD!
FINALLY, ITS TRUE FORM!
CHIEF SUZUSHIRO'S CHILD...
ゴゴゴゴ
コォオオ

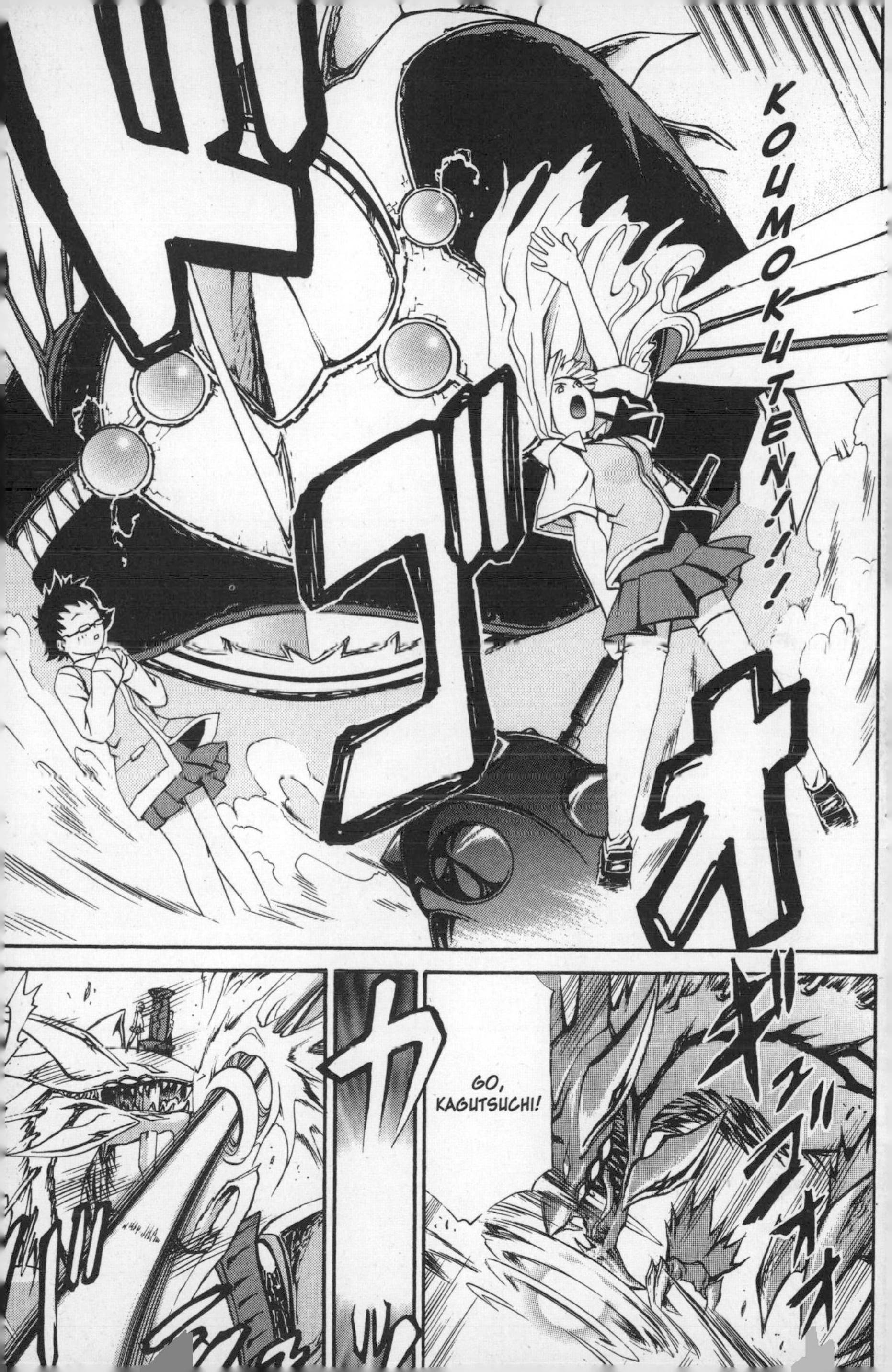
KOUMOKUTEN!!!!!
GO, KAGUTSUCHI!

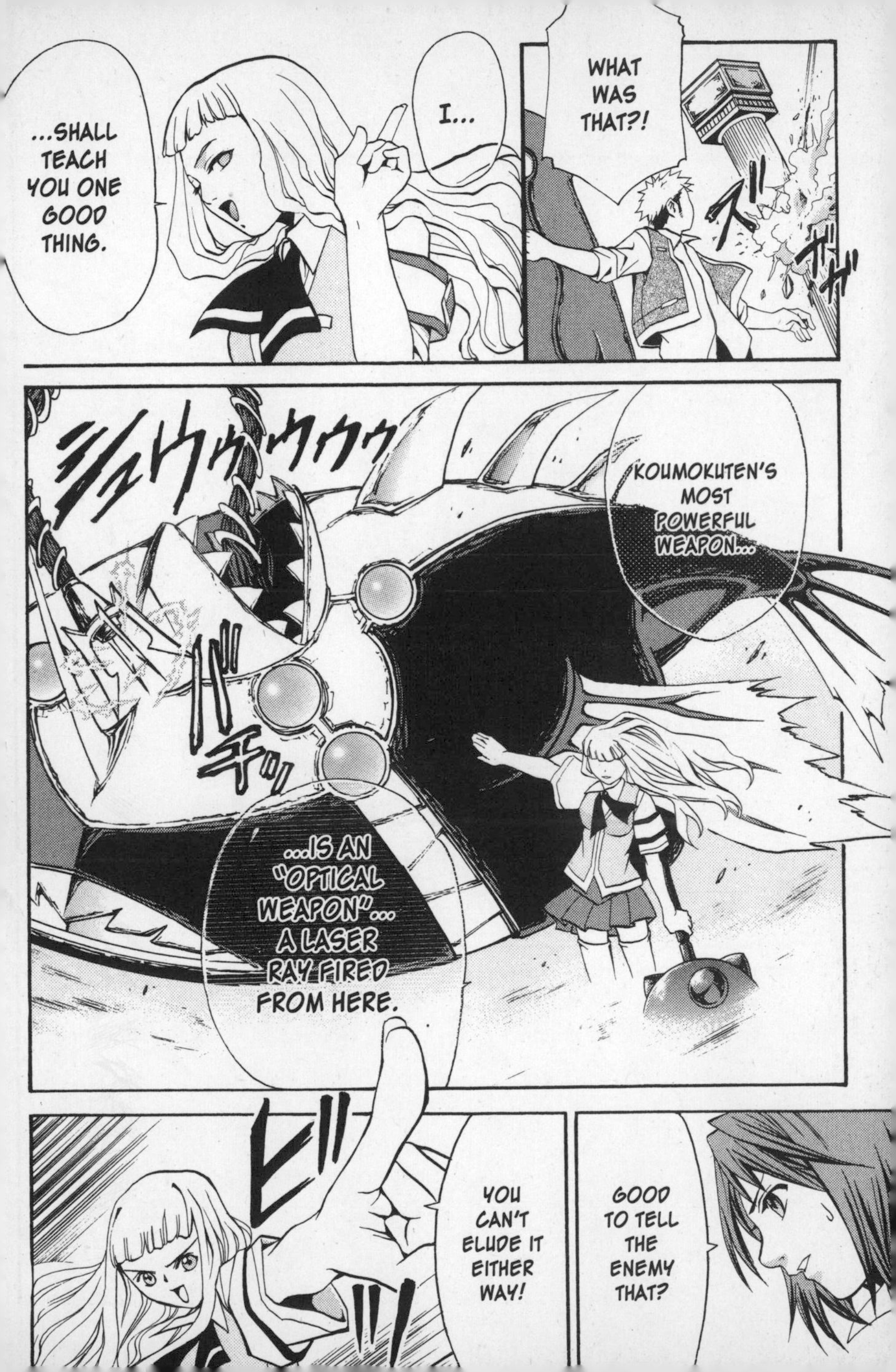
WHAT WAS THAT?!
I...
...SHALL TEACH YOU ONE GOOD THING.
KOUMOKUTEN'S MOST POWERFUL WEAPON...
...IS AN "OPTICAL WEAPON"... A LASER RAY FIRED FROM HERE.
GOOD TO TELL THE ENEMY THAT?
YOU CAN'T ELUDE IT EITHER WAY!

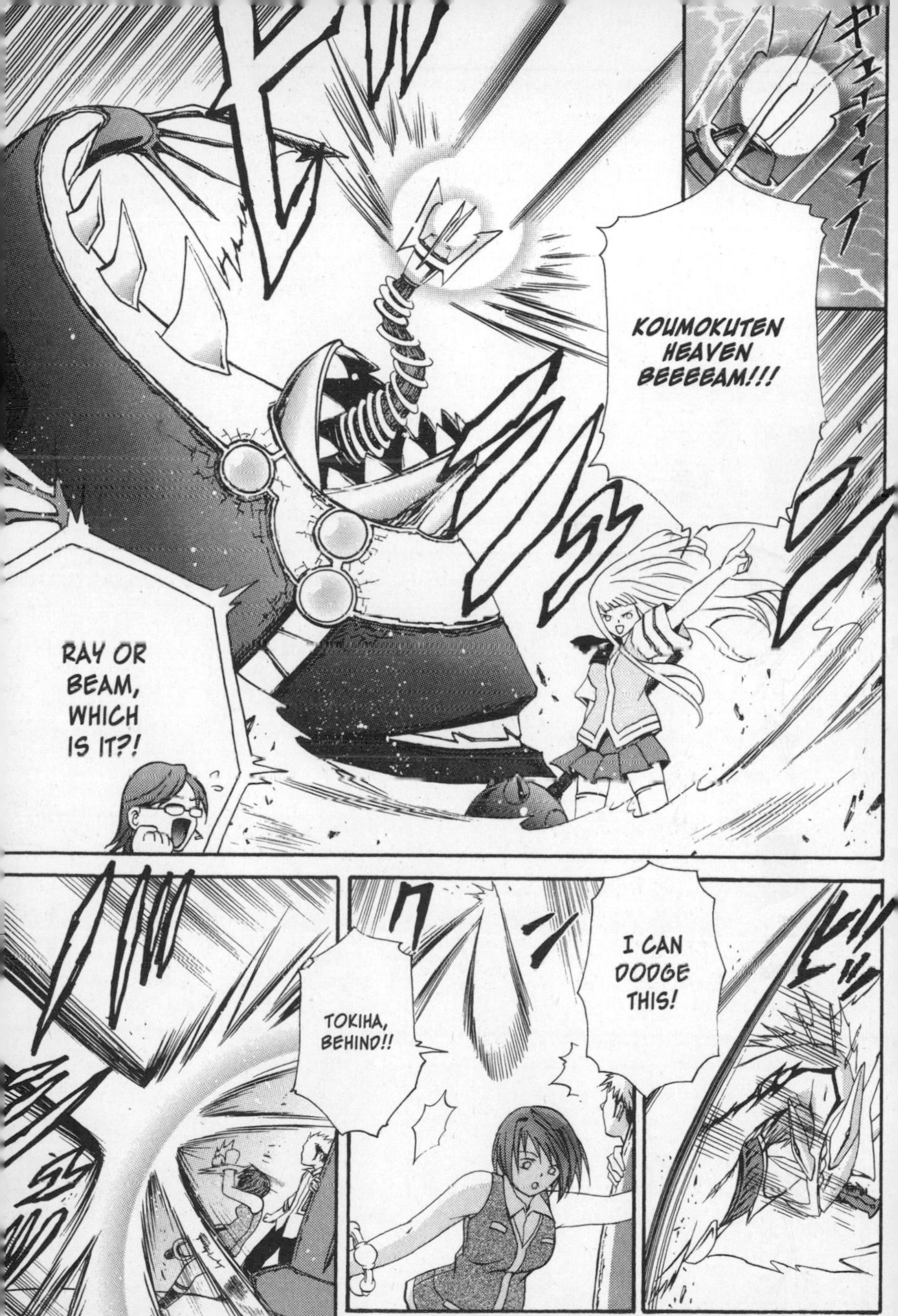
KOUMOKUTEN HEAVEN BEEEEAM!!!
RAY OR BEAM, WHICH IS IT?!
I CAN DODGE THIS!
TOKIHA, BEHIND!!

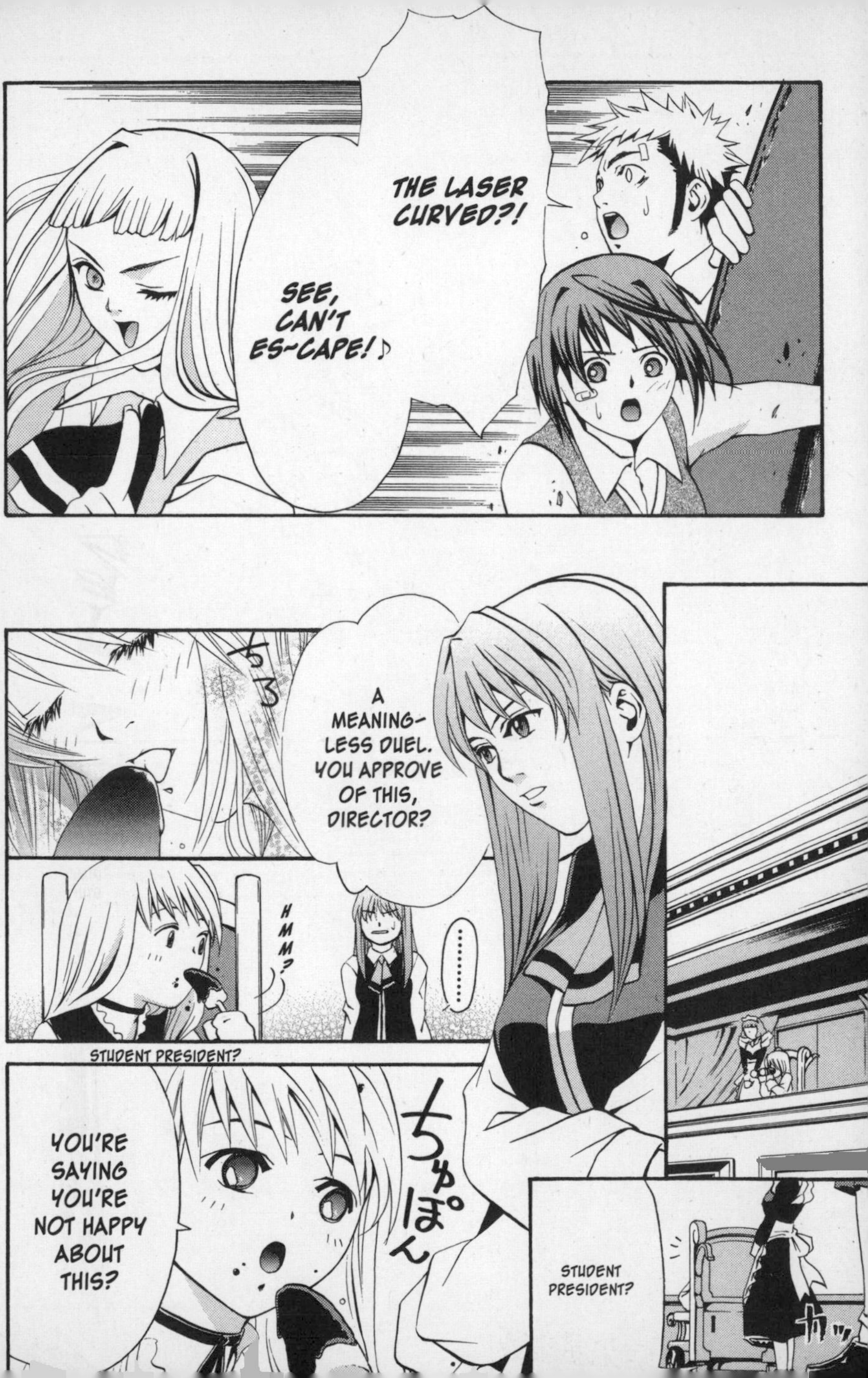
THE LASER CURVED?!
SEE, CAN'T ES-CAPE!♪
A MEANING-LESS DUEL. YOU APPROVE OF THIS, DIRECTOR?
ちろ
HMM?
......
STUDENT PRESIDENT?
STUDENT PRESIDENT?
カッ
ちゅぽん
YOU'RE SAYING YOU'RE NOT HAPPY ABOUT THIS?

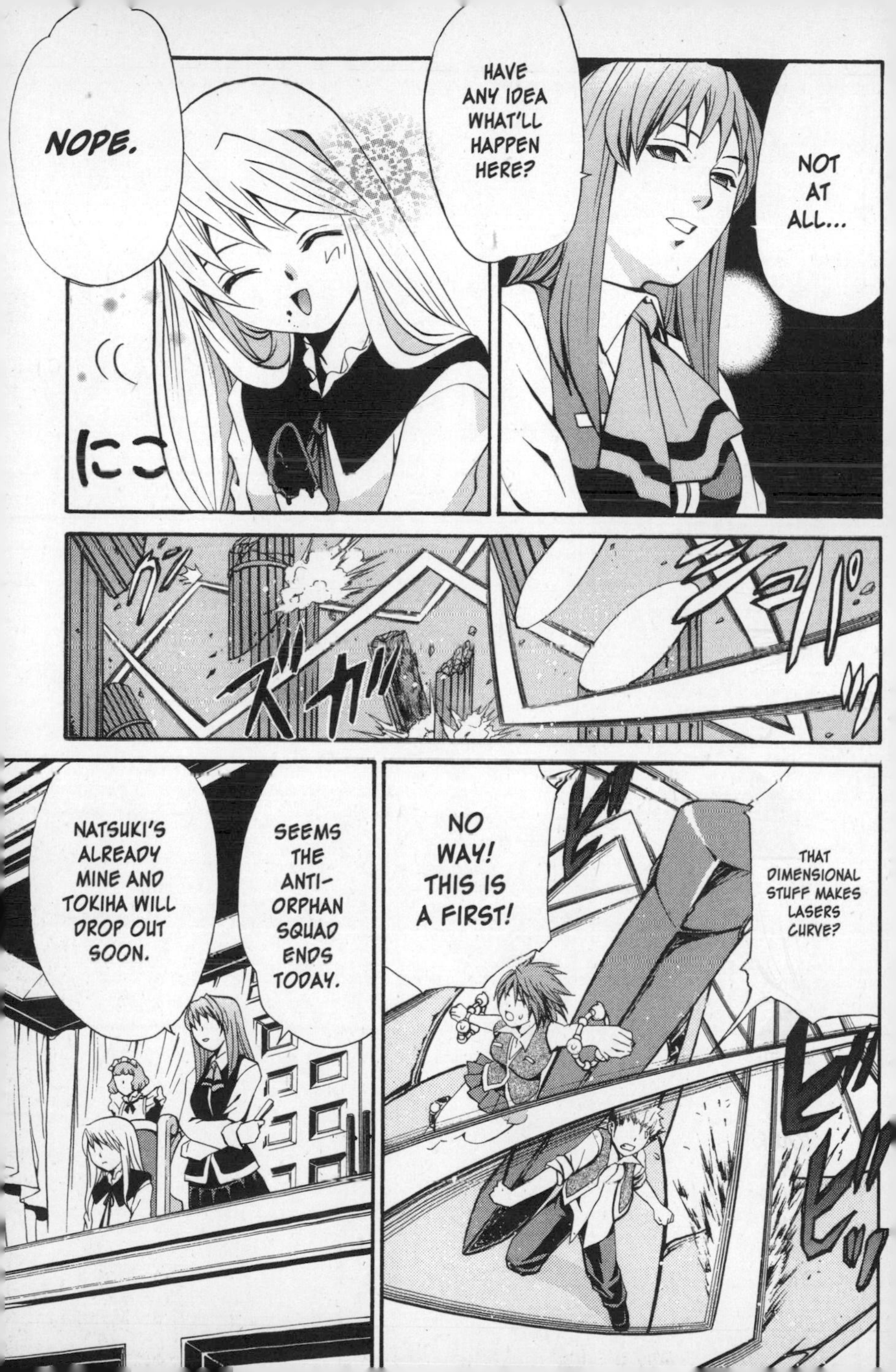
NOT AT ALL...
HAVE ANY IDEA WHAT'LL HAPPEN HERE?
NOPE.
にこ
THAT DIMENSIONAL STUFF MAKES LASERS CURVE?
NO WAY! THIS IS A FIRST!
SEEMS THE ANTI-ORPHAN SQUAD ENDS TODAY.
NATSUKI'S ALREADY MINE AND TOKIHA WILL DROP OUT SOON.

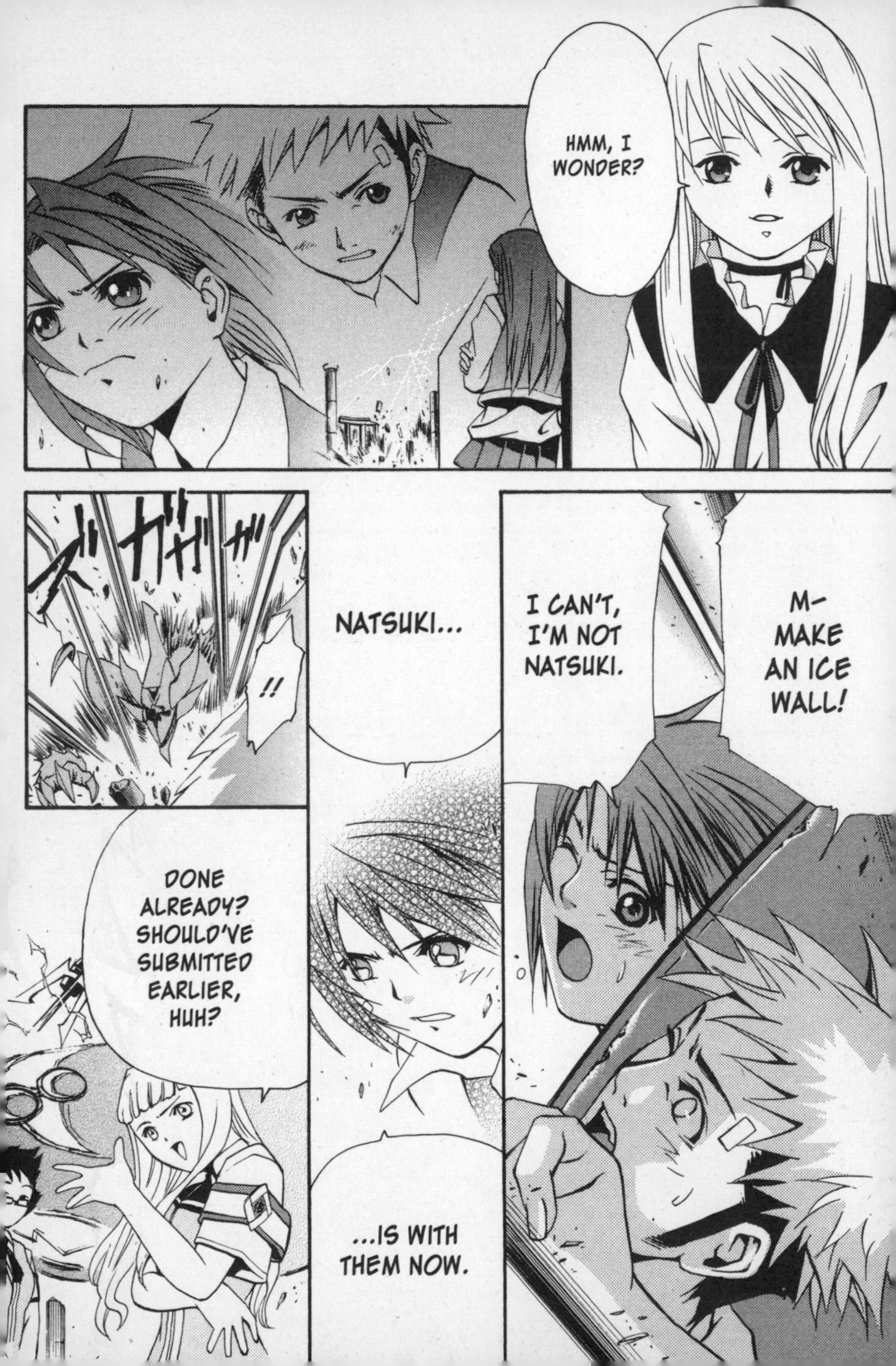
HMM, I WONDER?
M- MAKE AN ICE WALL!
I CAN'T, I'M NOT NATSUKI.
NATSUKI...
...IS WITH THEM NOW.
ズガガガ
!!
DONE ALREADY? SHOULD'VE SUBMITTED EARLIER, HUH?

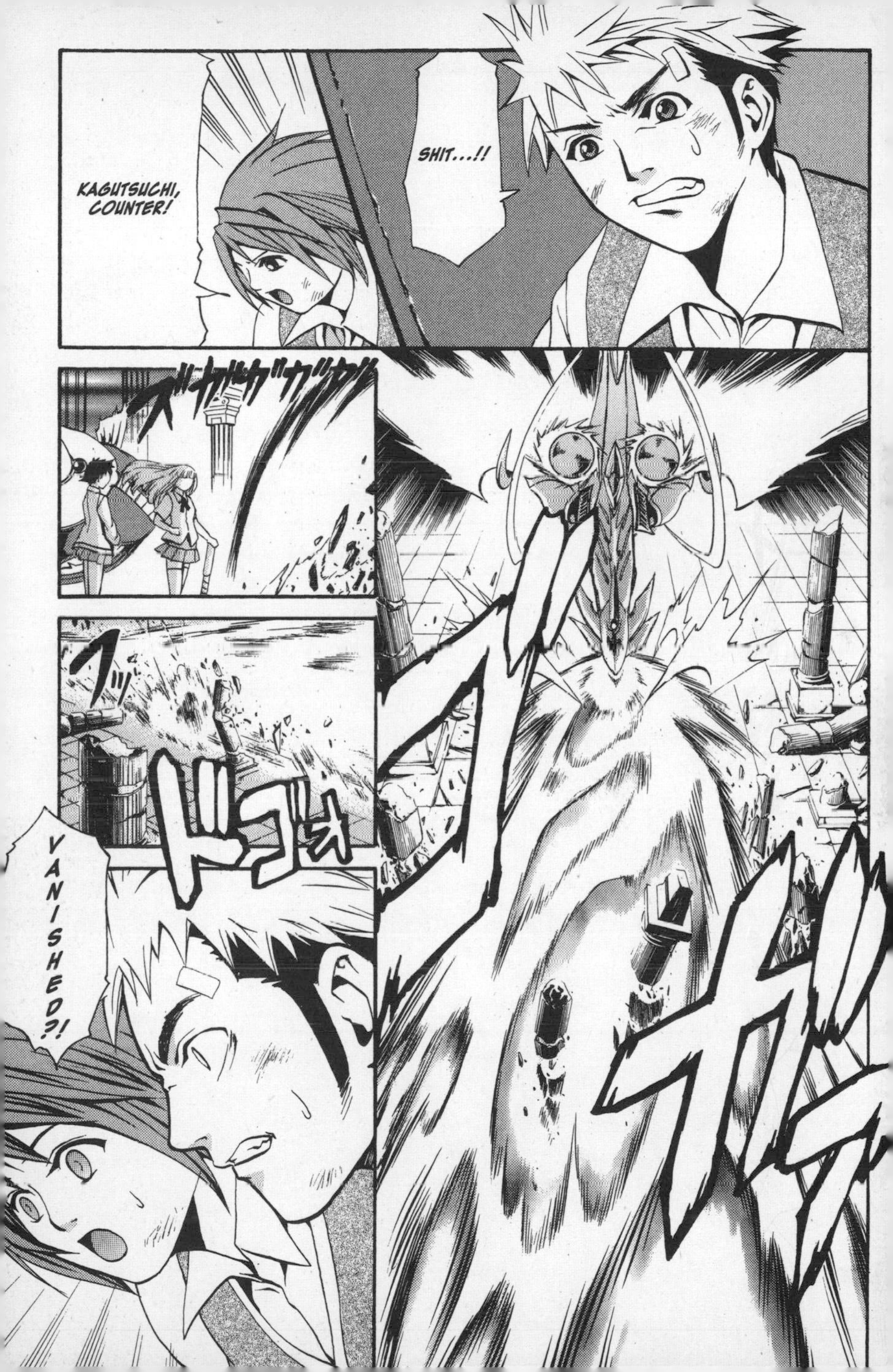
SHIT...!!
KAGUTSUCHI, COUNTER!
VANISHED?!

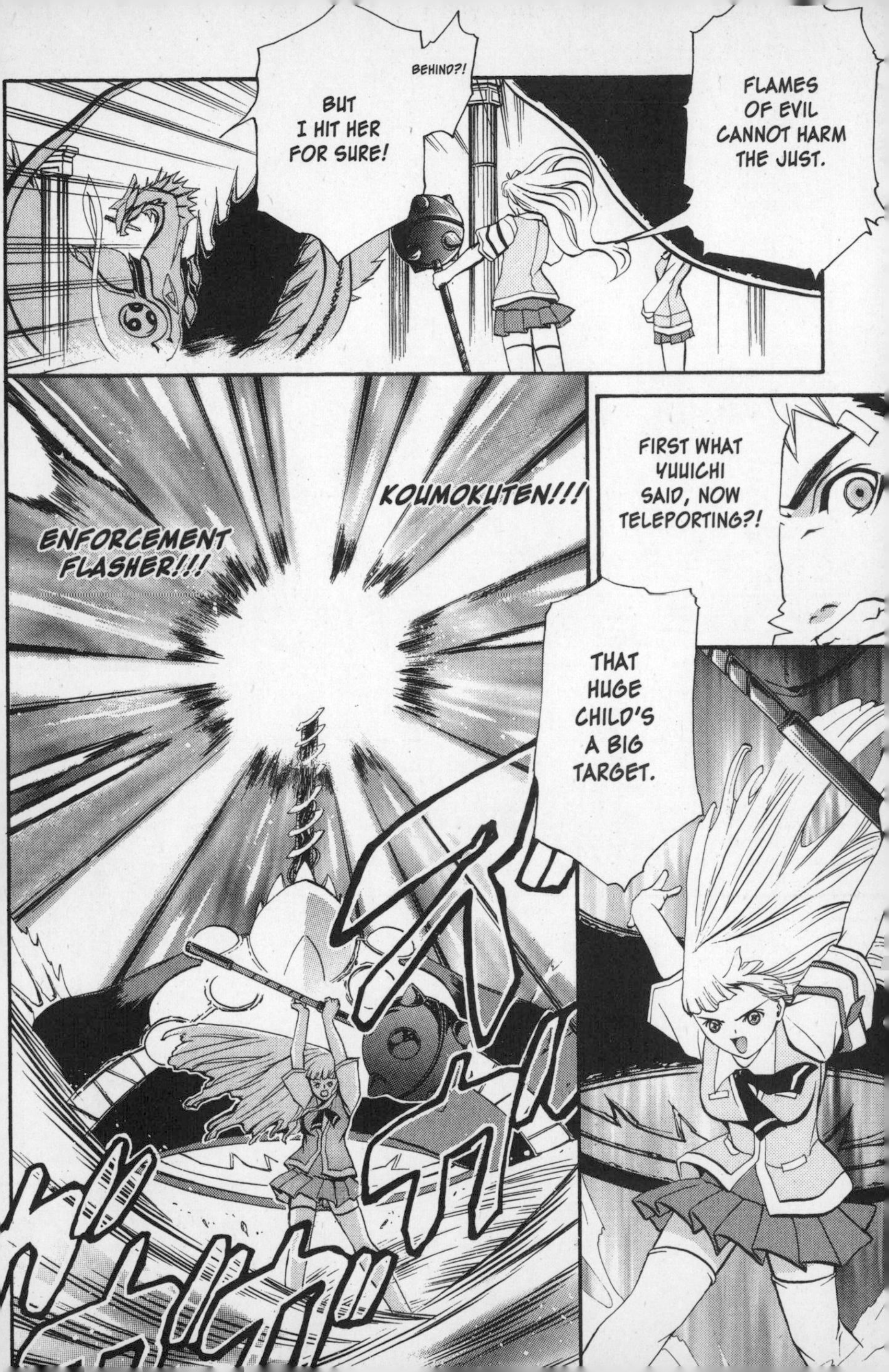
FLAMES OF EVIL CANNOT HARM THE JUST.
BEHIND?!
BUT I HIT HER FOR SURE!
FIRST WHAT YUUICHI SAID, NOW TELEPORTING?!
THAT HUGE CHILD'S A BIG TARGET.
KOUMOKUTEN!!!
ENFORCEMENT FLASHER!!!

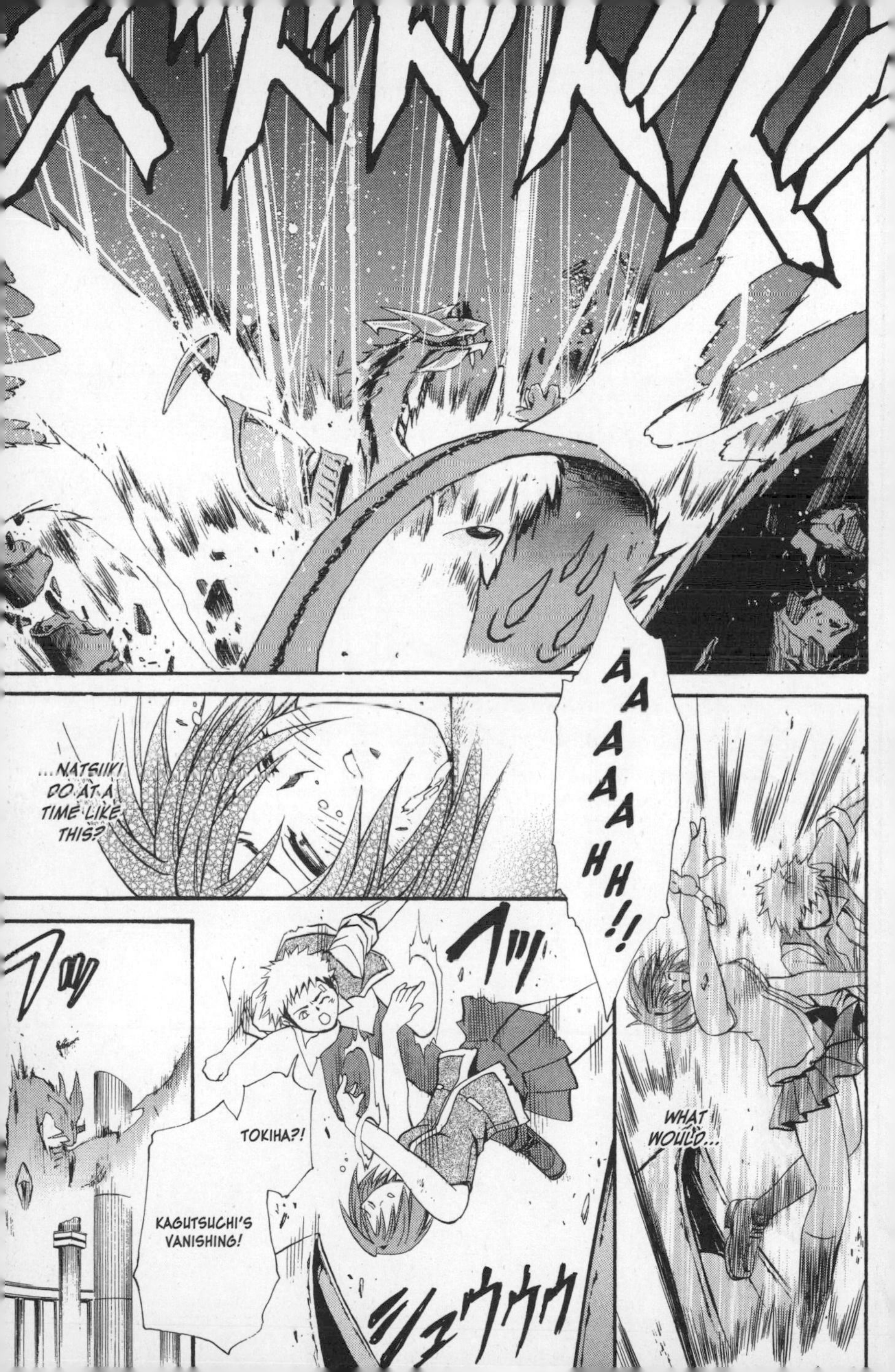

AAAAAHH!!
WHAT WOULD...
...NATSUKI DO AT A TIME LIKE THIS?
TOKIHA?!
KAGUTSUCHI'S VANISHING!
シュウウウ

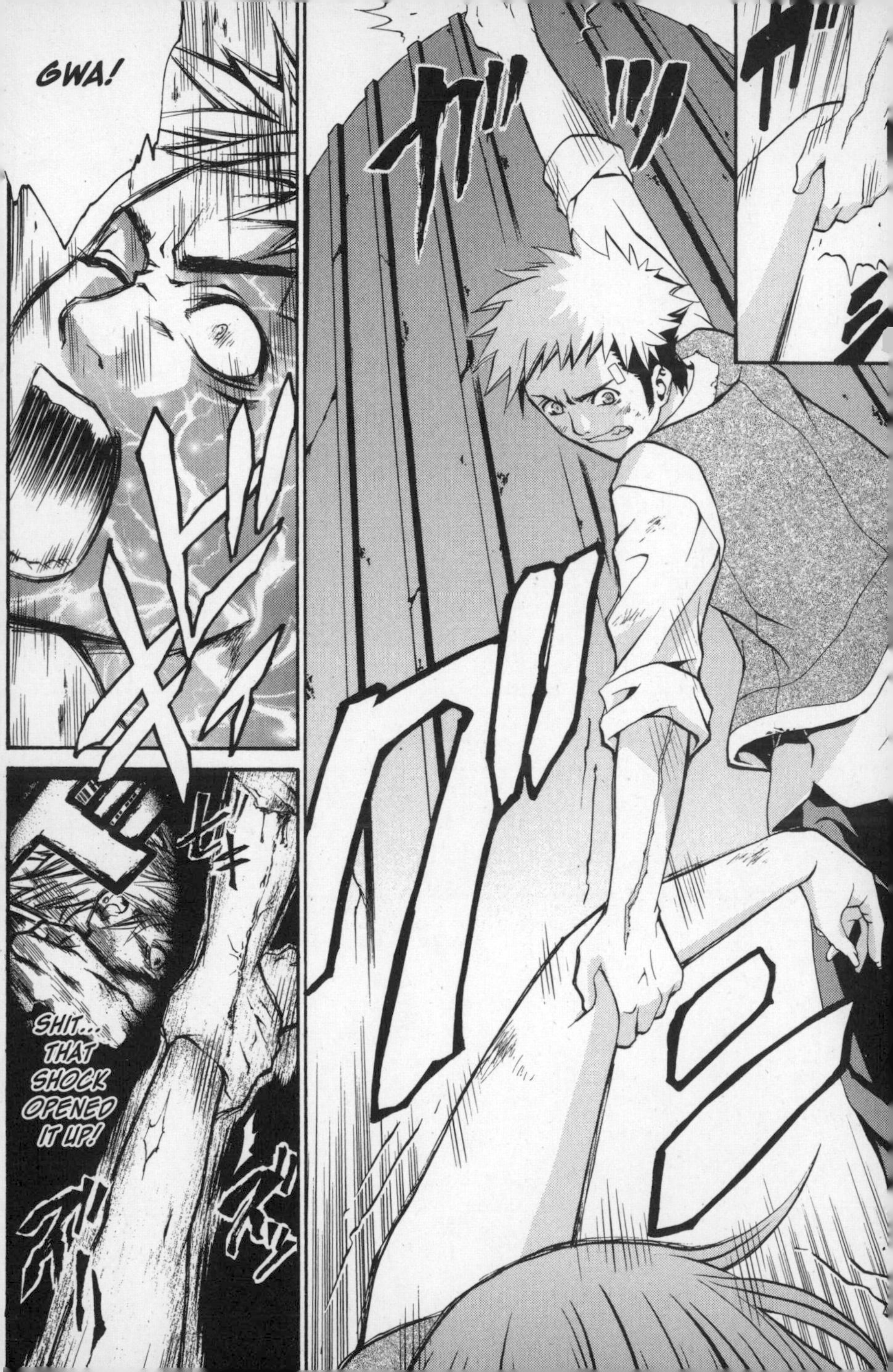
GWA!
SHIT... THAT SHOCK OPENED IT UP!

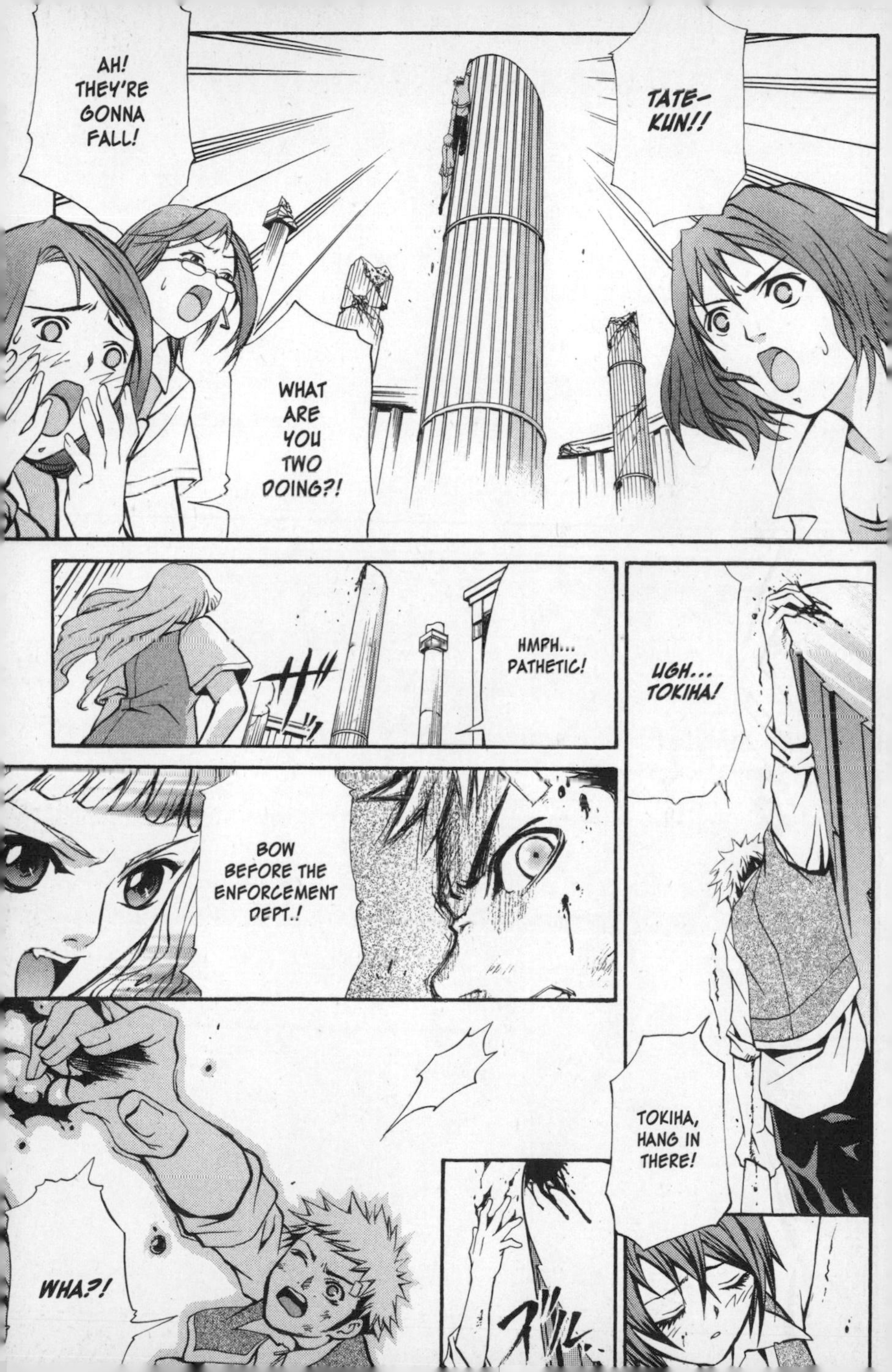
TATE-KUN!!
AH! THEY'RE GONNA FALL!
WHAT ARE YOU TWO DOING?!
UGH... TOKIHA!
TOKIHA, HANG IN THERE!
HMPH... PATHETIC!
BOW BEFORE THE ENFORCEMENT DEPT.!
WHA?!

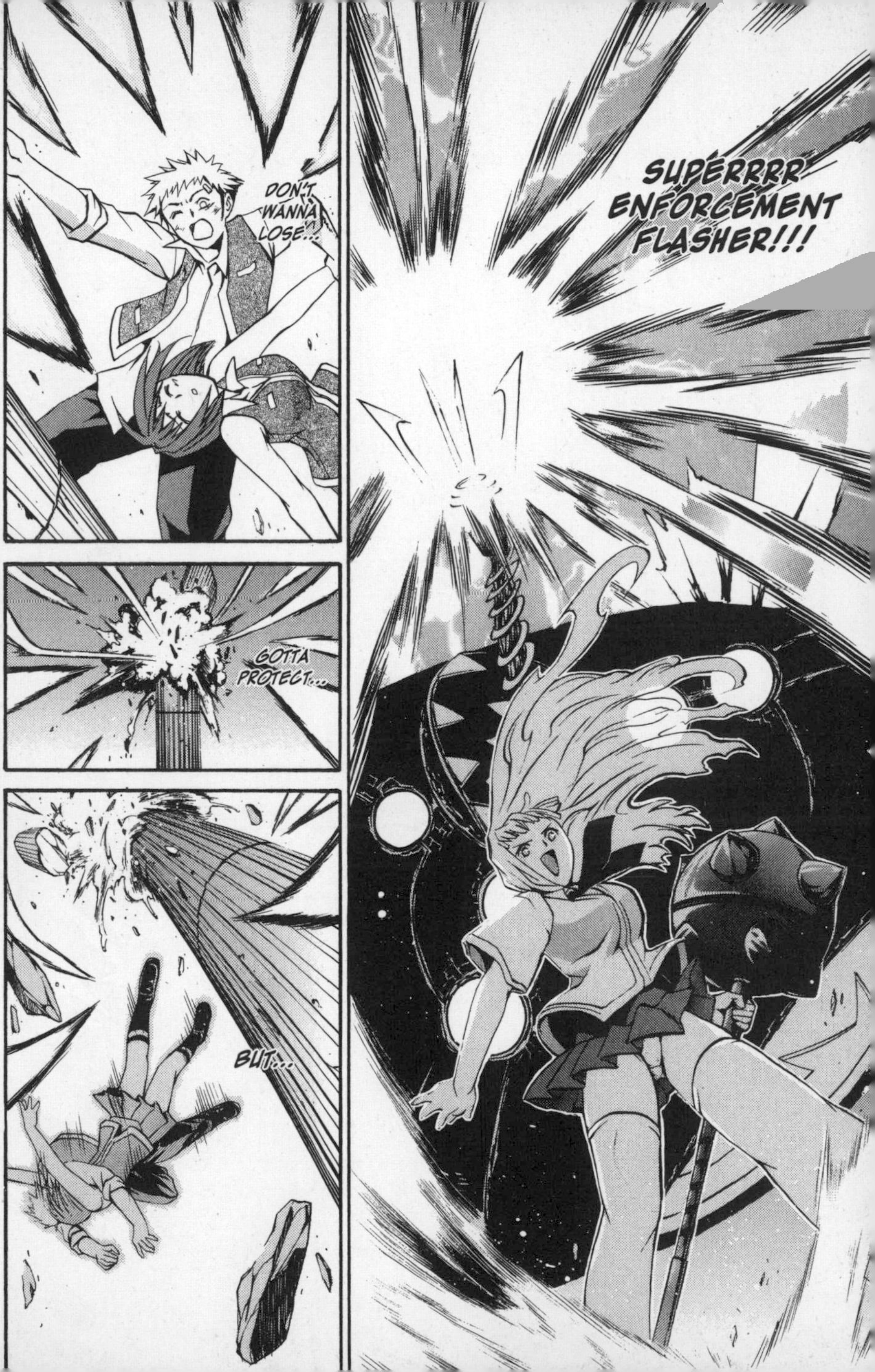
SUPERRRR ENFORCEMENT FLASHER!!!
DON'T WANNA LOSE...
GOTTA PROTECT...
BUT...

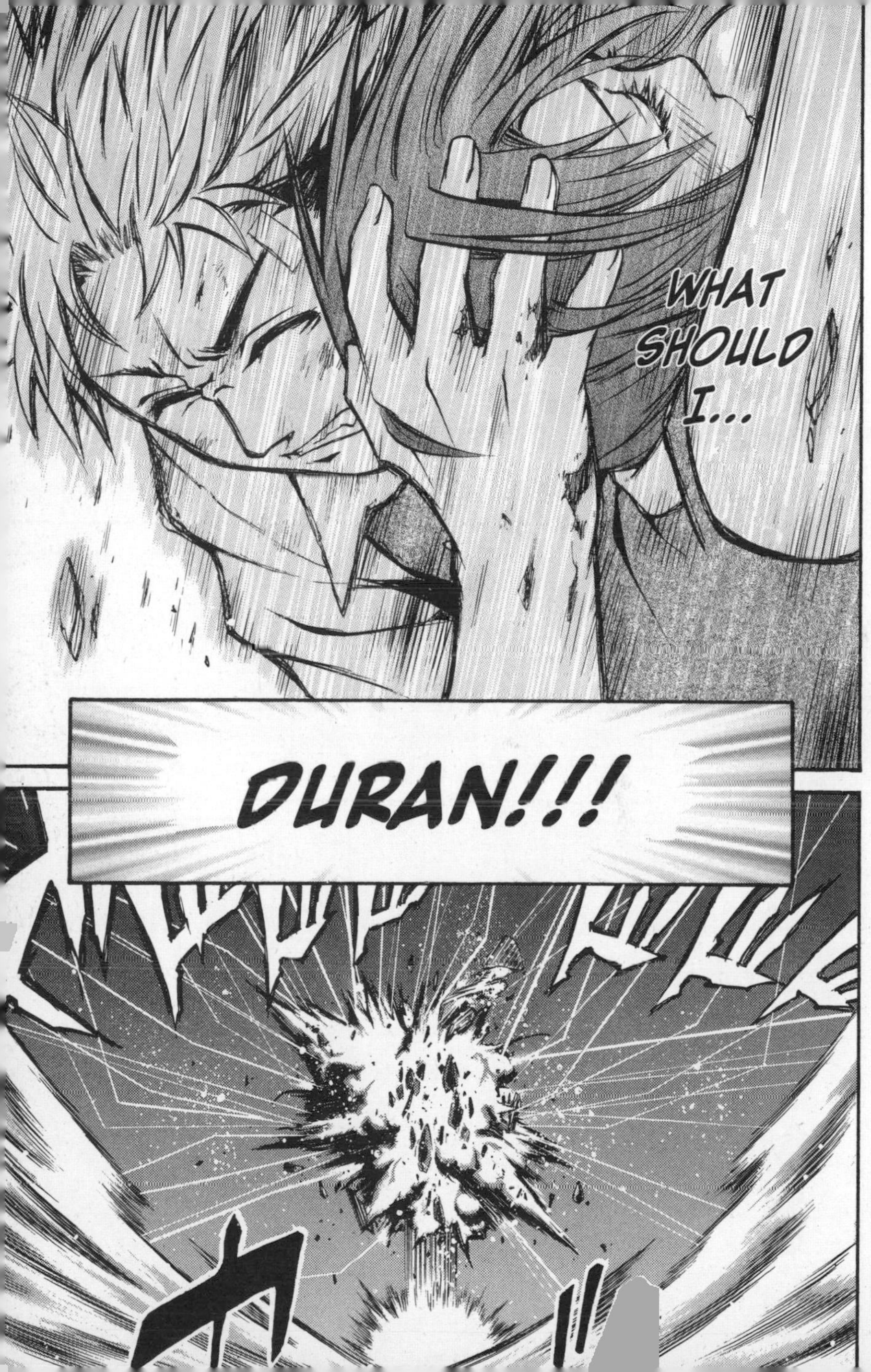
WHAT SHOULD I...
DURAN!!!

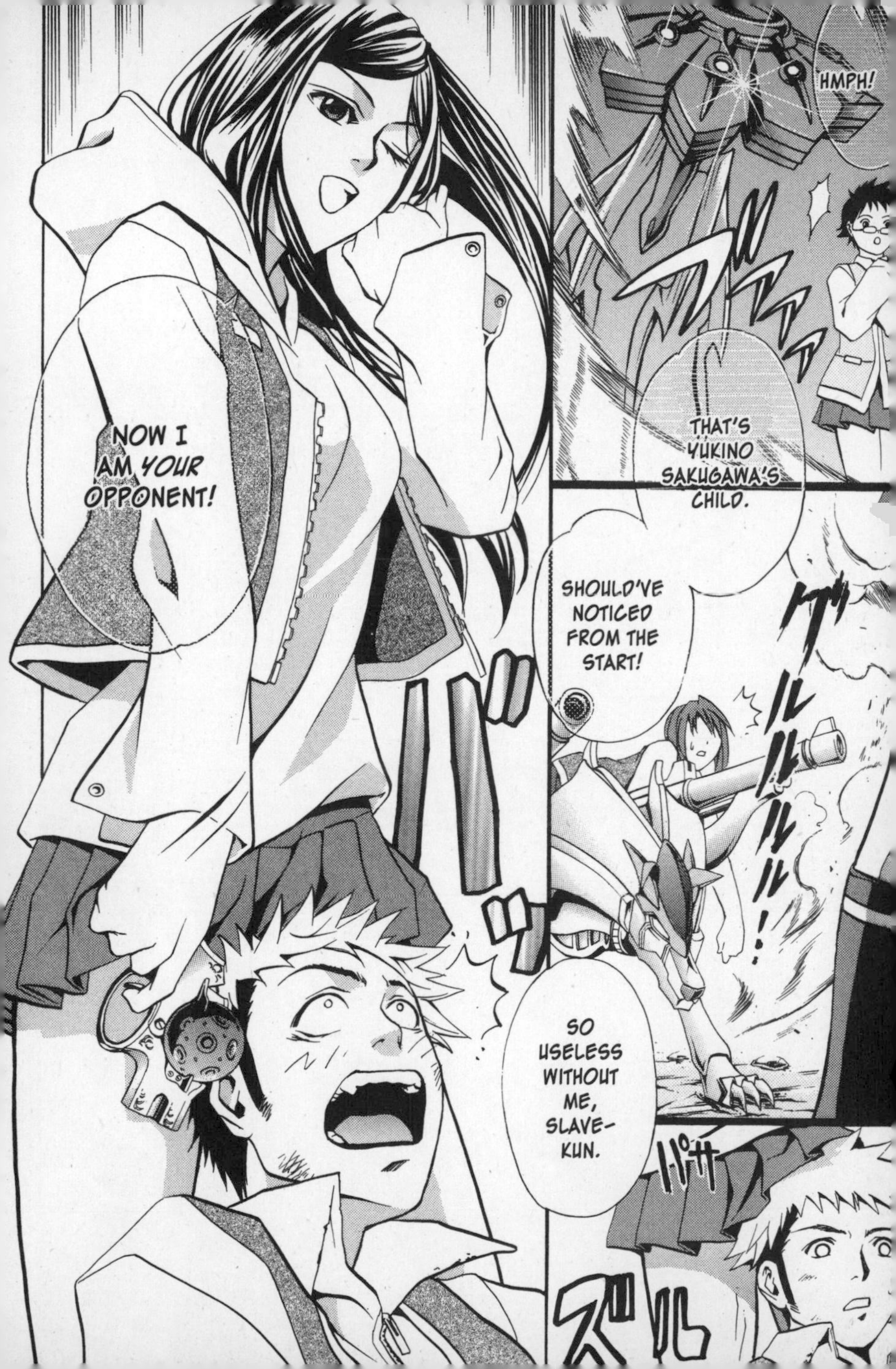
HMPH!
THAT'S YUKINO SAKUGAWA'S CHILD.
SHOULD'VE NOTICED FROM THE START!
NOW I AM *YOUR* OPPONENT!
SO USELESS WITHOUT ME, SLAVE-KUN.

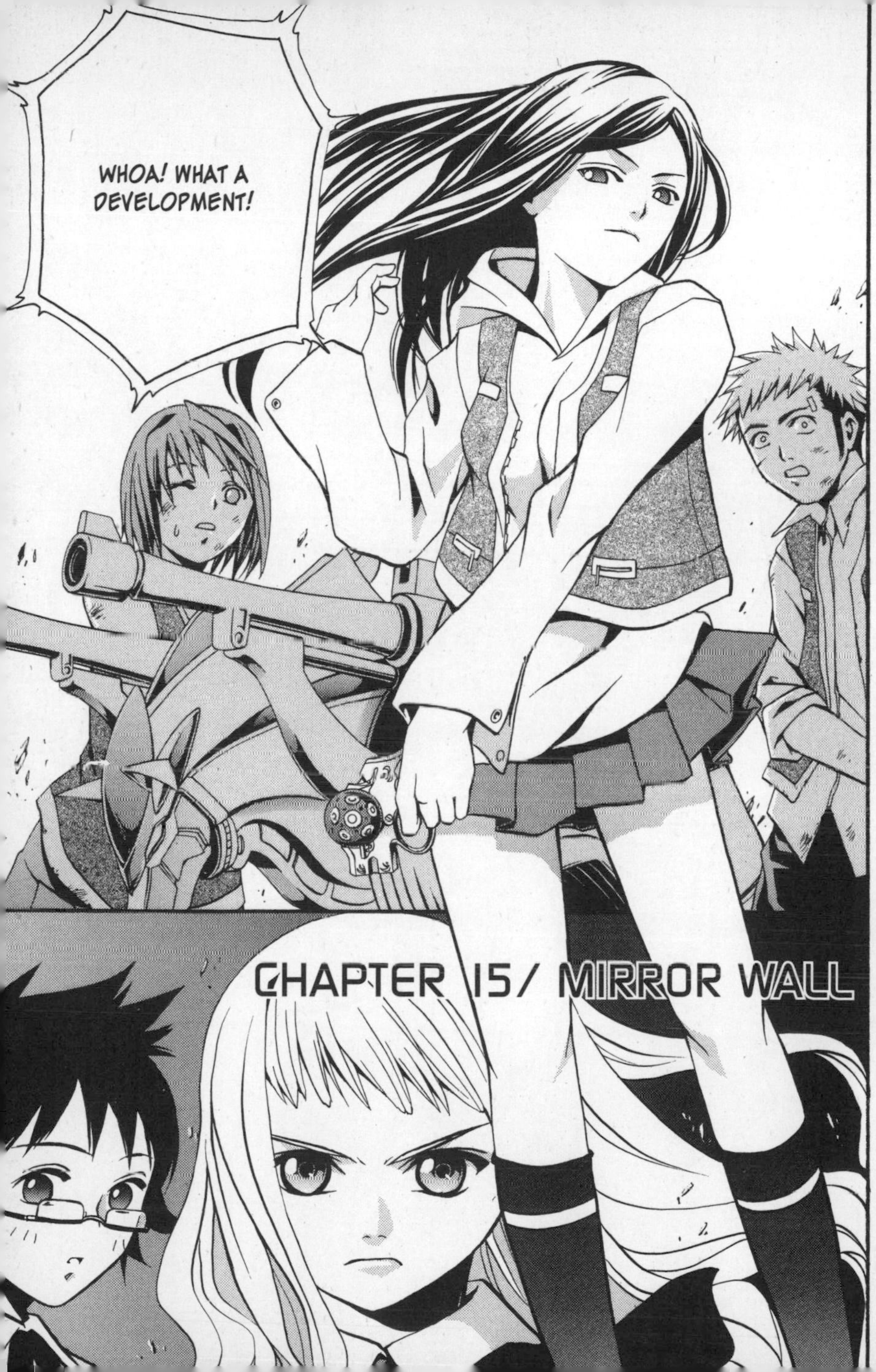
WHOA! WHAT A DEVELOPMENT!
CHAPTER 15/ MIRROR WALL

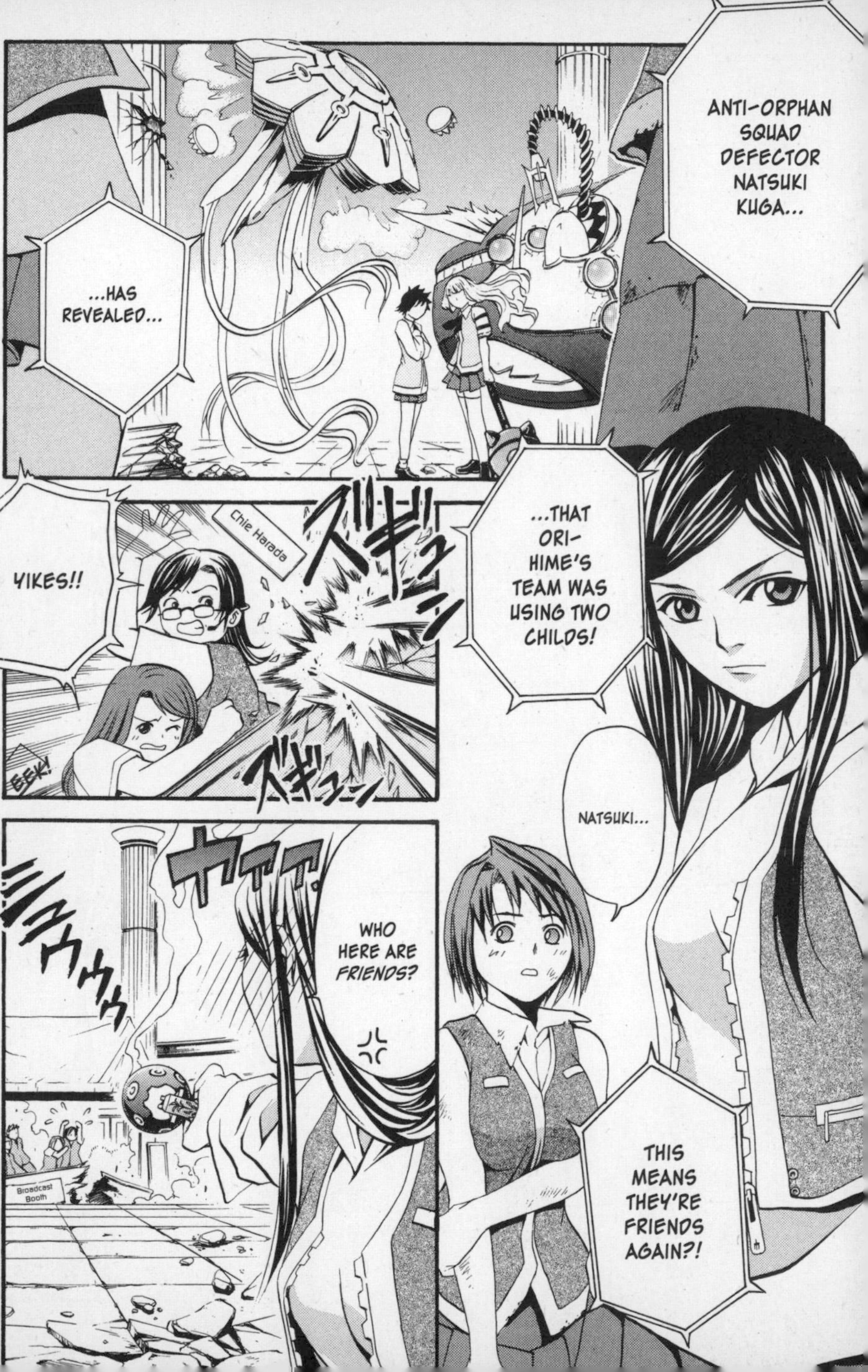
ANTI-ORPHAN SQUAD DEFECTOR NATSUKI KUGA...
...HAS REVEALED...
...THAT ORI-HIME'S TEAM WAS USING TWO CHILDS!
YIKES!!
Chie Harada
EEK!
NATSUKI...
THIS MEANS THEY'RE FRIENDS AGAIN?!
WHO HERE ARE FRIENDS?
Broadcast Booth

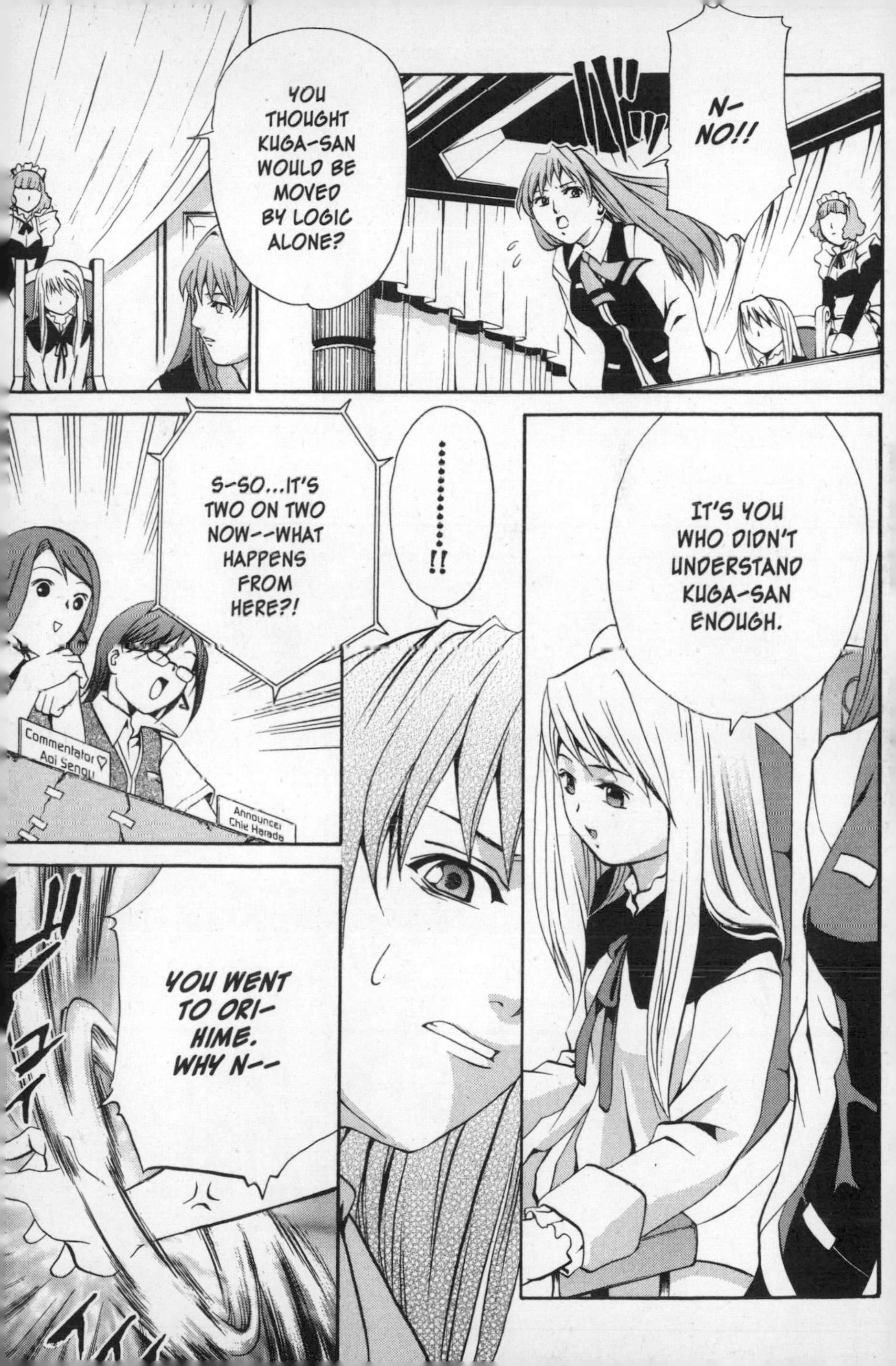
N-NO!!
YOU THOUGHT KUGA-SAN WOULD BE MOVED BY LOGIC ALONE?
IT'S YOU WHO DIDN'T UNDERSTAND KUGA-SAN ENOUGH.
........!!
S-SO...IT'S TWO ON TWO NOW--WHAT HAPPENS FROM HERE?!
Commentator ♡ Aoi Sengu
Announcer: Chie Harada
YOU WENT TO ORI-HIME. WHY N--

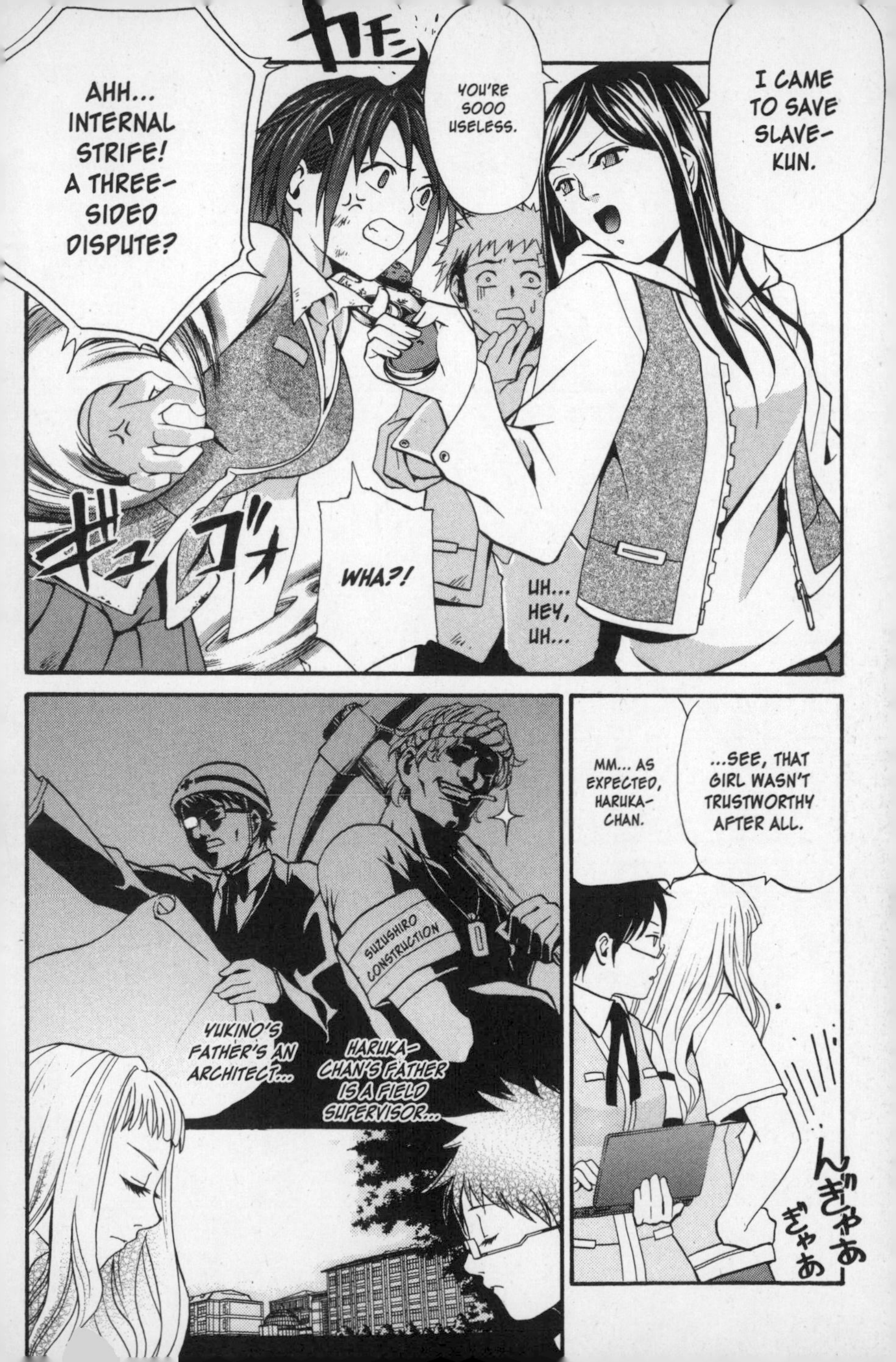
I CAME TO SAVE SLAVE-KUN.
YOU'RE SOOO USELESS.
カチ
AHH... INTERNAL STRIFE! A THREE-SIDED DISPUTE?
WHA?!
UH... HEY, UH...
ギュゴォ
...SEE, THAT GIRL WASN'T TRUSTWORTHY AFTER ALL.
MM... AS EXPECTED, HARUKA-CHAN.
んぎゃあぎゃあ
SUZUSHIRO CONSTRUCTION
HARUKA-CHAN'S FATHER IS A FIELD SUPERVISOR...
YUKINO'S FATHER'S AN ARCHITECT...

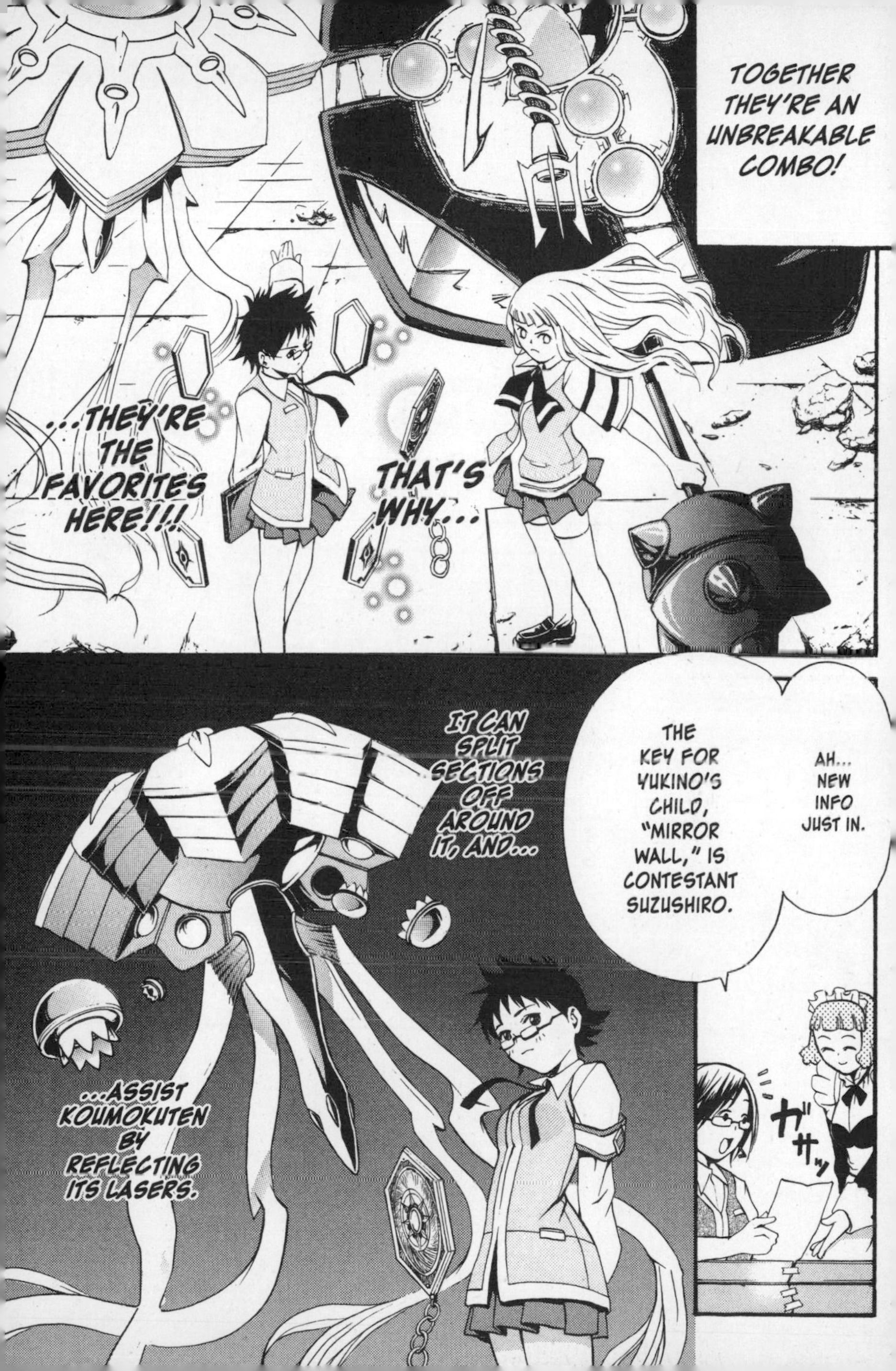
TOGETHER THEY'RE AN UNBREAKABLE COMBO!
THAT'S WHY...
...THEY'RE THE FAVORITES HERE!!!
AH... NEW INFO JUST IN.
THE KEY FOR YUKINO'S CHILD, "MIRROR WALL," IS CONTESTANT SUZUSHIRO.
ガサッ
IT CAN SPLIT SECTIONS OFF AROUND IT, AND...
...ASSIST KOUMOKUTEN BY REFLECTING ITS LASERS.

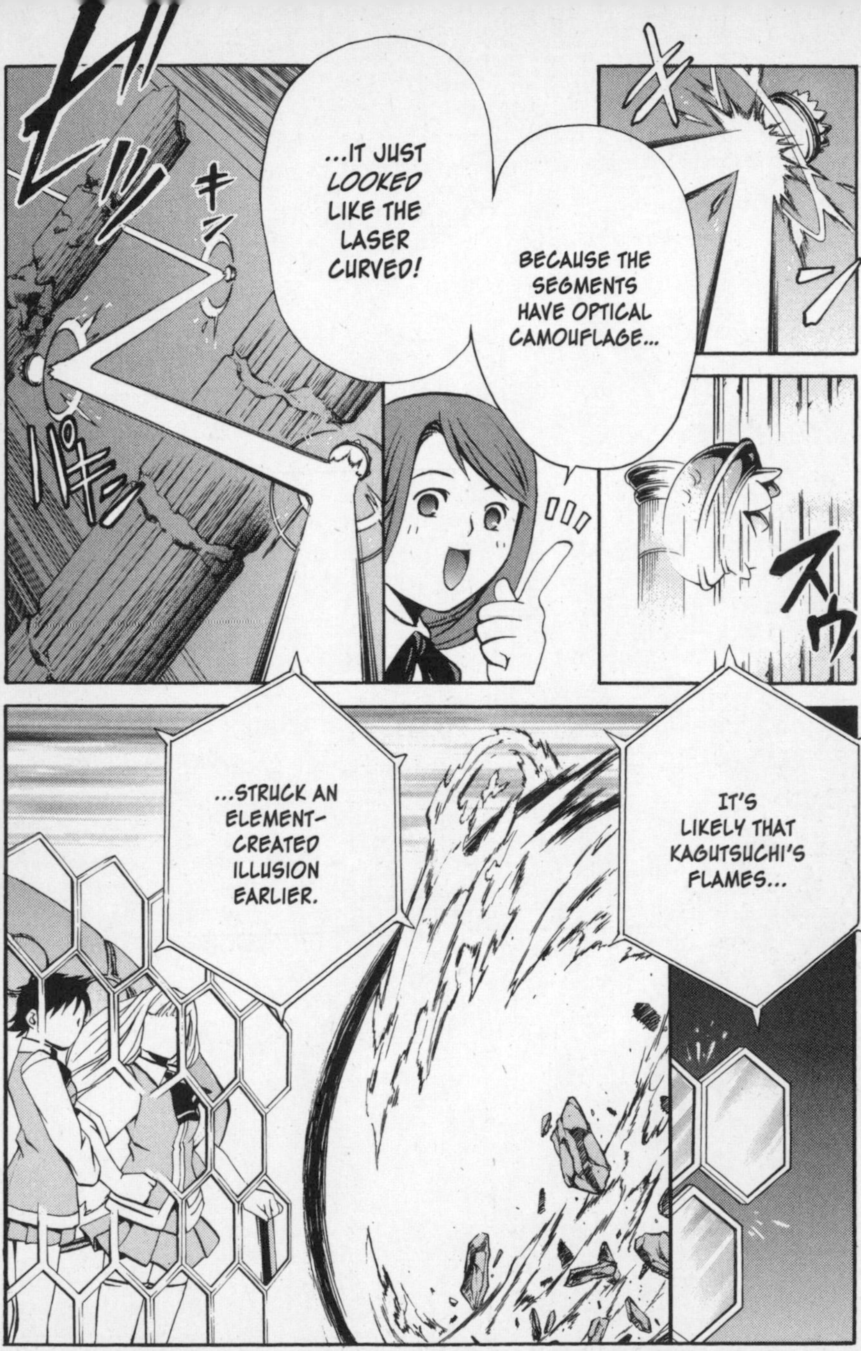

BECAUSE THE SEGMENTS HAVE OPTICAL CAMOUFLAGE...
...IT JUST LOOKED LIKE THE LASER CURVED!
IT'S LIKELY THAT KAGUTSUCHI'S FLAMES...
...STRUCK AN ELEMENT-CREATED ILLUSION EARLIER.

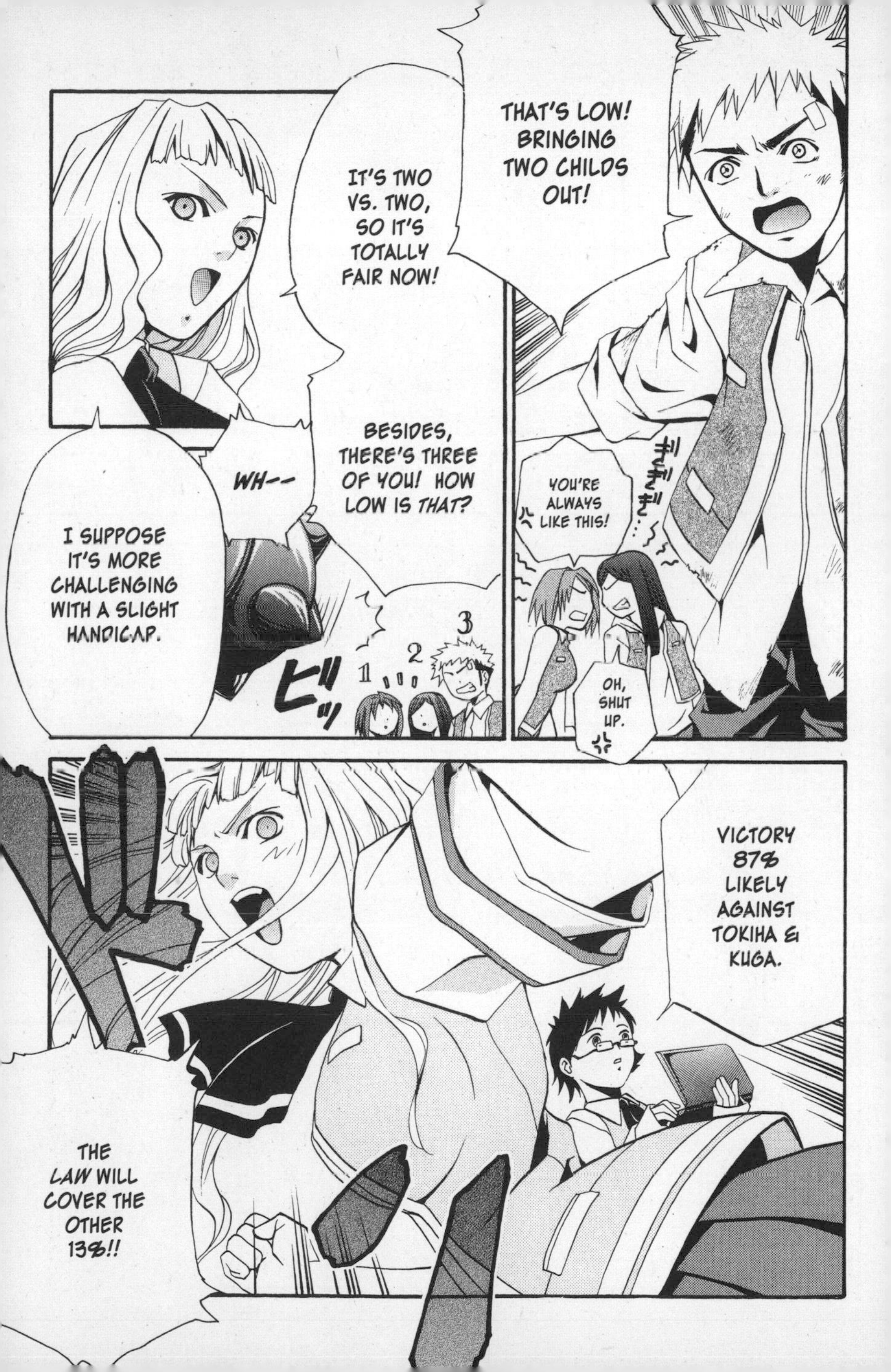
THAT'S LOW! BRINGING TWO CHILDS OUT!
IT'S TWO VS. TWO, SO IT'S TOTALLY FAIR NOW!
YOU'RE ALWAYS LIKE THIS!
OH, SHUT UP.
BESIDES, THERE'S THREE OF YOU! HOW LOW IS *THAT*?
WH--
I SUPPOSE IT'S MORE CHALLENGING WITH A SLIGHT HANDICAP.
3
2
1
ビッ
VICTORY 87% LIKELY AGAINST TOKIHA & KUGA.
THE *LAW* WILL COVER THE OTHER 13%!!

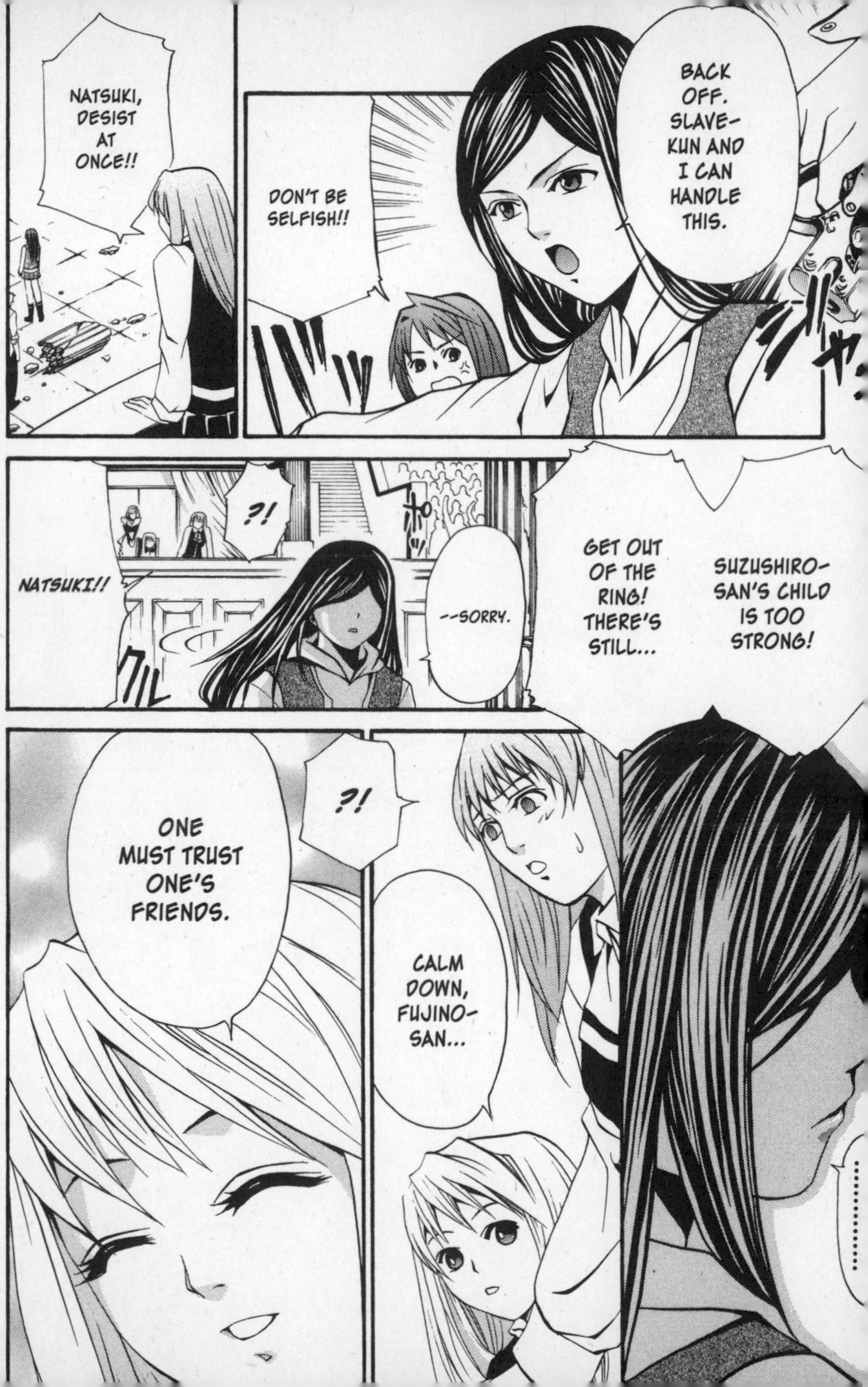
BACK OFF. SLAVE-KUN AND I CAN HANDLE THIS.
DON'T BE SELFISH!!
NATSUKI, DESIST AT ONCE!!
SUZUSHIRO-SAN'S CHILD IS TOO STRONG!
GET OUT OF THE RING! THERE'S STILL...
--SORRY.
?!
NATSUKI!!
......
CALM DOWN, FUJINO-SAN...
?!
ONE MUST TRUST ONE'S FRIENDS.

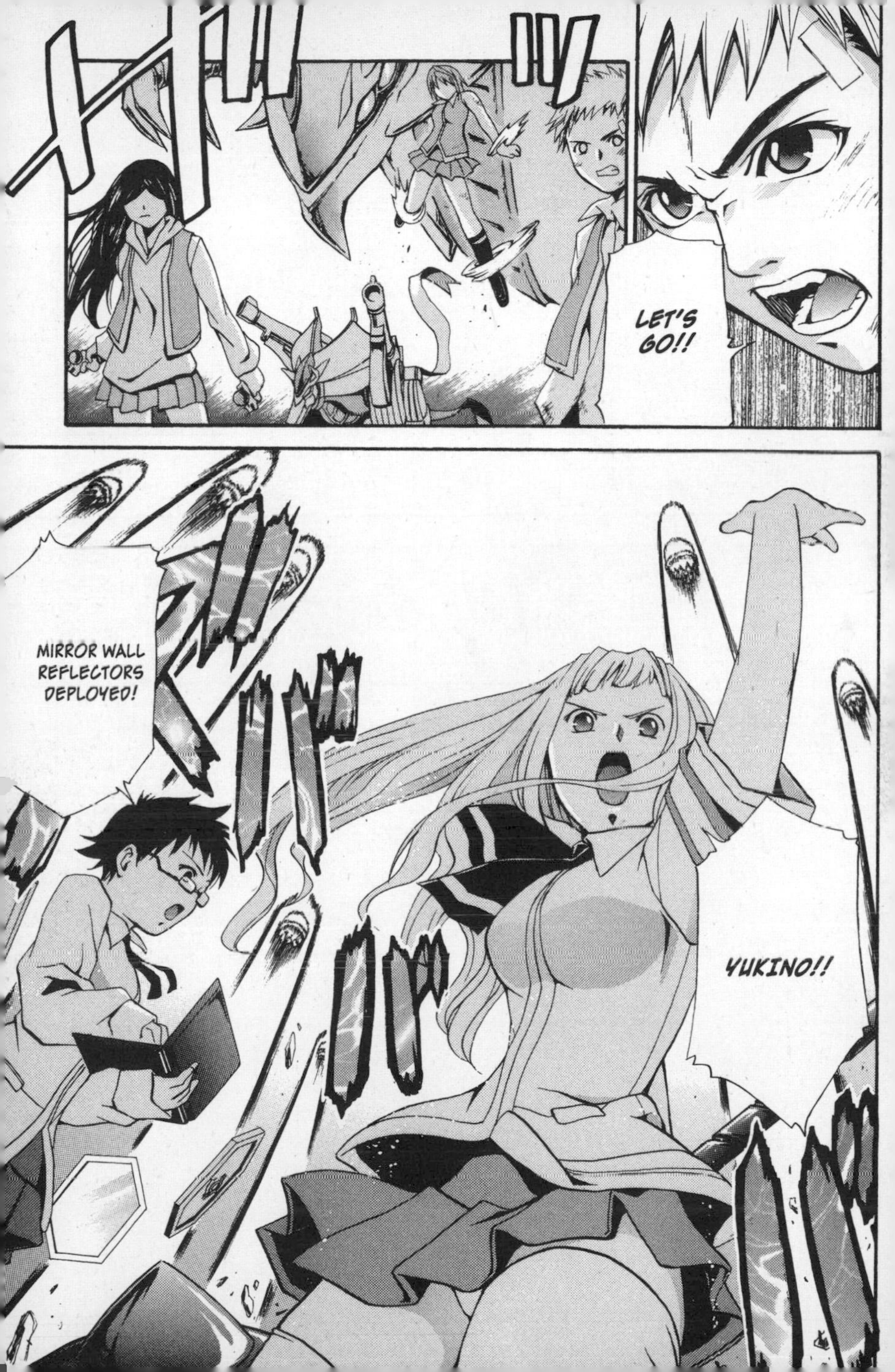
LET'S GO!!
YUKINO!!
MIRROR WALL REFLECTORS DEPLOYED!

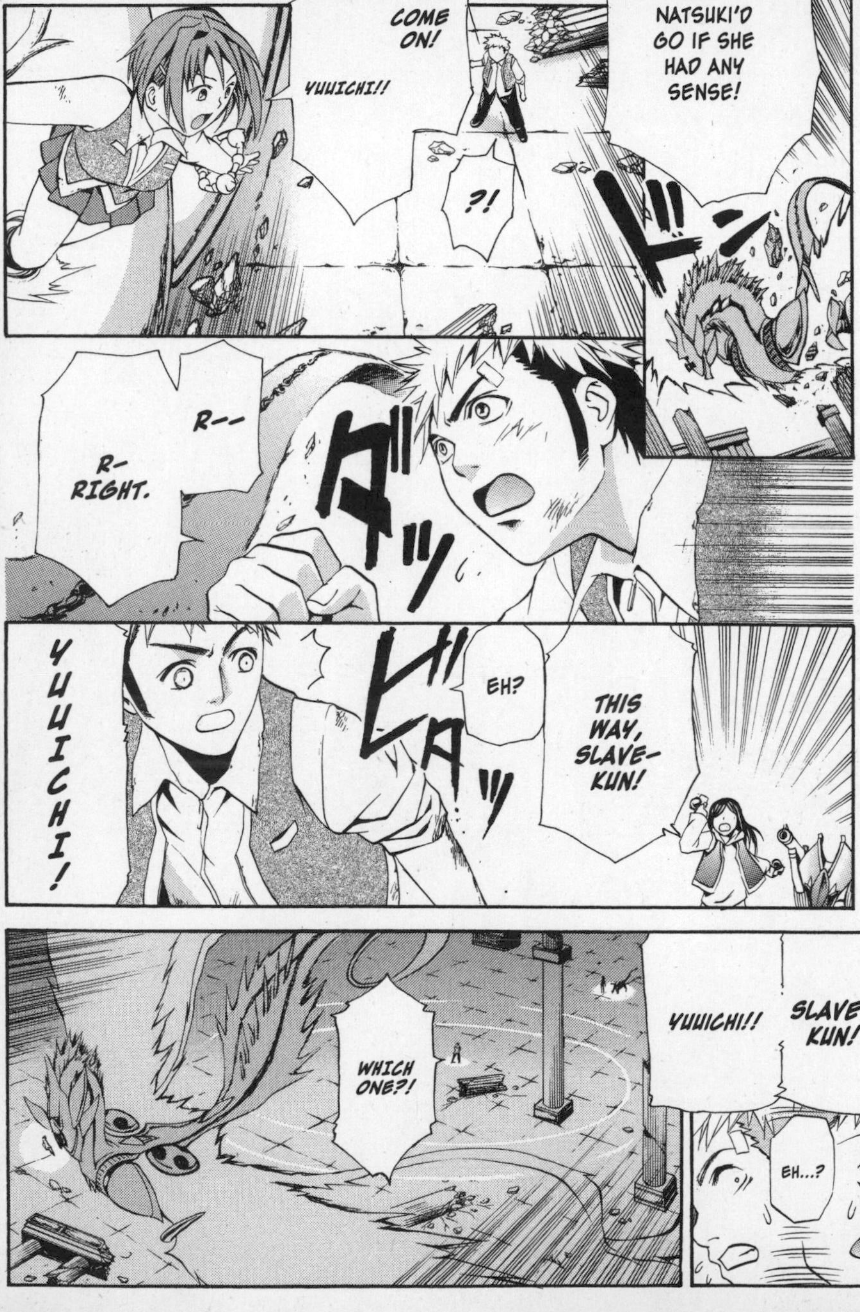
NATSUKI'D GO IF SHE HAD ANY SENSE!
COME ON!
YUUICHI!!
?!
R--
R-RIGHT.
THIS WAY, SLAVE-KUN!
EH?
YUUICHI!
SLAVE-KUN!
YUUICHI!!
EH...?
WHICH ONE?!

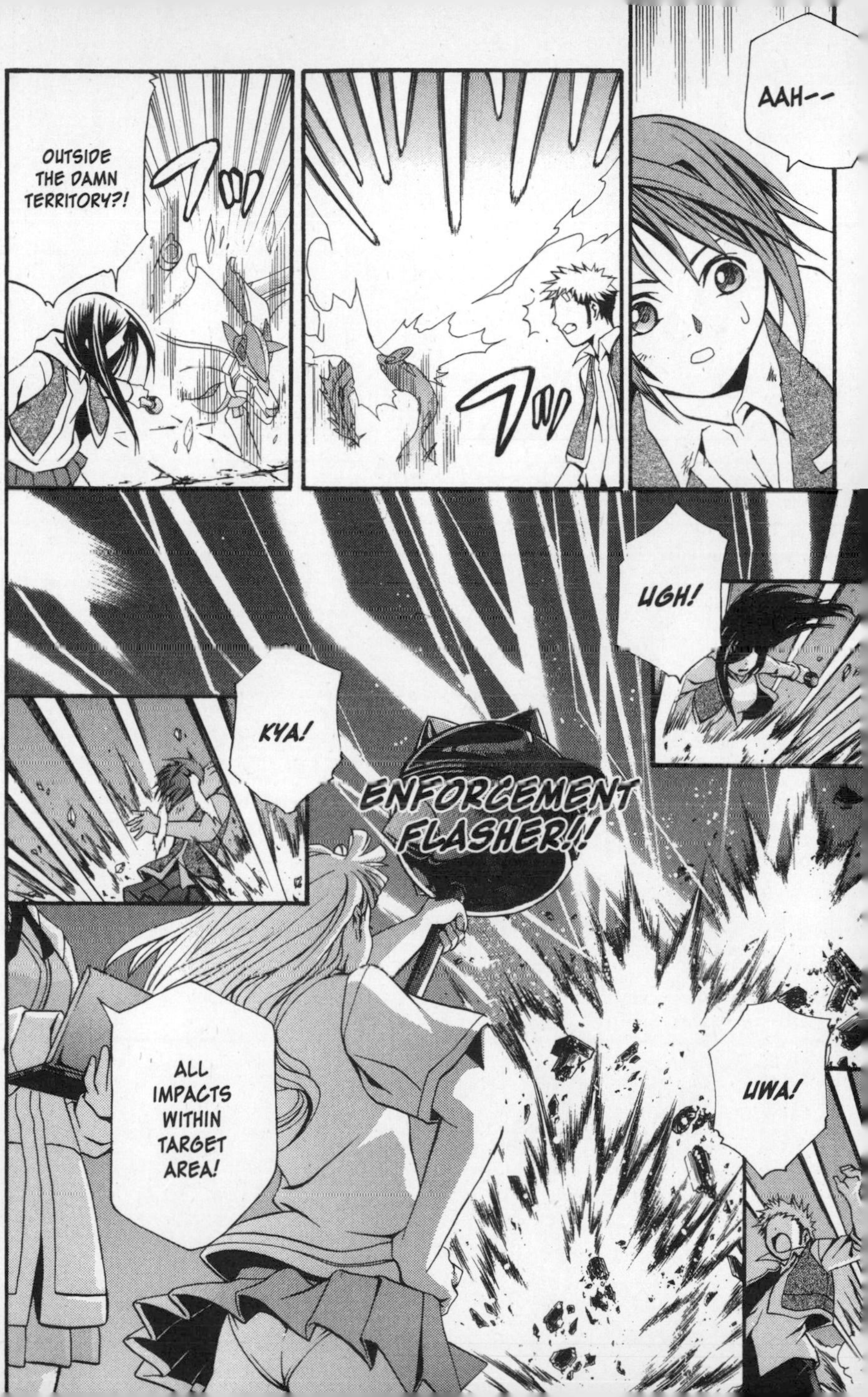
AAH--
OUTSIDE THE DAMN TERRITORY?!
UGH!
KYA!
ENFORCEMENT FLASHER!!
ALL IMPACTS WITHIN TARGET AREA!
UWA!

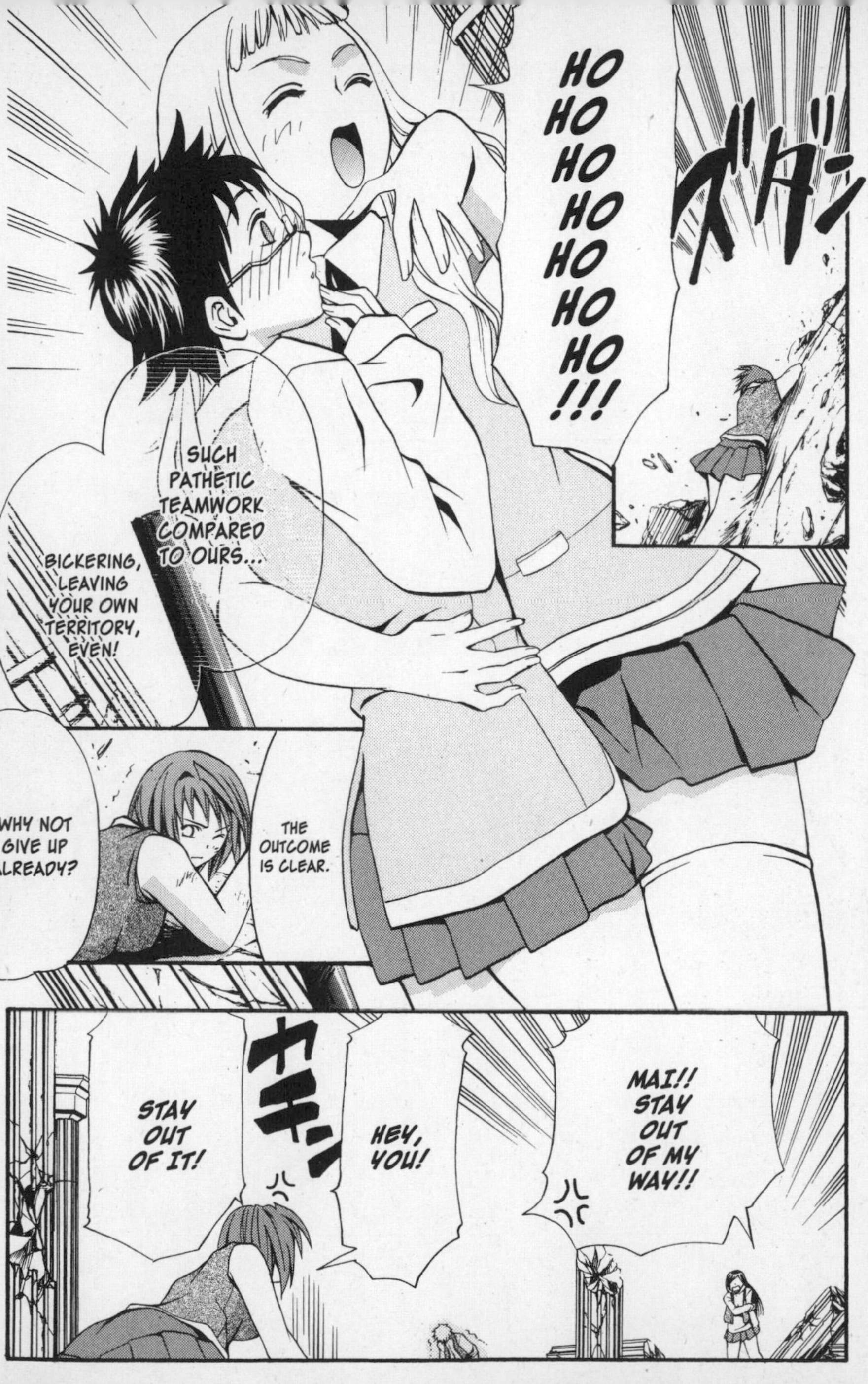
ズダン
HO HO HO HO HO HO HO!!!
SUCH PATHETIC TEAMWORK COMPARED TO OURS...
BICKERING, LEAVING YOUR OWN TERRITORY, EVEN!
THE OUTCOME IS CLEAR.
WHY NOT GIVE UP ALREADY?
MAI!! STAY OUT OF MY WAY!!
HEY, YOU!
カキン
STAY OUT OF IT!

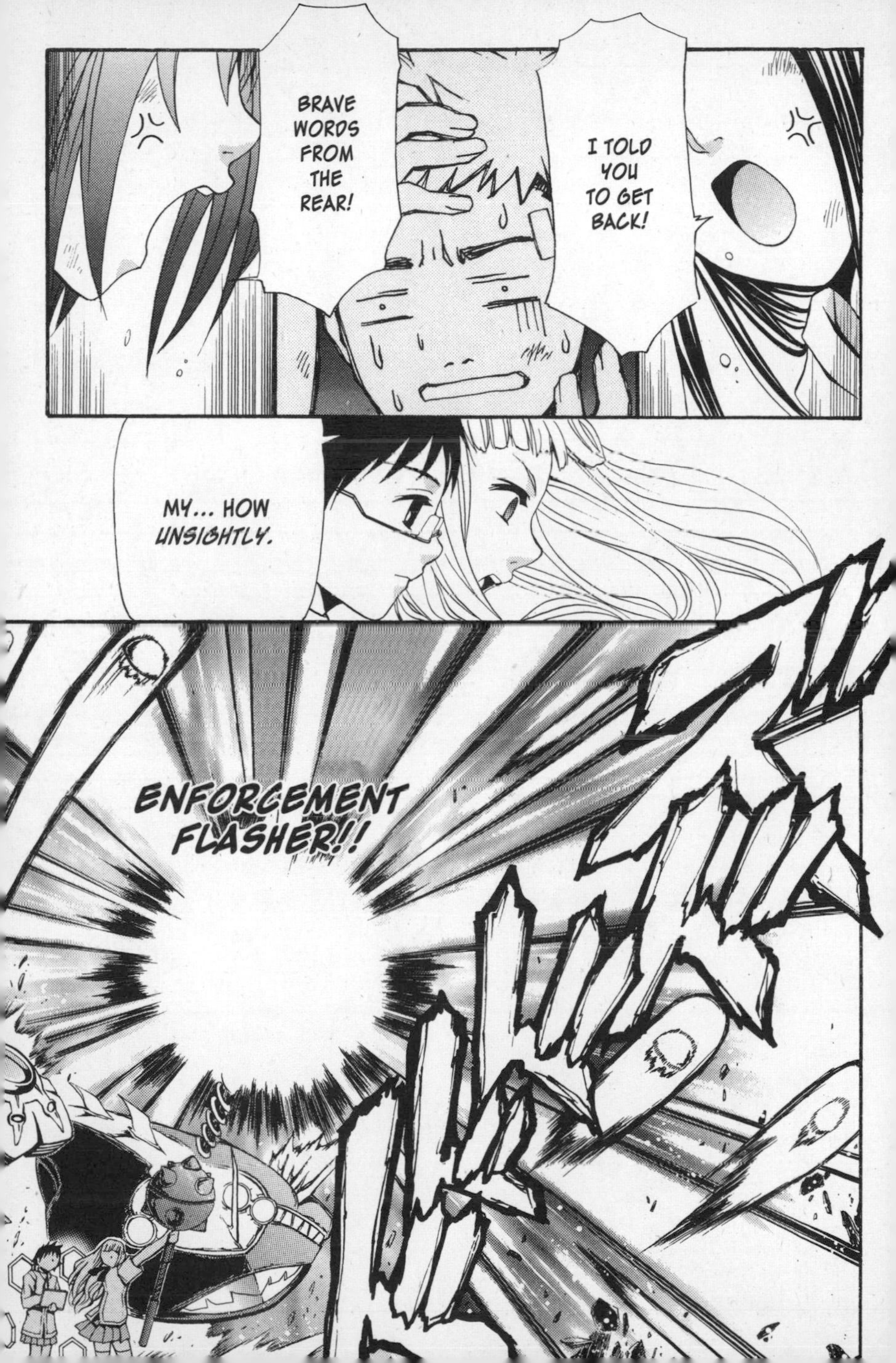
I TOLD YOU TO GET BACK!
BRAVE WORDS FROM THE REAR!
MY... HOW UNSIGHTLY.
ENFORCEMENT FLASHER!!

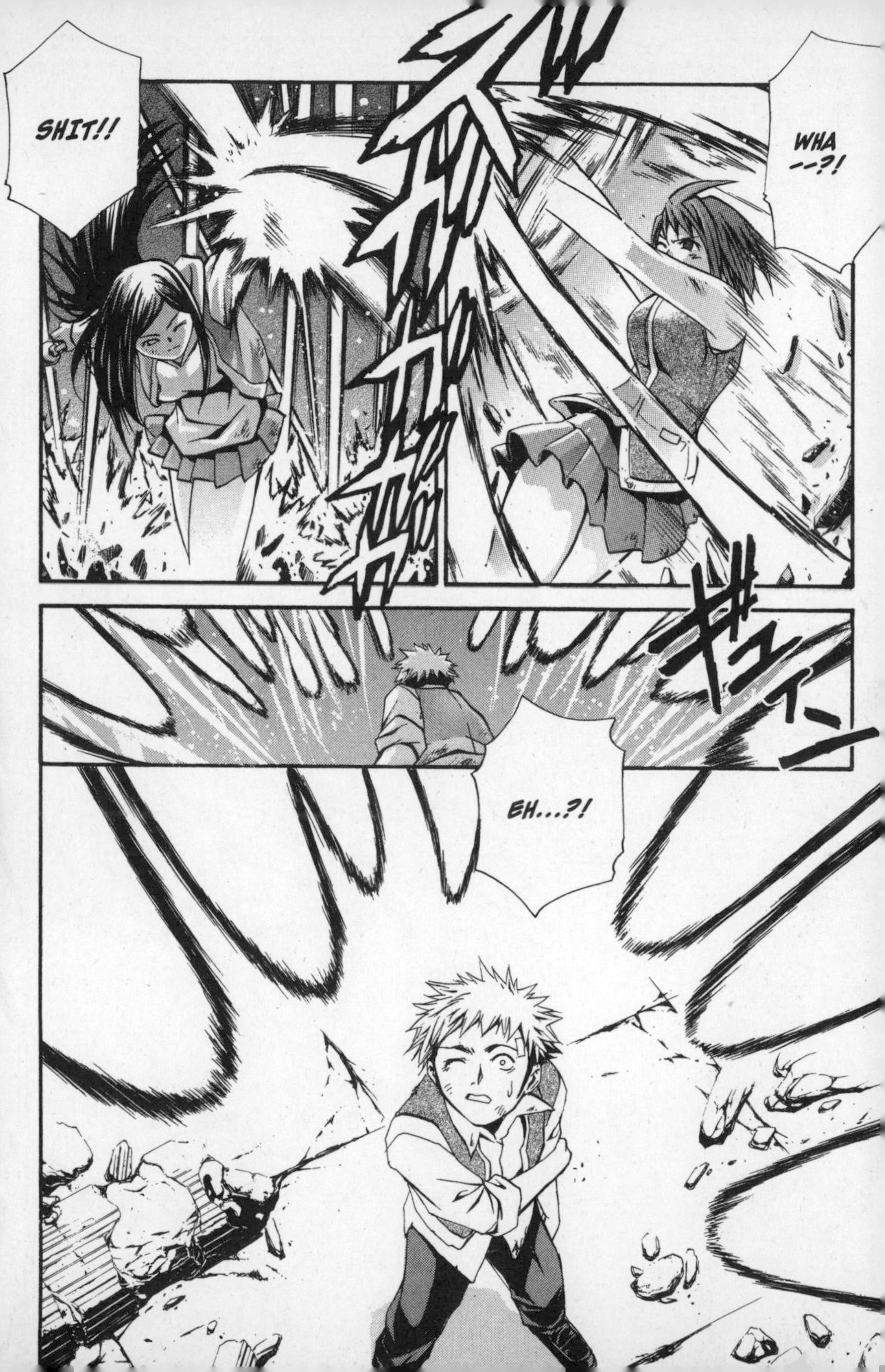
WHA--?!
SHIT!!
EH...?!

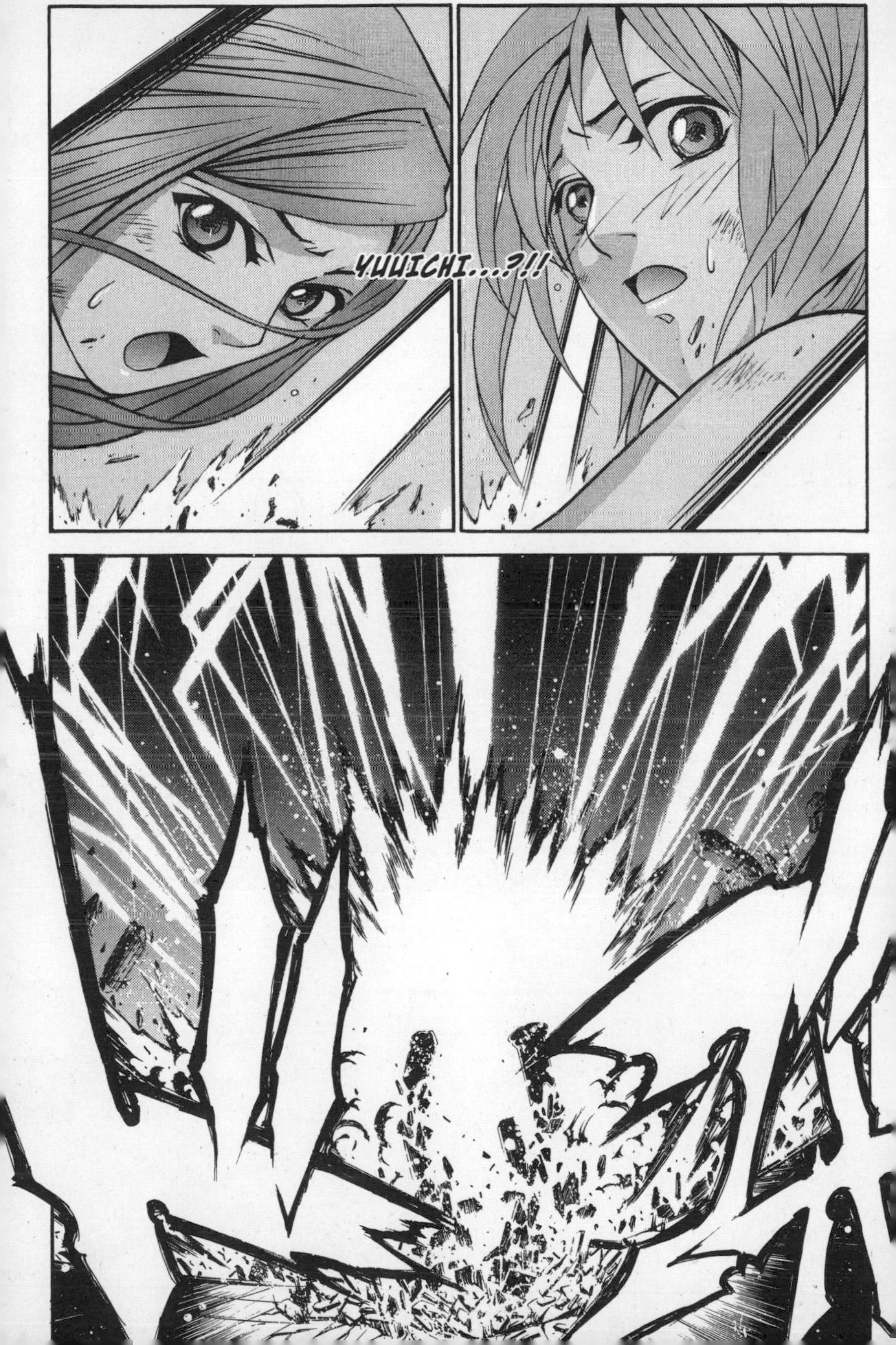
YUUICHI...?!!

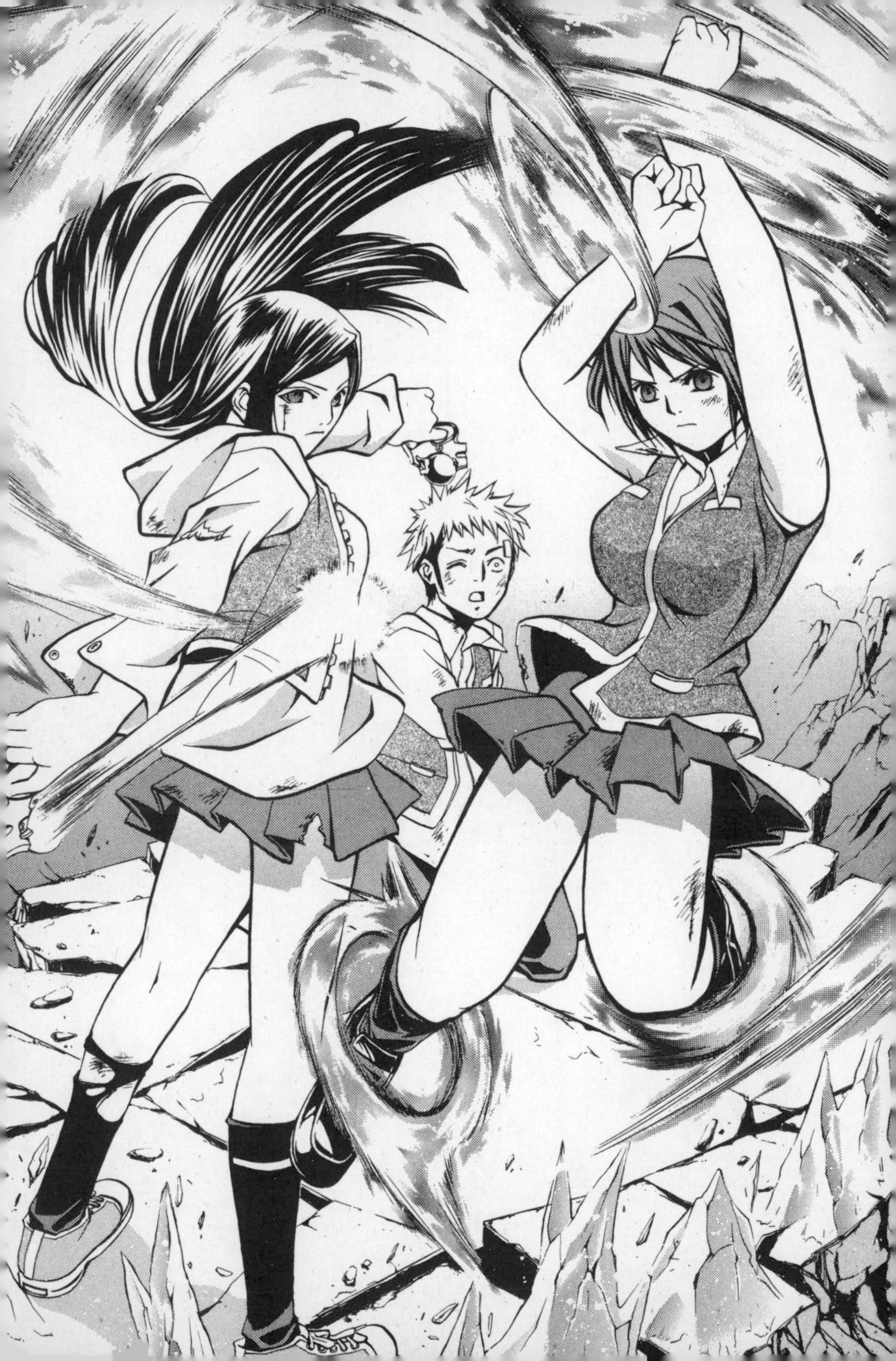

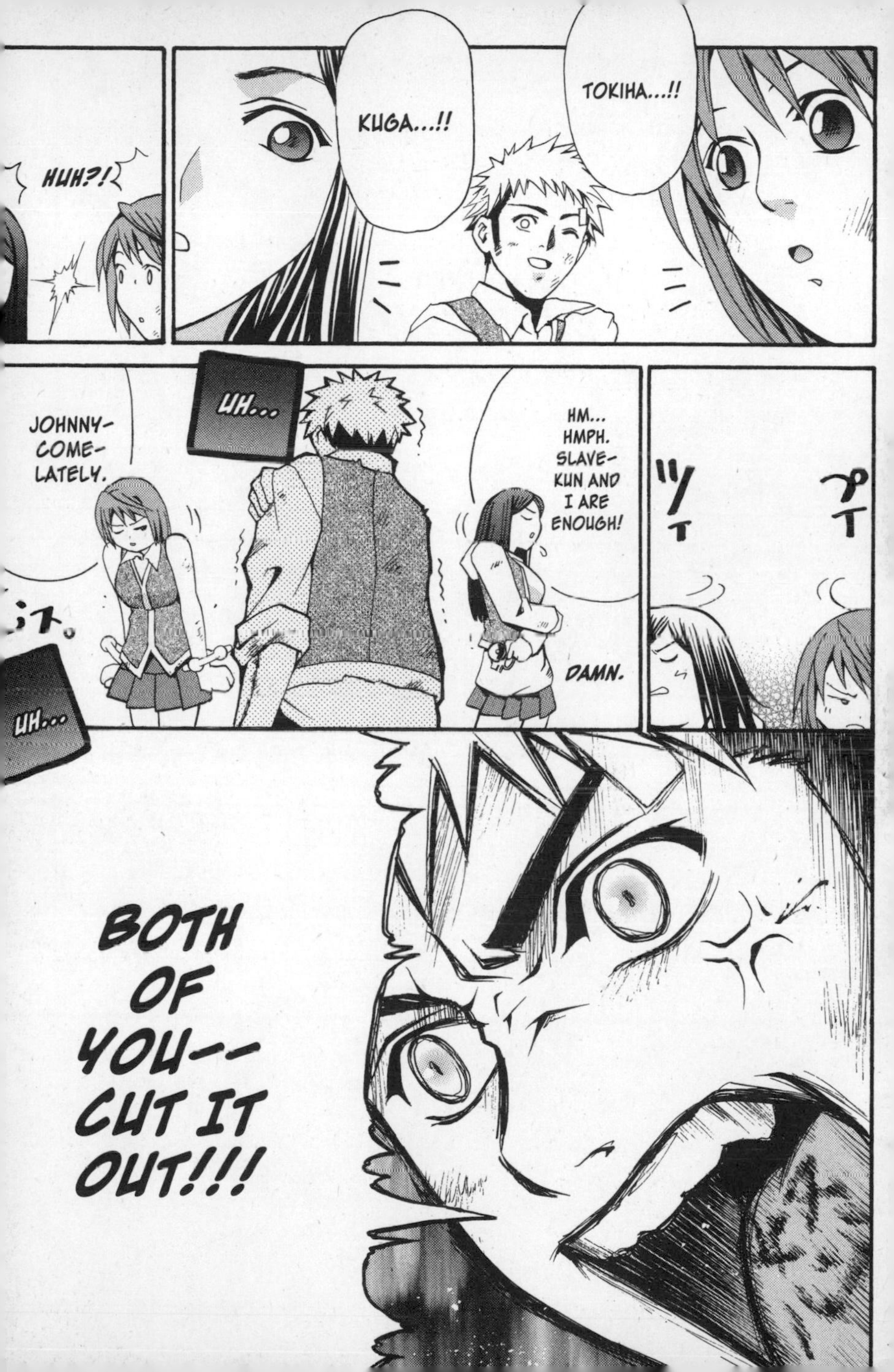
TOKIHA...!!
KUGA...!!
HUH?!
ツン
プイ
HM... HMPH. SLAVE-KUN AND I ARE ENOUGH!
DAMN.
UH...
JOHNNY-COME-LATELY.
UH...
BOTH OF YOU-- CUT IT OUT!!!

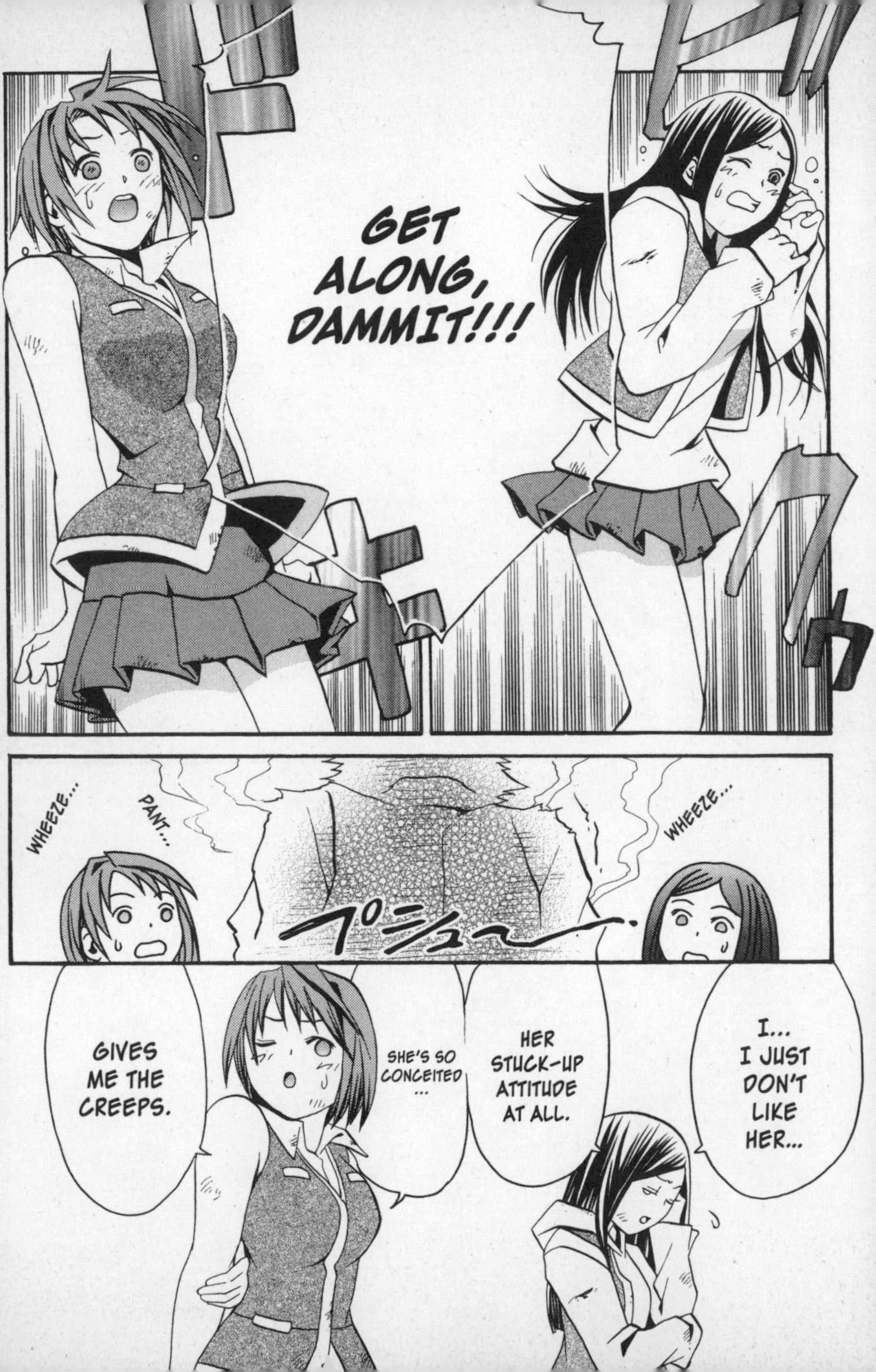
GET ALONG, DAMMIT!!!
WHEEZE...
PANT...
WHEEZE...
プシュ〜
I... I JUST DON'T LIKE HER...
HER STUCK-UP ATTITUDE AT ALL.
SHE'S SO CONCEITED ...
GIVES ME THE CREEPS.

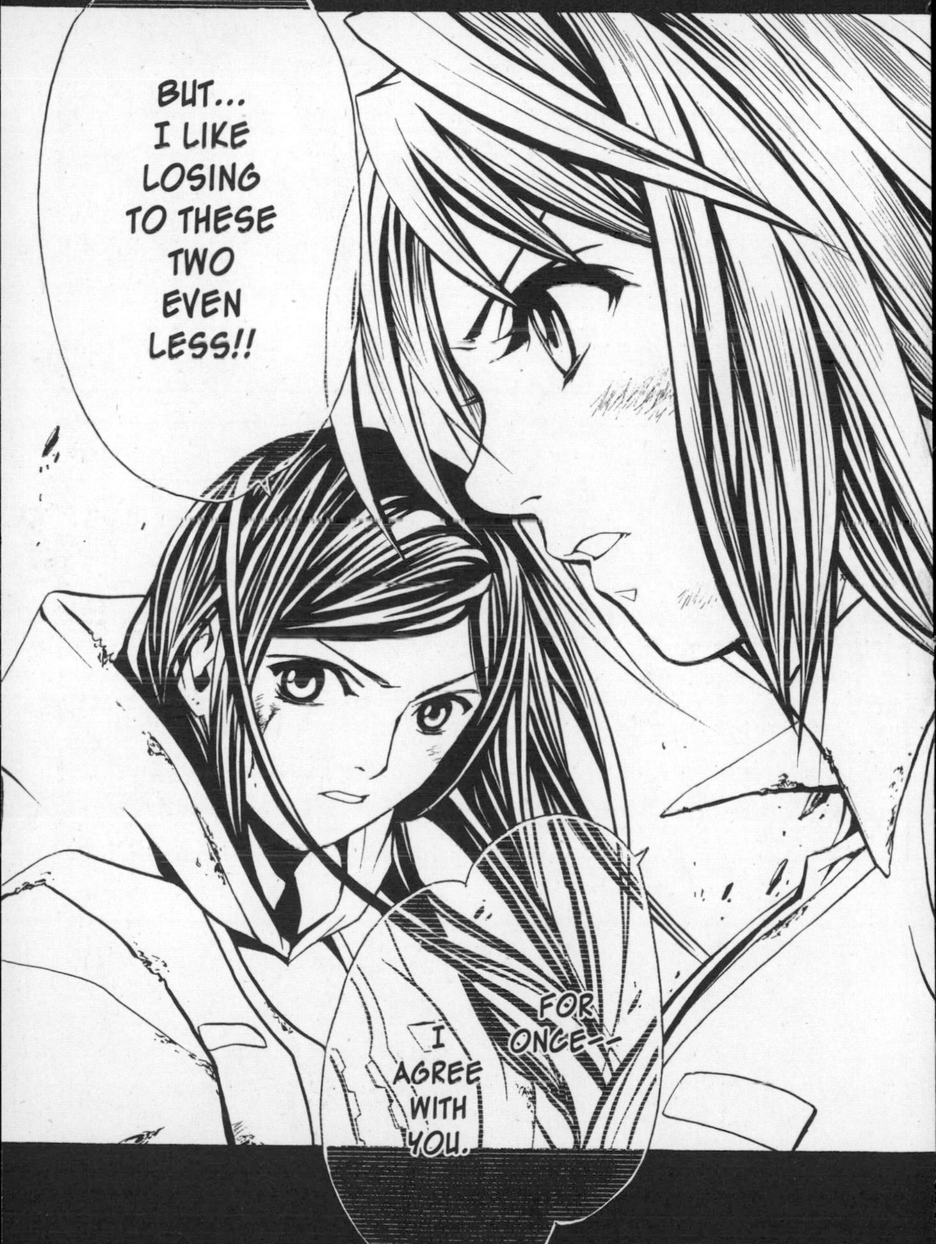
BUT... I LIKE LOSING TO THESE TWO EVEN LESS!!
FOR ONCE--
I AGREE WITH YOU.

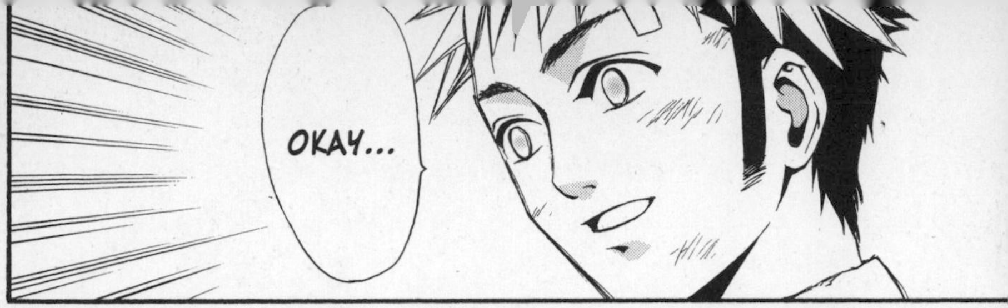
OKAY...
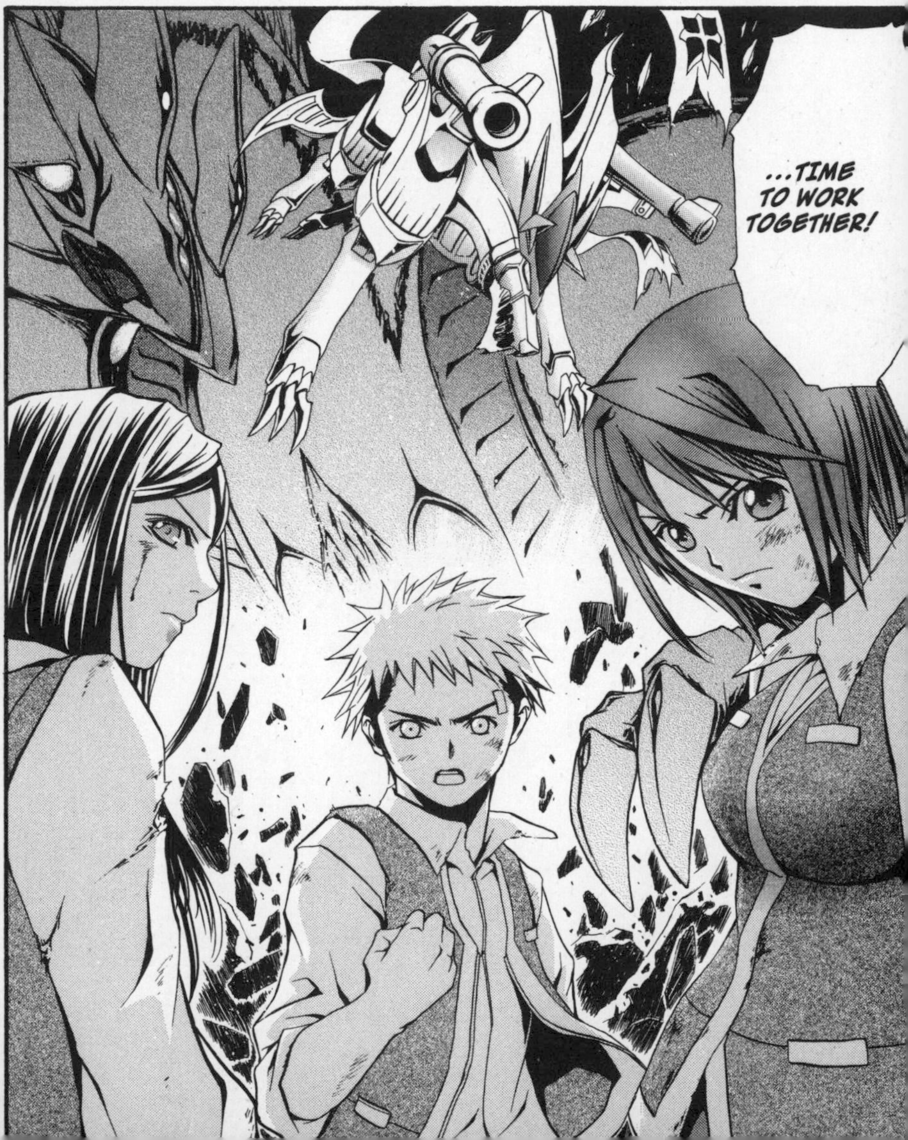
...TIME TO WORK TOGETHER!

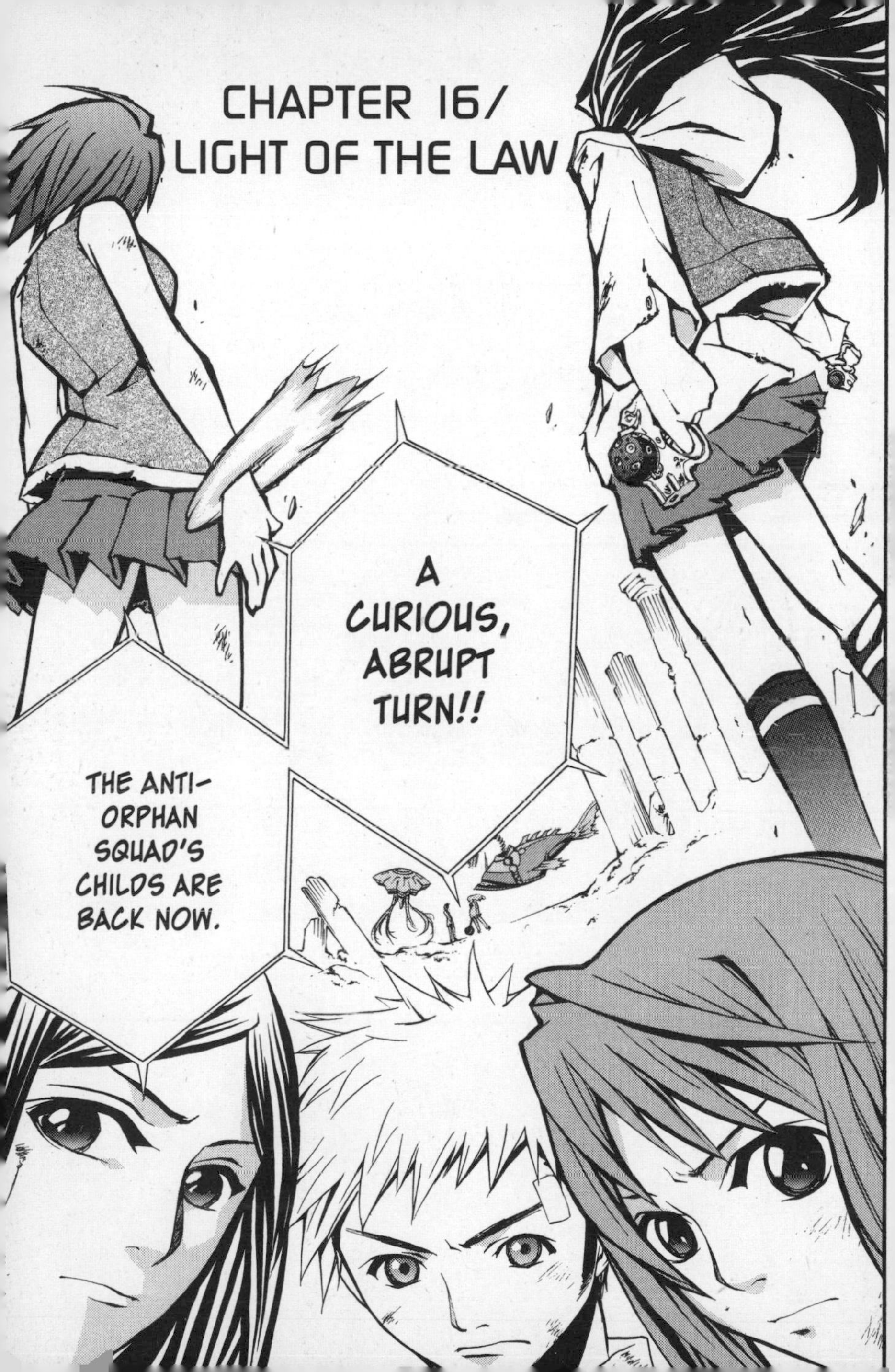
CHAPTER 16/
LIGHT OF THE LAW
A CURIOUS, ABRUPT TURN!!
THE ANTI-ORPHAN SQUAD'S CHILDS ARE BACK NOW.

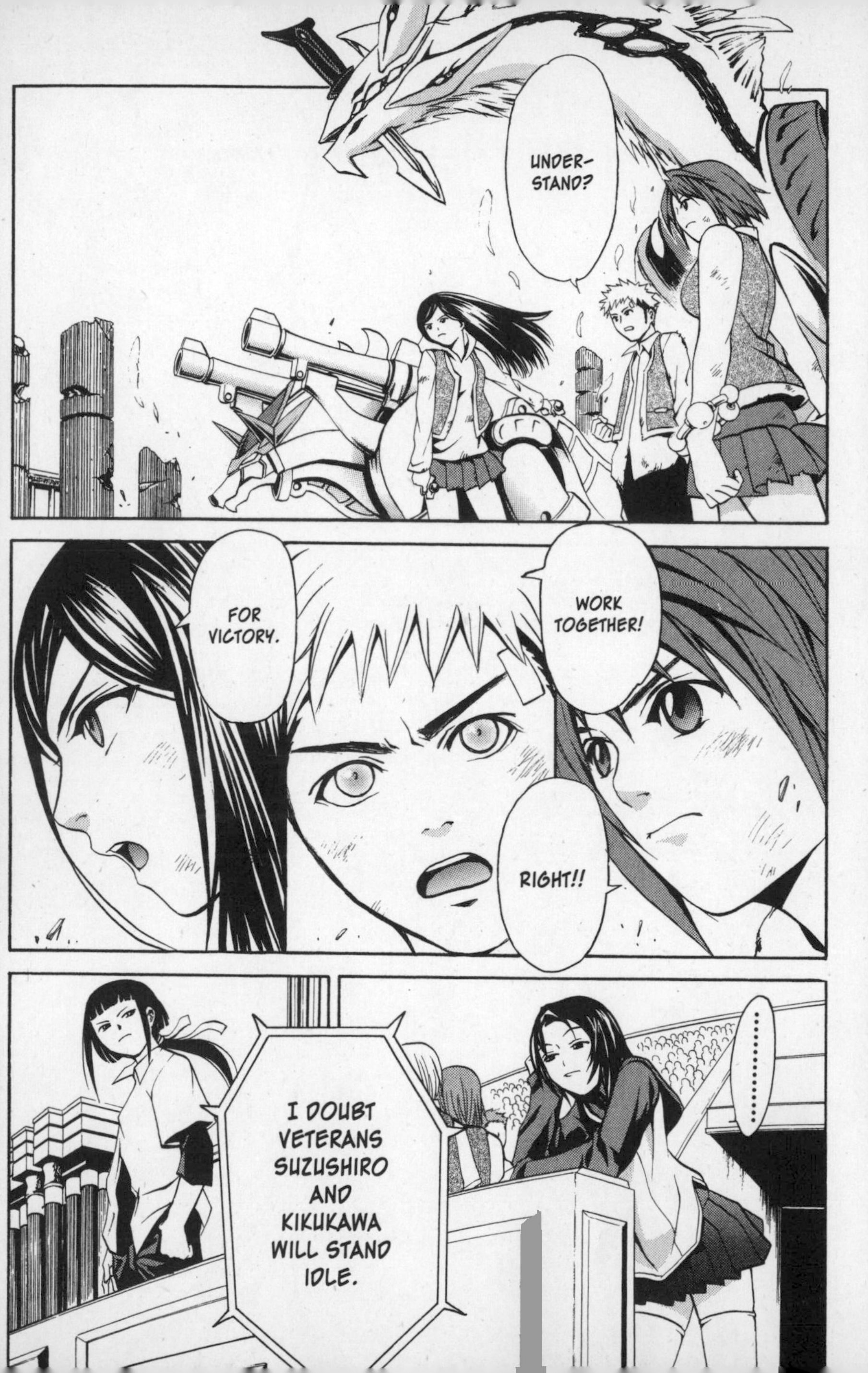
UNDER-STAND?
WORK TOGETHER!
FOR VICTORY.
RIGHT!!
....
I DOUBT VETERANS SUZUSHIRO AND KIKUKAWA WILL STAND IDLE.

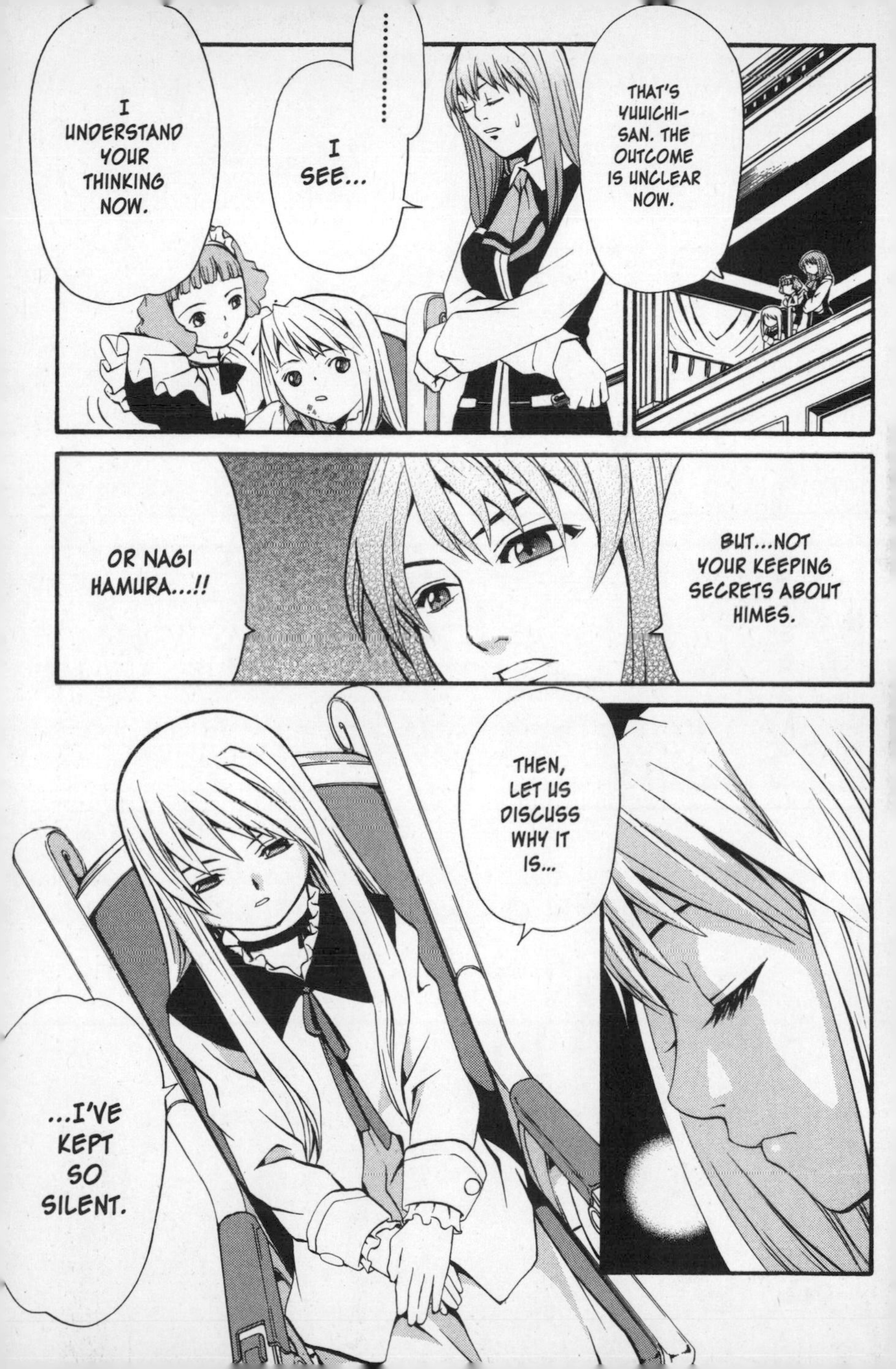
THAT'S YUUICHI-SAN. THE OUTCOME IS UNCLEAR NOW.
......
I SEE...
I UNDERSTAND YOUR THINKING NOW.
BUT...NOT YOUR KEEPING SECRETS ABOUT HIMES.
OR NAGI HAMURA...!!
THEN, LET US DISCUSS WHY IT IS...
...I'VE KEPT SO SILENT.

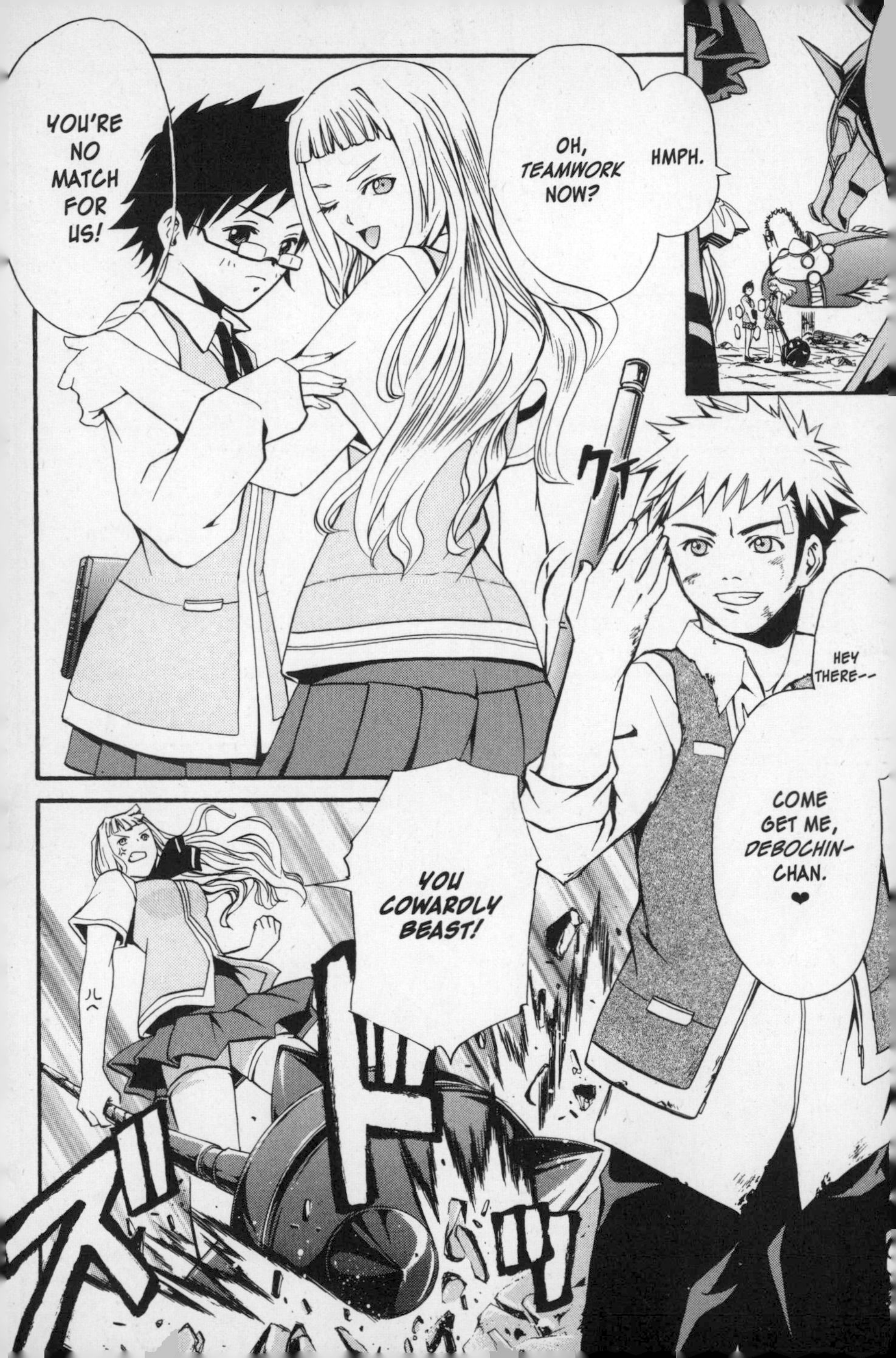
HMPH.
OH, TEAMWORK NOW?
YOU'RE NO MATCH FOR US!
HEY THERE--
COME GET ME, DEBOCHIN-CHAN. ❤
YOU COWARDLY BEAST!

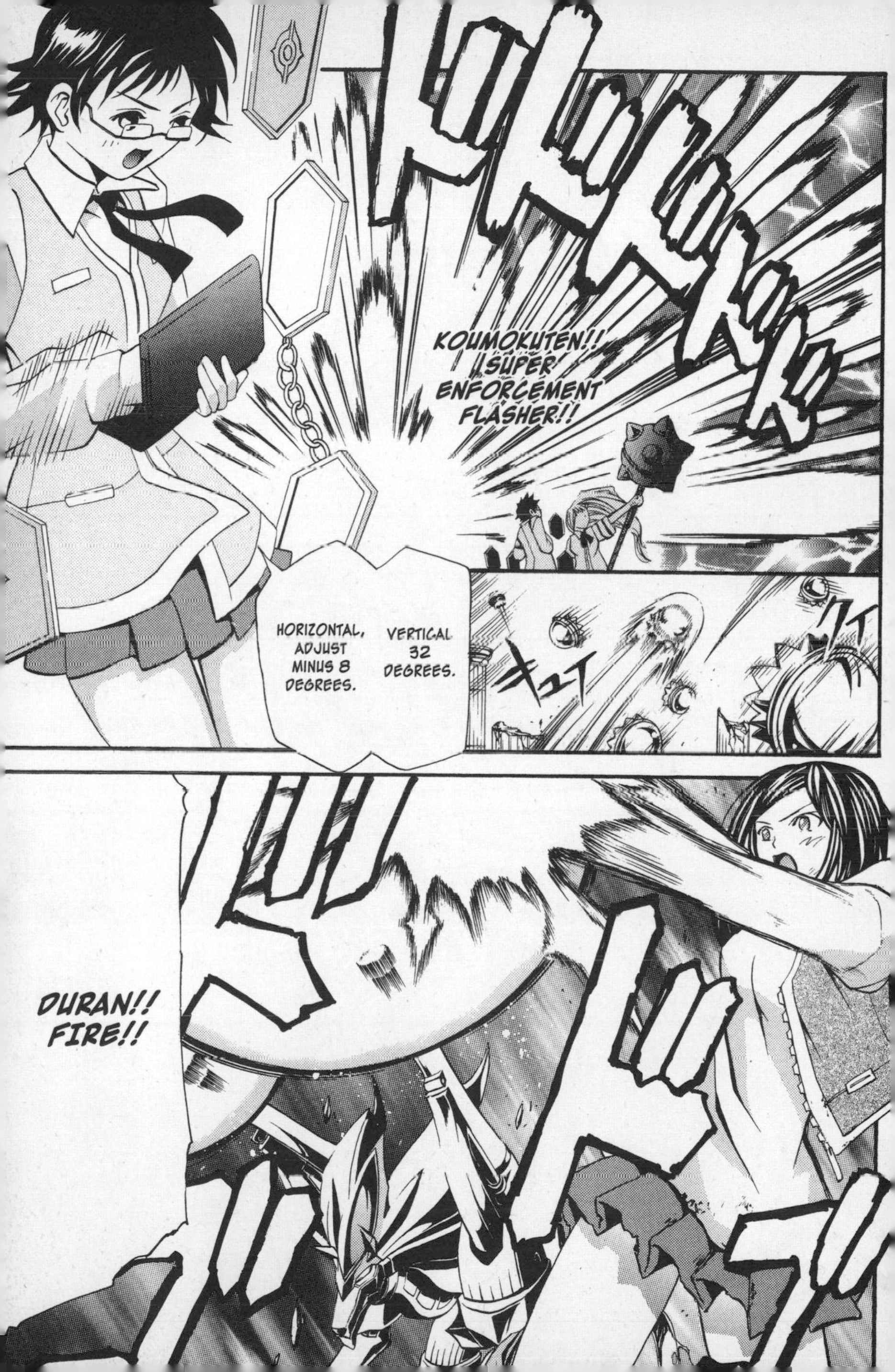
KOUMOKUTEN!! SUPER ENFORCEMENT FLASHER!!
HORIZONTAL, ADJUST MINUS 8 DEGREES.
VERTICAL 32 DEGREES.
DURAN!! FIRE!!

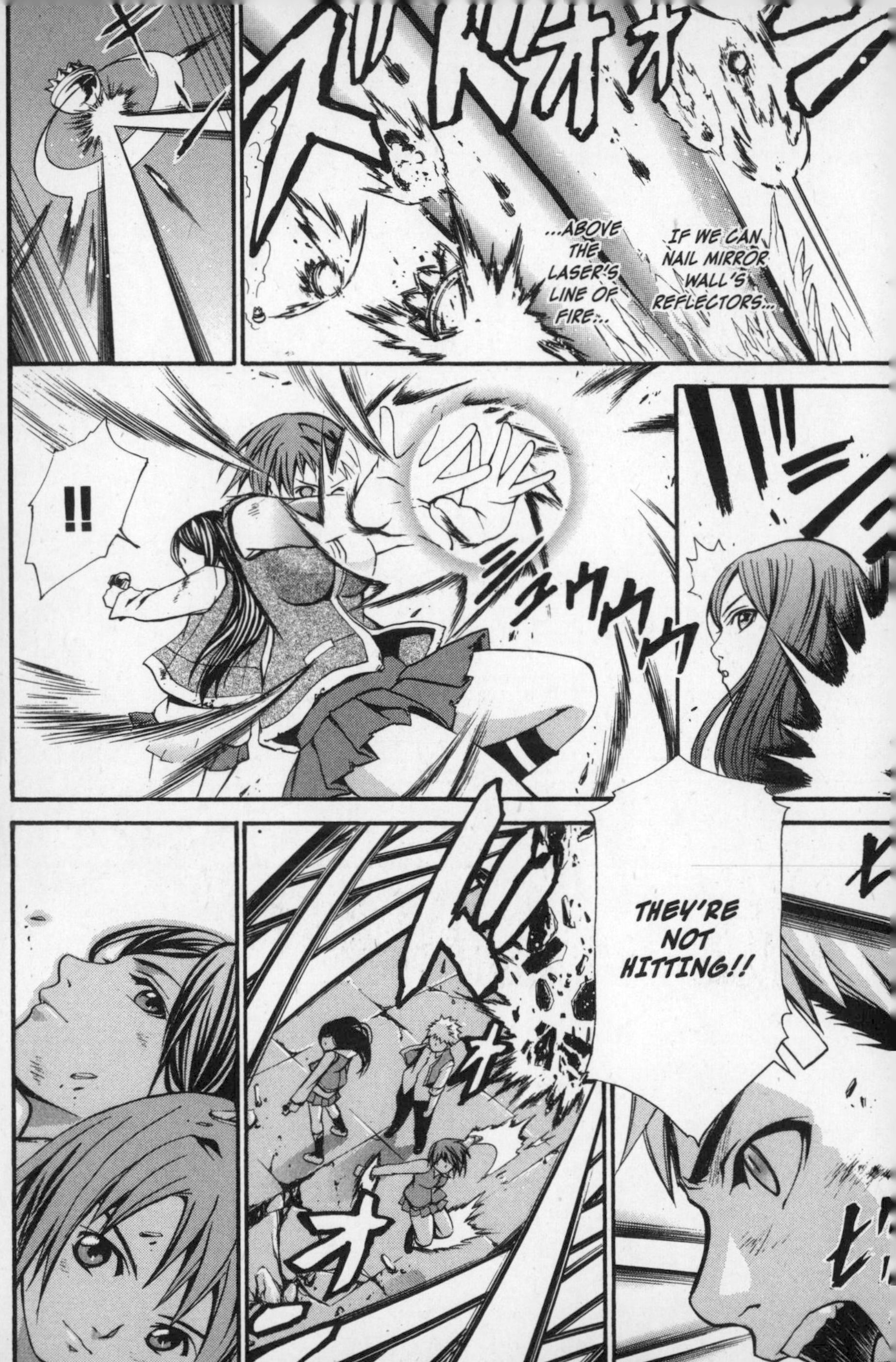
IF WE CAN NAIL MIRROR WALL'S REFLECTORS...
...ABOVE THE LASER'S LINE OF FIRE...
!!
THEY'RE NOT HITTING!!

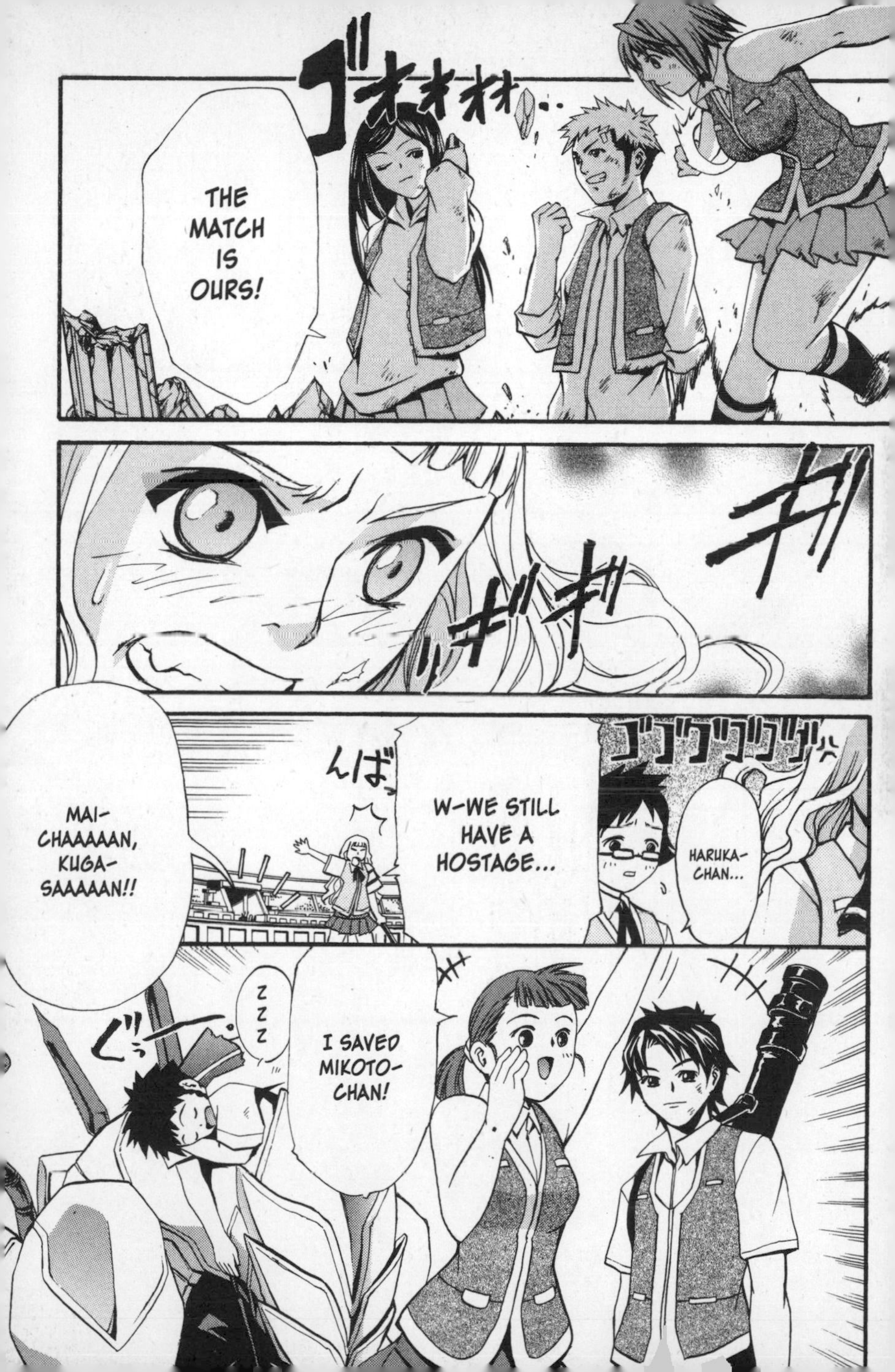
ゴオオオオ..
THE MATCH IS OURS!
HARUKA-CHAN...
W-WE STILL HAVE A HOSTAGE...
んばっ
MAI-CHAAAAAN, KUGA-SAAAAAN!!
I SAVED MIKOTO-CHAN!
ZZZ

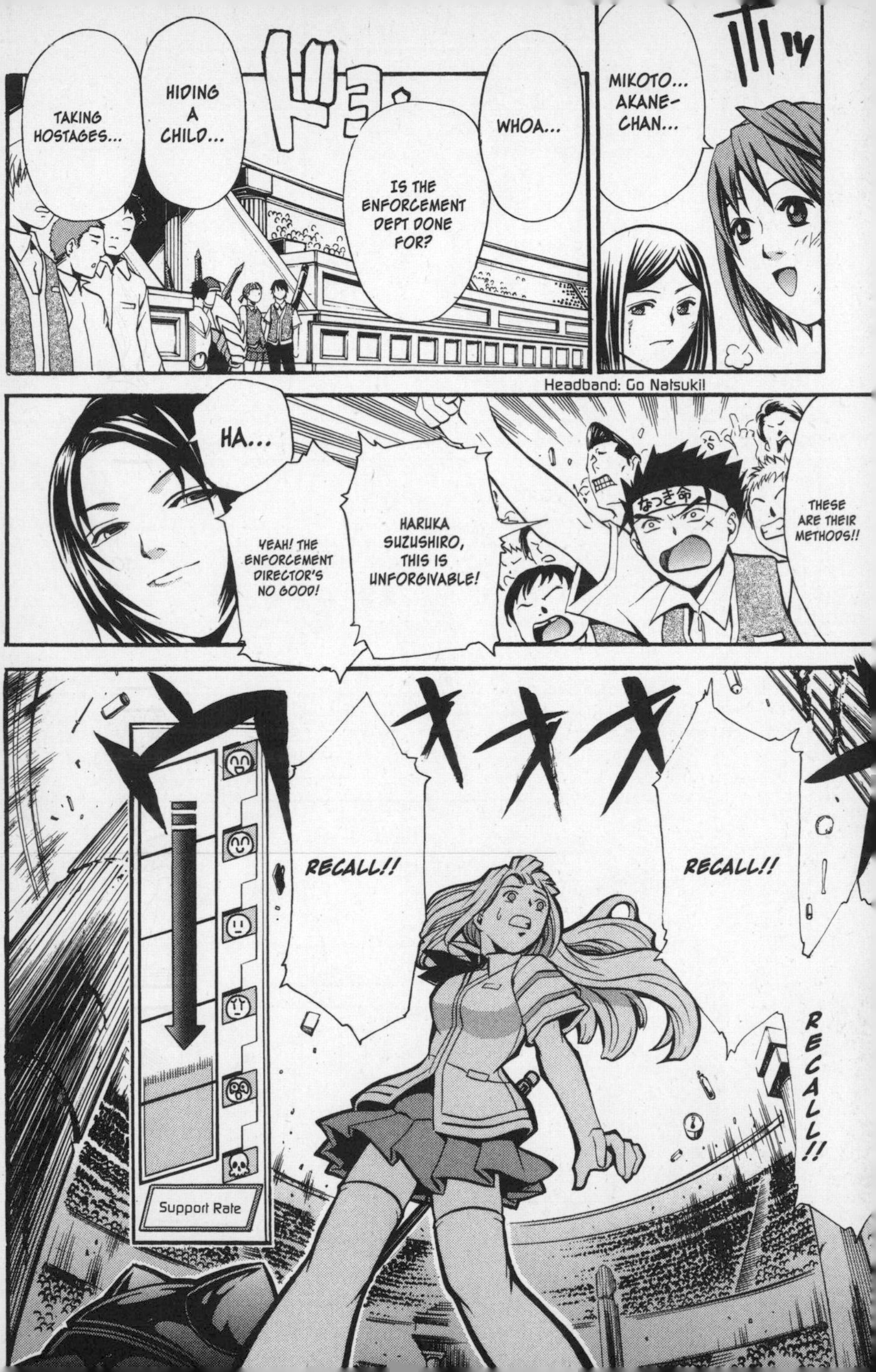
MIKOTO... AKANE-CHAN...
WHOA...
IS THE ENFORCEMENT DEPT DONE FOR?
HIDING A CHILD...
TAKING HOSTAGES...
Headband: Go Natsuki!
THESE ARE THEIR METHODS!!
なつき命
HARUKA SUZUSHIRO, THIS IS UNFORGIVABLE!
YEAH! THE ENFORCEMENT DIRECTOR'S NO GOOD!
HA...
RECALL!!
RECALL!!
RECALL!!
Support Rate

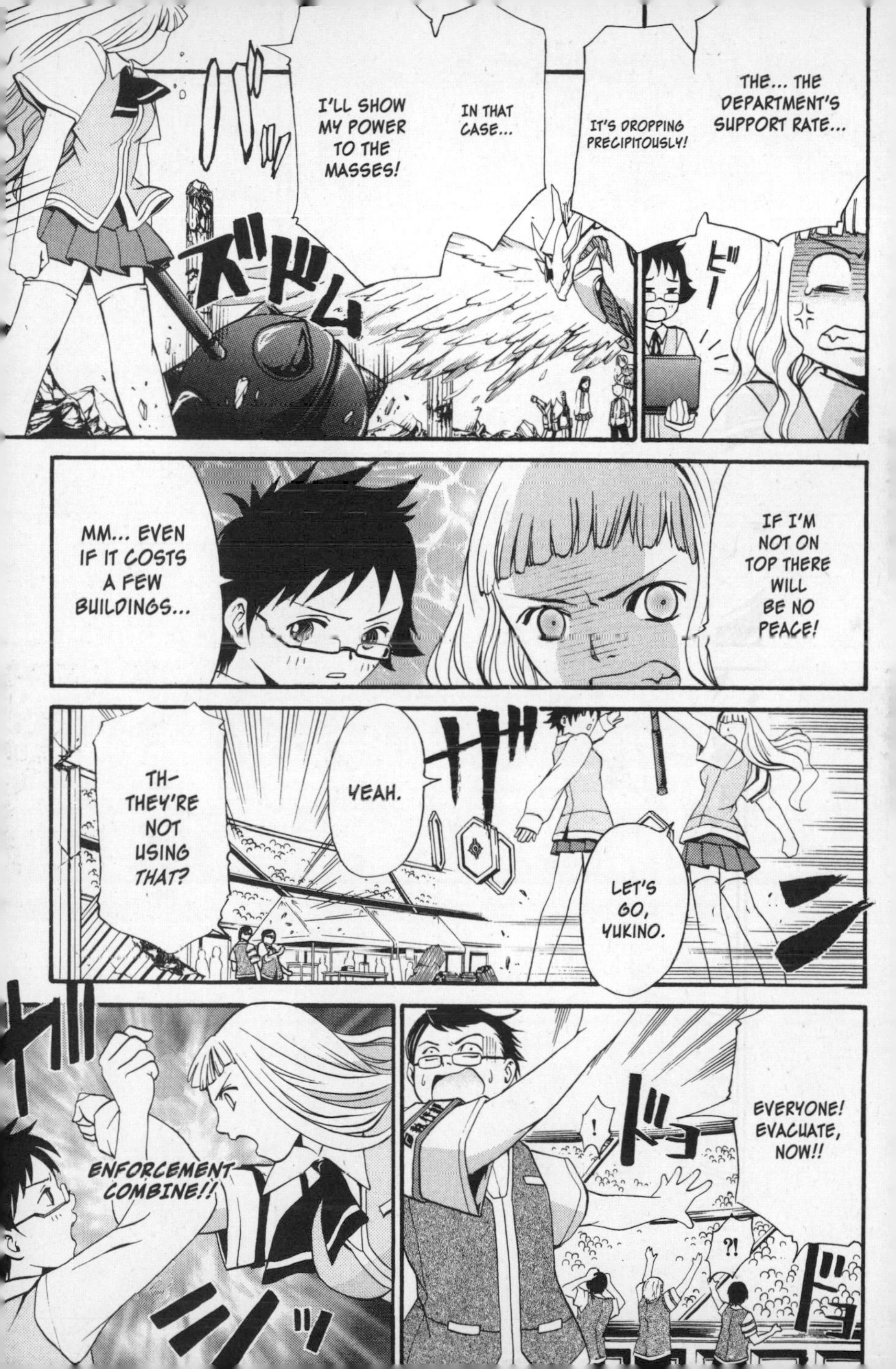
THE... THE DEPARTMENT'S SUPPORT RATE...
IT'S DROPPING PRECIPITOUSLY!
IN THAT CASE...
I'LL SHOW MY POWER TO THE MASSES!
ズドム
IF I'M NOT ON TOP THERE WILL BE NO PEACE!
MM... EVEN IF IT COSTS A FEW BUILDINGS...
LET'S GO, YUKINO.
YEAH.
TH- THEY'RE NOT USING THAT?
EVERYONE! EVACUATE, NOW!!
!
?!
ENFORCEMENT COMBINE!!

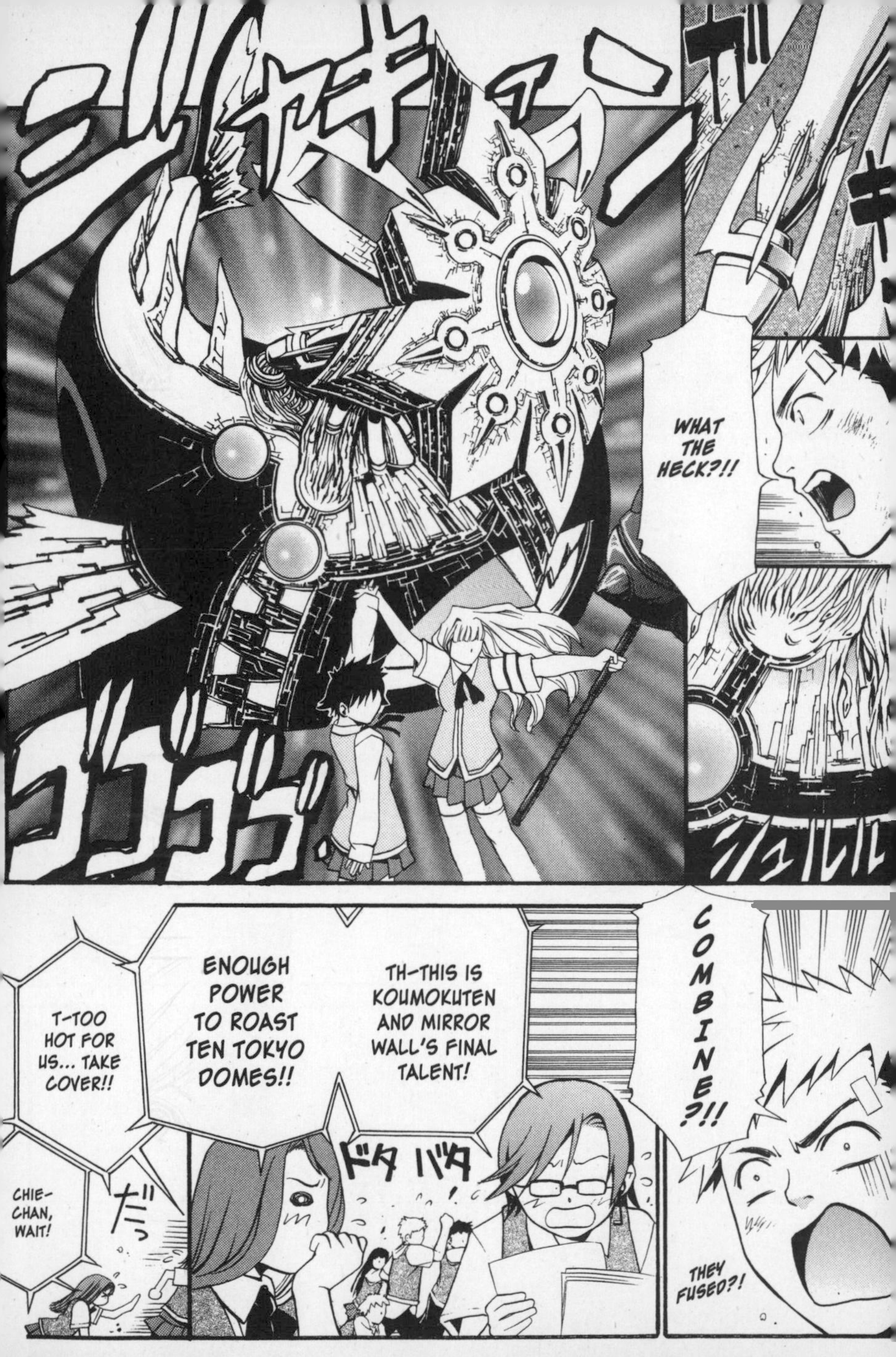

WHAT THE HECK?!!
COMBINE?!!
THEY FUSED?!
TH-THIS IS KOUMOKUTEN AND MIRROR WALL'S FINAL TALENT!
ENOUGH POWER TO ROAST TEN TOKYO DOMES!!
ドタ バタ
T-TOO HOT FOR US... TAKE COVER!!
CHIE-CHAN, WAIT!
だっ

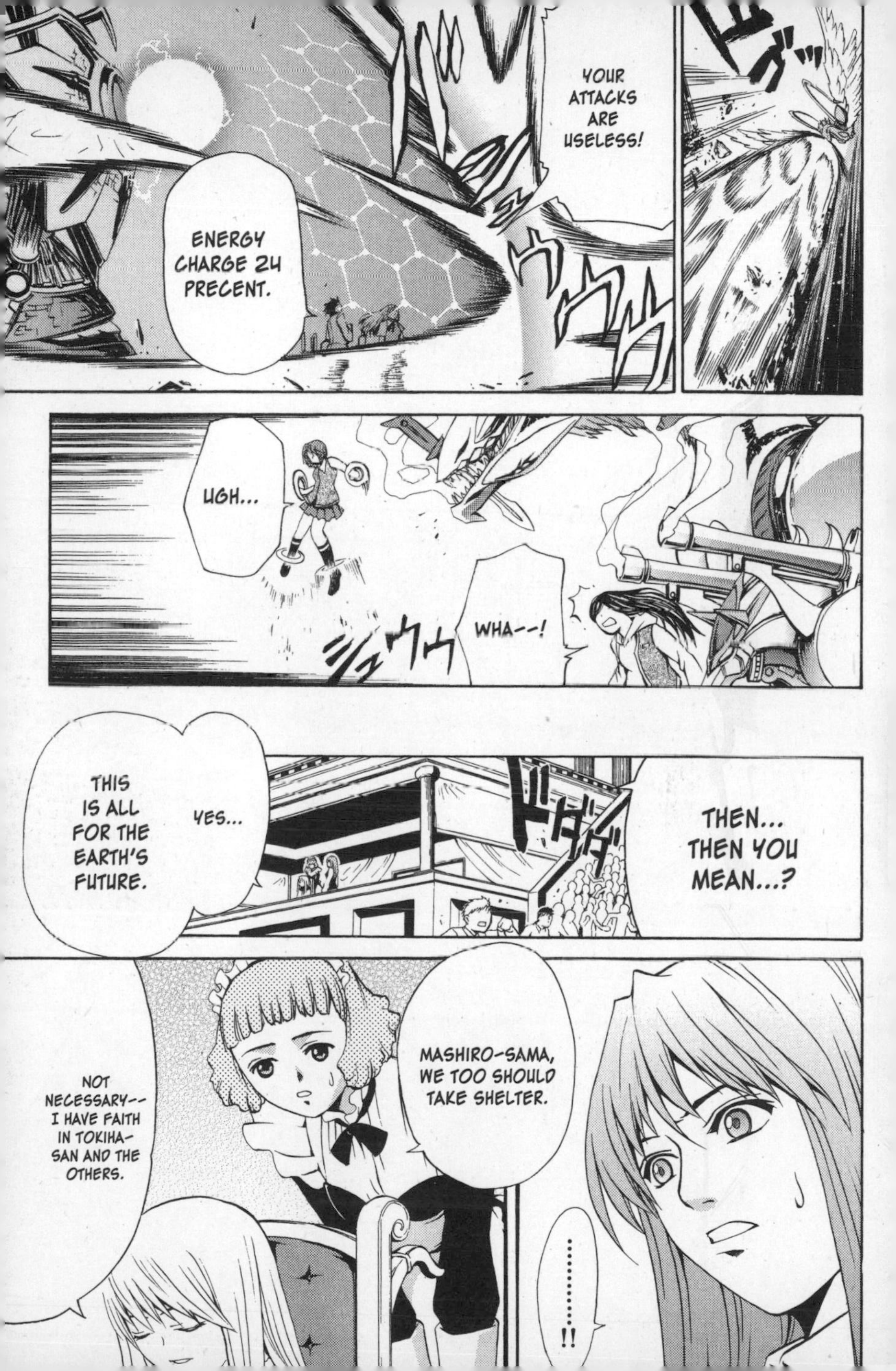
YOUR ATTACKS ARE USELESS!
ENERGY CHARGE 24 PRECENT.
WHA--!
UGH...
THEN... THEN YOU MEAN...?
YES...
THIS IS ALL FOR THE EARTH'S FUTURE.
MASHIRO-SAMA, WE TOO SHOULD TAKE SHELTER.
NOT NECESSARY-- I HAVE FAITH IN TOKIHA-SAN AND THE OTHERS.
......!!

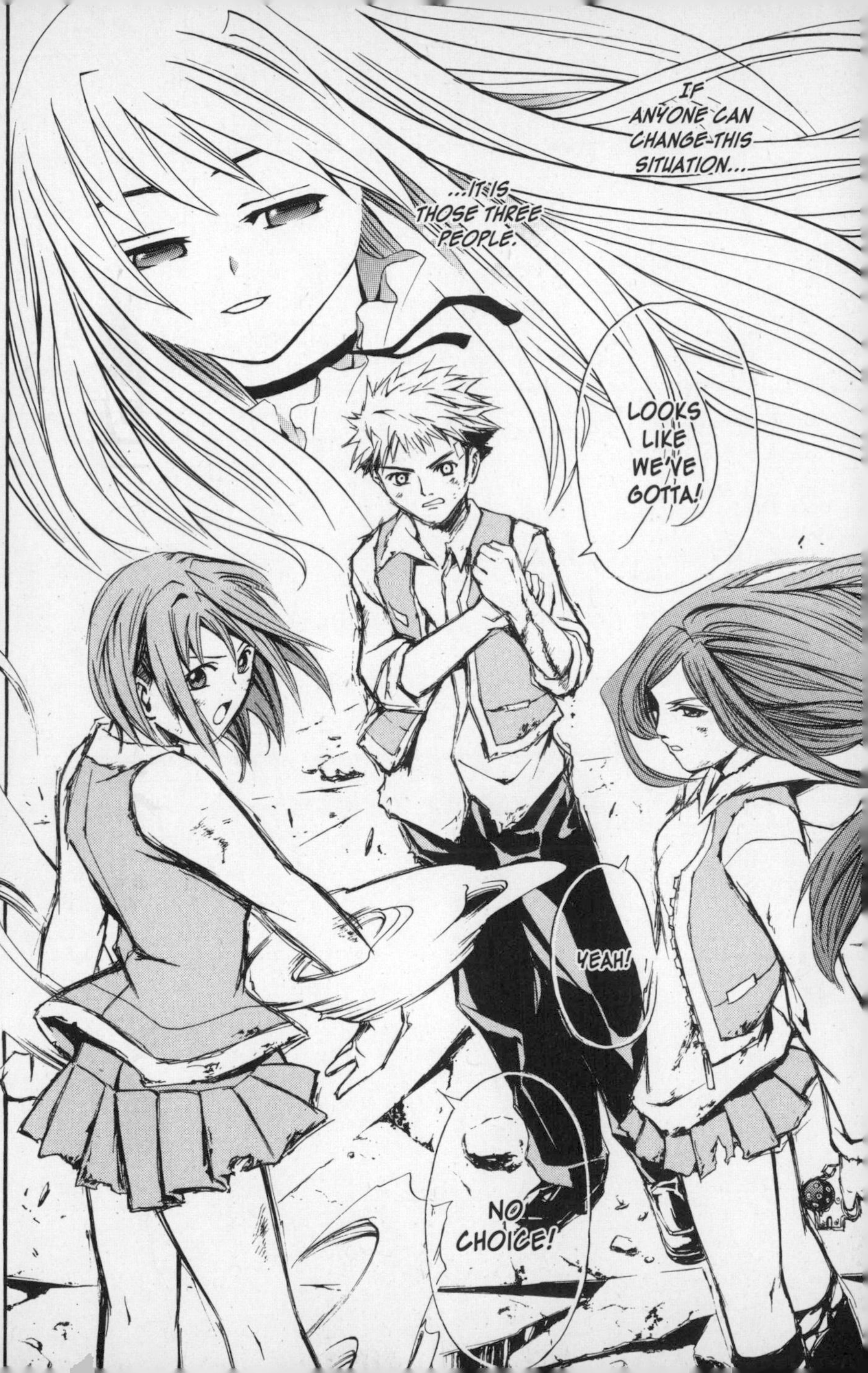
IF ANYONE CAN CHANGE THIS SITUATION...
...IT IS THOSE THREE PEOPLE.
LOOKS LIKE WE'VE GOTTA!
YEAH!
NO CHOICE!

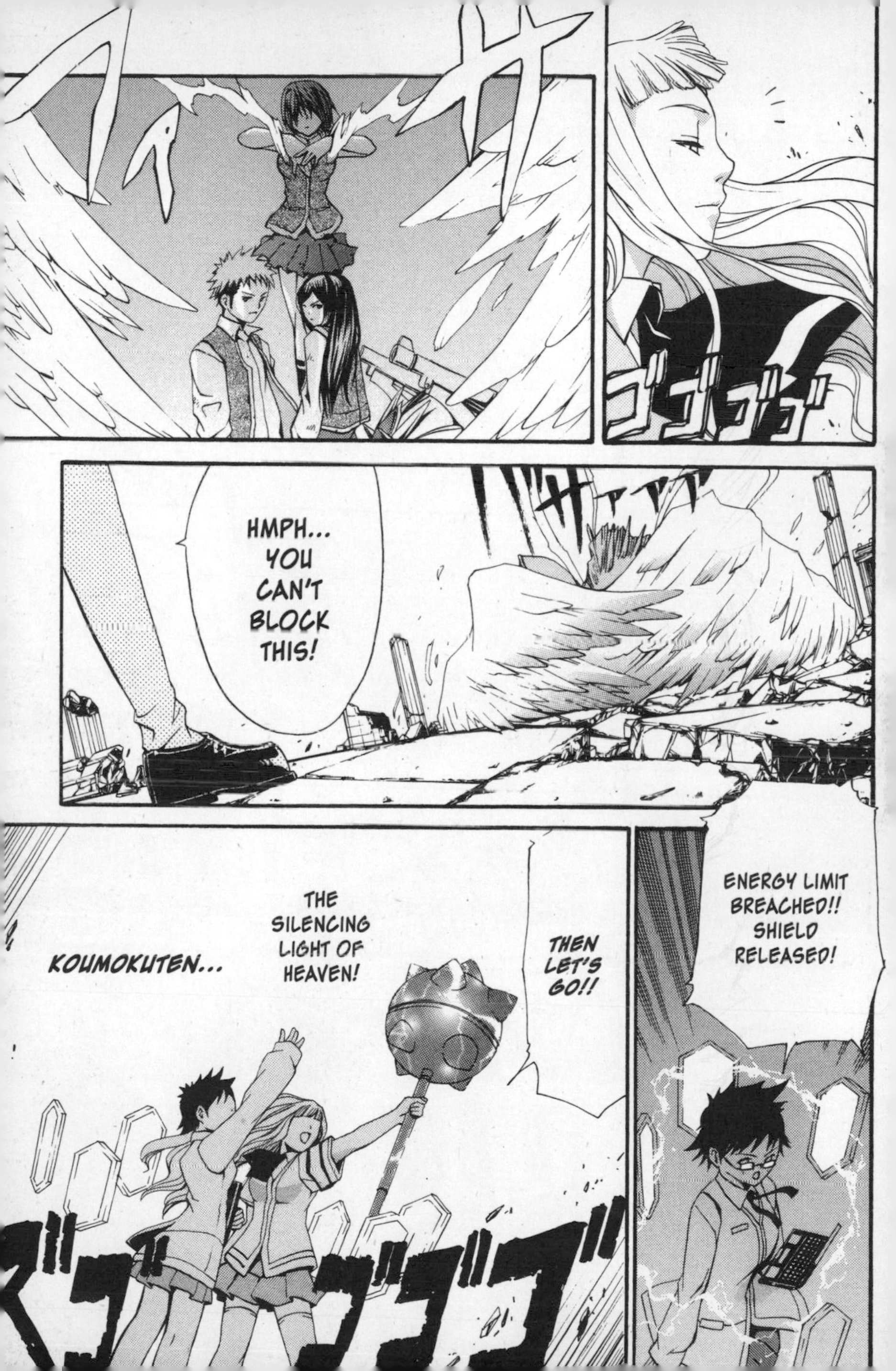
HMPH... YOU CAN'T BLOCK THIS!
ENERGY LIMIT BREACHED!! SHIELD RELEASED!
THEN LET'S GO!!
THE SILENCING LIGHT OF HEAVEN!
KOUMOKUTEN...

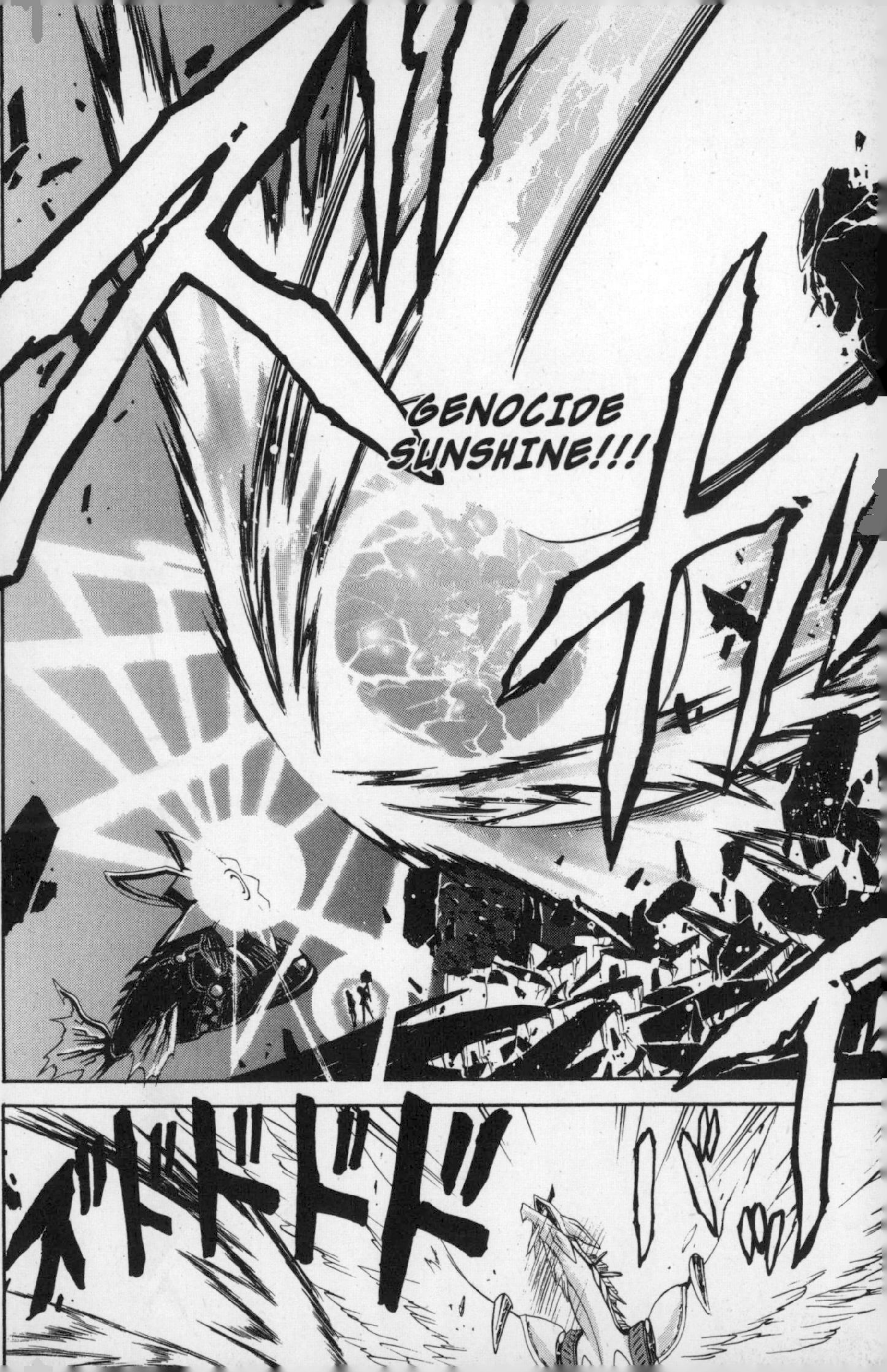
GENOCIDE SUNSHINE!!!
ズドドドド

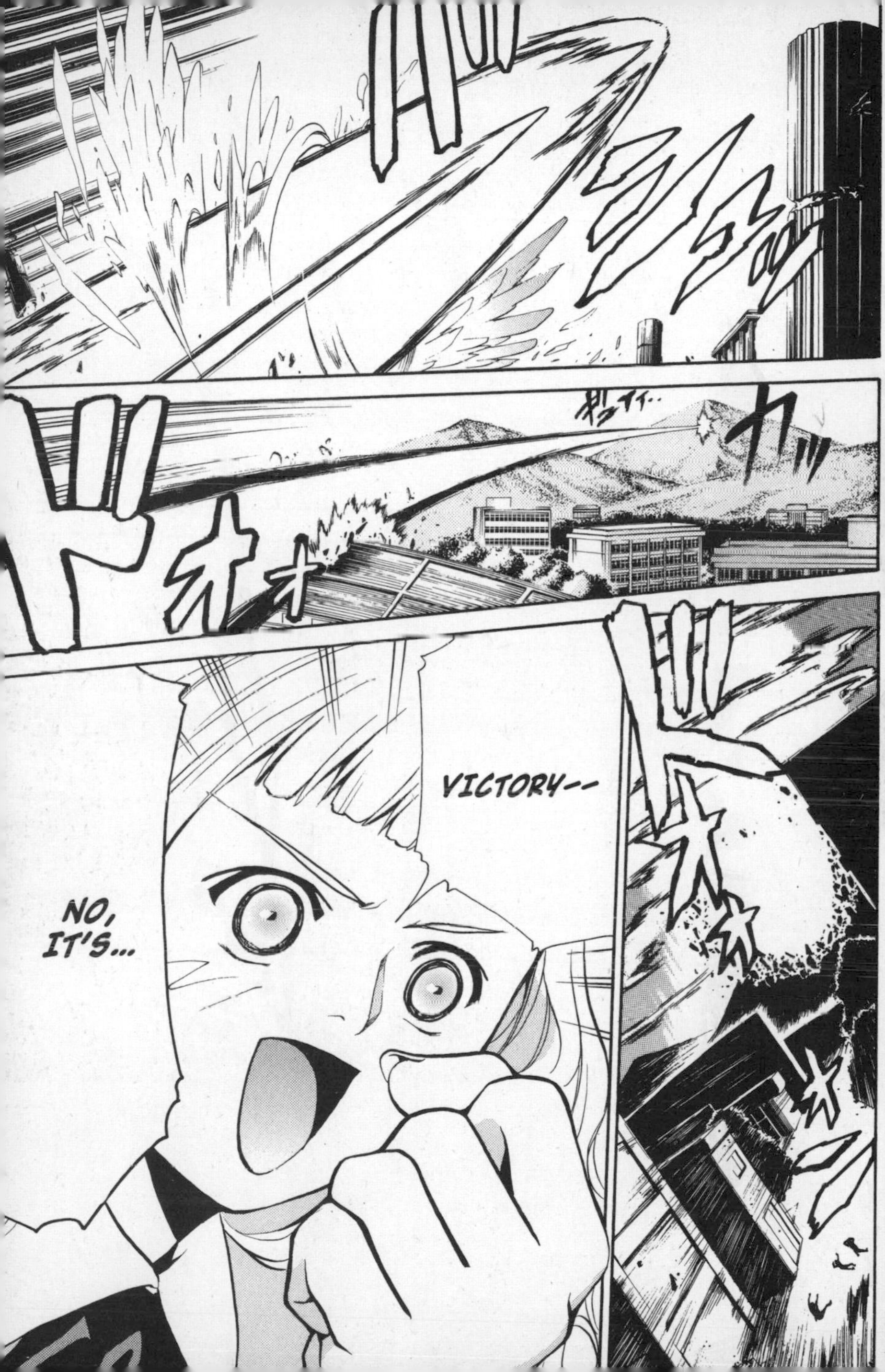
VICTORY--
NO, IT'S...

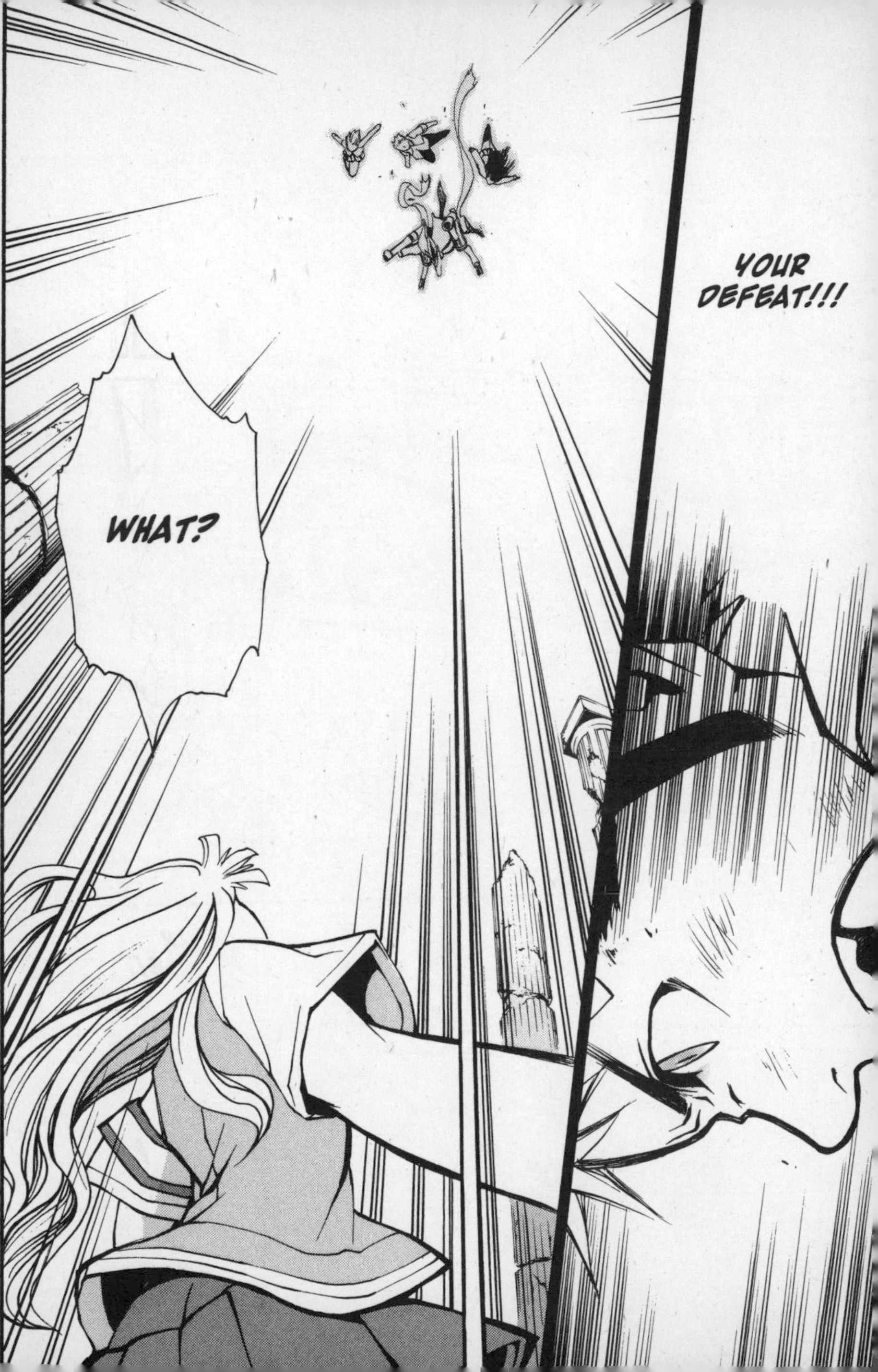
YOUR DEFEAT!!!
WHAT?

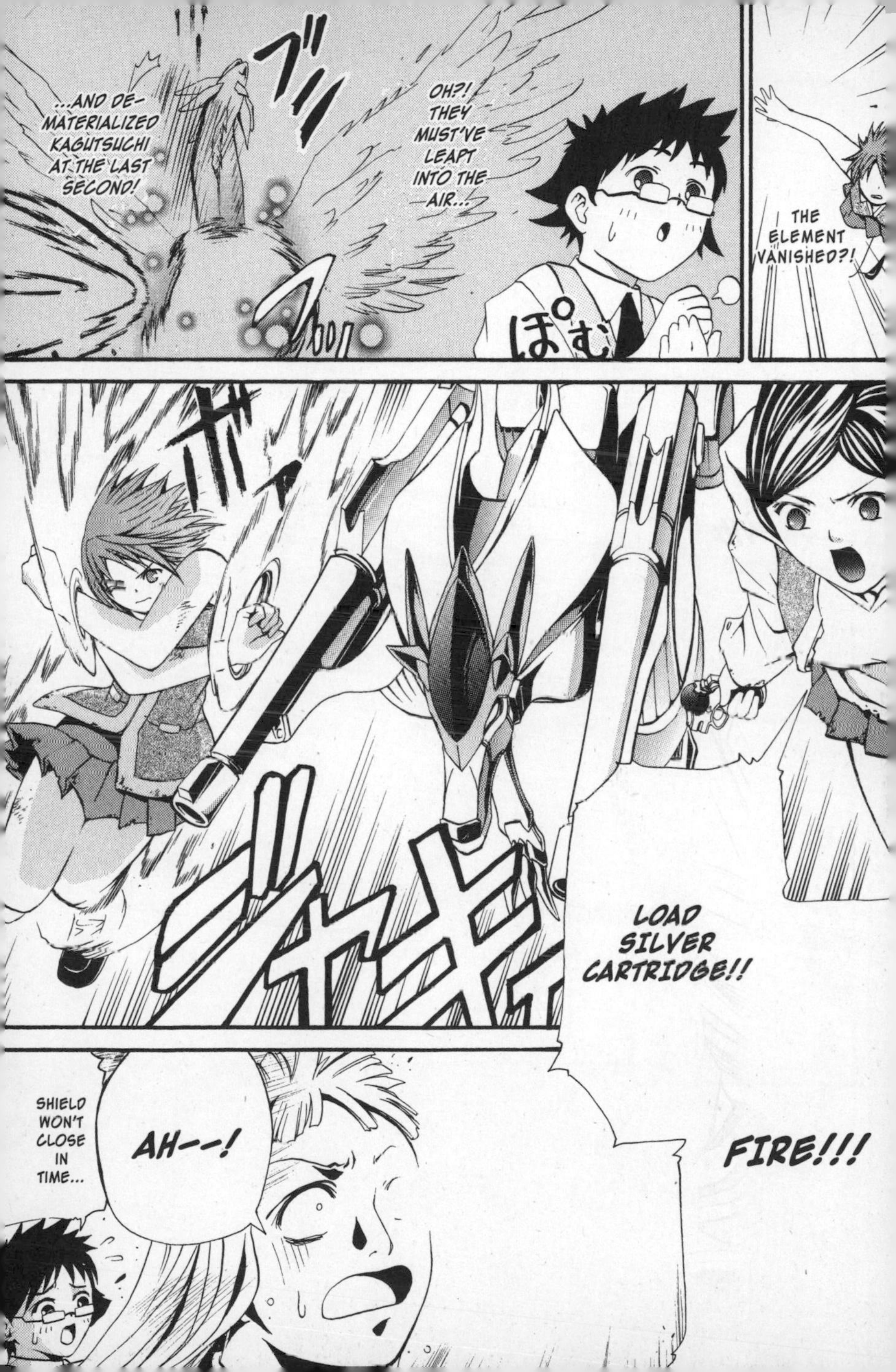
THE ELEMENT VANISHED?!
OH?! THEY MUST'VE LEAPT INTO THE AIR...
...AND DE-MATERIALIZED KAGUTSUCHI AT THE LAST SECOND!
ぽむ
LOAD SILVER CARTRIDGE!!
FIRE!!!
AH--!
SHIELD WON'T CLOSE IN TIME...

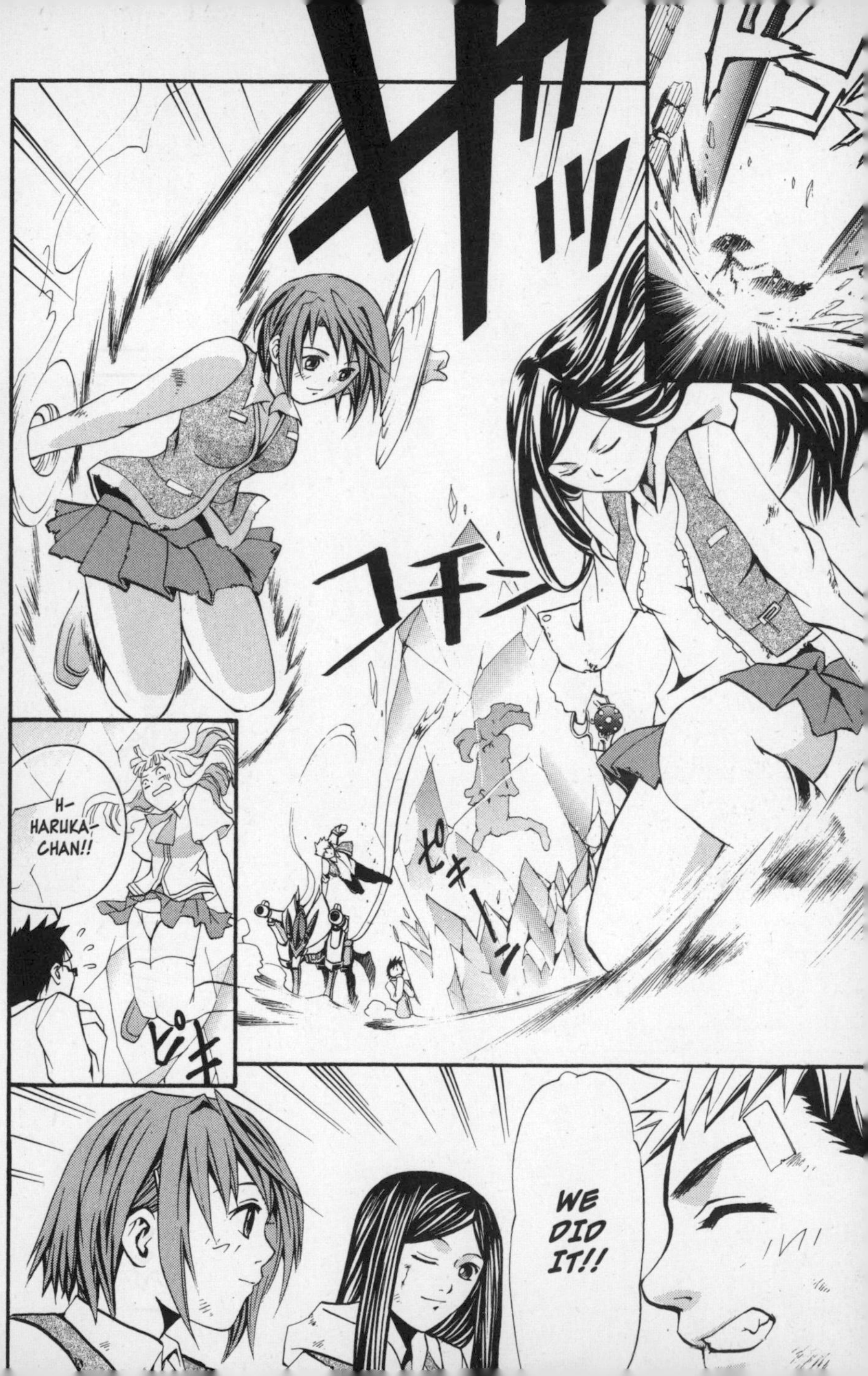
H-HARUKA-CHAN!!
WE DID IT!!

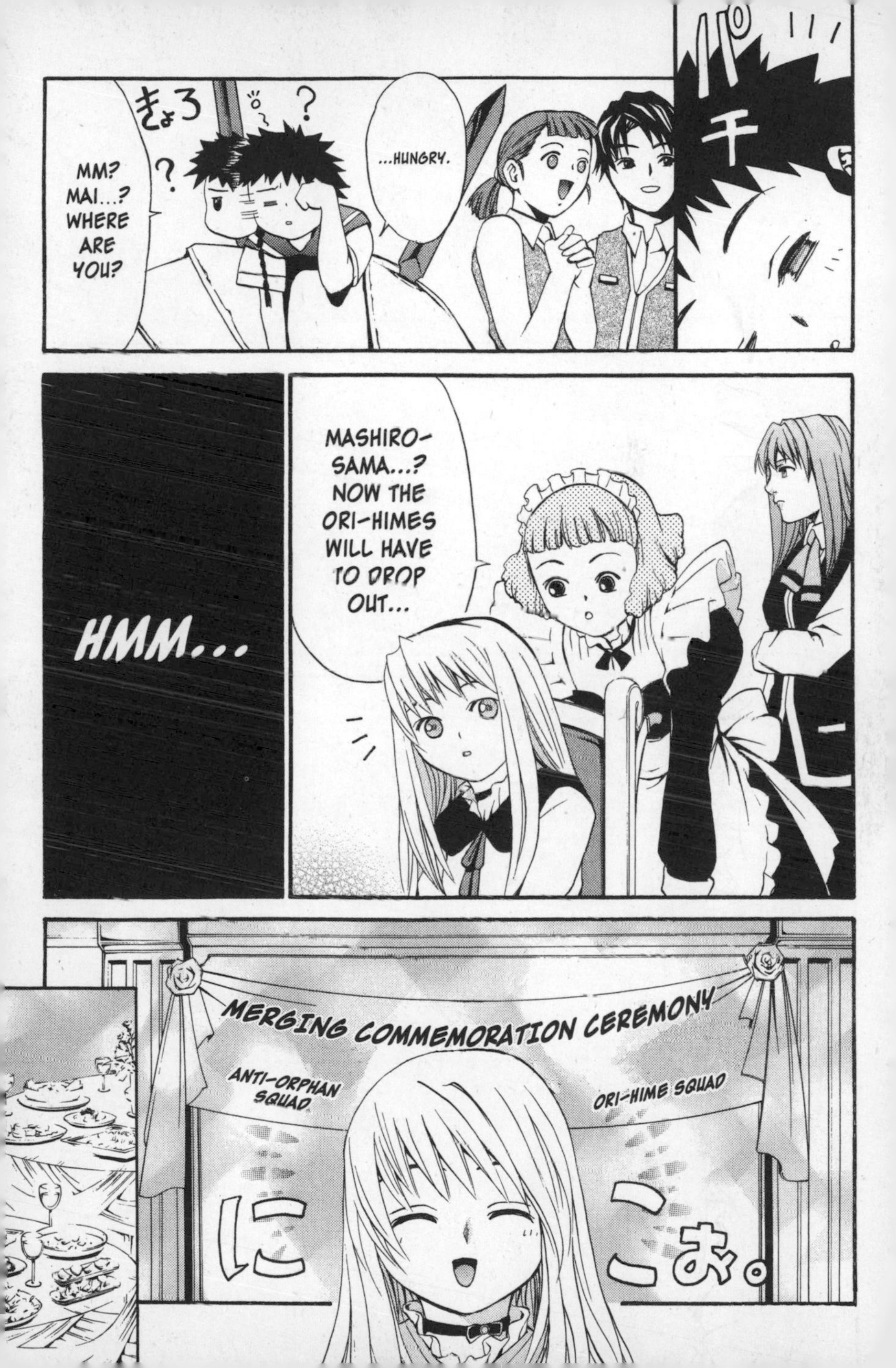
パチ
...HUNGRY.
きょろ
MM? MAI...? WHERE ARE YOU?
MASHIRO-SAMA...? NOW THE ORI-HIMES WILL HAVE TO DROP OUT...
HMM...
MERGING COMMEMORATION CEREMONY
ORI-HIME SQUAD
ANTI-ORPHAN SQUAD
にこぉ。

MERGING THE SQUADS FOR ACADEMY PEACE IS QUITE NATURAL.

PRESIDENT FUJINO AGREES, TOO, SO FROM NOW ON...

TH—TH—TH—TH——

きょと...ん。

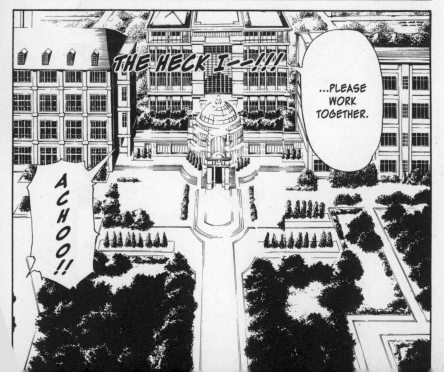

THE HECK I——!!!

...PLEASE WORK TOGETHER.

ACHOO!!

Chapter 17/ 17 Years Old

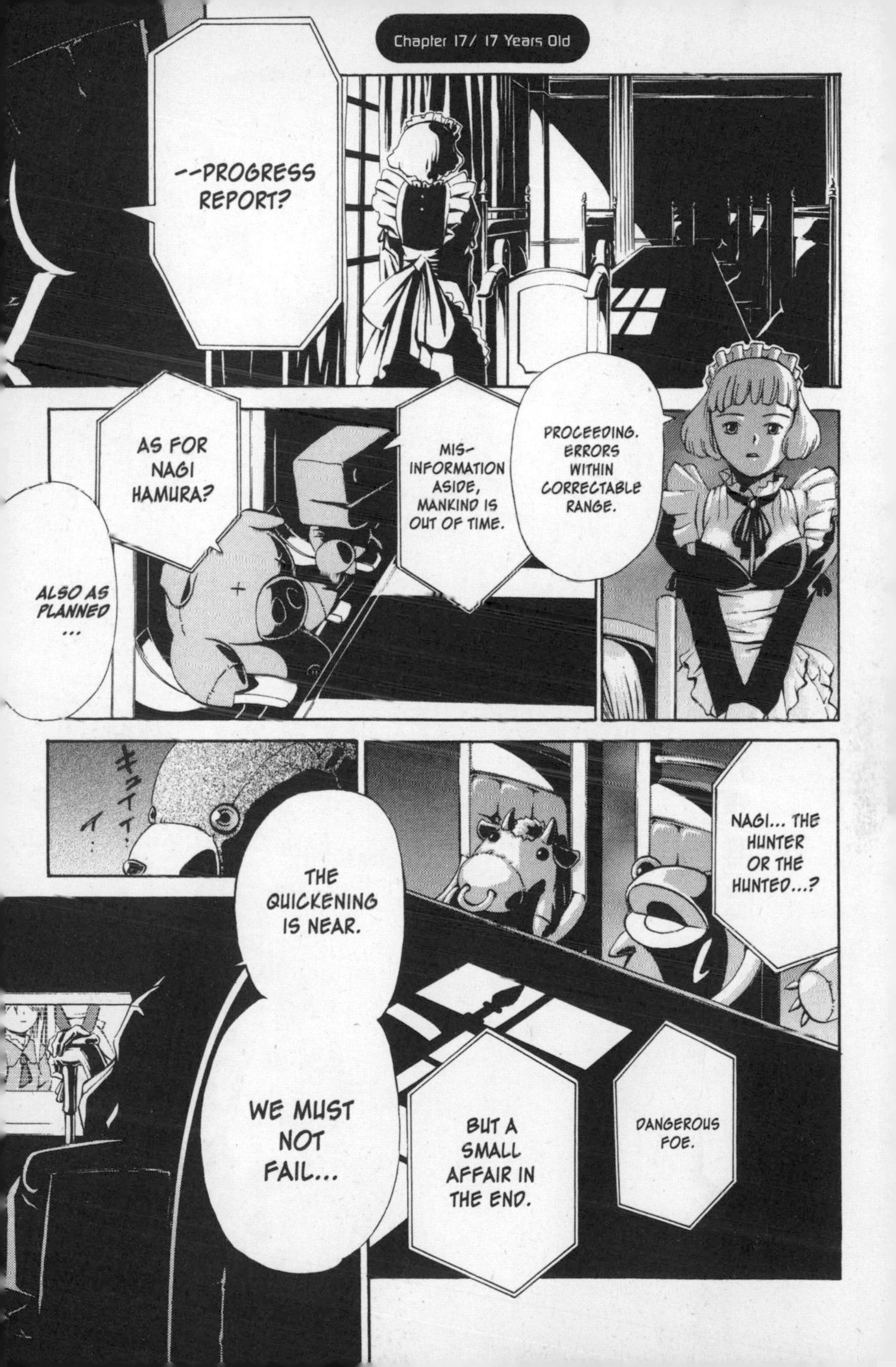
--PROGRESS REPORT?
PROCEEDING. ERRORS WITHIN CORRECTABLE RANGE.
MIS-INFORMATION ASIDE, MANKIND IS OUT OF TIME.
AS FOR NAGI HAMURA?
ALSO AS PLANNED...
NAGI... THE HUNTER OR THE HUNTED...?
THE QUICKENING IS NEAR.
キュイイイ…
DANGEROUS FOE.
BUT A SMALL AFFAIR IN THE END.
WE MUST NOT FAIL...

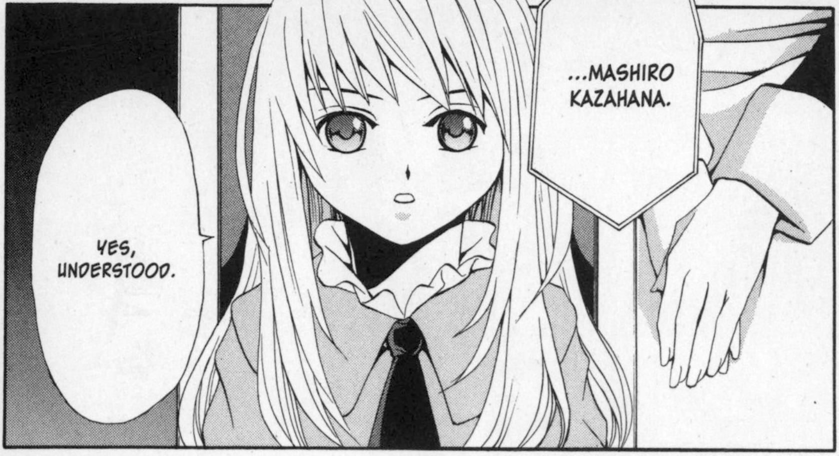
...MASHIRO KAZAHANA.
YES, UNDERSTOOD.

CHAPTER 17/ 17 YEARS OLD

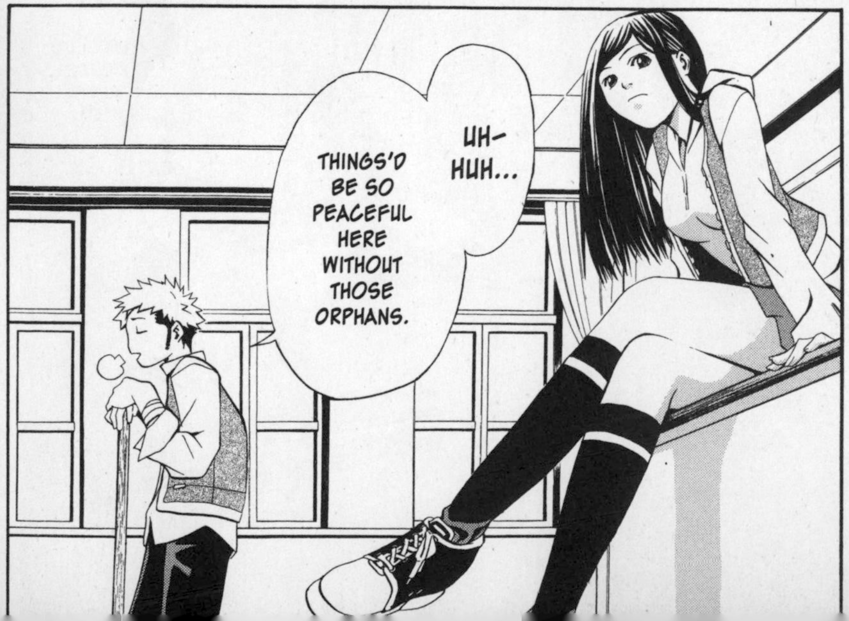
THINGS'D BE SO PEACEFUL HERE WITHOUT THOSE ORPHANS.
UH-HUH...

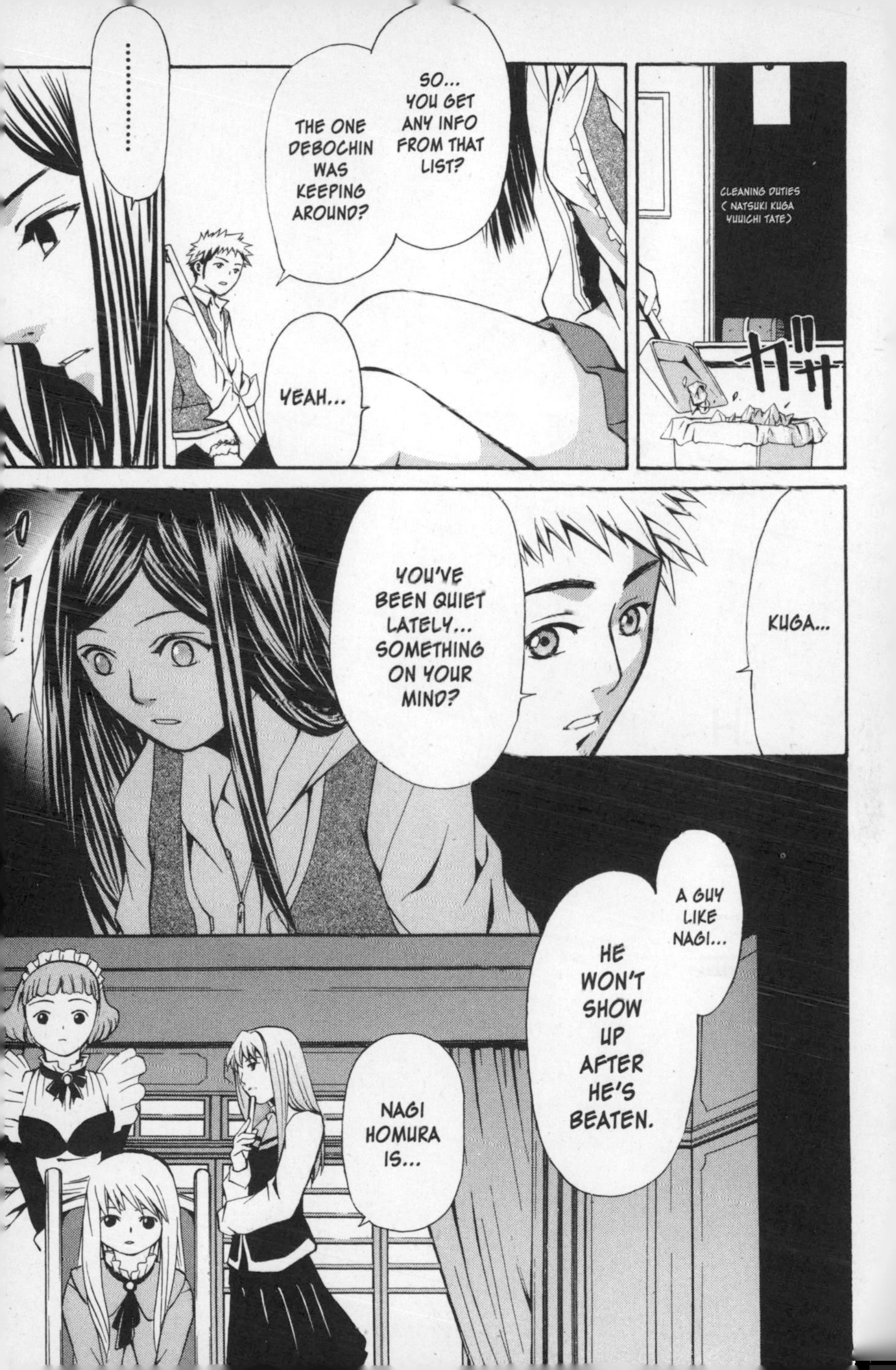
CLEANING DUTIES
(NATSUKI KUGA
YUUICHI TATE)
SO... YOU GET ANY INFO FROM THAT LIST?
THE ONE DEBOCHIN WAS KEEPING AROUND?
YEAH...
......
KUGA...
YOU'VE BEEN QUIET LATELY... SOMETHING ON YOUR MIND?
A GUY LIKE NAGI...
HE WON'T SHOW UP AFTER HE'S BEATEN.
NAGI HOMURA IS...

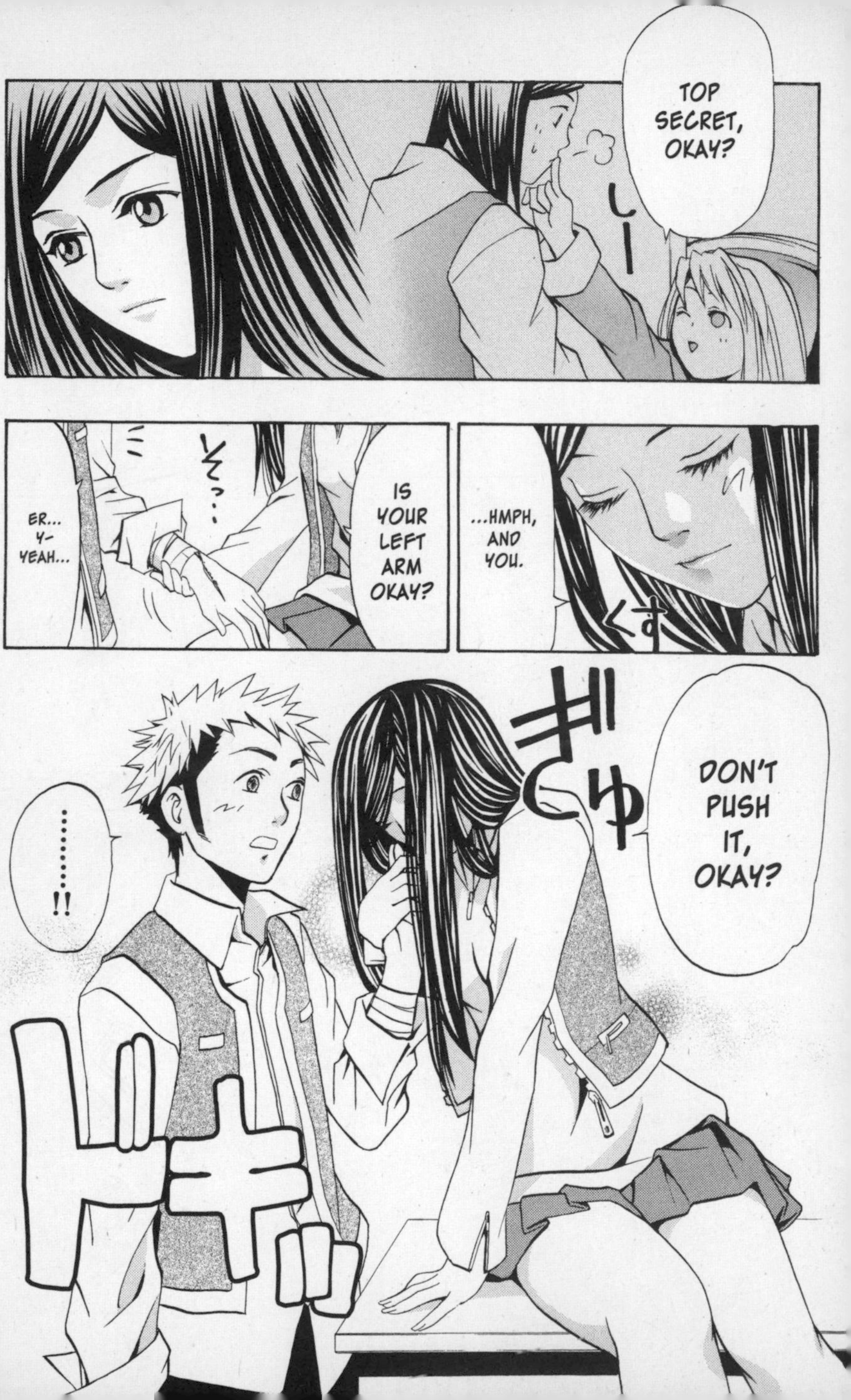
TOP SECRET, OKAY?
しー
...HMPH, AND YOU.
くす
IS YOUR LEFT ARM OKAY?
ぞっ…
ER... Y-YEAH...
DON'T PUSH IT, OKAY?
ぎゅ
......!!
ドキッ

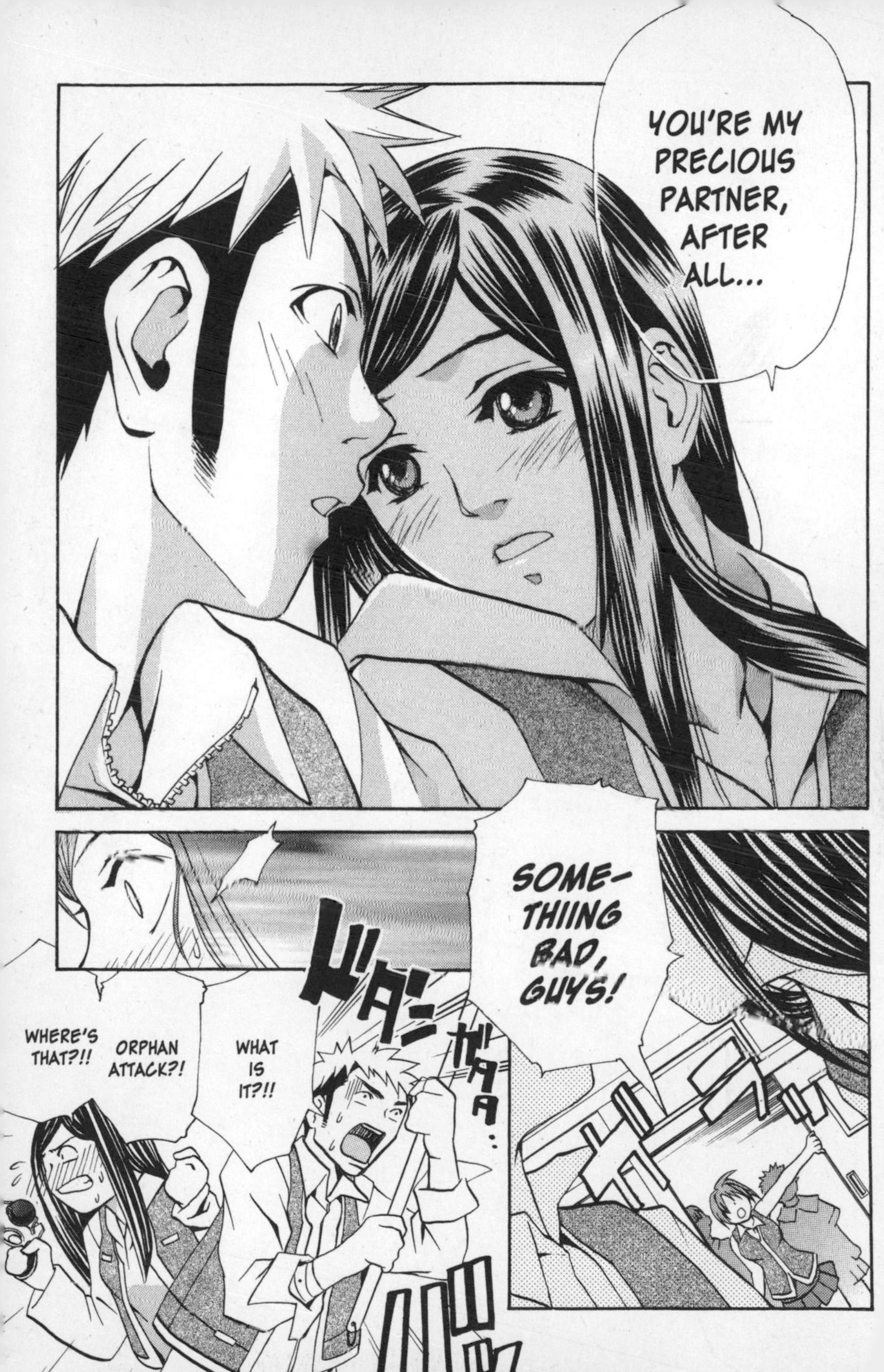
YOU'RE MY PRECIOUS PARTNER, AFTER ALL...
SOME-THIING BAD, GUYS!
WHAT IS IT?!!
ORPHAN ATTACK?!
WHERE'S THAT?!!

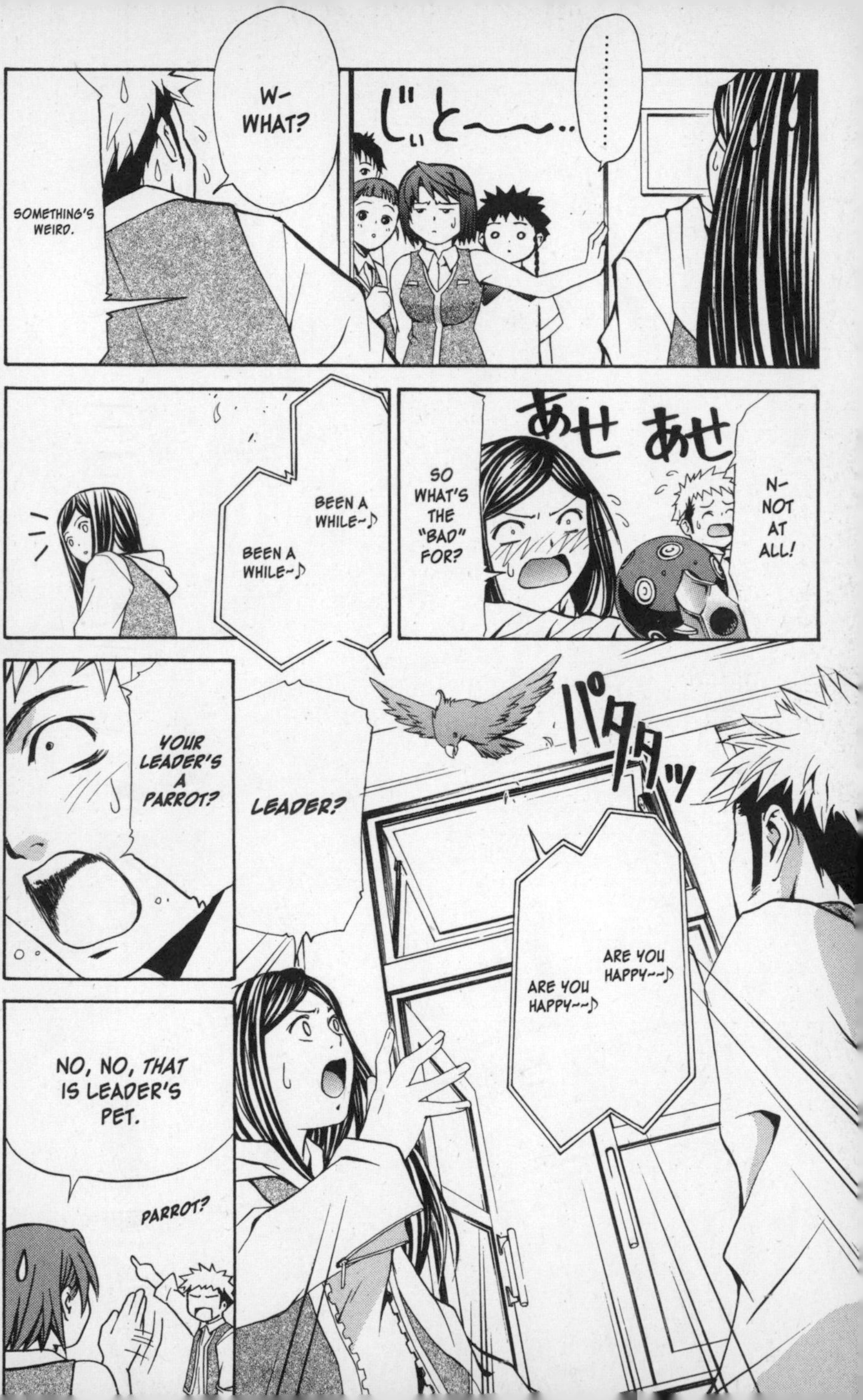

じぃと〜〜..
......
W- WHAT?
SOMETHING'S WEIRD.
あせ あせ
N- NOT AT ALL!
SO WHAT'S THE "BAD" FOR?
BEEN A WHILE~♪
BEEN A WHILE~♪
パタタッ
ARE YOU HAPPY~~♪
ARE YOU HAPPY~~♪
LEADER?
YOUR LEADER'S A PARROT?
NO, NO, THAT IS LEADER'S PET.
PARROT?

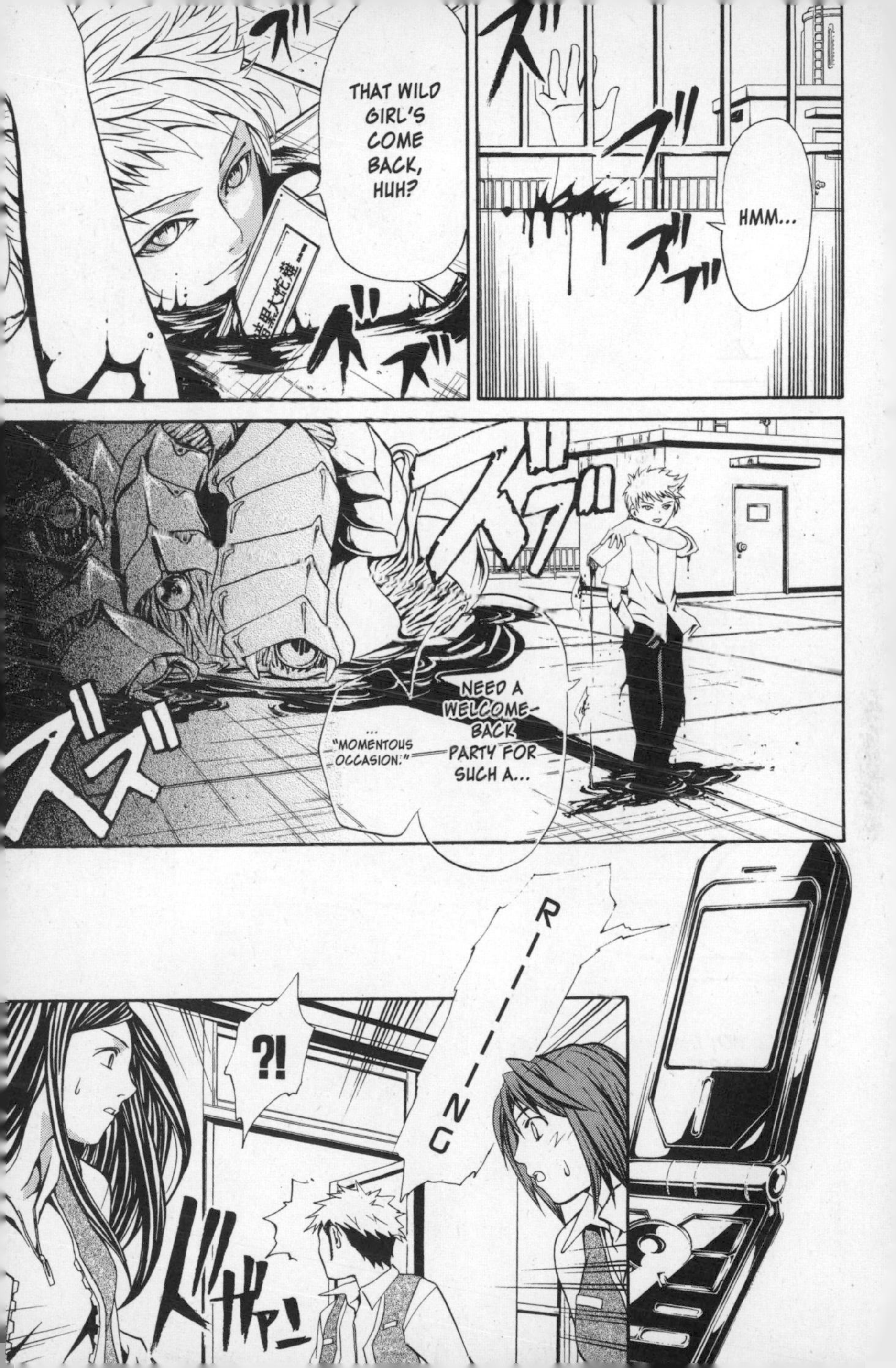
HMM...
THAT WILD GIRL'S COME BACK, HUH?
NEED A WELCOME-BACK PARTY FOR SUCH A...
..."MOMENTOUS OCCASION."
R-I-I-I-I-N-G
?!

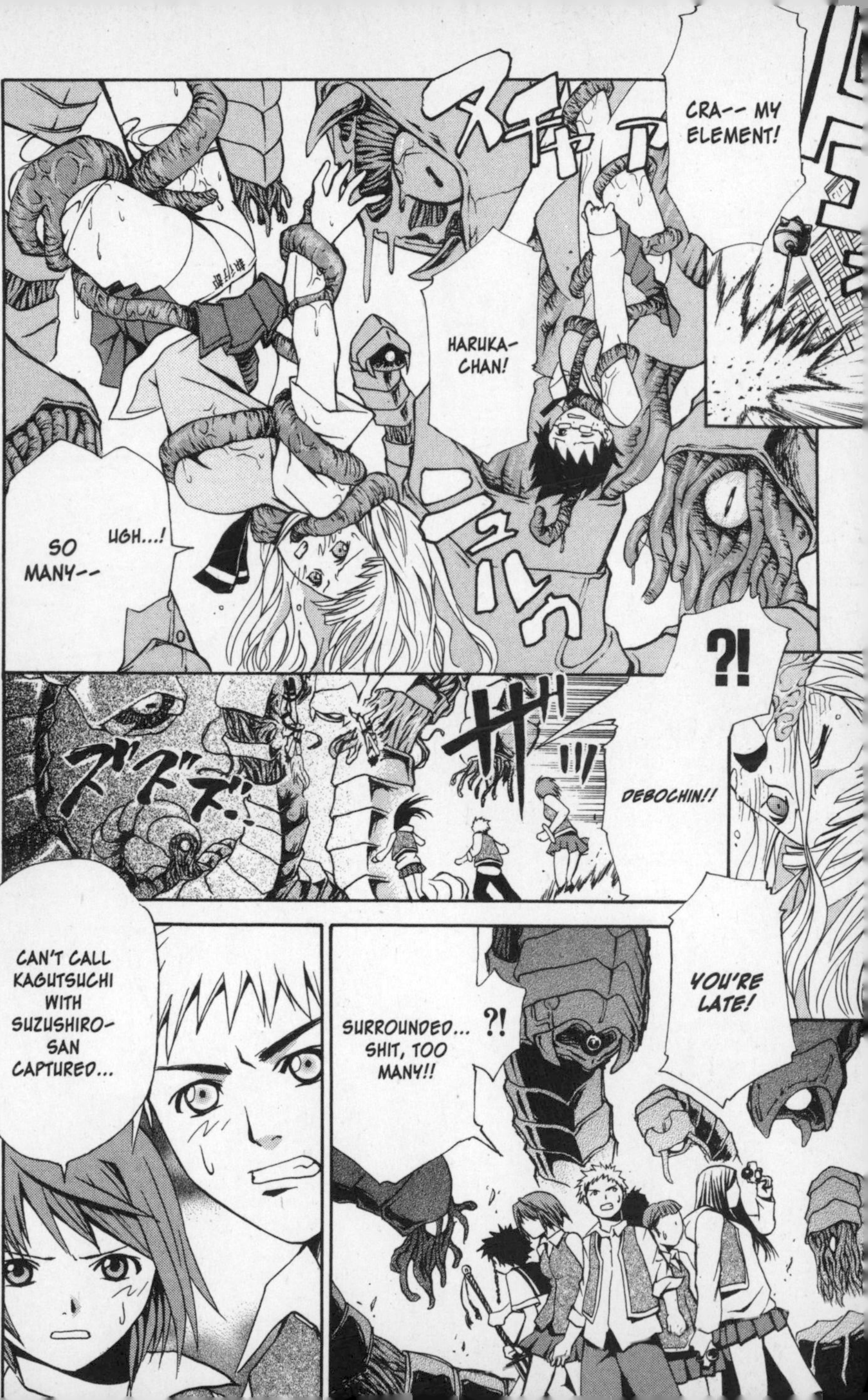

CRA-- MY ELEMENT!
HARUKA-CHAN!
UGH...!
SO MANY--
?!
DEBOCHIN!!
YOU'RE LATE!
?!
SURROUNDED... SHIT, TOO MANY!!
CAN'T CALL KAGUTSUCHI WITH SUZUSHIRO-SAN CAPTURED...

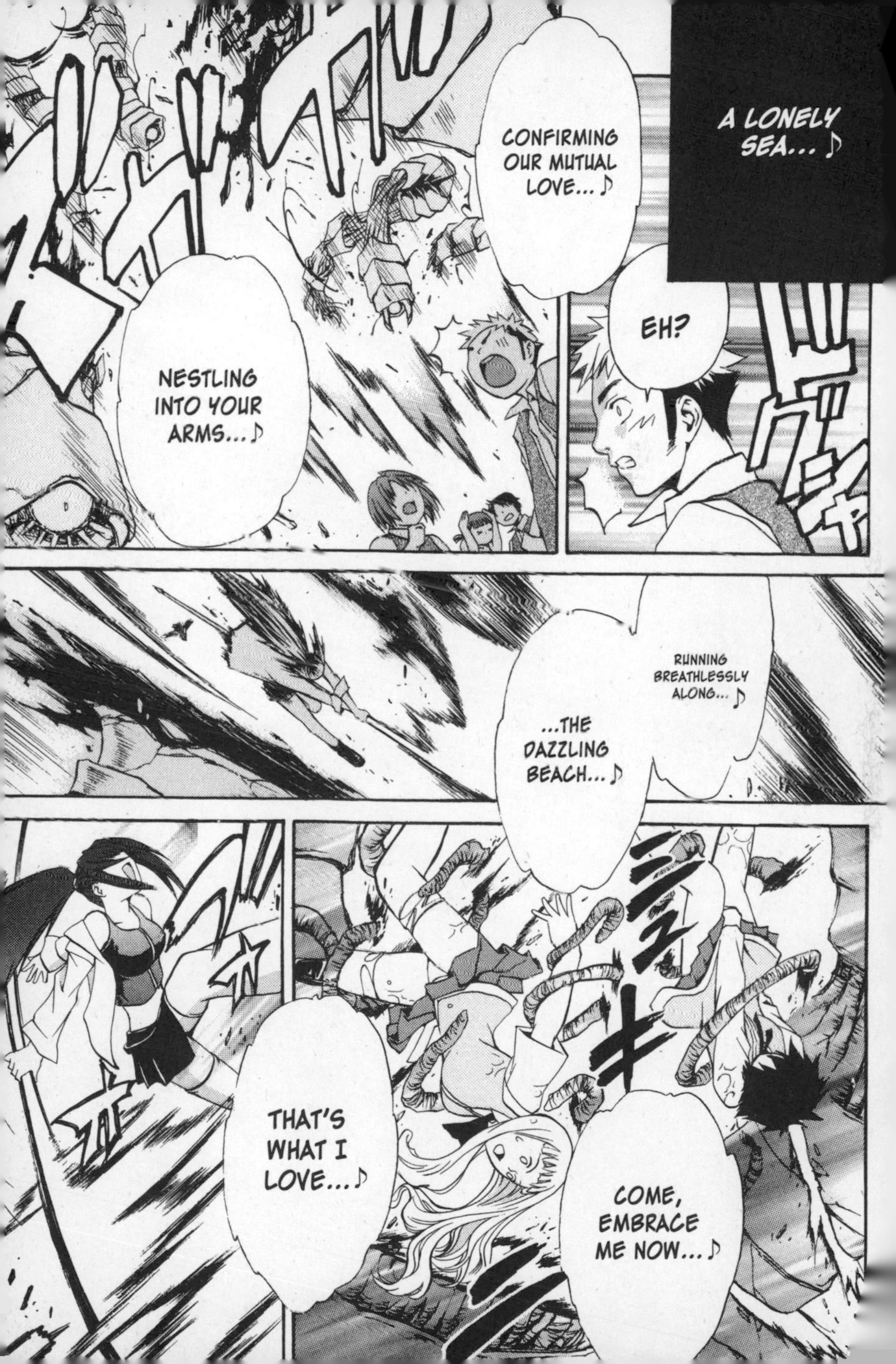
A LONELY SEA...♪
EH?
CONFIRMING OUR MUTUAL LOVE...♪
NESTLING INTO YOUR ARMS...♪
RUNNING BREATHLESSLY ALONG...♪
...THE DAZZLING BEACH...♪
COME, EMBRACE ME NOW...♪
THAT'S WHAT I LOVE...♪

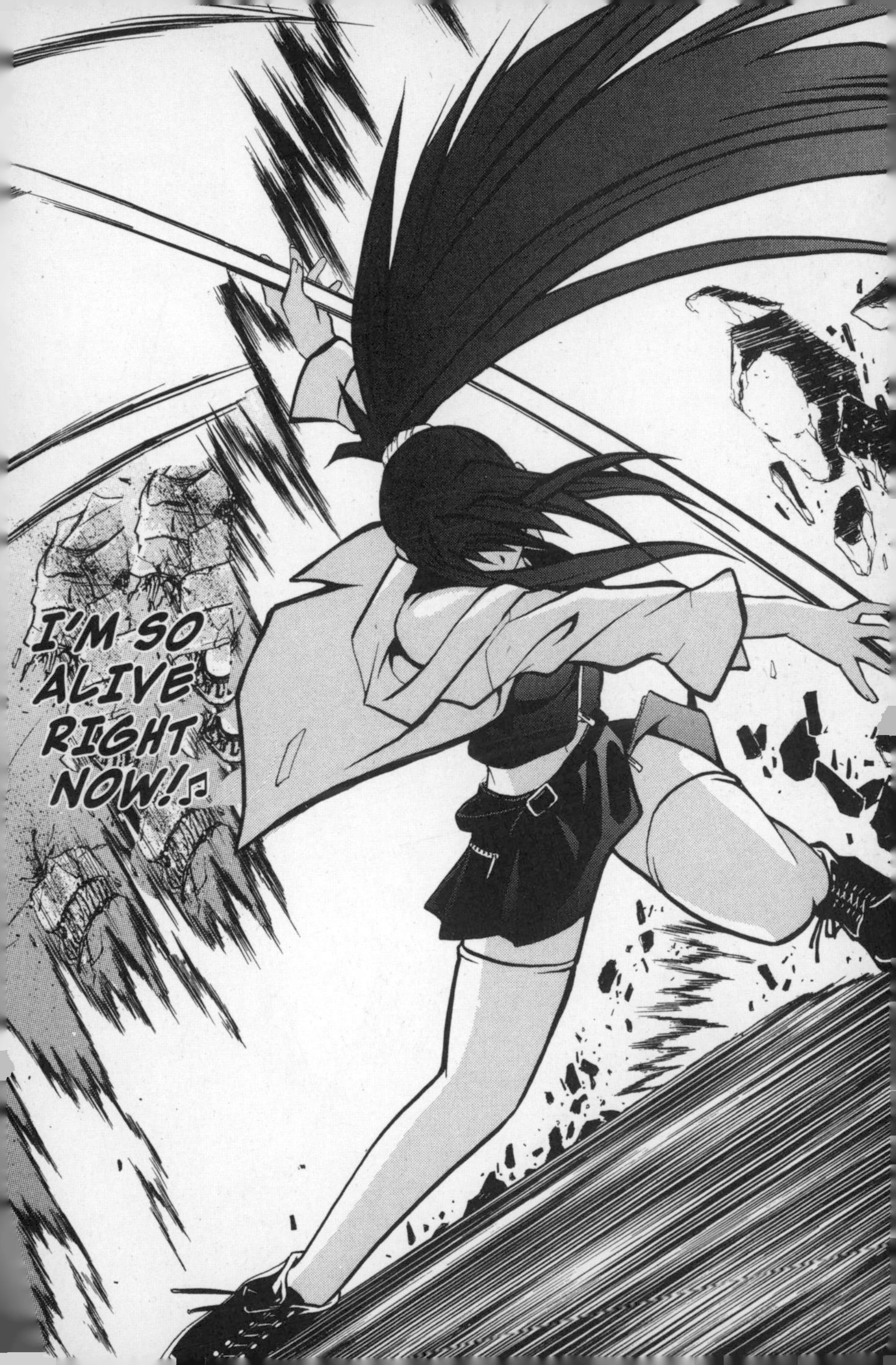
I'M SO ALIVE RIGHT NOW!♫

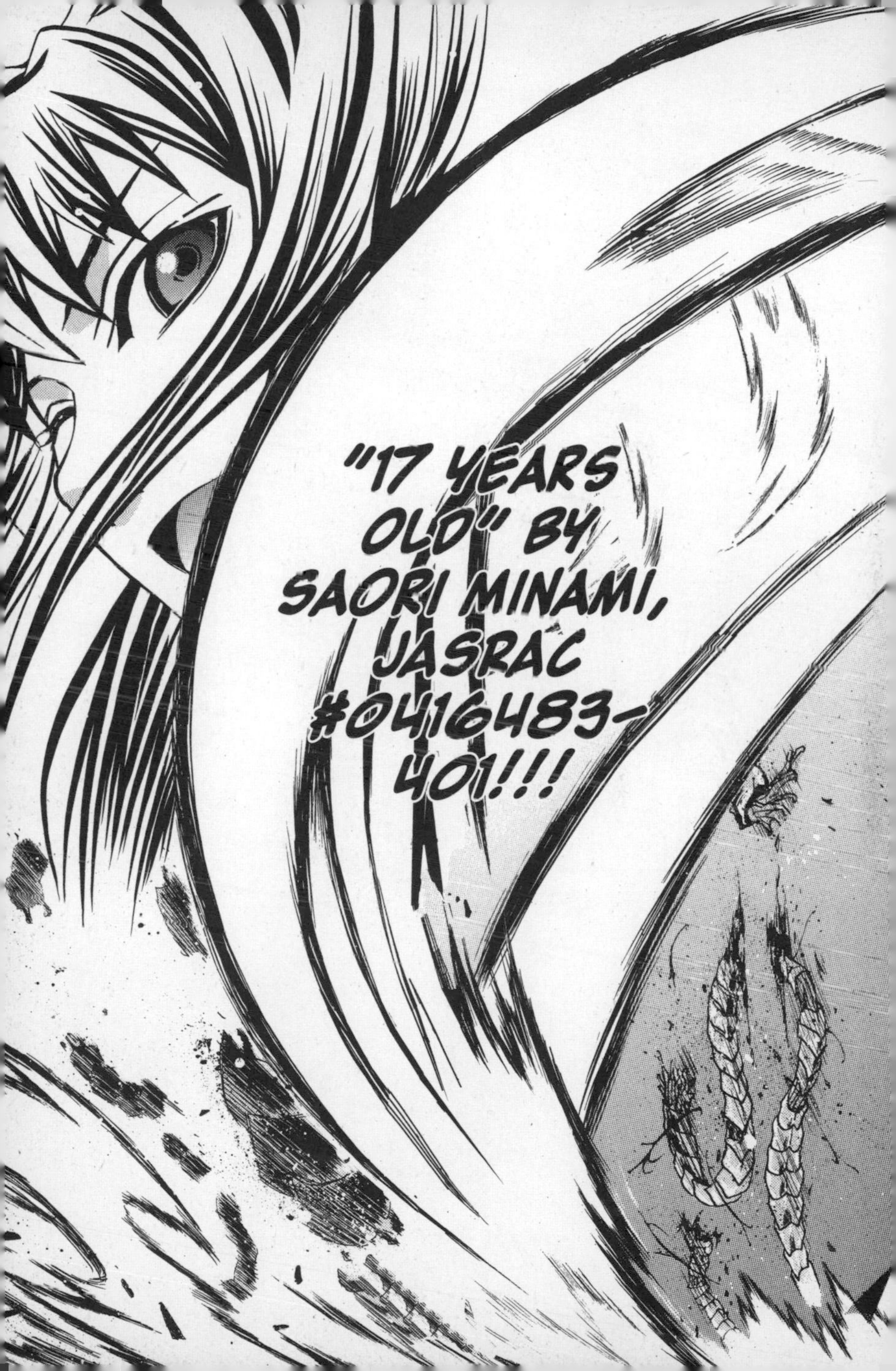
"17 YEARS OLD" BY SAORI MINAMI, JASRAC #0416483-401!!!

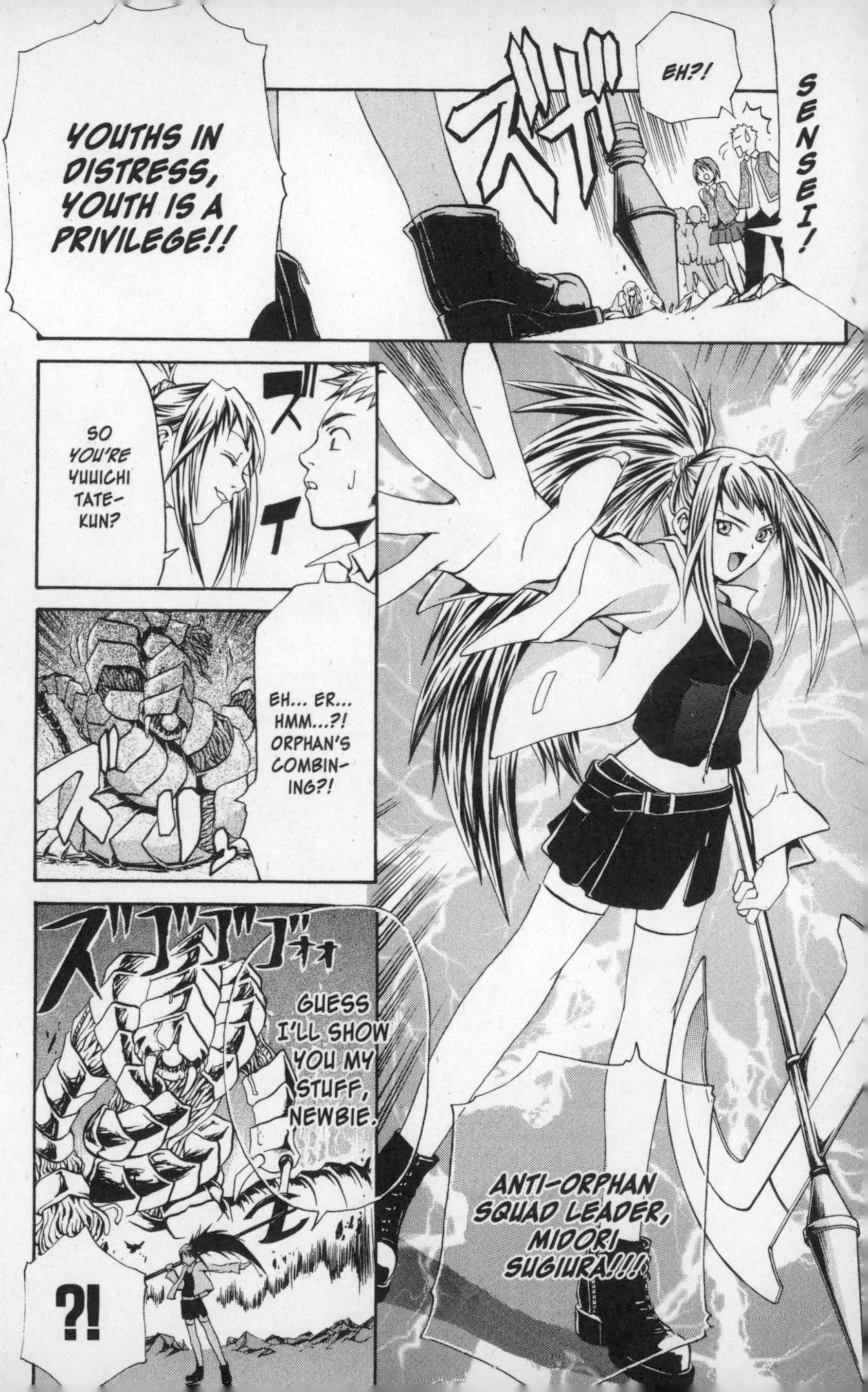
SENSEI!
EH?!
YOUTHS IN DISTRESS, YOUTH IS A PRIVILEGE!!
ANTI-ORPHAN SQUAD LEADER, MIDORI SUGIURA!!!
SO YOU'RE YUUICHI TATE-KUN?
EH... ER... HMM...?! ORPHAN'S COMBINING?!
GUESS I'LL SHOW YOU MY STUFF, NEWBIE.
?!

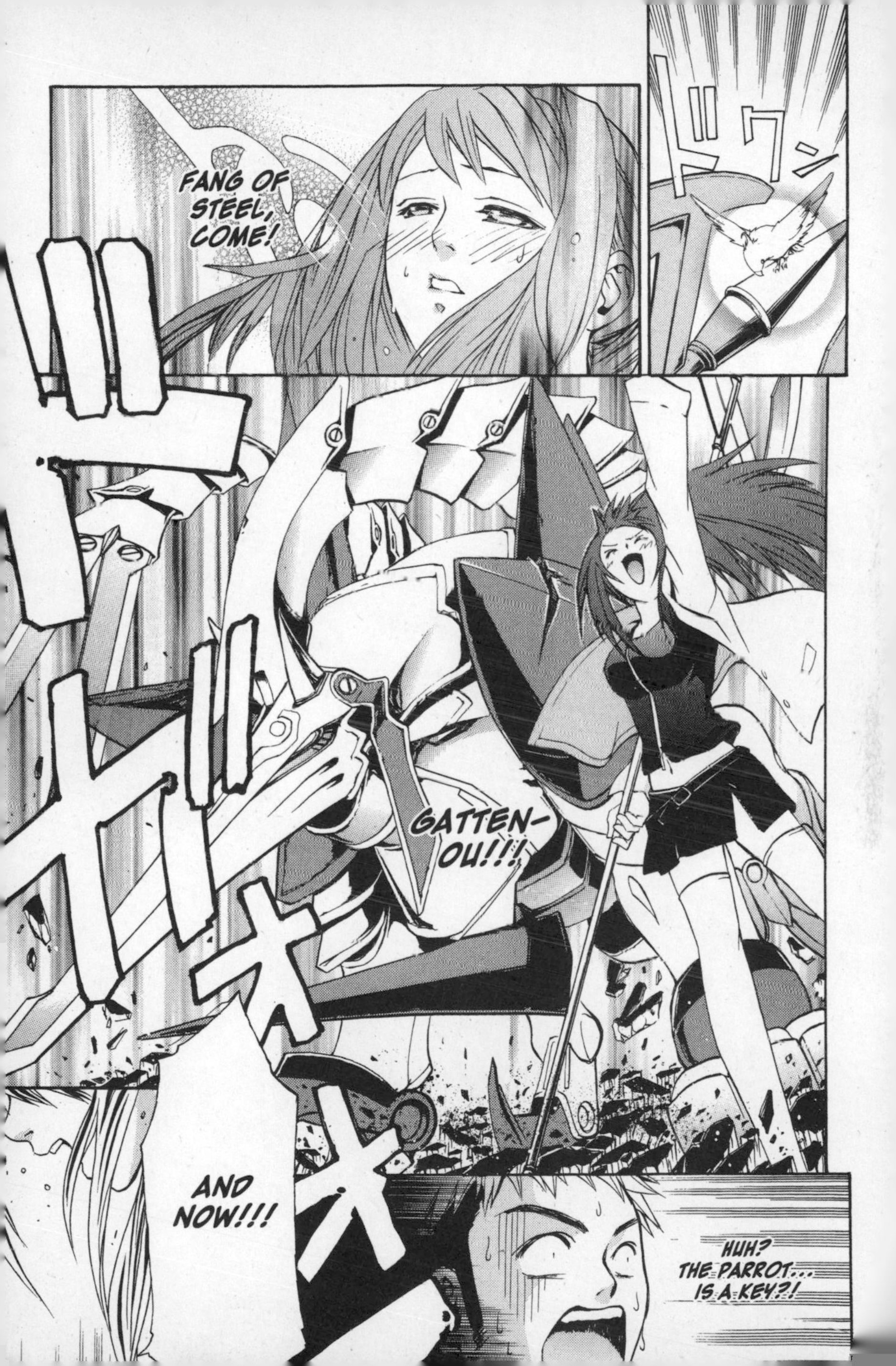
FANG OF STEEL, COME!
GATTEN-OU!!!
HUH? THE PARROT... IS A KEY?!
AND NOW!!!

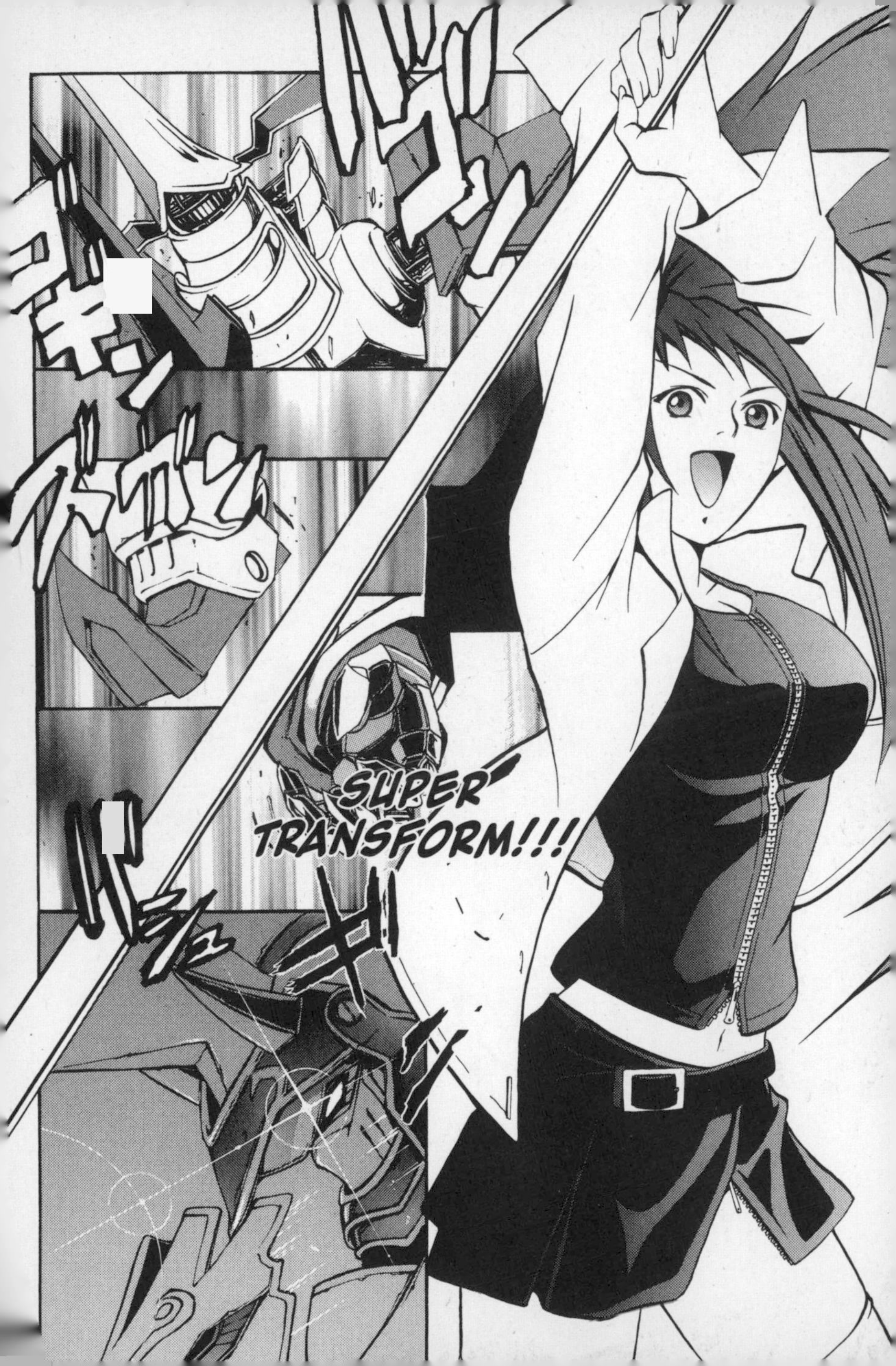
SUPER TRANSFORM!!!

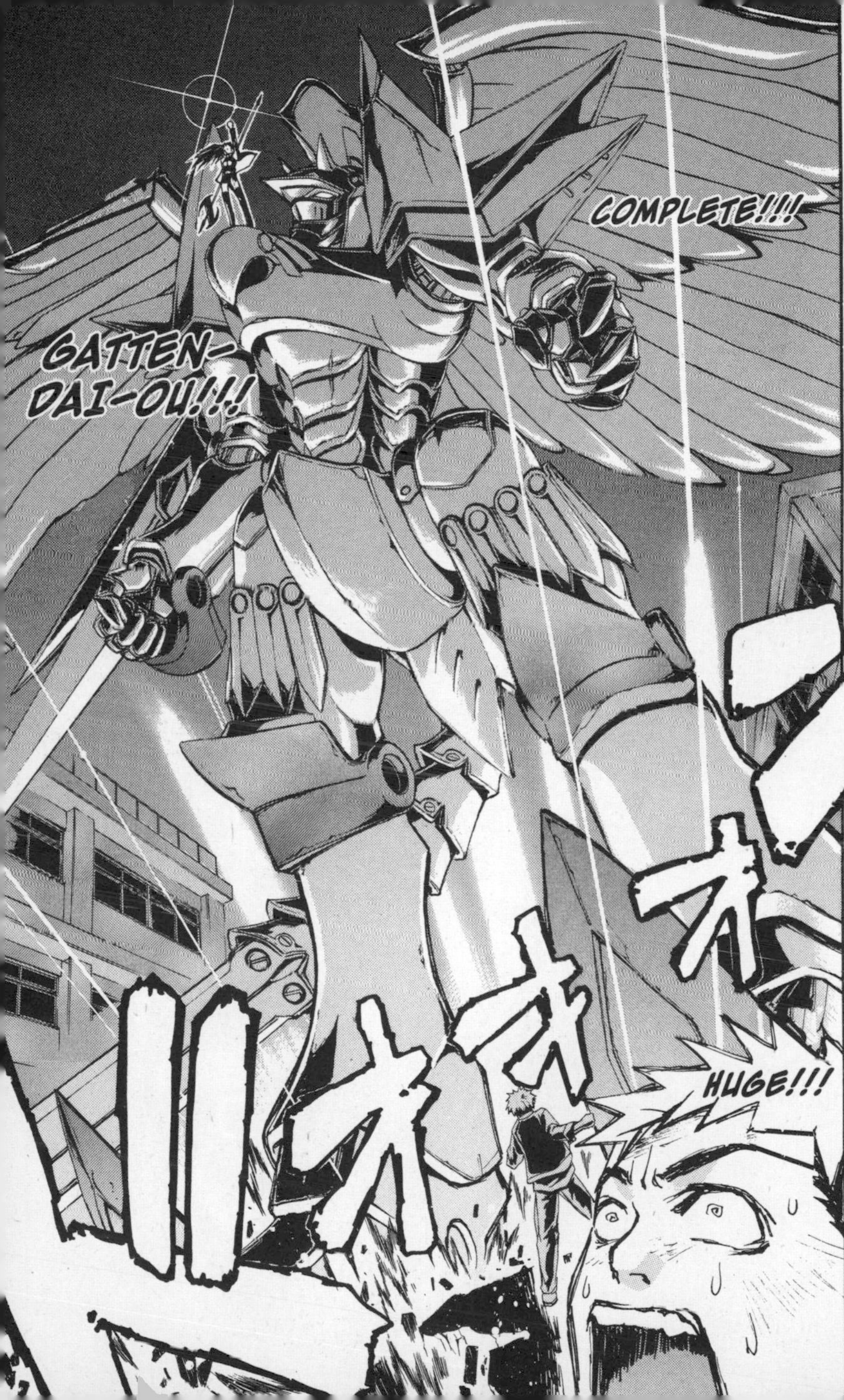
COMPLETE!!!
GATTEN-DAI-OU!!!
HUGE!!!

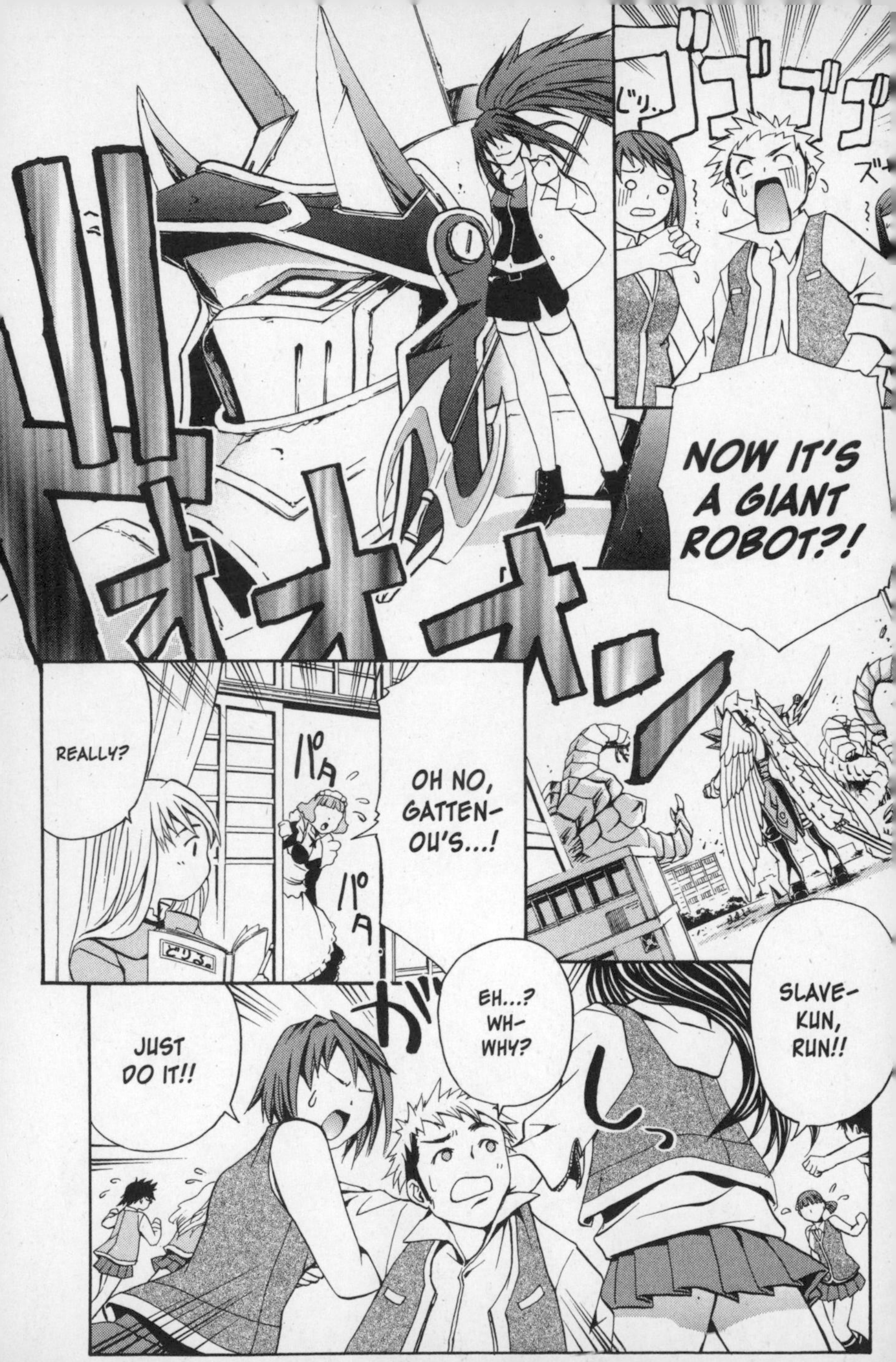

NOW IT'S A GIANT ROBOT?!
OH NO, GATTEN-OU'S...!
REALLY?
どりる。
SLAVE-KUN, RUN!!
EH...? WH-WHY?
JUST DO IT!!

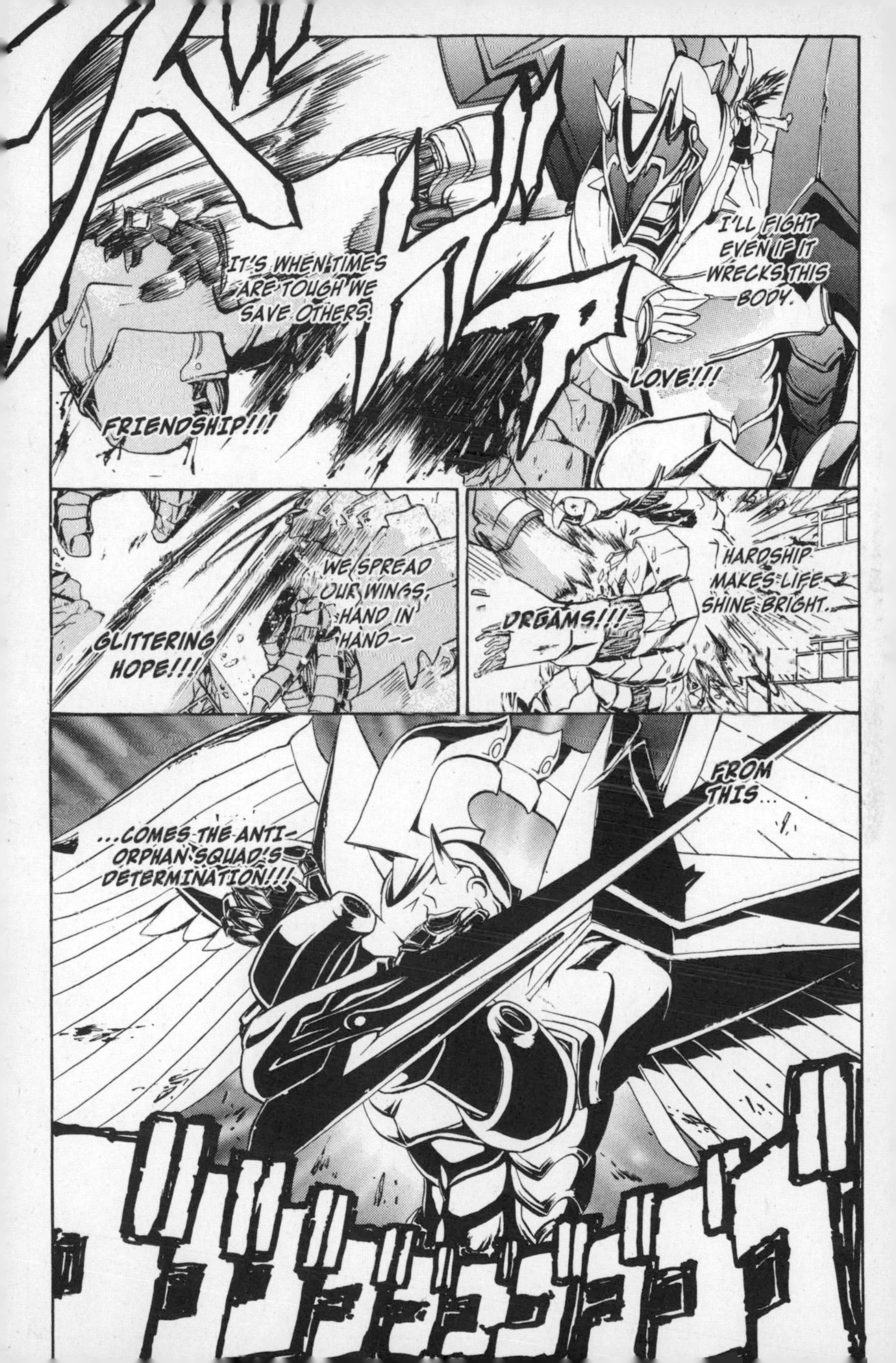
I'LL FIGHT EVEN IF IT WRECKS THIS BODY.
LOVE!!!
IT'S WHEN TIMES ARE TOUGH WE SAVE OTHERS.
FRIENDSHIP!!!
HARDSHIP MAKES LIFE SHINE BRIGHT.
DREAMS!!!
WE SPREAD OUR WINGS, HAND IN HAND--
GLITTERING HOPE!!!
FROM THIS...
...COMES THE ANTI-ORPHAN SQUAD'S DETERMINATION!!!

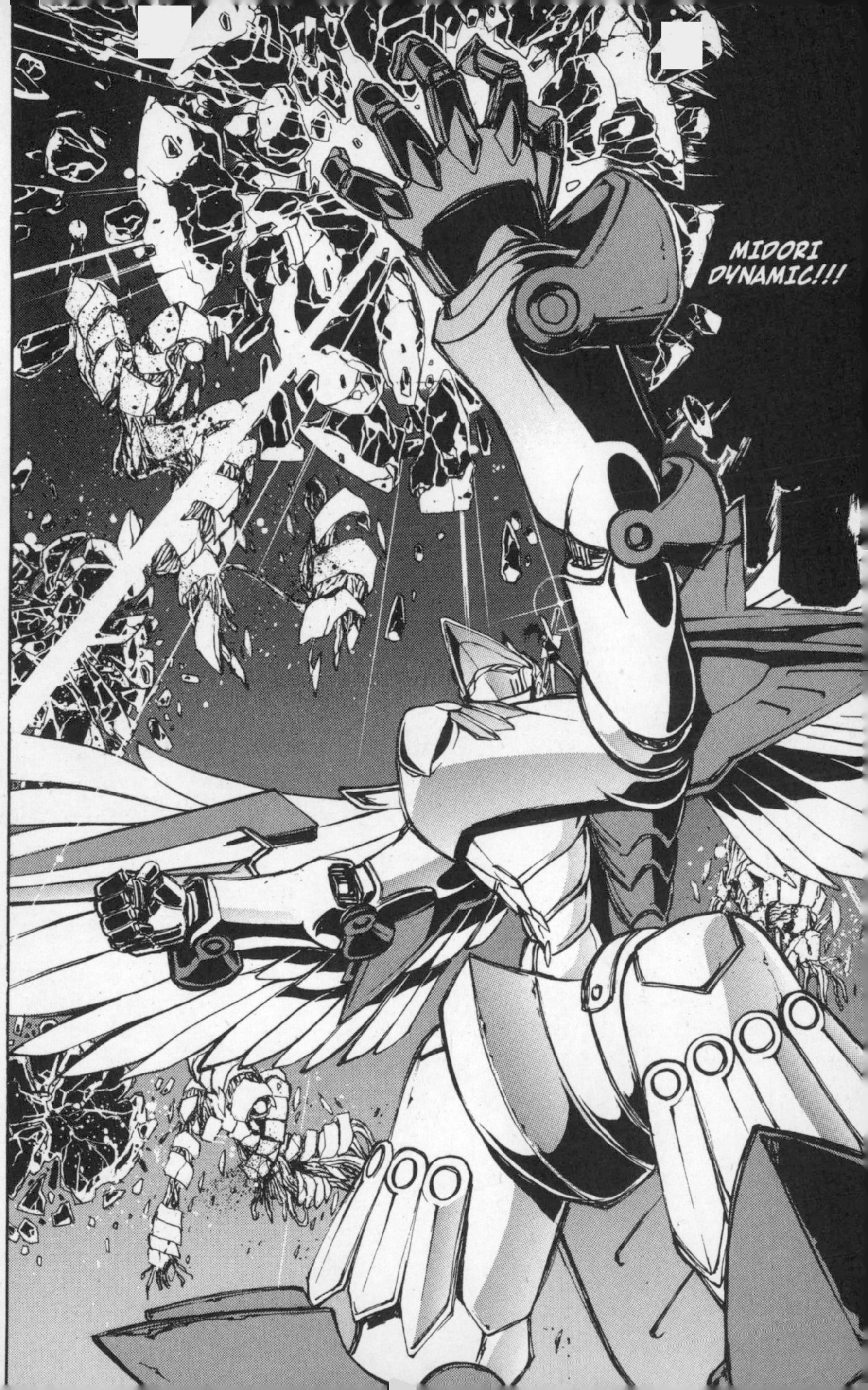
MIDORI
DYNAMIC!!!

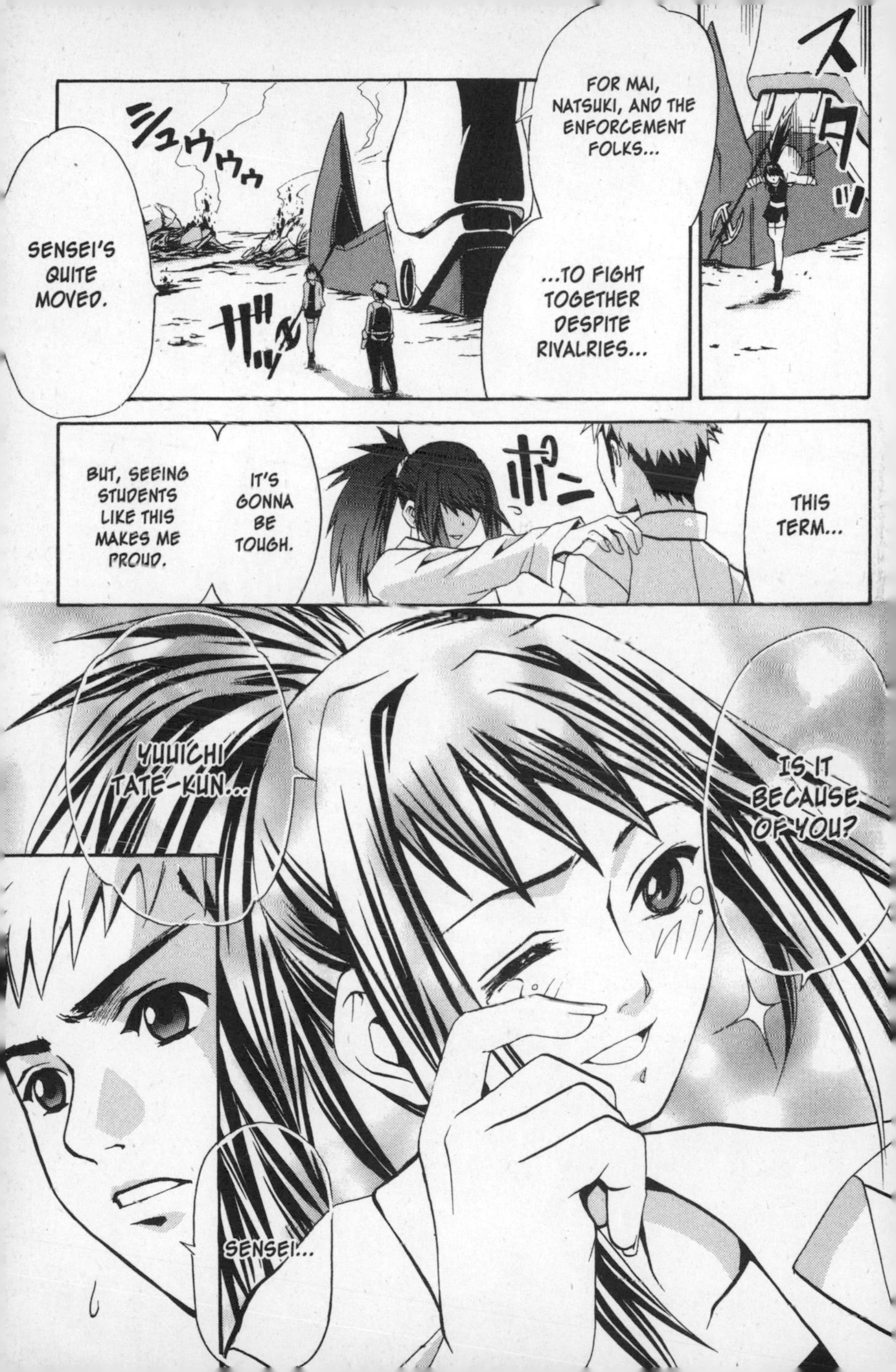
スタッ
FOR MAI, NATSUKI, AND THE ENFORCEMENT FOLKS...
...TO FIGHT TOGETHER DESPITE RIVALRIES...
シュウウゥゥ
ザッ
SENSEI'S QUITE MOVED.
THIS TERM...
ポン
IT'S GONNA BE TOUGH.
BUT, SEEING STUDENTS LIKE THIS MAKES ME PROUD.
IS IT BECAUSE OF YOU?
YUUICHI TATE-KUN...
SENSEI...

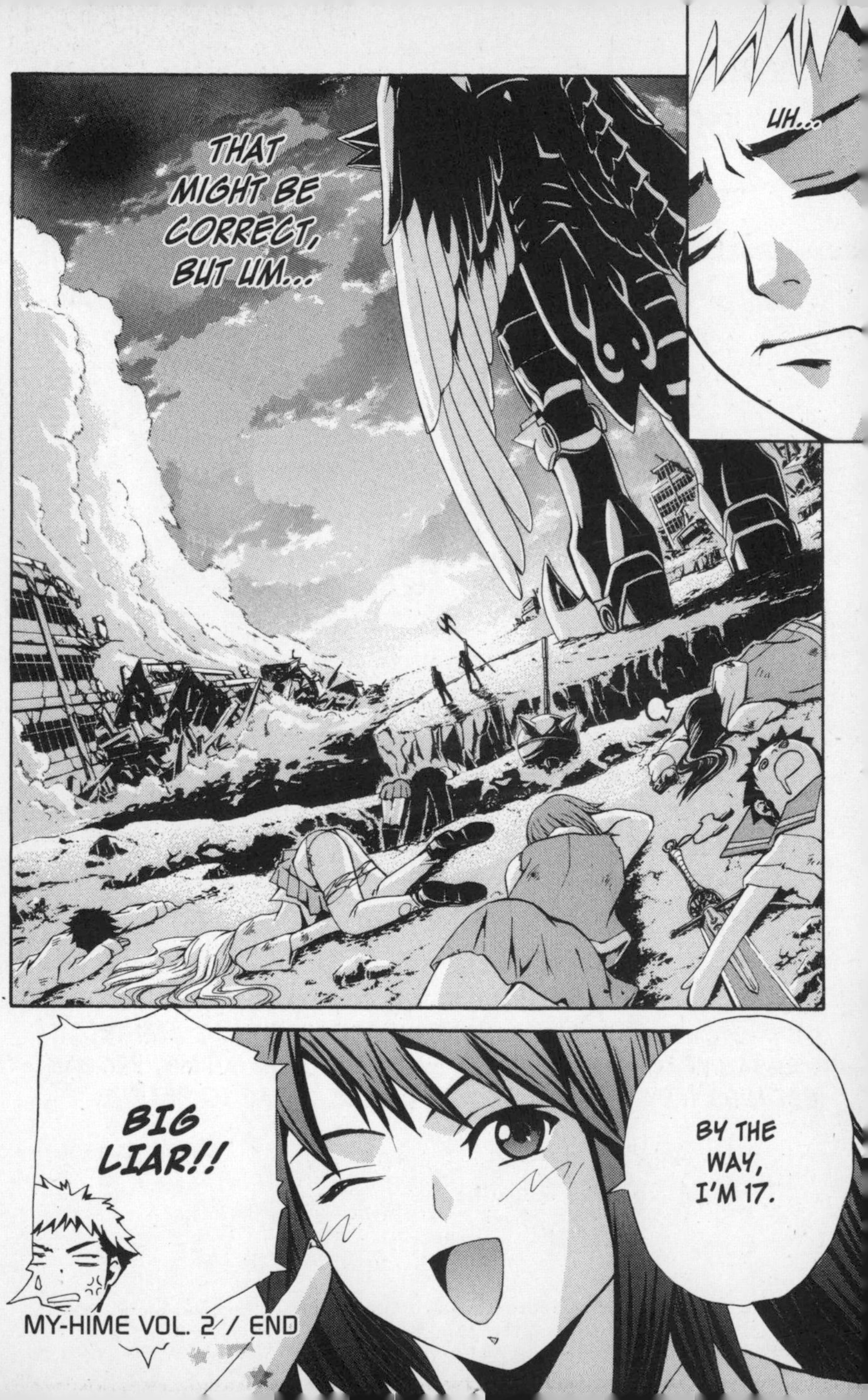
UH...
THAT MIGHT BE CORRECT, BUT UM...
BY THE WAY, I'M 17.
BIG LIAR!!
MY-HIME VOL. 2 / END

Voice Actress for Natsuki Kuga

Saeko Chiba

AT FIRST, I WAS OVERWHELMED BY A COOL, BUT AGGRESSIVE, LONE WOLF CHARACTER LIKE NATSUKI. I'M BAD AT DECISIVE, COOL LINES, SO WE HAD A LOT OF RE-RECORDING. HER CUTENESS AND OTHER ASPECTS BECAME CLEARER; THE ROLE FEELS COMPLETELY NATURAL NOW.

NATSUKI IS DISTANT, UNABLE TO TALK SOFTLY TO OTHERS, OBSESSIVELY SELF-RELIANT, AND VERY STINGY. I THINK HER HEART FINALLY OPENS BECAUSE OF HER WONDERFUL FRIENDS.

IT SEEMS BACKWARDS TO ME, BUT IN THE ANIME, THE MORE FATE HURTS PEOPLE, THE CLOSER THEIR FATES BECOME, AND THE MORE FATE BINDS THEM... I THINK THAT'S WHAT MADE EVERY WEEK COMPELLING. I REALLY HAD FUN WONDERING WHAT'D COME TO PASS IN THE NEXT EPISODE.

THE MANGA, WITH THE SAME CHARACTERS BUT A DIFFERENT PLOT AND BACKGROUND, IS INTERESTING, TOO. "OH, THAT'S WHAT THEY DID!" ETC. IN THE MANGA NATSUKI'S SO GENTLE. I CAN TELL THE MANGA CHARACTERS ARE VERY FAITHFUL TO THE ANIME, PROBABLY BECAUSE THEY STUDIED OUR WORK A LOT. GLAD TO READ IT.

I'M GLAD EVEN THOSE WHO HAVEN'T SEEN THE SHOW CAN "HEAR" OUR VOICES THROUGH READING.

SAEKO CHIBA: NUMEROUS STAGE/ SINGING/ VOICE-ACTING ROLES. HER 2ND ALBUM, "EVERYTHING" IS IN STORES. ROLES INCLUDE LAPIS-CHAN IN "TOTTOKO HAM TARO" AND AKIHO SUDOU IN "IRIA'S SKY, UFO SUMMER."

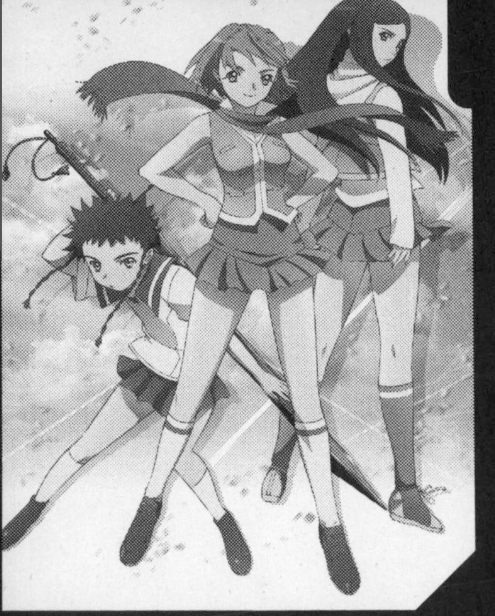

Hiroyuki Yoshino

TV Animation

My-HiME

Series Writer

VIA MY VAGUE "PLOT ASSISTANCE" TITLE, I'VE FOUND PARTICIPATING IN MANGA TO BE BOTH INTERESTING AND CHALLENGING. I REALIZE THE IMAGERY REQUIRES DIFFERENT METHODS THAN IN ANIME. EVEN SO, I CAN MAKE FUN SUGGESTIONS LIKE "SHORTEN MAI'S SKIRT, I WANT MORE PANTY SHOTS!" ...WELL, THE CIRCUMSTANCES ARE A BIT DIFFERENT FROM ANIME. BUT REALLY (^_^) , I HELPED WITH STORY AND CHARACTER IDEAS, THOUGH KIMURA AND SATO ARE 100% IN CHARGE OF THE MANGA VERSION (THANKS FOR PUTTING UP WITH ME, YOU TWO). IN THE HANDS OF DIFFERENT WRITERS, THE CHARACTERS FROM THE ANIME I DIRECTED STAR IN A DIFFERENT, BUT EXTRAVAGANT, ENGROSSING DRAMA. I THINK MANY WHO'VE SEEN BOTH VERSIONS WILL SHARE MY FEELINGS OF: "DARN, SHOULD'VE DONE THAT FOR THE ANIME!" AND SO ON.

THOUGH THE MANGA HAS A DIFFERENT FLAVOR, COMBINING BOTH VERSIONS OF "MY-HIME" DOUBLES--NO--QUADRUPLES THE FUN, I ASSURE YOU. PLEASE CHEER ON MAI, NATSUKI, MIKOTO AND YUUICHI IN THEIR ANIME AND MANGA ADVENTURES.

Fuka Academy Official Web Site

http://www.sunrise-inc.co.jp/my-hime/

MY-HIME VOLUME 2

THANK YOU FOR BUYING THIS!
WELL, I'M OFF.
SEE YOU AGAIN.
– NOBORU KIMURA

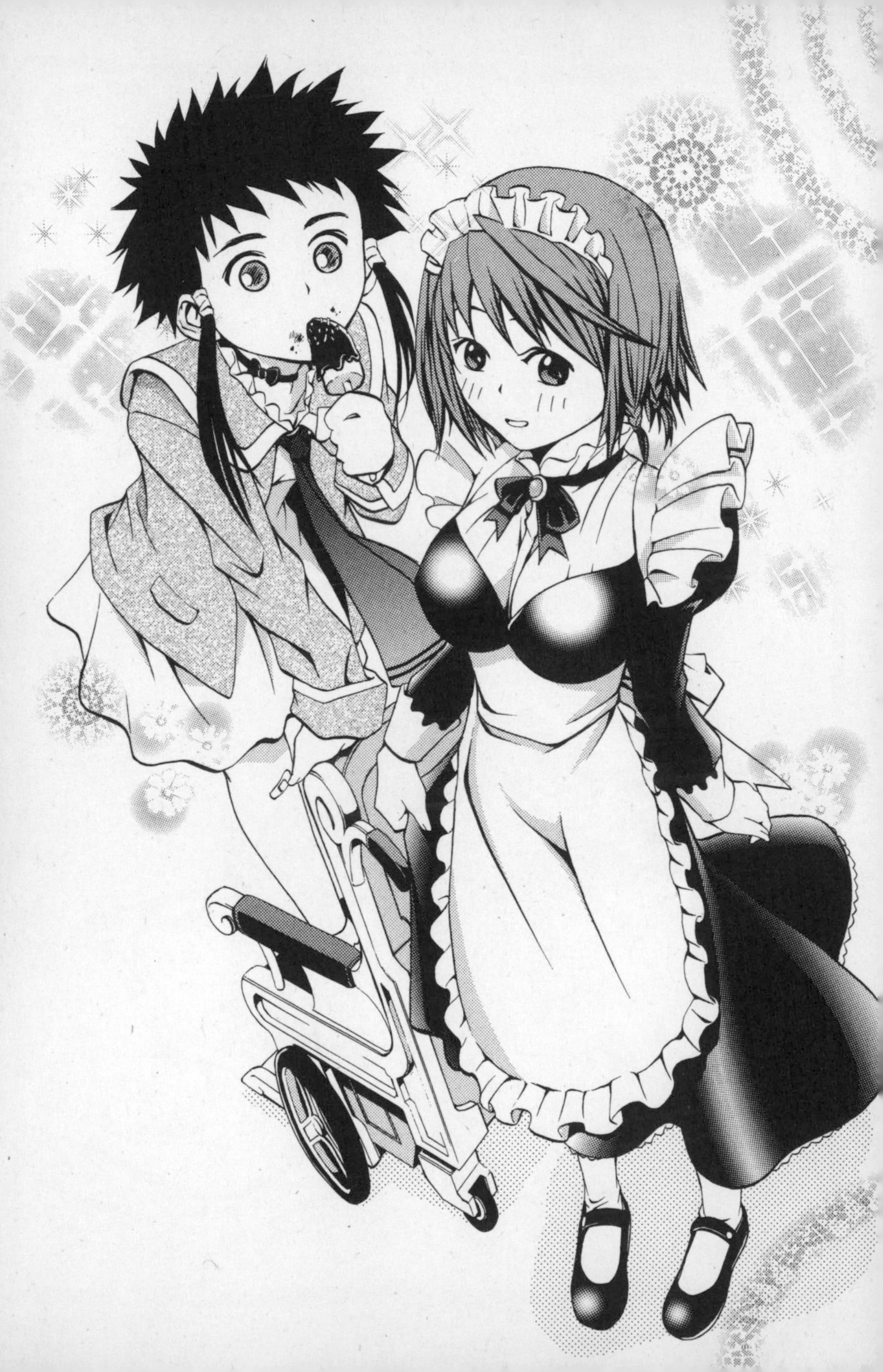

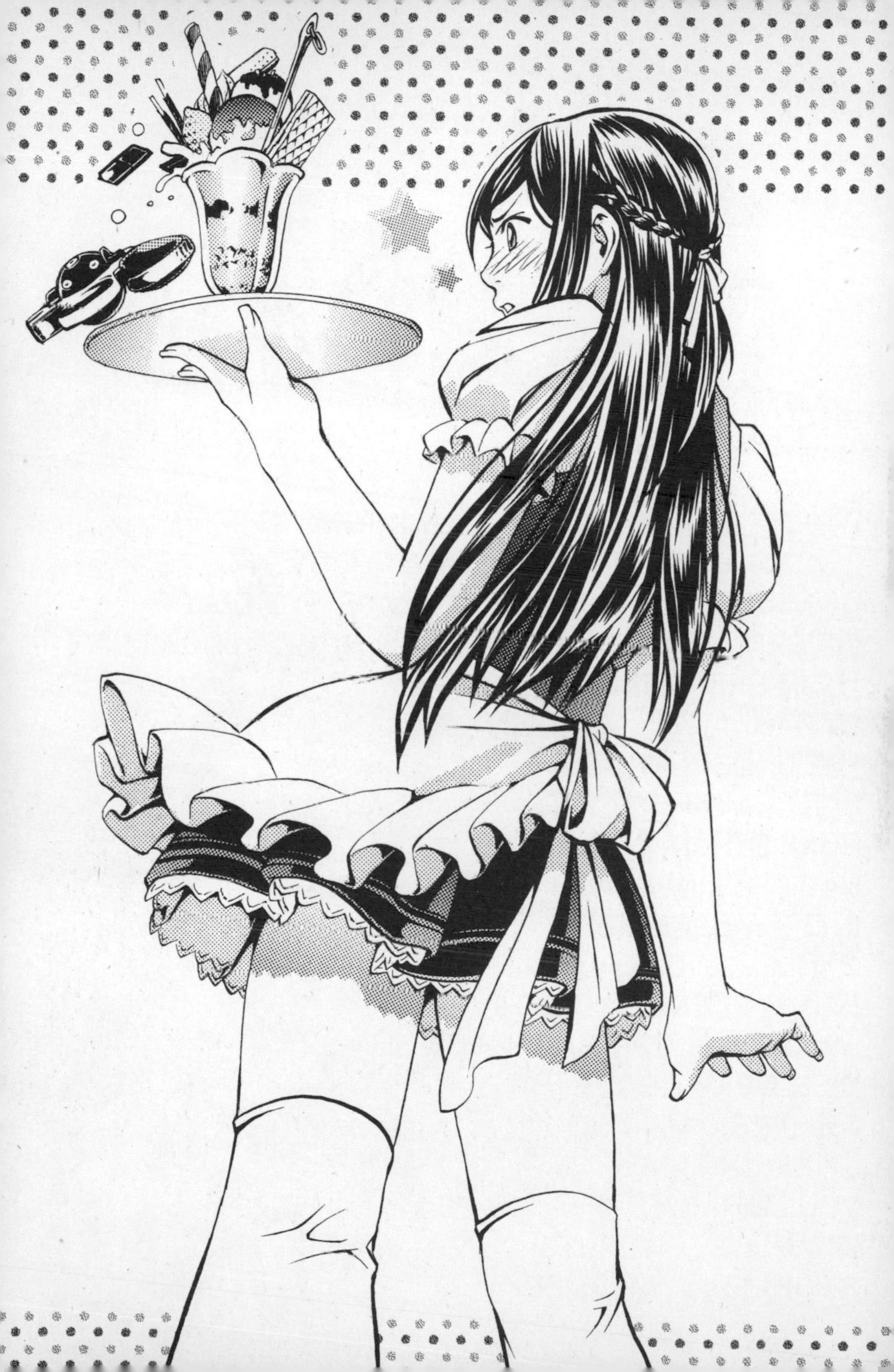

IN THE NEXT VOLUME OF

My-HiME

WHEN THE HIME TEAM FALLS INTO A MASSIVE
CRATER, CREATED BY THE DESTRUCTIVE FORCE
OF MIDORI, THEY DISCOVER A VAST SYSTEM OF
CAVERNS UNDER THE ACADEMY. NOW, IT LOOKS LIKE
THEIR BEST HOPE OF
FINDING A WAY OUT OF
THE UNDERGROUND
CATACOMBS LIES WITH
NONE OTHER THAN
NAO--YES, NAO! AND
IN BETWEEN BRIEF
BATTLES AND SULTRY
SAUNA SCENES, YUUICHI
MAKES A SURPRISING
DISCOVERY ABOUT
MIDORI'S PAST. AND
LATER, THE MAI –
YUUICHI – NATSUKI
TRIANGLE CONTINUES
TO GET EVEN MESSIER!

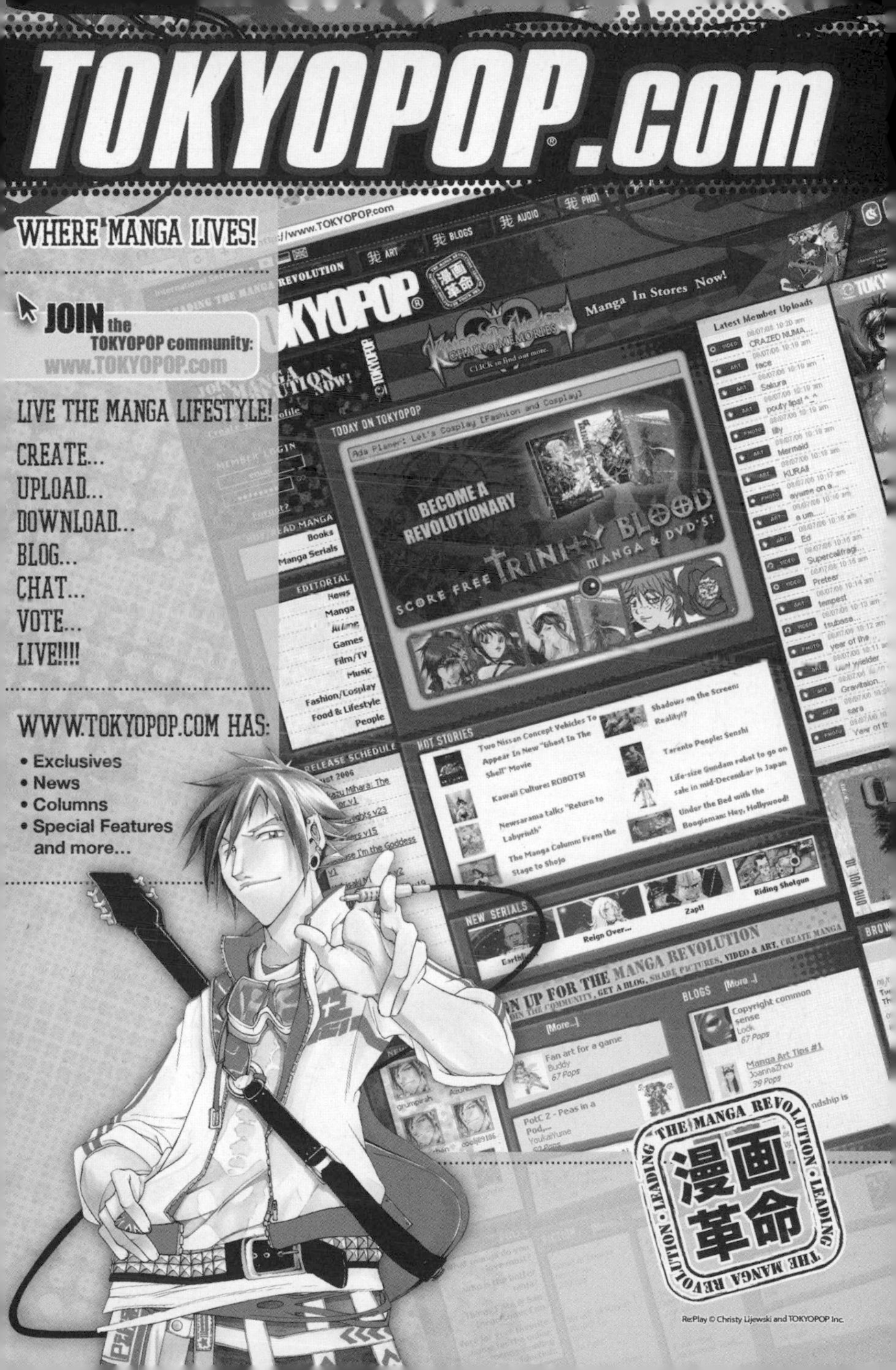
TOKYOPOP®.com
WHERE MANGA LIVES!
JOIN the TOKYOPOP community:
www.TOKYOPOP.com
LIVE THE MANGA LIFESTYLE!
CREATE...
UPLOAD...
DOWNLOAD...
BLOG...
CHAT...
VOTE...
LIVE!!!!
WWW.TOKYOPOP.COM HAS:
• Exclusives
• News
• Columns
• Special Features and more...
LEADING THE MANGA REVOLUTION
漫画革命
Re:Play © Christy Lijewski and TOKYOPOP Inc.

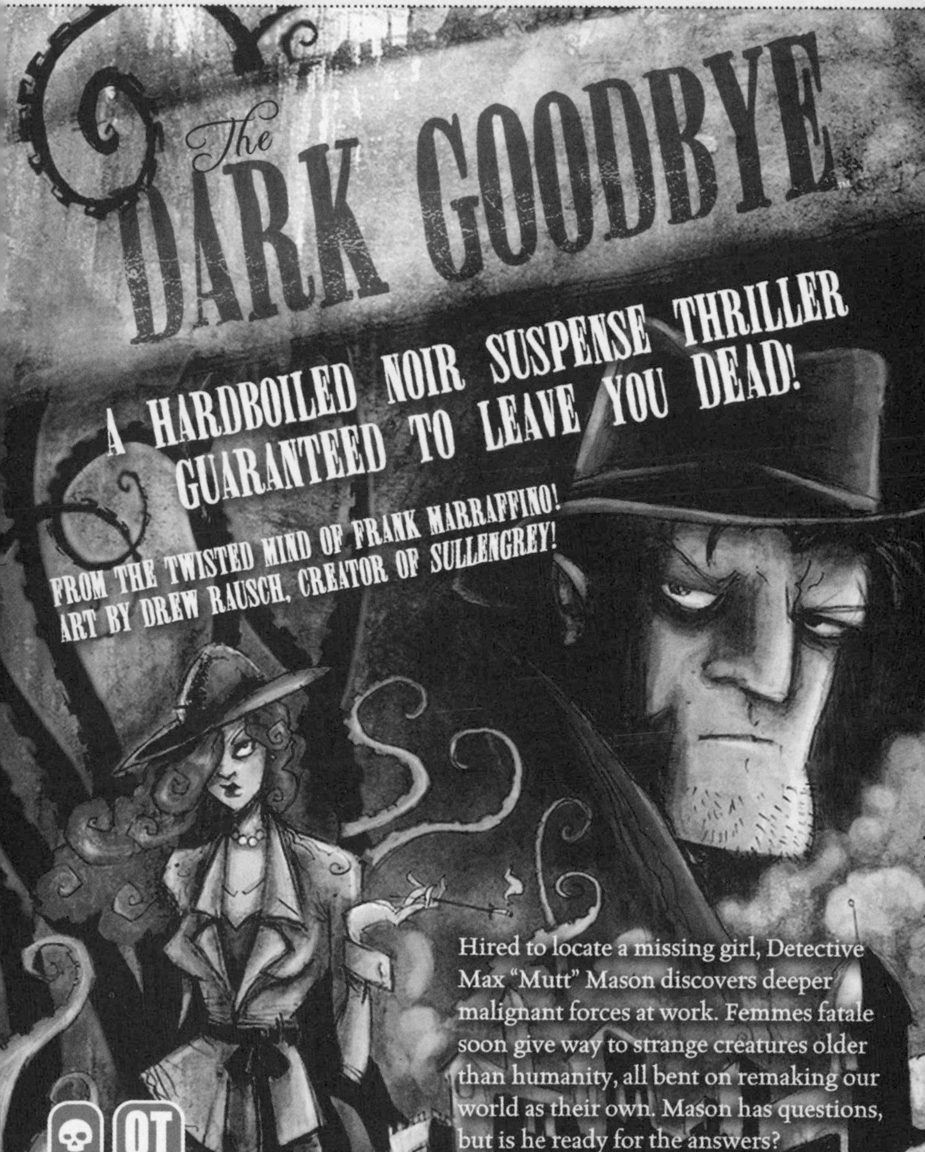

The DARK GOODBYE

A HARDBOILED NOIR SUSPENSE THRILLER GUARANTEED TO LEAVE YOU DEAD!

FROM THE TWISTED MIND OF FRANK MARRAFFINO!
ART BY DREW RAUSCH, CREATOR OF SULLENGREY!

Hired to locate a missing girl, Detective Max "Mutt" Mason discovers deeper malignant forces at work. Femmes fatale soon give way to strange creatures older than humanity, all bent on remaking our world as their own. Mason has questions, but is he ready for the answers?

HORROR

OT
OLDER TEEN
AGE 16+

©2007 Frank Marraffino and TOKYOPOP inc.

FOR MORE INFORMATION VISIT: WWW.TOKYOPOP.COM

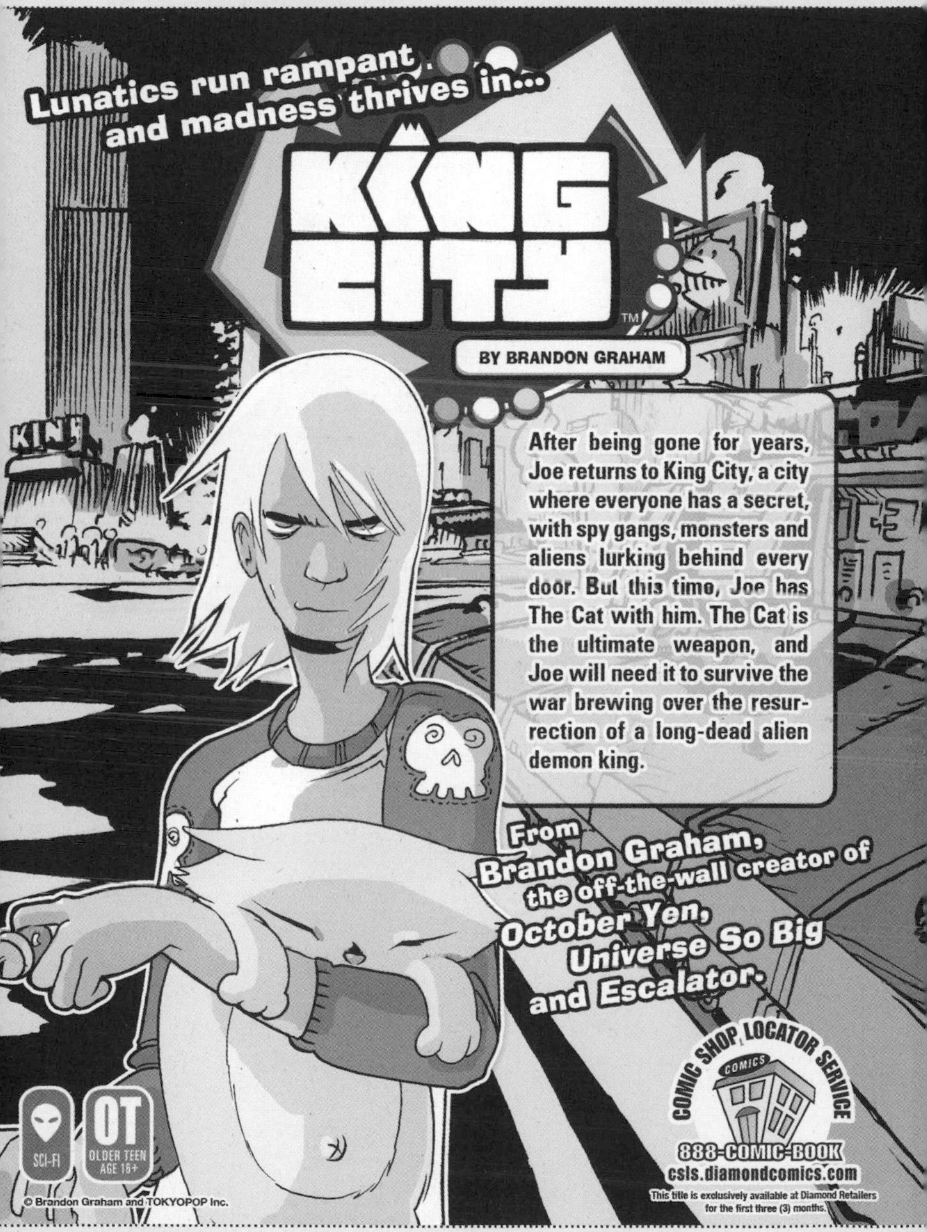
Lunatics run rampant...
and madness thrives in...
KING CITY™
BY BRANDON GRAHAM
After being gone for years, Joe returns to King City, a city where everyone has a secret, with spy gangs, monsters and aliens lurking behind every door. But this time, Joe has The Cat with him. The Cat is the ultimate weapon, and Joe will need it to survive the war brewing over the resurrection of a long-dead alien demon king.
From Brandon Graham, the off-the-wall creator of October Yen, Universe So Big and Escalator.
SCI-FI
OT
OLDER TEEN AGE 16+
© Brandon Graham and TOKYOPOP Inc.
COMIC SHOP LOCATOR SERVICE
COMICS
888-COMIC-BOOK
csls.diamondcomics.com
This title is exclusively available at Diamond Retailers for the first three (3) months.

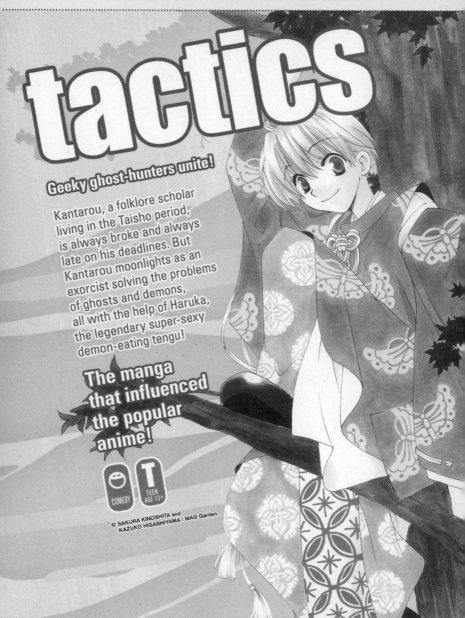

tactics

Geeky ghost-hunters unite!

Kantarou, a folklore scholar living in the Taisho period, is always broke and always late on his deadlines. But Kantarou moonlights as an exorcist solving the problems of ghosts and demons, all with the help of Haruka, the legendary super-sexy demon-eating tengu!

The manga that influenced the popular anime!

COMEDY

T
TEEN
AGE 13+

© SAKURA KINOSHITA and
KAZUKO HIGASHIYAMA / MAG Garden.

FOR MORE INFORMATION VISIT: WWW.TOKYOPOP.COM

TOKYOPOP MANGA SUPPLEMENT

ZAPT!

From the super team of Eisner-winner Keith Giffen, animation veteran Shannon Eric Denton & hot new talent Armand Villavert, Jr.!

An exciting heroic manga for 8-12-year-olds!

© Shannon Denton, Keith Giffen and TOKYOPOP Inc.

Twelve-year-old Armand Jones has to police the galaxy and finish his chores all before dinnertime!

Vol. 1 in stores now!
Vol. 2 coming soon!

WWW.TOKYOPOP.COM/MANGAREADERS

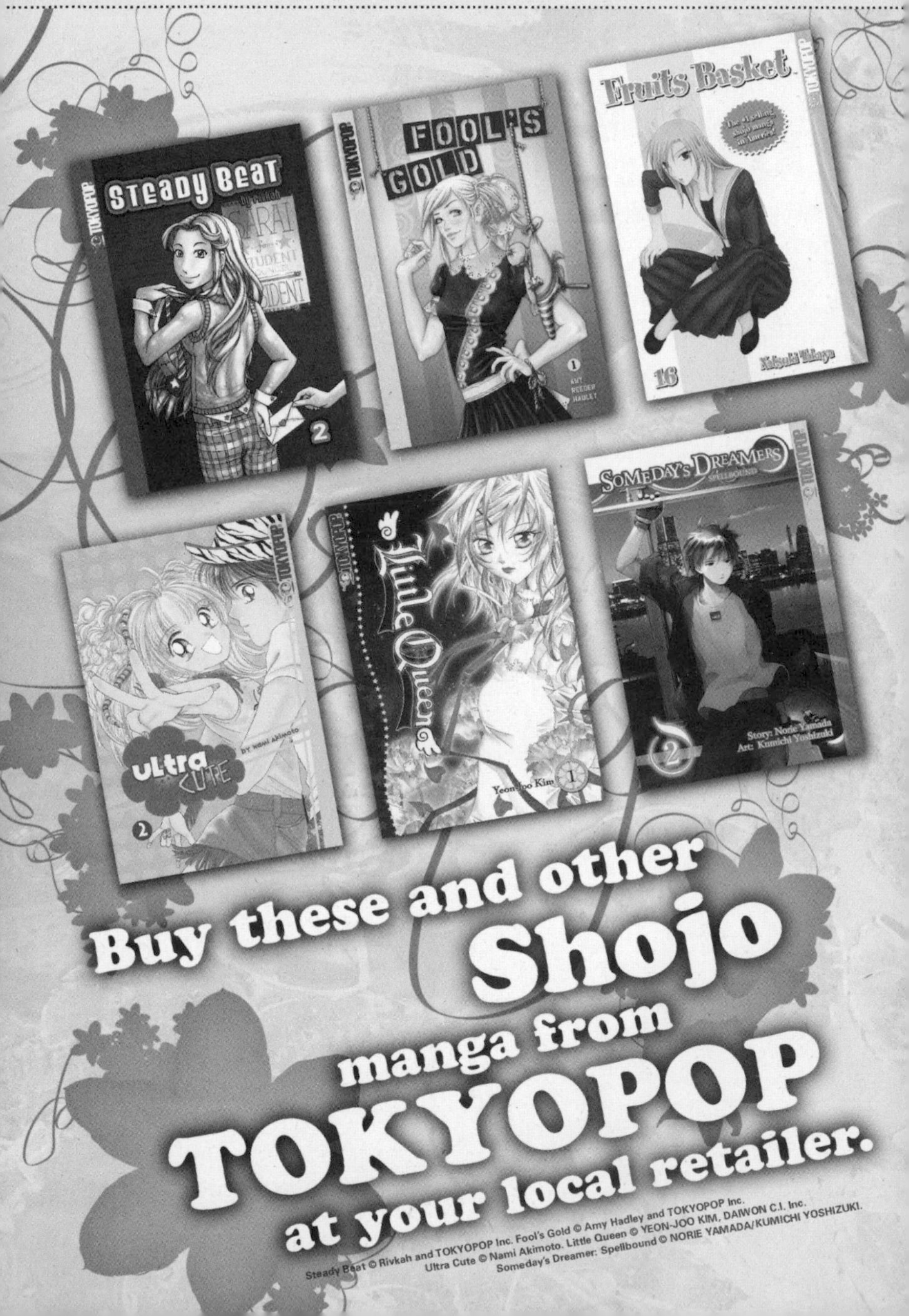
STEADY BEAT
FOOL'S GOLD
Fruits Basket
16
SOMEDAY'S DREAMERS
SPELLBOUND
Story: Norie Yamada
Art: Kumichi Yoshizuki
Little Queen
Yeon-Joo Kim
ultra CUTE
Buy these and other
Shojo
manga from
TOKYOPOP
at your local retailer.
Steady Beat © Rivkah and TOKYOPOP Inc. Fool's Gold © Amy Hadley and TOKYOPOP Inc.
Ultra Cute © Nami Akimoto. Little Queen © YEON-JOO KIM, DAIWON C.I. Inc.
Someday's Dreamer: Spellbound © NORIE YAMADA/KUMICHI YOSHIZUKI.

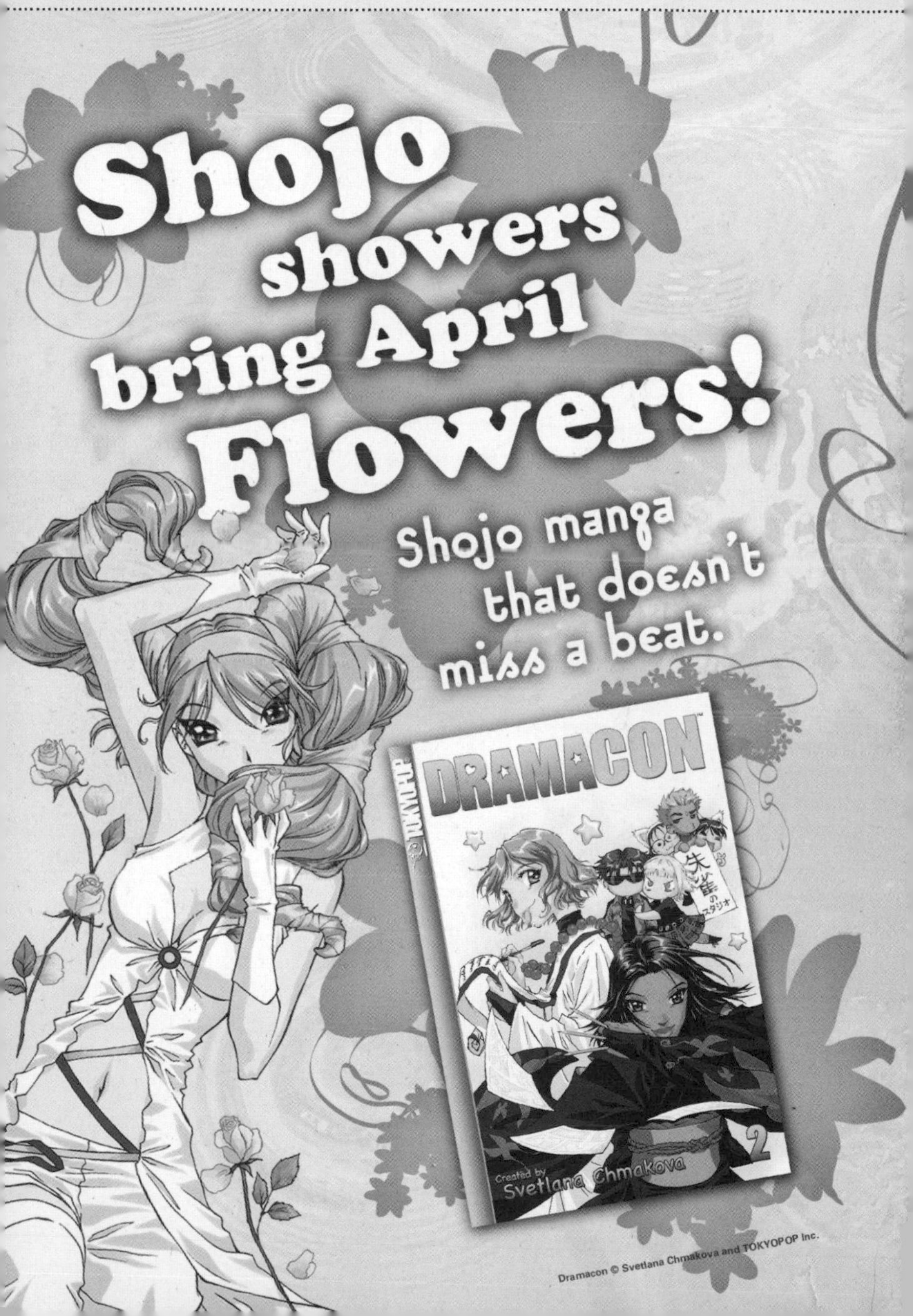
Shojo showers bring April Flowers!
Shojo manga that doesn't miss a beat.
DRAMACON
TOKYOPOP
2
Created by Svetlana Chmakova
Dramacon © Svetlana Chmakova and TOKYOPOP Inc.

STOP!

This is the back of the book.
You wouldn't want to spoil a great ending!

This book is printed "manga-style," in the authentic Japanese right-to-left format. Since none of the artwork has been flipped or altered, readers get to experience the story just as the creator intended. You've been asking for it, so TOKYOPOP® delivered: authentic, hot-off-the-press, and far more fun!

DIRECTIONS

If this is your first time reading manga-style, here's a quick guide to help you understand how it works.

It's easy... just start in the top right panel and follow the numbers. Have fun, and look for more 100% authentic manga from TOKYOPOP®!